A CENTURY *of*

Parks
Canada

Canadian History and Environment Series

Alan MacEachern, Series Editor

ISSN 1925-3702 (Print) ISSN 1925-3710 (Online)

It is a great pleasure to welcome this first book in the "Canadian History & Environment" series, a new partnership between NiCHE and the University of Calgary Press. The series will demonstrate the value of seeing Canadian history through an environmental lens and the environment through a historical lens.

Alan MacEachern, Director
NiCHE: Network in Canadian History & Environment
Nouvelle initiative canadienne en histoire de l'environnement
http://niche-canada.org

No. 1 · **A Century of Parks Canada, 1911–2011** Edited by Claire Elizabeth Campbell

A CENTURY *of*

Parks Canada

1911–2011

edited by

CLAIRE ELIZABETH CAMPBELL

UNIVERSITY OF
CALGARY
PRESS

CANADIAN HISTORY AND ENVIRONMENT SERIES
ISSN 1925-3702 (Print) ISSN 1925-3710 (Online)

University of Calgary Press
2500 University Drive NW
Calgary, Alberta
Canada T2N 1N4
www.uofcpress.com

LIBRARY AND ARCHIVES CANADA CATALOGUING IN PUBLICATION

A century of Parks Canada, 1911-2011 / edited by Claire Elizabeth Campbell.

(Canadian history and environment series, 1925-3702 ; 1)
Includes bibliographical references and index.
Also available in electronic formats.
ISBN 978-1-55238-526-5

1. National parks and reserves—Canada—History. 2. Parks Canada—History.
I. Campbell, Claire Elizabeth, 1974- II. Series: Canadian history and environment series ; 1

SB484.C3C45 2011   333.78'30971   C2011-900677-4

The University of Calgary Press acknowledges the support of the Alberta Foundation for the Arts for our publications. We acknowledge the financial support of the Government of Canada through the Canada Book Fund for our publishing activities. We acknowledge the financial support of the Canada Council for the Arts for our publishing program.

This book has been published with support from NiCHE: Network in Canadian History & Environment. This book has been published with the aid of a grant from Alberta Sport, Recreation, Parks and Wildlife Foundation (Government of Alberta). This book has been published with the help of a grant from the Canadian Federation for the Humanities and Social Sciences, through the Aid to Scholarly Publications Program, using funds provided by the Social Sciences and Humanities Research Council of Canada.

Printed and bound in Canada by Marquis Book Printing Inc.
∞ This book is printed on Rolland Opaque paper

Front cover image:
Takakkaw Falls, Yoho National Park, British Columbia [ca. 1921–37]. Photographer: Thomas B. Moffat S-20-336, Glenbow Museum.
Back cover images:
Princess Victoria Mary in Banff National Park, 1901, NA-3705-15, Glenbow Museum.
Greenwich, Prince Edward Island National Park, 2010. Photographer: Claire Elizabeth Campbell.
La Mauricie National Park, 1978. Photographer: T. Grant © Parks Canada: 05.51.04.04(16).
Pangnirtung, Auyuittuq National Park, 1981. Photographer: M. Beedell © Parks Canada: 13.03.12.04(02)
Jakes Landing, Kejimkujik National Park, 1995. Photographer: Barrett & MacKay © Parks Canada: 03.31.02.07(07).
Fundy National Park, 1950. Photographer: C. Lund © Parks Canada: 04.40.04.04(13).

Maps by Marilyn Croot: pages 82, 209, 276, 279, 280
Cover design, page design and typesetting by Melina Cusano

Table of Contents

Governing a Kingdom: Parks Canada, 1911–2011

𝕫

CLAIRE ELIZABETH CAMPBELL
DEPARTMENT OF HISTORY
DALHOUSIE UNIVERSITY

In May of 1911, the House of Commons was preparing to vote on Bill 85, a bill "respecting forest reserves and parks." It had been a busy enough session for the House that spring, and this particular bill was hardly the most important on the docket. In fact, the Toronto *Globe* counted it as one of a series – along with raising postal workers' salaries and standardizing bushel weights – designed "with a view of giving the Senate something to do," while Members of Parliament prepared to lock horns over the subject of free trade with the United States.[1] When forest reserves and parks *were* discussed, MPs focused on the wealth of timber contained on the eastern slopes of the Rocky Mountains, under the rule of the Department of the Interior. There was little discussion about national parks, which were still very much a novelty, and there was no mention of who would run them. The bill simply allowed Cabinet to appoint someone to oversee the forest reserves and to make any decisions necessary for the "protection, care and management" of public parks. But shortly before the vote, Alexander Haggart of Winnipeg rose in protest. Was Parliament, he asked, really about to "divest ourselves of the power of governing a kingdom," by handing it to an unknown "hired official"?[2] His question fell flat, the bill passed, and a month later Cabinet quietly approved the creation of a new unit within the Department of the Interior, to be called the Dominion Parks Branch.[3] It was the first time in history that a country had created an agency devoted to managing its national parks.

Haggart was right, but in ways he could not have foreseen. What began as a minor bureaucratic shuffle, simply to provide better management for the forest reserves and a handful of western parks, created an agency that over the next century would convince Canadians that in their national parks resided the true wealth of a kingdom. We prize our national parks because they are places of physical beauty, snapshots of the incredible diversity of the Canadian landscape. We may also think of them as ecological sanctuaries that protect nature for us and, increasingly, protect nature *from* us. But national parks are not "islands of wilderness" saved from history: they are the work of human hands and records of our history. They document our relationship to nature, not just as we wish it could be, but as it has been. Public demands, political strategy, environmental concern, cultural symbolism, and scientific debate have all been inscribed in our parks. And the agency created in 1911 has alternately guided and mirrored this dialogue between Canadians and their land. (Originally called the Dominion Parks Branch, the agency was renamed the National Parks Branch in 1930, the Parks Canada Program in 1973, the Canadian Parks Service in 1984, and the Parks Canada Agency in 1998. As we follow the agency through its history in this collection, we have tried to preserve the name in use at the time.) What began with a "hired official" and a handful of staff would come to govern some of the most iconic places in Canada, profoundly affecting how Canadians and the world see our country. No other government agency in Canada has had such imaginative power.

A Century of Parks Canada, 1911–2011 is about that agency, but it isn't a conventional institutional history. The essays in this collection set the changing philosophies and practices of Parks Canada in historical context, measuring its response to social and political circumstances, and seeing it as a barometer of Canada in the twentieth century. The agency's decisions about national parks – where to create them and how to manage them – reflected contemporary ideas and ideals even as they affected particular places and communities. The authors here explore the motivation, effect, and meaning of park policies that played out at different moments in Canadian history.

Parks Canada is a lens through which to understand the making of Canada: our sense of territory, as ideas, resources, and space; our changing relationship with First Nations peoples, with urban communities, with the North; the evolving framework of the Canadian state; and the evolution of environmental thought and practice as we struggle to find a sustainable place for ourselves in the natural world. National parks, then, invite us to look forward *and* back. In 1936, M.B. Williams reflected on the experience of the National Parks Branch in its first quarter-century: "But ideals seldom remain the same for that long together. They grow and develop and change, like everything else, with the passing years. An anniversary merely affords a convenient moment to stand back and look at the design and see how it is working out."[4] The centennial of that Branch, now Parks Canada, is such a fitting moment.

In 1985, Parks Canada celebrated a different centennial: that of its landmark creation, Banff National Park. The story of this first park is fairly well known because firsts tend to be, but also because it marked the beginnings of the national parks system, and because it became enmeshed in national iconography. In 1883 workers for the Canadian Pacific Railway accidentally discovered a hot springs – made popular by health-seeking tourists in the nineteenth century – and two years later an Order-in-Council reserved an area of ten square miles around the springs. Federal surveyors reported that the site had "features of the greatest beauty, and was admirably adapted for a national park" (although few would have been able to say what a "national park" actually looked like), and, in June 1887, Parliament passed the *Rocky Mountains Park Act*, creating "a public park and pleasure ground for the benefit, advantage and enjoyment of the people of Canada."[5] It says much about our early parks that this phrase, which defined park creation in this country for half a century, is less often cited than the blustery "if we can't export the scenery, we'll import the tourists," attributed to CPR director William Van Horne.[6] The CPR's approach was very much in keeping with federal plans for developing the newly acquired western interior. It was the allure of national parks en route, with luxurious hotels and dramatic mountain scenery, that transformed the mammoth but prosaic construction of the transcontinental railway into a true "national dream." In fact, Ottawa and the CPR owed the United States for the inspiration; Yellowstone National Park, created fifteen years before at another hot springs, was already a booming tourist destination.

Over the next two decades, Ottawa created four more parks in the mountains, all with much the same sensibility. National parks were not imagined as a way of preserving nature from people, but as reserving nature for the people's use. Selected sites favoured both the visually sublime and, with the rail line, the geographically convenient. "A forest reserve is withdrawn from occupation," Minister of the Interior Frank Oliver explained, "whereas a forest park is intended to primarily to be occupied for the purposes of pleasure."[7] The clarification was necessary partly because parks and reserves tended to be located near or adjacent to one another in the Rockies but also because they had been lumped together in the federal bureaucracy. From 1906 to 1911, the handful of national parks in existence were managed by the Dominion Forestry Branch, which had relatively little time for these small tracts of land. Parks and forests alike fell under the jurisdiction of the Department of the Interior, the powerhouse of the federal Cabinet in the decades following Confederation. The Department concentrated on nation-building projects and the development of resources contained in the western territories, and its attitude toward parks was as utilitarian as toward the rest of its lands.[8] Parks were reserved for "the people" from sale or settlement – but not from primary industries like timber or mining, or from those wanting to operate facilities for tourists. This meshed nicely with a growing public interest in the outdoors, and the new popularity of "getting back to nature" for spiritual and physical renewal. (Meanwhile, a small private bequest enabled the first eastern park in Ontario's tony holiday area of the Thousand Islands, closer to more of "the people of Canada" if somewhat out of keeping with the physical grandeur that Canadians had already come to expect of their parks.) Whether as an industrial or recreational resource, the concept of national parks suited the new ethos of conservation, which insisted that rational, modern management could ensure use in perpetuity. Management, of course, required bureaucracy.

The creation of a Dominion Parks Branch in 1911 thus represented a crucial step in establishing a public identity for national parks. While the *Dominion Forest Reserves and Parks Act* shrunk park borders,[9] the subsequent decision to create a separate agency proved nothing short of a saving grace for Canada's future national parks system. For one thing, a handful of small parks now actually constituted a system, with a public face in James B. Harkin, the first commissioner of the new branch. Harkin seems the quintessentially

Canadian hero: an "Ottawa mandarin" initially armed with little more than a piece of federal legislation, who in 1919 justified parks to his pragmatically minded department on the grounds that scenery was worth $13.88 an acre.[10] But as Alan MacEachern suggests here, the Branch flourished over the next twenty years, thanks in part to its development of an able corps of staff like M.B. Williams, but, more importantly, to its ability to present an image of parks that resonated with national and international audiences. It rapidly expanded the parks system, eastward into Saskatchewan, Manitoba, and Ontario – this last, in particular, to provide park space closer to where most Canadians lived – and created wildlife preserves for antelope, elk, and buffalo in Alberta and Saskatchewan.[11] By twinning use and protection, the Branch was laying the foundations of an approach to national park management that would remain in place throughout the twentieth century. "But though so many provisions are made for enjoyment and use," M.B. Williams would write in 1936, "it is never forgotten that the most precious possessions of the parks are their peace and solitude."[12]

Providing both enjoyment and solitude was a tall order but one that Canadians were coming to expect of the Parks Branch by the 1930s. If the idea of the national park dates to 1887, and its agency to 1911, then the national park landscape we have inherited really belongs to the interwar period, when the new automobile culture consistently shaped park design. John Sandlos shows that the Branch's enthusiasm for catering to highway tourism affected parks in nearly every part of the country. The original parks landscape of the mountain sublime was joined by the lake shoreline at Prince Albert and Point Pelee. This expansion raised the public profile of national parks, and they attained a heightened, even iconic, status as early as the 1920s. But the diversification of their social and ecological character also began to test the cohesion of a national system. Bill Waiser's essay is just one in this volume that demonstrates the tension emerging between a local community and the national authority, as the cottage community at Prince Albert National Park exhibited a proprietorial attachment to their particular holidaying spot. In 1930, the Prairie provinces finally received jurisdiction over their natural resources, making it far more difficult for Ottawa to create parks at will in the west. Ben Bradley raises the fascinating question of "failed" parks through Hamber, a national park that never existed because it in effect fell through the cracks of this new intergovernmental landscape.

The government of British Columbia created a massive provincial park in the western Rockies, hoping to lure the Parks Branch into adopting it – and the enormous expense of its highway construction. The gamble failed and most of Hamber was eventually reopened to development. Rich in forest resources, Hamber also reminds us how porous and fragile park boundaries can be when land is considered valuable.

With the passage of the *National Parks Act* in 1930, Parliament entrenched the philosophy developed within the Parks Branch – now the National Parks Branch – over its first two decades. This was another legislative watershed, because now the mandate of parks to provide for the "benefit, education and enjoyment" of the people was paired with a mandate for the people to maintain the parks "so as to leave them unimpaired for future generations." Industrial activities were excluded, park boundaries were made permanent, and a category of Historical Parks was formally recognized.[13] "Unimpaired for future generations" is so powerful a phrase that it remains the motto for Parks Canada's approach to ecological integrity, the core, if elusive, objective of parks management in the twenty-first century.[14] But it is important not to exaggerate the preservationist thinking of Canadians of 1930; like the creation of the Dominion Parks Branch, the implications of the *National Parks Act* would become clearer over time. In fact, with the onset of the Great Depression the parks system entered a period of remarkable stasis, and only four new parks were added over the next forty years. We are sorely in need of more research on this period, precisely because of this relative silence. Until recently historians have concentrated on the earliest years of the national parks system: the rail travel, elite hotels, and alpine culture of the mountain parks in the prewar years. And scientists and park planners have had more use for history since 1970, when national parks were governed by a new biophysical system plan and ecological language. But the middle part of the century may tell us much about what inhibits national park creation, the feasibility of legislating protection as well as use, and the character of the Parks Branch in different parts of the country. All four new parks were created in Atlantic Canada, giving the Branch a significant presence in the four eastern provinces for the first time. But these four clearly followed the old formula: whether along the Cabot Trail on Cape Breton or the north shore of Prince Edward Island, they were designed to provide scenic highway views.[15]

By the middle of the twentieth century, the National Parks Branch held a stated commitment to environmental protection but typically was preoccupied with managing parks for tourism and recreation. This contradiction would come to a head by the early 1960s amid a booming postwar economy, as families spurred by a heartily suburban and child-oriented culture made ever-more intense demands on park space. Meanwhile, national parks and their caretaker were having trouble finding a foothold in the byzantine world of federal bureaucracy. After the Department of the Interior was disbanded in 1936, the Parks Branch floated through a series of departments, from Mines and Resources to Indian and Northern Affairs, where, as David Neufeld indicates in his essay on Kluane, it was often overshadowed by more development-oriented players. But in responding to these new pressures, Parks began to evolve a distinctive organizational infrastructure, which in turn helped refine its thinking about parks themselves. A planning branch was established in 1957, followed by regional offices, to ease the tension between policies originating from a remote federal agency and local administration. (The attitude in Banff, according to C.J. Taylor, recalls a Chinese saying that "The mountains are high and the emperor is far away.") Several essays in this collection describe the Branch's efforts to locate a "middle ground" in this period within its old dual mandate. South of the border, the U.S. National Park Service likewise found itself facing conflicting demands from its public; an ambitious ten-year program to upgrade visitor facilities, known as "Mission 66" (to be completed by 1966, the fiftieth year of *their* national parks agency), suddenly ran counter to new concern about park overdevelopment and the preservationist directive introduced in 1964 with the *Wilderness Act*.[16]

Although the Parks Branch had no formal equivalent to Mission 66, Taylor shows how the wear and tear of park overcrowding, now reaching critical levels at Banff, and an increasingly vocal scientific community prompted significant changes in parks policy, including zoning to localize use and a new degree of public consultation. In 1964, the minister of Northern Affairs and Natural Resources tabled the first national parks policy, which stated that national parks were to preserve "for all time areas which contain significant geographical, geological, biological or historic features as a natural heritage for the benefit, education and enjoyment of the people of Canada." The contradiction was still present – how were Canadians to enjoy these places without visiting them? – but preservation was nudged ahead of recreation. In his 2007 book, *Taking the Air: Ideas and Change in Canada's National Parks*, Paul Kopas calls this "the era of state initiative," to distinguish it from the subsequent era of "public participation."[17] But the two cannot be so neatly divided. For one thing, the state was attempting to respond *to* the public, because Canadians were using and discussing national parks more than ever before. George Colpitts discusses how the National Film Board, like the Parks Branch, sought to both shape and respond to a significant shift in attitudes about just who or what parks should be for. While the NFB initially featured wildlife as a tourist attraction in order to promote park visits, by the late 1960s its films cast bears as park inhabitants endangered by those very tourists. After 1963 the National and Provincial Parks Association, later the Canadian Parks and Wilderness Society, emerged as an influential environmental lobby in Canada, sponsoring a conference on "Parks for Tomorrow" in 1968, where scholars leveled pointed criticism at user-oriented development.

This growing support for environmental protection, the energy of the new Trudeau government, and a new interest in Canada's northern territory gave national parks a new prominence on the federal agenda. All of these were summed up by Minister of Northern and Indian Affairs Jean Chrétien, flying over the dramatic fjords on Baffin Island, who turned from the window to his wife and promised grandly, "Aline, I will make these a national park for you." Sure enough, Aline's park is now Auyuittuq.[18] The federal government created new parks with remarkable speed, from sea (Gros Morne, Kejimkujik, and Kouchibouguac) to sea (Pacific Rim) to sea (Kluane, Nahanni, and Auyuittuq). But romantic impulse and ministerial hubris reached their limit here, for future parks would not be as arbitrary. In 1970, the Branch adopted the National Parks System Plan, which divided the country into thirty-nine "natural regions" and promised to someday have at least one park representative of each. This meant not only more parks but parks with a concrete basis in ecological diversity rather than (or at least in addition to) scenery and political advantage. By recognizing regional landscapes and local specificity, the System Plan also brought Parks Canada, as it was called after 1973, closer to the ground. But Olivier Craig-Dupont argues that the agency was able to use the ecological language of the System Plan to support a more symbolic and conventional federal goal: generating national pride in Canada's natural beauty. Completing the System Plan remains a stated

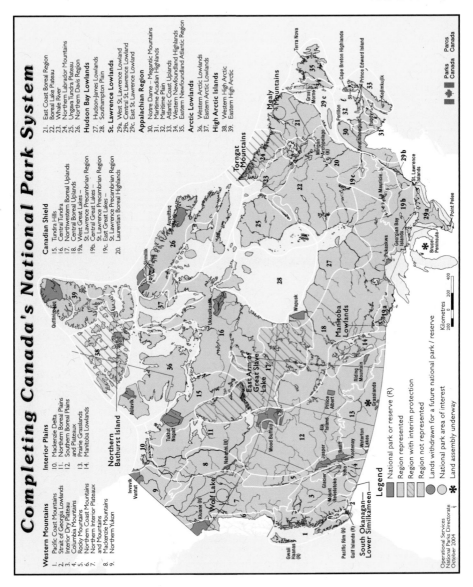

Completing Canada's National Park System

Western Mountains
1. Pacific Coast Mountains
2. Strait of Georgia Lowlands
3. Interior Dry Plateau
4. Columbia Mountains
5. Rocky Mountains
6. Northern Coast Mountains
7. Northern Interior Plateaux and Mountains
8. Mackenzie Mountains
9. Northern Yukon

Interior Plains
10. Mackenzie Delta
11. Northern Boreal Plains
12. Southern Boreal Plains and Plateaux
13. Prairie Grasslands
14. Manitoba Lowlands

Northern Bathurst Island

Canadian Shield
15. Tundra Hills
16. Central Tundra
17. Northwestern Boreal Uplands
18. Central Boreal Uplands
19a. West Great Lakes – St. Lawrence Precambrian Region
19b. Central Great Lakes – St. Lawrence Precambrian Region
19c. East Great Lakes – St. Lawrence Precambrian Region
20. Laurentian Boreal Highlands
21. East Coast Boreal Region
22. Boreal Lake Plateau
23. Whale River
24. Northern Labrador Mountains
25. Ungava Tundra Plateau
26. Northern Davis Region

Hudson Bay Lowlands
27. Hudson-James Lowlands
28. Southampton Plain

St. Lawrence Lowlands
29a. West St. Lawrence Lowland
29b. Central St. Lawrence Lowland
29c. East St. Lawrence Lowland

Appalachian Region
30. Notre Dame – Megantic Mountains
31. Maritime Acadian Highlands
32. Maritime Plain
33. Atlantic Coast Uplands
34. Western Newfoundland Highlands
35. Eastern Newfoundland Atlantic Region

Arctic Lowlands
36. Western Arctic Lowlands
37. Eastern Arctic Lowlands

High Arctic Islands
38. Western High Arctic
39. Eastern High Arctic

Legend

National park or reserve (R)

Region represented

Region with interim protection

Region not represented

Lands withdrawn for a future national park / reserve

National park area of interest

* Land assembly underway

Operational Services
National Parks Directorate
October 2004

Kilometres
200 0 200 400

Parks Canada
Parcs Canada

Fig. 1.
Completing Canada's National Park System (2008). [Parks Canada Agency.]

objective for Parks Canada, but history suggests that ecological science can be as political as many other elements of parks policy.[19]

At the same time, parks had to be located where land was available – and where the federal government was particularly concerned with showing the flag. This meant that after 1970 new parks were overwhelmingly concentrated in the north, in federal territory, and where they could be drawn on a vast scale. But the "available" space was deceptive because Parks Canada found itself confronting resident communities responding to park creation in an unprecedented way. The stories in this volume of La Mauricie, Kouchibouguac, Kluane, and Ivvavik all document the agency's efforts to deal with community resistance, the politics of land appropriation, and competing kinds of use. Aboriginal communities in the north most effectively challenged conventional thinking about national parks. In 1974 the *National Parks Act* was amended to include provisions for traditional hunting and fishing practices, and the new concept of a national park reserve: land set aside for a *future* national park pending settlement of any land claims. Ironically, the turn to the great spaces of the north was redefining our sense of parks as "wilderness," and Parks Canada began to adopt the concept of cultural landscape.[20] For the first time in its history, the agency acknowledged the role of people in shaping the physical face of park environments and the different cultural meanings that people might find there. According to Gwyn Langemann, by the early 1970s, archaeologists with the agency had firmly established a record of longstanding human presence in the mountain parks. And as I.S. MacLaren argues forcefully, other countries provide useful models of how to recognize human habitation within national parks, thereby offering an alternative to the idea of parks as wilderness sanctuaries. Meanwhile, high-profile land claims in the face of northern development and increasing disputes over Arctic sovereignty drew international attention to Canada's parks. More positively, so too did our ratification of the World Heritage Convention in 1976. As the federal representative, Parks Canada acquired the authority for nominating World Heritage Sites, and a showcase for its possessions; national parks presently make up half of Canada's World Heritage Sites. Regardless of the contested nature of park politics at home, parks now enjoyed an international cachet, and Parks Canada gained a priceless form of advertising.

This heightened attention at home and abroad reinforced concerns about the ecological health of the national parks. So by the early 1980s Parks Canada found itself defining not one but two core paradigms for park management: cultural landscapes and ecological integrity. It was a new and ironic twist on an historical duality. The agency, which had finally accepted the role of people in making national parks, was now also insisting that the health of natural ecosystems would be "paramount" in all governance decisions.[21] The contradiction became apparent within parks themselves: by the late 1980s, precisely when Parks Canada's mandate for environmental protection was stronger than at any point in its history, the actual environmental quality *in* the parks reached its nadir. Despite – or because of – a new climate of green politics and a new fashion for green living, national parks were more popular than ever and were eroding under the strain of our enthusiasm for them; environmentalists began to talk about "loving the parks to death." Ottawa commissioned a series of semi-independent investigations into the state of the parks, culminating in the Panel on the Ecological Integrity of Canada's National Parks in 2000. These reports consistently described national parks as "under serious threat," especially the smallest parks like Point Pelee and Prince Edward Island.[22] In response, the *Canada National Parks Act* of 2000 provided the strongest language to date, stating that "maintenance or restoration of ecological integrity, through the protection of natural resources and natural processes, shall be the first priority ... when considering all aspects of the management of parks." Yet it retained the old dualist language of 1930, dedicating the parks to "the people of Canada for their benefit, education and enjoyment," and promising that "the parks shall be maintained and made use of so as to leave them unimpaired for the enjoyment of future generations."

Perhaps this is why Parks Canada has always struggled to find a foothold in the federal bureaucracy, for it is a political creature with responsibilities to Canadians as well as to the environment we inhabit. In 1979, the agency was transferred from Indian and Northern Affairs to the Department of the Environment: a reasonable choice, given the emerging emphasis on ecological integrity. But in 1993 its responsibility for historic places as well as national parks as "natural heritage" prompted another relocation, this time into the new Department of Heritage. This contradicted the trajectory of several decades, and within five years Parks Canada was reconstituted as a special operating agency, answerable to the Minister of the Environment but

Fig. 2. Forillon National Park, 1987. [Photo: Neil Campbell.]

as a quasi-corporate body with a degree of independence.[23] This realigned the agency with its mandate for ecological protection, but it also heightened its need for public support. Introducing Canadians to "the beauty and significance of our natural world" gives Parks Canada both a civic function and a political *raison d'être*; in other words, bringing Canadians into national parks allows Parks to teach us about the natural environment but also about the agency that has brought us there.[24] Although it is easy to see successive pieces of legislation – 1930, 1964, 2000 – as progress toward more stringent environmental protection, we need to remember that Parks Canada remains responsible for, and invested in, ensuring our "benefit and enjoyment" of national parks.

Our history in these parks is clearly important, yet we do not possess a great deal of history about our national parks. One scholar has called national parks a "black hole for historical research" because we prefer to think of them as natural sanctuaries instead of human creations.[25] Indeed, Parks Canada's emphasis on ecology as non-human nature may prevent us from seeing the ways in which we humans encounter nature within its parks. As several of these essays demonstrate, these encounters occur in very human landscapes: in the campgrounds and scenic roadways dating from precisely the same era as the phrase "unimpaired for future generations," which Parks Canada takes as its directive. Meanwhile Parks Canada itself, the first agency in the world devoted to managing national parks, has remained astonishingly anonymous, and its complex relationship with these "sanctuaries" is rarely discussed. Histories relating to the Canadian national parks system have been sparse; those that exist tend to be celebratory and rooted in institutional chronology. While three "Parks for Tomorrow" conferences (in 1968, 1978, and 2008) generated critical discussions about human impact on parks, they were framed by scientific findings and policy language.[26] But the dramatic growth of environmental history as a field in recent years has set the stage for new research. Despite a rhetoric of wilderness, parks epitomize "hybrid landscapes," defined by one historian as "a compromise between human design and natural processes."[27] In this, they are perfectly suited to historical study.

A Century of Parks Canada captures this curiosity about our place in the natural world and the new sense of community among environmental historians in Canada. In 2005, a national Network in Canadian History and Environment (NiCHE) was established to support collaborative projects like this collection, whose contributors come from universities across Canada and within Parks Canada itself. We met twice to discuss themes and connections – an unusual step in putting together edited collections, but valuable when talking about a subject that refracts across the spectrum of Canadian history. The essays here locate Parks Canada in a cottage community and a mining frontier; in the Rocky Mountains and the sub-boreal forest of the Canadian Shield; in political disputes, travel writing, and town newspapers. In other words, we can learn as much about *Canada* as about *parks* from this history. Despite our different starting points in time and place, we were struck by the common themes or clusters that emerged. In the early part of the twentieth century automobile-based tourism had an enormous impact on the face of national parks. By the 1960s the presence and application of ecological science became central to the debate amid concerns about the health of the parks. And by the 1970s, expansion into the far north, and growing involvement by aboriginal communities, forced Parks Canada to rethink parks as cultural landscapes.

But one theme that stretches across the century and appears in nearly every essay is the tension between national agendas and local interests. Bill Waiser describes a moment when John Diefenbaker – one can almost imagine him shaking his fist in regionalist indignation – insisted that Prince Albert National Park was "a place for the people … not a playground for bureaucrats in Ottawa." But which people? Parks Canada is a federal agency, tasked with preserving "nationally significant" places for "the people of Canada." In reality, though, these places are located in very diverse ecosystems, and among very different communities. Sometimes these communities have been displaced by "bureaucrats in Ottawa" in the name of a national ideal – as with Acadians at Kouchibouguac, or Métis families in Jasper – and sometimes Parks officials have responded to local demands, as in the Georgian Bay, Prince Albert, or Ivvavik. In this, it is in many ways a microcosm of the tensions of federalism, in a country famously said to have too much geography.

An anniversary is, as M.B. Williams suggested, a convenient moment to stand back and ask what we have learned. Created in a legislative aside in 1911, yet charged with "governing a kingdom," Parks Canada one hundred years later is recognized as a global leader in the environmental challenges of protected places. But as these essays show, this has been hard-won, earned through a century of dealing with diverse communities, diverse geographies, and changing historical circumstances. So its history is a rich repository of experience, of lessons learned, and even of paths not taken.[28] Asking what has or hasn't worked, and where, and why, is critical for making informed decisions about how to sustain the environmental and social health of our national parks. At the same time, environmental policy needs the perspective of the humanities – the study of people who inhabit, use, and value that environment – in order to be effective.[29] The authors here are citizens as well as scholars; we write about these places because we care about them, because we feel invested in their future. While we see the heavy footprint of the past century, these essays are still "tinged with idealism," much as John Sandlos describes Parks Canada itself in its early years. We hope the stories we present here will add to our ability to make wise choices about these places in the future. And we hope, finally, that the 2011 centennial of Parks Canada kindles interest in our national parks and their place in Canada's history.

NOTES

1. "Government bills put through Commons," *Globe* (29 April 1911) and "What Parliament has done so far," *Globe* (22 May 1911). I would like to thank Alan MacEachern for his comments on an earlier draft of this introduction.

2. House of Commons, *Debates*, 9 May 1911, column 8666; *An Act respecting Forest Reserves and Parks*, Statutes of Canada 1–2 Geo. V., chap. 10.

3. Department of the Interior, *Annual Report for the fiscal year ending March 31, 1912*, J.B. Harkin, "Report of the Commissioner of Dominion Parks," Sessional Paper no. 25 (1913); E.J. Hart, *J.B. Harkin: Father of Canada's National Parks* (Edmonton: University of Alberta Press, 2010).

4. M.B. Williams, *Guardians of the Wild* (London: Thomas Nelson and Sons, 1936), 138.

5. *Annual Report of the Department of the Interior for the year 1886*, Part I: Dominion Lands, Sessional Paper no. 7 (Ottawa, 1887), 9.

6. Van Horne saw tourist revenue as a way to pay for the astronomical costs of the transcontinental construction project. See, for example, Walter Vaughan, *The Life and Work of Sir William Van Horne* (New York: Century, 1920) 151, and E.J. Hart, *The Selling of Canada: The CPR and the Beginnings of Canadian Tourism* (Banff: Altitude, 1983) 7, and "See this world before the

next: Tourism and the CPR," in *The CPR West: The iron road and the making of a nation*, ed. Hugh A. Dempsey, 151 (Vancouver: Douglas & McIntyre, 1984). Prime Minister John A. Macdonald shared this point of view, telling the House of Commons that a park at the Banff hot springs would "recuperate the patients, and recoup the Treasury." House of Commons, *Debates*, 3 May 1887.

7. House of Commons, *Debates*, 13 January 1911.

8. With jurisdiction over the vast federal territories in the northwest, Interior's portfolios included federal lands, Indian Affairs, the Geological Survey and the Dominion Survey, immigration, leases for homestead lands, timber, ranching, and mining, reclamation and water, the Forest Service, and, from 1911, the Parks Branch.

9. See Peter Murphy, "'Following the Base of the Foothills': Tracing the Boundaries of Jasper Park and its Adjacent Rocky Mountains Forest Reserve," in *Culturing Wilderness in Jasper National Park: Studies in Two Centuries of Human History in the Upper Athabasca River Watershed*, ed. I.S. MacLaren, 71–122 (Edmonton: University of Alberta Press, 2007).

10. Paul Kopas, *Taking the Air: Ideas and Change in Canada's National Parks* (Vancouver: UBC Press, 2007), 29; J.B. Harkin, "Report of the Commissioner,"

Annual Report of the Department of the Interior, 1919, Sessional Paper no. 25 (Ottawa, 1920), 3–4.

11 These were Menissawok (1914–30) in Saskatchewan and Wawaskesy (1914–38) and Nemiskam (1915–47) in Alberta, all of which were renamed national parks in 1922. This is the first and last time we see the use of aboriginal names until the creation of Kejimkujik National Park in Nova Scotia in 1968. Also see Jennifer Brower, *Lost Tracks: Buffalo National Park, 1909–1939* (Edmonton: AU Press, 2008), for the story of another wildlife preserve (1908–47) that was eventually eliminated.

12 Williams, *Guardians of the Wild,* 136–37.

13 C.J. Taylor, "Legislating Nature: The National Parks Act of 1930," in *To See Ourselves / To Save Ourselves: Ecology and Culture in Canada,* ed. Rowland Lorimer et al., 125–37 (Montreal: Association for Canadian Studies, 1991); also Taylor, *Negotiating the Past: The Making of Canada's National Historic Parks and Sites* (Montreal: McGill-Queen's University Press, 1990).

14 For more on this, see Shaun Fluker, "Ecological integrity and the law: The view from Canada's National Parks," Parks for Tomorrow 40th Anniversary Conference, Calgary, Alberta, 8–12 May 2008.

15 See Alan MacEachern, *Natural Selections: National Parks in Atlantic Canada, 1935–1970* (Montreal: McGill-Queen's University Press, 2001). Another study of the interwar period is Bill Waiser's *Park Prisoners: The Untold Story of Western Canada's National Parks, 1915–1946* (Calgary: Fifth House, 1995).

16 Ethan Carr, *Mission 66: Modernism and the National Park dilemma* (Amherst: University of Massachusetts Press in association with Library of American Landscape History, 2007); Richard West Sellars, *Preserving Nature in the National Parks: A History* (New Haven, CT: Yale University Press, 1997).

17 Kopas, *Taking the Air,* 37–66.

18 Jean Chrétien, *Straight from the Heart* (Toronto: Key Porter, 1985), 68.

19 Catriona Mortimer-Sandilands argues strongly for the nationalist message in park creation and presentation throughout the twentieth century, even after "the ecological turn." See "The Cultural Politics of Ecological Integrity: Nature and Nation in Canada's National Parks, 1885–2000," *International Journal of Canadian Studies* 39/40 (2009): 161–89. On the System Plan, see the *National Parks System Plan,* 3d ed. (Hull, QC: Canadian Heritage and Parks Canada, 1997); http://www.pc.gc.ca/eng/docs/v-g/nation/nation1.aspx. The Agency's stated goal remains to have at least one national park and one national marine conservation area in each of Canada's terrestrial and marine regions; currently 28 of the 39 terrestrial regions and 3 of the 29 marine regions are represented. See *Parks Canada Agency Corporate Plan, 2009/10–2013/14/ Agence Parcs Canada plan d'entreprise, 2009–2010 à 2013–2014* (Gatineau, QC: Parks Canada, 2009), 6. http://www.pc.gc.ca/eng/docs/pc/plans/plan2008-2009/sec1/page01.aspx) (However, in 1989, CPAWS and World Wildlife Canada complicated the neat jigsaw visual by launching an Endangered Spaces campaign, which called for protecting sample landscapes

in *350* regions). In 2010, Parks Canada proposed two future parks, both in Eastern Canada: Mealy Mountains, Labrador, as representative of the "East Coast Boreal Natural Region," and Sable Island, Nova Scotia. In the west, a memorandum of understanding with the province of British Columbia in 2003 enabled Parks to undertake a feasibility study for a park in the "Interior Dry Plateau Region" in the south Okanagan Valley, to be called the South Okanagan–Lower Similkameen National Park Reserve.

20 For a view of how this affected parks practice within the agency, see David Neufeld, "The development of community-based cultural research and management programs: The Canadian Parks Service (CPS) experience in the northwest," *Canadian Oral History Association Journal* 12 (1992): 30–33.

21 Parks Canada uses this definition of ecological integrity: "'An ecosystem has integrity when it is deemed characteristic for its natural region, including the composition and abundance of native species and biological communities, rates of change and supporting processes.' In plain language, ecosystems have integrity when they have their native components (plants, animals and other organisms) and processes (such as growth and reproduction) intact." Panel on the Ecological Integrity of Canada's National Parks, *Unimpaired for Future Generations? Conserving Ecological Integrity with Canada's National Parks* (Ottawa, 2000). It was established as paramount in the 1988 *National Parks Act* and the 1994 *Parks Canada Guiding Principles and Operational Policies*, which also acknowledged the importance of ecosystem health outside of

park boundaries and introduced new categories of designation, including national marine conservation areas.

22 David Bernard et al., *State of the Banff–Bow Valley, prepared for Banff-Bow Valley Study* (Banff, 1996); *State of the Parks Report*, especially for 1997 and 1999 (Parks Canada, 1998 and 2000) – continued as *State of Protected Heritage Areas*, reported in 2005 and 2007; *Unimpaired for Future Generations?* (2000).

23 While some agencies were related to Parks Canada, primarily in its historic sites mandate – notably Library and Archives Canada, and the National Battlefields Commission – the Department of Canadian Heritage is responsible for a primarily cultural portfolio, including, for example, the national museums, film and television, cultural property, and public servants. On the Parks Canada Agency, see *An Act to Establish the Parks Canada Agency* S.C. 31 (1998).

24 I owe this idea to a point made by Catriona Mortimer-Sandilands in "Calypso Trails: Botanizing on the Bruce Peninsula," *Dalhousie Review* 90, no. 1 (2010): 21. Also Parks Canada Agency charter (2002), http://www.pc.gc.ca/agen/chart/chartr_E.asp. The Agency's recent insistence on "visitor experience" betrays its quasi-market concerns; Chief Executive Officer Alan Latourelle recently highlighted Parks Canada's success in winning awards from the tourism industry. See *Parks Canada Agency Corporate Plan, 2008/09–2012/13/Agence Parcs Canada plan d'entreprise, 2008–2009 à 2012–2013* (Gatineau, QC: Parks Canada, 2008), 5.

25 Eric Higgs, "Twinning Reality, or how taking history seriously changes how we understand ecological restoration in Jasper National Park," in *Culturing Wilderness*, ed. MacLaren, 292.

26 At the 2008 conference, Alan MacEachern suggested that parks history actually was now more marginalized than it had been at the original "Parks for Tomorrow" conference forty years before. MacEachern, "Writing the History of Canadian Parks: Past, Present, and Future," Parks for Tomorrow 40th Anniversary Conference (Calgary, 2008) http://dspace.ucalgary.ca/bitstream/1880/46876/1/MacEachern.pdf. The 1968 conference proceedings were published as *The Canadian National Parks: Today and Tomorrow*, ed. J.G. Nelson and R.C. Scace (Calgary: National and Provincial Parks Association of Canada and the University of Calgary, 1969) and *Canadian Parks in Perspective: Based on the Conference The Canadian National Parks: Today and Tomorrow, Calgary, October 1968*, ed. J.G. Nelson with R.C. Scace (Montreal: Harvest House, 1970). R.C. Brown's essay "The Doctrine of Usefulness," from the 1968 conference, is one of the most cited for evidence of the exploitative or development-oriented agendas of early national parks, but a few years earlier A. Roger Byrne pointed to the diverse effects of human activity on a park in his M.Sc. thesis, "Man and landscape change in the Banff National Park area before 1911" (Calgary: University of Calgary, 1964). Brown's criticism was amplified by Leslie Bella in *Parks for Profit* (Montreal: Harvest House, 1987). Rick Searle, in *Phantom Parks: The Struggle to Save Canada's National Parks* (Toronto: Key Porter, 2000),

expresses concern over parks' long-term ecological integrity. On the other hand, the more prosaic institutional history is W.F. Lothian's *A Brief History of Canada's National Parks* (Ottawa: Environment Canada, 1987). Sid Marty, *A Grand and Fabulous Notion: The First Century of Canada's Parks* (Toronto: NC Press, in co-operation with Cave and Basin Project, Parks Canada, and Supply and Services Canada, 1984), the centennial publication, is predictably celebratory in tone, as is Robert J. Burns with Mike Schintz, *Guardians of the Wild: A History of the Warden Service of Canada's National Parks* (Calgary: University of Calgary Press, 2000). Janet Foster's *Working for Wildlife: The Beginnings of Preservation in Canada* (Toronto: University of Toronto Press, 1978, 1998) also looks favourably on the efforts of civil servants involved in wildlife policy. But the publication with the most public impact is likely the beautifully photographed *National Parks of Canada* by J.A. Kraulis and Kevin McNamee, rev. ed. (Toronto: Key Porter, 2004).

27 Mark Fiege, *Irrigated Eden: The Making of an Agricultural Landscape in the American West* (Seattle: University of Washington Press, 1999), 205. See also Richard White, "From Wilderness to Hybrid Landscapes: The Cultural Turn in Environmental History," *The Historian* 66 (2004): 558. The "cultural turn" is apparent in the park history that has proliferated in Canada in recent years. Such work includes MacEachern, *Natural Selections*; the essays in MacLaren, ed., *Culturing Wilderness*; Kopas, *Taking the Air*; Bill Waiser, *Saskatchewan's Playground: A History of Prince Albert National Park* (Saskatoon: Fifth House, 1989); John

S. Marsh and Bruce W. Hodgins, ed., *Changing Parks: The History, Future and Cultural Context of Parks and Heritage Landscapes* (Toronto: Natural Heritage/Natural History, 1998); Lyle Dick, *Muskox Land: Ellesmere Island in the Age of Contact* (Calgary: University of Calgary Press, 2001); George Colpitts, *Game in the Garden: A Human History of Wildlife in Western Canada to 1940* (Vancouver: UBC Press, 2002); John Sandlos, *Hunters at the Margin: Native People and Wildlife Conservation in the Northwest Territories* (Vancouver: UBC Press, 2007); C.J. Taylor, *Jasper: A History of the Place and Its People* (Calgary: Fifth House, 2009).

28 As Alan MacEachern has argued elsewhere, "In attempting to make decisions, we may as well draw on the experiences of those who came before us, who may have had to make similar decisions. The past is by no means a sure guide to the future, but then again it is the only database we have." "Writing the History of Canadian Parks" (2008), 2.

29 Environmental history is somewhat unusual because it is often oriented toward public engagement, even political application. Catherine A. Christen and Lisa Mighetto, "Environmental History as Public History," *The Public Historian* 26 (2004): 9–19.

M.B. Williams and the Early Years of Parks Canada

ALAN MACEACHERN
DEPARTMENT OF HISTORY
UNIVERSITY OF WESTERN ONTARIO

I remember, I remember the place where "Parks" was born
The dirty wind was where no sun came creeping in at morn
Yet nine never came a wink too soon, nor brought too long
    a day
For working under J.B.H. was less like work than play.
There were Maxwell, Byshe and Johnson and good F.H.W.
Wise A.K. and witty F.V. and quiet M.B. too.
There were piles and piles of dusty files about leases, lots and
    land
Way back when business was polite and memos were writ by
    hand.

The opening of "An Interminable Ode," a poem read to J. B. Harkin at a party following his retirement as first commissioner of national parks in Canada. Portions of the poem begin each section of this chapter.[1]

In a scratchy tape-recorded interview conducted by her niece in 1969, Mabel Williams recalls how she had first come to work with the Canadian Dominion Parks Branch almost sixty years earlier. She was working in Ottawa in 1911 as a clerk for the Department of Interior, cutting out newspaper clippings that related to the department's business. It was the sort of low-level position available to a single woman of the day, even one in her thirties and university-educated. (She had been one of the first female students at the University of Western Ontario, and a member of the University of Toronto's "Double Duck Egg" class that graduated in 1900.) One day, Williams was visited by her boss, James Bernard Harkin, the private secretary to Minister Frank Oliver. Do you ever get sick of politics, he asked. "I'm fed up to my teeth now," she said. He told her that he was to be commissioner of a new branch devoted to national parks, and wondered if she would like to join him.

"What in the world are national parks?" Williams asked.

"Blessed if I know," Harkin replied, "but it sounds easy."[2]

It's a lovely story, when you know what followed. James B. Harkin directed the Parks Branch, the first agency in the world devoted to national parks, through its first quarter century and became the parks' greatest advocate. The Branch and the system it oversaw flourished in those decades. And Mabel – M.B. – Williams rose in the 1910s from clipping newspapers to helping formulate and communicate the Branch's philosophy. In the 1920s, despite a recurring, poorly diagnosed illness that kept her bedridden for long periods of time throughout her entire life, she explored the parks by foot, by horse, and by car, as research for writing the guidebooks that would be that decade's centrepiece of tourism promotion of the parks, of the Canadian Rockies, and even of Canada itself.

It's also a familiar story in Canadian parks history, but with an important twist. In the standard telling, Harkin is the novice invited to join the Parks Branch by his boss, Oliver; Williams does not appear. That standard version originated in a 1961 booklet of posthumously published extracts from Harkin's personal papers and has been replayed in histories of Canadian national parks ever since.[3] The story constitutes an important step in the veneration of Harkin: his initial ignorance of parks, rather than being an impediment, ends up magnifying the extent of his conversion to conservation, symbolizing the

transformative power of parks. Today, Harkin is considered one of our nation's environmental heroes. The Canadian Parks and Wilderness Society names its highest honour the Harkin Award, for example, and sums up his reputation by stating, "Often called 'The Father of National Parks', J. B. Harkin developed the idea of conservation in Canada."[4] Nothing, by contrast, has ever been written about M.B. Williams; she has been entirely lost to history.

FIG. 2.
J.B. HARKIN,
FIRST
COMMISSIONER OF
NATIONAL PARKS
IN CANADA, 24
FEBRUARY 1937.
[SOURCE: LIBRARY
AND ARCHIVES
CANADA/
CREDIT: YOUSUF
KARSH/YOUSUF
KARSH FONDS/
E010767606.]

But interestingly, the sole source of the story about Harkin joining the Branch is Williams herself; it was she who lovingly compiled his memoirs and saw them to publication in 1961. Yet it was also she who, when interviewed in 1969, reframed the story as her own. Whether the incident actually happened to Williams or Harkin or both or neither is largely beside the point. Rather, the story – stories – serve as a reminder of the hazards of biography, and most especially the care that must be taken in seeing the history of an organization through the lens of a single person, whether a renowned man or a forgotten woman. Groups are, almost by definition, the product of more than one person.

Using as a basis M.B. Williams' newly available archival papers and oral interview, and the guidebooks published under her name, this chapter will explore the 1911 to 1930 development of the Dominion Parks Branch, forerunner to Parks Canada.[5] This period saw the parks system experience a phenomenally rapid maturity: it cultivated a loyal staff, a national and international reputation, a claim to permanent consideration, and most importantly – and unusual for a government agency – a coherent and well-accepted philosophy that would help constantly regenerate all of these other elements. Whereas the Branch was born in 1911 with a staff of seven and a budget of $200,000 (just 4% of its department's overall budget), with the parks attracting 50,000 visitors per year, by the onset of the Great Depression the Branch had a staff of 44 and a budget of $1,400,000 (more than 16% of the department's budget), and the parks welcomed 550,000 annual visitors.[6]

Williams' papers and publications do more than document this growth: they help explain it, because she was deeply involved in the development and dissemination of the emerging philosophy of parks, a philosophy that stressed both their humanitarian and commercial value to the nation. In the 1910s, she was instrumental in linking parks to tourism, giving Harkin the ammunition he would need in annual reports, speeches, and newspaper columns to justify parks and spending on them. In the 1920s, she was the chief author of the parks system's series of promotional guidebooks, which taught that parks are the birthright of all Canadians, and that they make one physically stronger, psychologically renewed, spiritually fulfilled, and aesthetically aware. The goal of this chapter is not to argue that M.B. Williams, rather than J.B. Harkin, was the mastermind behind the development of Canadian national parks – to replace one hero myth with another – but instead to use her story to show that the germinating parks philosophy was the product of the entire agency.[7] More than that, the literature generated by the agency to win over Canadian politicians and the public had the unforeseen effect of also unifying the Branch's own staff around a core philosophy. Nowhere is this more evident than in the experience of M.B. Williams herself, who arrived having no knowledge of national parks but remained their champion, and even compiled her boss's memoirs, long after her retirement.

But [Harkin] cried Gadzooks to his waiting staff, "Ye must
    shoulder spade and axe
The House is full of Scotsmen, we must hit them hard with
    facts!
Get facts bedad" (with none to be had for who knew of Park's
    existence?
But a newspaperman's life is as good as a wife to stiffen a
    man's persistence)
So he drove us forth, east, west, south, north, with noses close
    to the ground
Hard on the trail of the Lonesome Facts and at last one fact
    was found
But J. B. cried "By the Buffalo's hide, one fact is enough for
    me
'Tis a great deal more than I had of yore when I wrote polit-
    icly."
And out of that small and modest fact, with the single yeast
    of his mind
He fashioned a Tourist Gospel that struck those Scotsmen
    blind.
Till even Mr. Meighen said, "That Harkin man is a honey
This is far less painful than taxes, let us give the lad some
    money!"

In September 1911, the Dominion Parks Branch set up its office in the new
Birks Building on Sparks Street in Ottawa. With just seven employees, most
of them transferred from the Forestry and Survey Branches, it constituted
about one-hundredth of the overall Department of the Interior. Mabel Williams would later state,

> There was little in the new office at Ottawa to serve for guide
> or inspiration. The files which had been transferred to the new
> organization were for the most part dreary compilations of cor-
> respondence concerning transfers of land in the townsites of

Banff and Field, the collection of rates and telephone charges, complaints concerning dusty roads and the absence of garbage collection. There were few photographs and no books, with the exception of Government records and bulletins. Three thousand miles away from their inspiring reality, it was difficult to visualize these national parks, and far more difficult to realize to what manifold uses they might be put.[8]

In Williams' memory, the very fact that the challenge seemed so daunting – the Branch so small, the lands it was to oversee so vast – helped to bring the unit together. And the staff quickly became devoted to Harkin, as he encouraged both collaboration and independence. The Commissioner "never wanted anything for himself, never wanted to make a sensation. You'd go to a meeting, and he'd always be in the backseat."[9] Williams undoubtedly had another reason for growing loyal to Harkin: at a time when the civil service commission actively kept women out of all but the most junior positions, he gave her increasingly important responsibilities and supported her rise in the office.[10]

The Dominion Parks Branch had been born in spite of national parks' insignificance, or perhaps even because of it.[11] Between 1885 and 1911, Rocky Mountains (Banff), Glacier, Yoho, Jasper, and Waterton Lakes National Parks had been created by a variety of mechanisms, under a variety of regulations, and under no central control. As Williams would later write, "the Government straightaway forgot about them, and for years the reserves were left to look after themselves."[12] This began to change early in the twentieth century, thanks to two strands of the era's conservation movement. On the one hand, there was a growing societal interest in going back to nature, drawing more attention to the seemingly unspoiled wilderness of parks. On the other hand, the rise of the principle of resource conservation encouraged the development of federal forest reserves, places where forests would be efficiently and scientifically managed so that their timber would be available forever. Since forests hold and protect both water and wildlife, forest reserves became associated with water and wildlife conservation, too. In effect, they took on many of the features that we today associate with national parks, minus the tourism development and the not insignificant difference that their forests were to be regularly harvested. In 1908, when the Canadian government under Wilfrid Laurier decided that national parks should be administered more centrally, the forest reserve model was at its very peak, so it was natural that the government placed the parks under the care of the division already administering forest reserves, the Forest Branch. Howard Douglas, until then Superintendent of Rocky Mountains Park, was moved to Edmonton and given responsibility for all the parks.

The 1911 *Dominion Forest Reserves and Parks Act* was meant to formalize the relationship between these two types of government properties. The Act defined parks as distinct entities but *within* forest reserves – bordered by them on all sides, and so literally subsumed by them. (Elk Island and Waterton Lakes had been defined as parks within forest reserves in 1906 and 1907 respectively.) This provided national parks with buffer zones from development and exploitation, but it also had two negative consequences. First, it reduced the size of most existing parks by turning some of their boundary lands into forest reserves. Rocky Mountains Park, for example, was shrunk from 4,500 to 1,800 square miles. Second, it meant that parks would, in the words of Minister Frank Oliver, "look to the enjoyment by the people of the natural advantages and beauties of those particular sections of the reserves, while the regulations regarding the remainder of the forest reserves looks rather to the exclusion of people from them."[13] Put another way, parks were defined by virtue of being developed, and reserves by virtue of being undeveloped. The *Forest Reserves and Parks Act* both signalled and made official how insignificant Canadian national parks really were in this period. They could easily have become places separated entirely from environmental concern and dedicated solely to tourism. Indeed, in terms of parks that was the Act's intention.

What prevented this outcome was that the Act also created a new Dominion Parks Branch. It may seem strange that at the very moment the Laurier government explicitly defined parks as places within reserves, it also severed administrative responsibility for the two. It may seem even stranger that it made the Parks Branch equivalent rather than subservient to the Forest Branch. This decision would lead to considerable confusion in the coming years – but it also supports the notion that the government considered parks and forest reserves as conceptually quite distinct.[14] The new Parks Branch could easily have defined its responsibilities conservatively, as being whatever the Forest Branch was not already doing, in whatever parks already existed.[15]

Such an interpretation would have not only been justified, it might have been thought politically expedient. After all, the new Branch was headed by James Harkin, who was closely tied to the Laurier administration but who was taking up his new position in September 1911, the very month that the Conservatives swept Laurier's Liberals from power.

There can be no greater testimony to national parks' obscurity in this era than the fact that Harkin expressed complete ignorance of them (or at least Williams wrote that he did), despite having been private secretary to the minister responsible for parks for the previous decade. Harkin directed his new staff to find out as much as possible about national parks. The American parks were contacted, as were Canadian government departments. Harkin also travelled out west to visit the parks, to the great appreciation of those working and living there. The townspeople of Banff were especially impressed because they had long complained that their concerns were ignored and the park under-managed. The parks commissioner made at least twelve trips to Banff in the 1910s, and the local *Crag and Canyon* reported on every one. As early as Harkin's second visit, the editor was already crowing, "J. B. is a friend of the Canadian National Park. He sleeps, eats, and smokes on the Canadian National Park. In fact he almost gets tiresome the way he talks about this park – stay with it – 'O you J. B.' *Crag and Canyon* is with you now and always."[16] The editor might have expressed reservations had he known that one of Harkin's first letters to the Banff Superintendent quizzed him as to whether a regulation concerning the weight of bread sold within park boundaries was being enforced.[17] The people of Banff would soon be complaining that the parks were being micromanaged from afar.

In M.B. Williams' recollection, Harkin's first task for her was to examine the timber leasing system; she found violations in nineteen of twenty leases.[18] An unsigned Branch memo reported that Forest Commissioner R.H. Campbell's second-in-command had been involved in "a crooked deal" in the years prior to the Parks Branch's creation, selling the parks' timber leases for personal gain. To the memo's author, such corruption signalled that parks and forest reserves were inherently incompatible: "The primary function of the Forestry Branch is to provide lumber. The primary function of the Parks Branch is to provide health, pleasure and patriotism grounds [*sic*] for the nation. The work of the Forestry Branch is closely allied to the business of the lumberman; that of the Parks Branch to that of the landscape artist."[19] Harkin and his staff grew convinced that the parks suffered by being associated with reserves, that the Dominion Forest Reserves and Parks Act had erred in forcing the Forest Branch and the Parks Branch together in a shotgun wedding. Mind you, the Parks Branch may have launched its timber lease investigation in the hopes of coming to just that conclusion.

So almost immediately after the 1911 Act brought forest reserves and national parks together, work began on pulling them apart. The Act was amended in 1913 to state unequivocally that parks were under the control of the parks commissioner and to allow for the creation of new parks that were not within forest reserves. Further amendments were passed the following year. Also in 1914, Jasper and Waterton Lakes National Parks were enlarged – tellingly, at the expense of their surrounding forest reserves. The Parks Branch and Forests Branch feuded constantly throughout the 1910s, with the former seeking to establish its authority on all matters within parks boundaries and the latter attempting to quash the upstart and at minimum retain control of forest matters within the parks. In the middle of the First World War, Harkin and his Forest Branch equal, R. H. Campbell, even met for a "conference" to carve up responsibilities for the lands they oversaw. But the department's lawyer – decrying the "foolish repeal" of the old *Rocky Mountains Parks Act* and bitterly criticizing its replacement – pointed out that the present Act gave them no such power.[20] The Parks Branch ultimately spent a considerable portion of its energies in its first decade working to overcome the legislation that had created it.

M.B. Williams' next major project for Harkin after tackling the timber lease issue was to strengthen the justification for parks. Government members who controlled the parks' budget appropriation gave no thought to them, too often confusing national parks with the urban variety. Williams would recall that after scouring the Parliamentary and Ottawa Public Libraries,

> I came across an old volume of the Scenic and Historic Preservation Society of America. And in one of their annual sessions, one old chap got up and said, "You know, when you think of it, these beautiful places are worth money." He says, "It brings tourists, it brings people in to see them." And I thought, "Here's my clue." And I brought it up to Mr. Harkin and he seized on it. "That's what we want!" And the words

"Tourist Traffic" had never been mentioned before in the government as a policy.[21]

Tourism had been growing in Canada since the late nineteenth century, and there were a few provincial tourism bureaus by the first decade of the twentieth century, but no federal agency had yet gauged the industry's significance. In retrospect, it seems natural that the new Parks Branch would be the first to do so. The national parks had been established in large part to draw traffic on the CPR, and more generally to attract tourists to the Rocky Mountains. What's more, by 1911 attendance to the parks was just starting to rise, thanks to the automobile. When cars had started arriving in the mountain parks at the turn of the century, the government's response had been to ban them outright. This was in part to protect horseback riders and in part to protect the automobile travellers themselves from hazardous mountain roads. The prohibition lasted until 1910, when cars were permitted on certain roads, and they were soon allowed everywhere, bringing increased visitation to parks in that decade.[22]

The economics of tourism could help justify appropriations for parks, but how to induce the tourists to come in the first place? For that, a more philosophical argument was needed. Harkin, Williams, assistant commissioner F.H.H. Williamson, and other Branch staff crafted this together. They propped up their case with the writings of American, British, and Canadian conservationists, naturalists, and civic leaders, but the amalgamation was their own. Harkin would later say of this effort, when in retirement and asked by Williams to share his memories of the Branch's early days,

> You will re-call our first worry was to satisfy ourselves as to whether Parks were worth-while or not. And the worth-while-ness had to be measured in terms of human welfare, first spiritual; second mental; third, physical. No, not exactly that way, we really felt that these were so intimately mixed up in life, that they were mutually dependent. So all three were requisite. You did more than anyone else to provide the proof. And you convinced the rest of us Parks could pay great dividends in these terms.[23]

For her part, Williams would credit Harkin, who had been a journalist before joining the civil service, for helping make the team's writing come alive.[24] The culmination of their work was a coherent, multifaceted philosophy, one that would serve as the basis for descriptions and defences of national parks for decades to come. The best summary of this philosophy is a long paragraph noteworthy because it concluded two 1914 Parks Branch documents, an internal memo under Harkin's name, "Dominion Parks – Their Values and Ideals," and the agency's first promotional booklet, *A Sprig of Mountain Heather*. That is, the same sentiment was used to inculcate the public and the organization itself with the value of parks. The paragraph read,

> To sum up then, Dominion Parks constitute a movement that means millions of dollars of revenue annually for the people of Canada; that means the preservation for their benefit, advantage and enjoyment forever, of that natural heritage of beauty – whether it be in the form of majestic mountain, peaceful valley, gleaming glacier, crystalline lake or living birds and animals, – which is one of our most precious national possessions; that means the guarantee to the people of Canada today and to all succeeding generations of Canadians of those means of recreation which serve best to make better men and women, physically, morally and mentally; the protection of the country's beauty spots equally for the poor and the rich; the preservation of those places which stand for historic events that have been milestones in Canada's development; they represent a movement calculated to arouse and develop that national pride which Canada's history and Canada's potentialities justify. Canada's parks exist to render the best possible services to Canada and Canadians. Their establishment and development is based upon this idea that Canada's greatness as a nation depends so much upon her natural resources of soil, of minerals or of timber as upon the quality of her men and women.[25]

Throughout the 1910s, this general theme, always bearing Harkin's name, was communicated by the Parks Branch in newspaper columns, magazine articles, and memos to the minister and prime minister. But the Branch chose as its prime forum the lowly annual report. This was certainly unconventional: no other government body so brazenly used its annual report as a means to lobby government and reach the broader public. According to Williams, the ex-newspaperman Harkin did not believe in paid print advertising, and his goal was always to get as much free publicity as possible.[26] So Harkin's early annual reports as commissioner, for example, contained series of images of the mountain parks and outlined in detail the commercial and humanitarian benefits of parks.[27] The Branch then sent these reports to Members of Parliament and newspapers across Canada – effectively turning a mandatory accounting into a marketing plan – earning favourable responses in both the House and editorial pages. The first report was even quoted at length when the U.S. Congress discussed creation of an American park service in 1916.[28] In Harkin's recollection to Williams, the high point of their efforts with these reports was formulating "the famous calculation" that, whereas wheat fields were worth only $4.91 per acre to Canada, scenery was worth $13.88.[29]

The government reacted very positively to the Parks Branch's message, although appropriations did not rise until after the First World War.[30] In working to justify the parks' existence, the Branch had effectively achieved the greater accomplishment of simply drawing attention to the parks' existence, something that had not really happened before. In 1919, Liberal member Lucien Cannon sought explanation from Conservative Prime Minister Arthur Meighen as to why the parks were to be given the power of expropriation. "For what purpose are those Dominion parks established?" he asked.

"For Dominion parks," Meighen answered.

This did not satisfy Cannon, so he tried again: "What is the purpose of a Dominion park?"

Meighen replied, "I do not know that any words could do other than obscure the very plain meaning of the term 'Dominion Park.'"[31] This terminological *pas de deux* could only have occurred at the moment when parks were moving from unfamiliar to self-explanatory in the public mind.

*****

And once he had the stuff to spend there soon was the
  Heather Pamph
(Poor Mr. Knechtel down on his knees gathering sprigs at
  Banff)
And so it went from year to year like a snowball getting bigger
And some of us lost our hair at last and some of us lost our
  figger

In 1914, J. B. Harkin had the idea of creating a guide to Banff that would have a souvenir sprig of heather attached to its cover. It was to be the sort of book that people would take home and display on their parlour table, and so advertise the park to others. Harkin assumed that writing *A Sprig of Mountain Heather* would be easy, but when he set to work on it found himself blocked at the very first sentence. He called in the whole office and asked help to get started. Mabel Williams gave him the first lines – "'The top o' the world to you' is an old greeting in Ireland, but this little sprig of Mountain Heather brings to you in very reality a bit of the top o' the world" – and eventually much of what followed. Having discovered that Williams had a flair for this kind of writing, the commissioner handed more and more public writing assignments over to her.[32]

Not that there was much promotional work in that period: the Dominion Parks Branch may have discovered tourism in the 1910s, but it was not really until the 1920s that it began to actively foster tourism by publishing promotional literature. Because of tightened budgets during the First World War, and perhaps also because Harkin preferred his publicity free, the office in its first decade tended only to publish guidebooks when an opportunity easily presented itself, such as when Alpine Club of Canada President A.P. Coleman wrote *Glaciers of the Rockies and Selkirks* or M.P. Bridgland and Robert Douglas wrote *Description of and Guide to Jasper Park* to accompany Bridgland's survey of the park.[33] Otherwise, travel guides were a low priority. The parks constantly hounded headquarters for more copies of what few there were – which certainly suggested a market demand – but Ottawa offered little help. When the superintendent at Jasper pleaded for more copies of his park's guide, he was told that since there were only 850 copies left he should raise their price from 30¢ to 50¢ or even 75¢ as a means of restricting their sale and distribution.[34] But the dearth of tourism material was no longer considered acceptable. By 1920 there were about 100,000 visitors to the Canadian parks each year, with many arriving by car, so the system could no longer depend solely on the tourism literature generated by the railroads.[35]

It was in this context that Mabel Williams was sent west to explore and write about the parks. Giving the job to Williams indicates either how much faith Harkin was coming to have in her or how relatively unimportant tourism promotion was still thought to be, or both. True, she had proven herself capable in every writing assignment given her. But she had no experience in travel writing and not much in travel. She had passed her fortieth birthday without ever having been to Western Canada, let alone their parks, and was not in the least bit outdoorsy. She also suffered from a number of ailments, including a poorly understood form of anemia; her personnel file shows six sick leaves in the late 1920s, ranging from eight days to three months.[36] Things began inauspiciously when at the end of her first day riding through Jasper National Park she got off the horse and fainted.[37]

Yet Williams ended up riding, hiking, and driving the parks of Western Canada from end to end. From this research she authored a string of guidebooks – all of the travel guides published by the Dominion Parks Branch in the 1920s – beginning with *Through the Heart of the Rockies and Selkirks* in 1921 and continuing through *The Banff-Windermere Highway, Waterton Lakes National Park, Kootenay National Park and the Banff-Windermere Highway, Jasper National Park, Prince Albert National Park, Jasper Trails*, and *The Kicking Horse Trail*. In retrospect, Williams' timing was impeccable. Of the 1921–22 fiscal year, Harkin declared, "For the first time since the outbreak of the war it was possible to devote part of the appropriation to publicity," so the Branch could afford to make *Through the Heart of the Rockies and Selkirks* its first mass-market guidebook, available to whoever wanted a copy. The agency's expenditures in the government's printing department jumped in a single year from $2,000 to almost $13,000.[38]

The Branch reprinted at least 10,000 copies of Williams' first guidebook five of the next six years.[39] And having convinced the department once to invest in such a travel guide, it was easier to do so again. As Harkin told his deputy minister, "It is a generally accepted axiom that advertising to be successful must be kept up. If we stop advertising these parks I think it probable we shall see a falling off of tourist travel."[40] The Parks Branch formed a Publicity Division, which quickly became the foremost government body

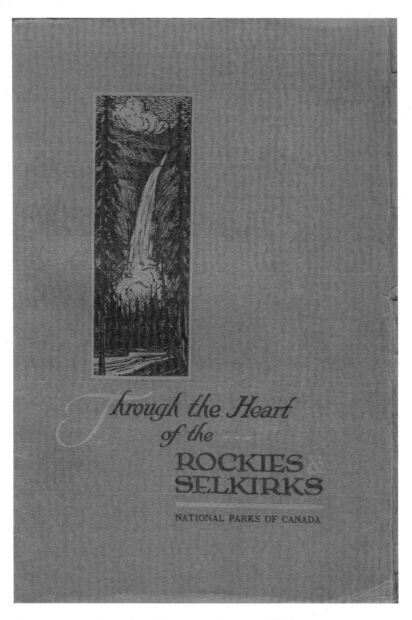

Fig. 3. Cover of *Through the Heart of the Rockies and Selkirks*, 4TH ED. [Ottawa: Department of the Interior, 1929 (1921).]

JASPER
NATIONAL PARK

by
M.B.WILLIAMS

1928

Camp in Byng Pass, Jasper National Park

FIG. 4. TITLE PAGE OF *Jasper National Park*. [OTTAWA: DEPARTMENT OF THE INTERIOR, 1928.]

for promoting Canada through guidebooks, public lectures and slide presentations, and motion pictures. By the end of the 1920s, the Division had twenty-five employees. Ironically, its success helped lead to the establishment of agencies that would ultimately displace it, the Canadian Government Travel Bureau and the National Film Board.[41]

All this changed Mabel Williams' career, and her life. Her salary had risen only from $1,200 to $1,300 in the 1910s – while, by comparison, Deputy Commissioner Williamson's rose from $1,300 to $2,500 – but it climbed to $1,560 when her job title shifted to "publicity assistant" in 1921, and to $2,160 when she became "publicity agent" the following year. She was soon overseeing much of the work in the new Publicity Division, and when the agency started making travel and wildlife documentaries, she penned the script for fifty of them. By 1930, she was making $3,000 per year.[42] With her first guidebook she adopted the gender-neutral "M.B." for her writing career, and, more tellingly, for the life she assumed off the page as well. The travel guides made M.B. Williams an author, and she subsequently identified as one.

Comparing Williams' 1928 *Jasper National Park* with M.P. Bridgland and Robert Douglas's 1917 *Description of and Guide to Jasper Park* helps to demonstrate how her writing built on what little parks literature there was, while moving considerably beyond it, accentuating both the maturing parks philosophy and the related changing approach to parks promotion. The two books are superficially similar, in terms of being text-heavy with many small scattered photographs, predominantly of distant mountains. They have similar structures, with an early chapter on the Jasper region's history followed by area-by-area excursions to sites of interest throughout the park. In the historical chapter, Williams uses some of the very same quotations that Bridgland and Douglas do, from David Thompson, Gabriel Franchère, and Alexander Ross, to define Jasper in terms of Canada's exploration and fur trade history. And yet the key difference between the two books is evident in their very first sentences. Bridgland and Douglas set to work immediately to lay a factual foundation: "Jasper Park is historic ground. More stirring scenes in the upbuilding of Canada have been staged in it than in any other part of the Rockies."[43] In contrast, Williams seeks a more relaxed, literary effect, opening with an epigraph from the British socialist writer Edward Carpenter, and then commenting on it:

> To make some share of 'the wild places of the land sacred,' is the avowed object of the national parks. Everywhere else the continent over, the swift tide of civilization rushes onward; the land our fathers knew disappears; the ancient forests fall back before the lumberman; waterfalls are impoverished to turn the wheels of industry; the wild game is driven even farther and farther back. But within the boundaries of the great national reservations lie a few thousand square miles, safe and inviolate, so far as it is within the power of man, from change and invasion. Of these national possessions in Canada the greatest is Jasper Park.[44]

This became Williams' trademark device: associating the Canadian national parks with a noted thinker – from Pauline Johnson to Johann Goethe – by way of a quotation and having that lead into a description of how the parks were fulfilling important social, spiritual, or environmental goals. Her style was more artistic and her intent more ambitious than that of her predecessors. Williams treated the Parks Branch's 1920s guidebooks as extension of the 1910s annual reports, using them to develop and disseminate the justification for parks directly to the public.

But the fact that Williams used some of the same quotations in her Jasper book as Bridgland and Douglas had a decade earlier raises an obvious question: how can we know which of the guidebooks were truly *hers*? After all, Parks Branch staff were already accustomed to writing prose as a team but giving credit to one person. And Williams' authorship was indeed treated fluidly at times. Her name appears nowhere on the 1923 *The Banff-Windermere Highway* (although she listed it among her works in her archival papers), but the 1928 *Kootenay National Park and Banff-Windermere Highway*, borrowing heavily on its predecessor, is credited to her. On the other hand, having being listed as author of the 1928 *Prince Albert National Park*, her name was removed entirely from the 1935 edition: a draft typescript pasted in large portions of the original text and also pasted a blank sheet of paper over her name.[45] Perhaps the best evidence that M.B. Williams wrote the guidebooks bearing her name – besides her rising salary, parks correspondence about the books' production, and her own claims in her archival papers and oral interview – is simply that, whereas it made sense for the Parks Branch to credit most parks literature to Commissioner Harkin, there was no reason to credit the guides to the unknown (and, on the book jackets, unidentified) Williams. Still, one can and should read Williams' guidebooks as not only expressive of her personal opinions but also as indicative of where the Branch's thinking was headed in the 1920s. Her work relied on information supplied by government biologists and geologists, it was produced with the aid of staff photographers and designers, it was vetted by her colleagues and superiors, and, of course, she was heavily involved in shaping the broader parks philosophy and promotional strategy of which it was a part.

Two elements found in M.B. Williams' guidebooks may show how they helped develop and communicate the Branch's values: their celebration of the automobile and their treatment of First Nations. The automobile was

FIG. 5. COVER OF *The Banff-Windermere Highway*. [OTTAWA: DEPARTMENT OF THE INTERIOR, 1923.]

in a very real sense the impetus for these guidebooks, both because it increased traffic to the parks and because it, unlike the train, spread that traffic throughout the parks. Yet in Williams' first book, the 1921 *Through the Heart of the Rockies and Selkirks*, the car does not really figure; how tourists get to and around the parks is unimportant. But the inroads the Parks Branch had made the previous decade in winning over government led in the 1920s to actual roads: the completion of the Banff-Windermere Highway crossing Banff and Kootenay parks in 1923 and the Kicking Horse Trail from Lake Louise through Yoho to Golden four years later. (John Sandlos discusses 1920s parks roadbuilding in more detail in the chapter that follows.) In Williams' travel guides to the parks along these highways, the roads become symbols of a modern nation working with the individual to achieve personal betterment. *The Banff-Windermere Highway* opens, "The building of a motor highway across the central Canadian Rockies adds one more thrilling chapter to the romance of modern engineering" and ends, "Out of the dreams of a few far-visioned men have come the National parks and the National highways of to-day. Is there not room to believe that the final outcome will exceed all their imaginings and that both are only entering upon their possible service to humanity; that they may in the end prove for all the people to be roads back to a healthier and fuller contact with nature, to a wider and deeper love of country and a richer and more joyous life?"[46] By the time *The Kicking Horse Trail* was published, there was no need to frame the argument tentatively, as a question – the dream is being fulfilled. Williams rhapsodizes about the automobile:

> the "horseless carriage," fantastic chimera for so many centuries of wildly imaginative minds. ... Already, in two short decades, have we not seen it practically revolutionize our way of life, sweeping away with one gesture, the old measures of time and distance, and enabling man, for the first time since he exchanged his nomadic existence for the warm security of the fireside, to escape from the narrow boundaries of his local parish and to enter upon a wider, more joyous, more adventurous life.[47]

The quotation could go on – the entire book is a paean to the automobile – but that is the point: the guidebooks provided Williams with an extensive, targeted, public platform for communicating the Parks Branch's message. Earlier guidebooks had already positioned the mountain parks as much in terms of Canada's history as of nature's timelessness, but Williams went further in downplaying past native occupation of the parks. In her first book, *Through the Heart of the Rockies and Selkirks*, she states that the parks were long vacant because "the Indians seem to have feared and avoided the mountains." The Stonies had only entered the Bow Valley "possibly less than a century ago" and the Shuswaps "built their half-buried dwellings at the base of mount Rundle where now the tourist plays golf, but the Indians left few more marks of their habitation than the wild animals."[48] Such an argument threads through all her 1920s guidebooks. The aboriginal presence was worth mentioning only because of their alleged legends, which helped give the parks a sense of enchantment. On the second page of *Waterton Lakes National Park*, the reader is told that "The Indians, who, like all primitive peoples, weave stories about the places they particularly love, have a legend that this region was miraculously created." After recounting it, Williams ends, "A primitive folk tale? Too childish for our rational and scientific minds? Assuredly. Yet certain it is that a special aura of happiness seems to encircle this charming reservation."[49] And when the First Nations' presence was not inconsequential or charming, it was downright harmful: whereas Bridgland and Douglas's booklet had blamed the decimation of big game around Jasper on workers constructing the transcontinental railways, Williams blamed Indian hunters.[50] It may well be that Williams did not consider her treatment of natives and their history disparaging, let alone racist, but she must surely have recognized it was convenient: erasing the native presence in the parks allowed her to start the parks' history with European exploration and the fur trade, better positioning the parks in the broader history of Canadian nation-building and so defining them more easily as part of our national birthright. Williams did not invent this strategy, either in terms of the Parks Branch or the society at large, but she did help entrench it in the parks.

The guidebooks and other promotional work that Williams and the rest of the Parks Branch initiated in the 1920s evidently yielded results: attendance in parks surged from 150,000 in 1921 to 250,000 in 1925 and 550,000 by 1928.[51] Perhaps the greatest surprise was how many of those visitors were

Canadian. Harkin's annual reports had always preached how valuable parks were, not only financially, but also in terms of improving Canadians themselves; in 1916, he described how parks rejuvenated a nation's "human units" during war.[52] Nonetheless, the focus of tourism in the early years was on visitors to Canada, not from within Canada – an indication that a nation's trade balance was more easily measured than the well-being of her human units. But in the 1920s the national parks were opened up to Canadians: logistically and financially by the automobile, and philosophically and emotionally by the literature the Parks Branch was busily producing. In 1919, Harkin noted the "very substantial increase" of Canadian visitors. By 1927, the commissioner wrote as if Canadian tourists had been favoured all along, saying, "It is especially gratifying to note the large percentage of Canadians among parks' visitors."[53] The truth was that the Parks Branch had never expected the parks to so quickly become so much more accessible to so many more Canadians, nor that their own attempts to promote the parks to tourists and the *idea* of parks to all Canadians would be so quickly successful. In her 1936 *Guardians of the Wild*, M.B. Williams would write that "No development in respect of the National Parks and Sanctuaries during the past twenty-five years can have been more gratifying, if less expected, than the wholehearted support the National Parks have finally won from the Canadian people." That book opens with another epigraph by Edward Carpenter: "I see a great land waiting for its own people to take possession of it."[54] The line served well by this time as something of a mission statement for the Canadian parks system, even if it was a sentiment that had itself waited for the Parks Branch to take possession of it.

*****

So many years, such happy years, under a leader kind
Broad visioned, wise and generous and tolerant of mind
Who never sought for fame or pelf, advancing others not himself!
But history will record his share in building up a land more fair
Praising his dream of man's release through contact with Nature's peace

And men unborn will better be because his heart and mind
could see
That though one half of us be clod, through Beauty we rise
to God.

It is difficult to imagine how Canada's Dominion Parks Branch could have
accomplished more in its first two decades than it did. It had made the national parks much more well-known and popular. It oversaw a considerable
expansion of the parks system, with nine new parks established. Its staff
and appropriation had increased markedly, and it had grown into a government leader in terms of publicity, engineering, and what we today would
call environmental or resource management. And it had developed and was
communicating to Canadians a coherent philosophy that, not only defined
the parks as outstanding examples of Canada's natural landscapes, but also
stressed that parks were to be inviolable, that these places being preserved
today were being preserved forever.[55] The parks system's rapid development
is in sharp contrast to that of the forest reserve system, which had largely
withered away in the same period.[56]

Yet the choices the Branch made in its early years also brought negative
consequences. Focusing on a philosophy and defining parks in terms of all
Canadians for all time tended to alienate some potential here-and-now allies.
The people of Banff, for example, grew furious over how Ottawa managed
their town on the basis of timeless principles rather than their more immediate needs. The editor of the *Crag and Canyon*, who in 1913 had promised
unending loyalty to Harkin, by 1926 wrote an article that stated in its entirety, "J.B. Harkin, Commissioner of Parks, is registered at the Banff Springs
Hotel. Who the hell cares?"[57] (The sentiment would linger through much of
the century, as C.J. Taylor notes in his essay on Banff.) When the Depression hit and a new Conservative government took power in 1930, the Parks
Branch learned the hard way the risk of choosing principles over politics. The
new prime minister was R.B. Bennett, Member of Parliament for Calgary
West, which included the community of Banff. Bennett had long battled
with Harkin over his handling of the parks, and his government proceeded
to gut the Parks Branch. Thirty-two positions were lost in the Ottawa office,
and the prime minister phoned Harkin regularly asking him to resign.[58] For
the entire Depression and the Second World War which followed, the Parks

FIG. 6. FROM *The Kicking Horse Trail.* [OTTAWA: DEPARTMENT OF THE INTERIOR, 1930 (1927).]

Branch wandered in the wilderness, its appropriations and its spirit curtailed dramatically.[59]

But the parks system re-emerged in the mid-1940s, thanks in great part to the firm foundation lain in the 1910s and 20s. When the government became more interested than ever in tourism and cultural development, and when Canadians became more interested than ever in exploring Canadian nature, the Parks Branch already had intact an extensive parks system, strong guiding legislation, and a committed staff. Above all, it had a largely understood and accepted philosophy, one that had been simultaneously developed and promoted in the pages of the Parks Branch's annual reports and guidebooks in the 1910s and 1920s.

As for M.B. Williams herself, when R.B. Bennett cut the parks system's staff and budget, she took it personally, because she knew Bennett personally. She was a longtime friend and companion of Mary Bird Herridge, the stepmother of William Duncan Herridge, who was Benett's policy advisor and husband to his beloved sister Mildred.[60] In a letter home to family, M.B. wrote of attending Parliament with Bennett's sister, and having to watch R.B. as he "perspired in gold lace and white satin trousers, cocked hat with the same grim determination with which he raises the tariff and cuts down the Civil Service."[61] Her own job in the civil service was likely safe, given both her seniority – by this time she oversaw a large staff, including all the women in the Parks Branch headquarters – and her proximity to the Bennett family. But when told to lay off most of her staff, she resigned in solidarity.[62]

M.B. then "ran away"[63] to Europe for a number of years, travelling with Mary Bird Herridge throughout the continent and setting up a home in London, England as a base. She continued writing, though she published nothing. But in 1936, as a favour to staff in the Parks Branch, she helped chaperone Grey Owl on his tour of England. That seemed to reawaken her love of the Canadian parks system, and in the space of five months, she proposed, wrote, and saw to publication the first history of Canada's national parks and the Dominion Parks Branch, titled *Guardians of the Wild*. In it Williams never writes about her own work with the Parks Branch; all credit is given instead to "the Commissioner," who possesses the vision and prescience of the Creator. Shortly after Williams published the book, she and Herridge returned to Canada. M.B. continued to try to make her name as a writer – vigorously researching book projects on subjects as diverse as David Thompson and Carl Jung – but as a career it went nowhere. She saw work to completion only when it involved the parks, such as when she compiled Harkin's papers posthumously as *The History and Meaning of the National Parks of Canada* and reworked her old guidebooks in the 1940s and 1950s as *The Banff-Jasper Highway* and *The Heart of the Rockies*.[64] She lived until 1972, more than forty years after quitting the Parks Branch, but it seemed that only when working on the national parks that she had the passion and commitment to see things through. The devotion for national parks that the Branch had engendered in its first decades was nowhere more apparent than in the life of M.B. Williams, who had done so much to engender it.

1 "An Interminable Ode," National Parks Branch file, M.B. Williams papers, R12219-0-3-E, Library and Archives Canada [henceforth, "Williams papers, LAC"]. The poem's misspellings and patchy punctuation have been corrected here for the sake of readability. The staff members mentioned in the passage above are James Bernard Harkin ("J.B.H."), Maxwell Graham ("Maxwell"), Frederick Byshe ("Byshe"), Duncan Johnson ("Johnson"), Frank H.H. Williamson ("good F.H.W."), Abraham Knechtel ("wise A.K."), Fredericka Von Charles ("witty F.V."), and M.B. Williams ("quiet M.B."); all but Knechtel were with the Branch at its establishment in 1911.

This essay owes a great debt to Williams' niece, Frances Girling, who passed away in 2010. Frances was in possession of her aunt's personal papers until 2007, when I assisted her in donating them to Library and Archives Canada. She was very pleased that they were deemed of national interest. (Having had access to the papers before they were catalogued by LAC, and minimal contact with them since, I will reference the titles then listed on the files – titles they may no longer carry.) I wish to thank editor Claire Campbell and the other contributors to this volume, in particular Ian MacLaren, for their aid in writing this chapter. I also wish to acknowledge the assistance provided by the University of Western Ontario's Academic Development Fund.

2 M.B. Williams interview [henceforth, "Williams interview"], conducted by Ruth and Len Wertheimer, October 1969 and June 1970; in possession of the author.

3 J.B. Harkin, *The History and Meaning of the National Parks of Canada* (Saskatoon: H.R. Larson, 1957), 5. The incident is cited, for example, in Janet Foster, *Working for Wildlife: The Beginning of Preservation in Canada*, 2nd ed. (Toronto: University of Toronto Press, 1998 [1974]), 78; Leslie Bella, *Parks for Profit* (Montreal: Harvest House, 1986), 61; and Paul Kopas, *Taking the Air: Ideas and Change in Canada's National Parks* (Vancouver: UBC Press, 2007), vii.

4 Canadian Parks and Wilderness Society, http://www.cpaws.org/about/harkin.php; accessed 30 September 2009. See also E.J. (Ted) Hart, *J.B. Harkin: Father of Canada's National Parks* (Edmonton: University of Alberta Press, 2010); and Gavin Henderson, "James Bernard Harkin: The Father of Canadian National Parks," *Borealis* (Fall 1994): 28–33.

5 The agency went through a number of names over its history, beginning with "Dominion Parks Branch" for its first decade. I tend to use "National Parks Branch" because that was its most common appellation prior to becoming Parks Canada in 1973.

6 See Auditor-General, *Annual Reports*, 1911–30; C.J. Taylor, "A History of National Parks Administration," unpublished manuscript (no pagination), 1989, table 1; and J.B. Harkin, Commissioner of National Parks, *Annual Report*, 1929–30, 99.

7 This is an elaboration of an argument I made in *Natural Selections: National Parks in Atlantic Canada, 1935–1970* (Montreal: McGill-Queen's University Press, 2001), 25–33. Harkin's biographer

E.J. (Ted) Hart has taken exception to this interpretation, suggesting that by spotlighting the Branch, rather than its commissioner, I make Harkin "rather ineffectual and even redundant to the parks story" (xvi). While there is no doubt that Harkin played a leading role in the Canadian parks system's development, it is also perfectly clear in the archival record that many of the policy and promotional documents attributed to Harkin, and which have built his reputation, were written by or with the aid of others. Hart himself cites such cases a number of times, on one occasion crediting it as proof of the "commissioner's willingness to listen to and adapt the ideas of his colleagues into branch policies" (64).

8   Williams, *Guardians of the Wild* (London: Thomas Nelson and Sons, 1936), 7.

9   Williams interview. It may be worth noting that Harkin was younger than half of his staff, and only three years older than Williams.

10   A useful summary of women's position in the Canadian civil service in the early twentieth century may be found in John Hilliker, *Canada's Department of External Affairs*, vol. 1: *The Early Years, 1909–1946* (Montreal: Institute of Public Administration of Canada and McGill-Queen's University Press, 1990), 47–49.

11   In understanding this period of Canadian parks history, I have been aided greatly by C.J. Taylor's "A History of National Parks Administration" and "Legislating Nature: The National Parks Act of 1930," in *To See Ourselves / To Save Ourselves: Ecology and Culture in Canada*, ed. Rowland Lorimer et al., 125–38 (Montreal: Association for

Canadian Studies, 1991); R. Peter Gillis and Thomas R. Roach, *Lost Initiatives: Canada's Forest Industries, Forest Policy, and Forest Conservation* (Westport, CT: Greenwood, 1986), especially 62–70; and Peter J. Murphy, "'Following the Base of the Foothills': Tracing the Boundaries of Jasper Park and its Adjacent Rocky Mountains Forest Reserve," in *Culturing Wilderness: Studies in Two Centuries of Human History in the Upper Athabasca River Watershed*, ed. I.S. MacLaren, 71–121 (Edmonton: University of Alberta Press, 2007).

12   Williams, *Guardians of the Wild*, 4.

13   Frank Oliver, House of Commons, *Debates*, 28 April 1911, columns 8083-4. For more on the ideas behind the 1911 Act, see Oliver, ibid., 13 January 1911, columns 1640-1; Owen Ritchie, Barrister, to Frank Oliver, Minister, Department of the Interior, 16 November 1910, RG 39, vol. 259, file 38305, pt. 1, LAC; and RG 39, vol. 259, file 38305, pt. 2, LAC. Though the law was passed just months before the end of the Liberal government's fifteen-year time in power, its timing does not seem to have been related to the coming election. The coming coronation of George V was said to be putting greater pressure on legislation. See Sir Richard Cartright, Senate, *Debates*, 19 May 1911, 742.

14   R. Peter Gillis and Thomas R. Roach believe that the 1911 act contributed to the fragmentation of conservation in Canada. Although the Forestry Branch retained responsibility for firefighting on Dominion land, including parks, the responsibility for wildlife conservation was turned over to the Parks Branch. Rather than having one organization oversee resources on a more ecological model, the resources were being carved

up between agencies. Gillis and Roach, *Lost Initiatives*, 66.

15   The 1911 Act allowed for the establishment of new national parks, but only within forest reserves. See RG 39, vol. 259, file 38305, pt. 2, LAC.

16   *Crag and Canyon*, 13 June 1913.

17   Harkin to A.B. Macdonald, Superintendent, Rocky Mountains Park, 26 January 1912, RG 84, vol. 80, file U3, pt. 3, 1911–1914, LAC.

18   Williams interview. On suspected corruption in the timber berth system prior to 1911, see Gillis and Roach, 70.

19   Unsigned memo to Harkin, 19 January 1914, RG 84, vol. 80, file U3, pt. 3, 1911–1914, LAC.

20   Rothwell to Deputy Minister of the Interior, 24 April 1917, RG 84, vol. 654, file B2-1, vol. 1, LAC; and surrounding correspondence.

21   Williams interview.

22   See RG 84, vol. 80, file U3, pt. 2, 1908–1911, LAC.

23   Harkin to Williams, 23 November 1941, National Parks Branch file, Williams papers, LAC.

24   Williams interview. Williams and Harkin's mutual admiration was longstanding. A 1936 review of Williams' history of the Canadian national parks system, *Guardians of the Wild*, states, "She gives all praise to J. B. Harkin: yet, and this betrays her secret, Mr. Harkin, in June this year, told Mr. Harper Cory that Miss Williams had been an inspiring and dominant factor in the works of the Parks Branch for some twenty years." Reviews of *Guardians of the Wild* file, ibid.

25   Harkin, "Memorandum re National Parks – Their Values and Ideals," 14 March 1914, Harkin papers, MG30 E169, vol. 2, LAC; and *A Sprig of Mountain Heather; Being a Story of the Heather and Some Facts about the Mountain Playgrounds of the Dominion* (Ottawa: Department of the Interior, 1914), 16. The paragraphs are not quite identical. In the booklet, mention of "living birds and animals" is removed, and "one of our most precious national possessions" becomes "men's rightful heritage." As John Sandlos mentions in the following chapter of this book, the passage's first sentence captures the dual economic and preservationist purposes of parks.

26   Williams interview.

27   Harkin, *Annual Report*, 1913.

28   In a 5–16 April 1916 hearing before the U.S. House of Representatives' Committee on Public Lands, Secretary of the American Civic Association Richard B. Watrous used the report both to detail the commercial and humanitarian value of parks and to demonstrate the important work done by the agency already in existence in Canada.

29   Harkin to Williams, 23 November 1941, National Parks Branch file, Williams papers, LAC. The calculation first appears in Harkin, *Annual Report*, 1920, 3. This was the "small and modest fact" of the poem that begins this section of the chapter.

30   Asked in Parliament in 1916 "What is the use of these parks?" the Minister of the Interior began his reply, "I think they are of great utility. They attract a large number of foreign tourists and cause to be spent in Canada much more money that would not otherwise come into the country." William Roche,

House of Commons, *Debates*, 15 February 1916, 844.

31 Cannon and Meighen, House of Commons, *Debates*, 12 May 1919, 2303.

32 Williams interview. On *A Sprig of Mountain Heather*, see *The Globe*, 14 August 1914; and I.S. MacLaren with Eric Higgs and Gabrielle Zezulka-Mailloux, *Mapper of Mountains: M.P. Bridgland in the Canadian Rockies, 1902–1930* (Edmonton: University of Alberta Press, 2005), 104–5 and 152 note 15.

33 M.P. Bridgland and R. Douglas, *Description of & Guide to Jasper Park* (Ottawa: Department of the Interior, 1917); A.P. Coleman, *Glaciers of the Rockies and Selkirks* (Ottawa: Dept. of the Interior, [between 1912 and 1917]).

34 Surveyor General Deville to Maynard Rogers, Superintendent, Jasper National Park, 4 September 1920, RG 84, vol. 146, file J113-200, pt.2, LAC.

35 On the role of railroads in promoting tourism in the parks, see Gabrielle Zezulka-Mailloux, "Laying the Tracks for Tourism," in *Culturing Wilderness*, 233–59; and E.J. Hart, *The Selling of Canada: The CPR and the Beginnings of Canadian Tourism* (Banff: Altitude, 1983).

36 RG 32, vol. 480, file Williams Mabel B., LAC. Also, Frances Girling interview with the author, 28 January 2006. It should be noted, however, that during her paid sick leave in May–July 1929, Williams went to Europe with longtime travelling companion Mary Greene (later, Herridge). See MB 1931, file, Williams papers, LAC.

37 Frances Girling interview with the author, 28 January 2006.

38 Harkin, *Annual Report*, 1923, 112; 1922, K-121; and 1923, K-119.

39 See RG 84, vol. 170, file U113-2, vol. 2, LAC.

40 Harkin to W.W. Cory, 3 December 1923, ibid.

41 W.F. Lothian, *A History of Canada's National Parks*, vol. 2 (Ottawa: Parks Canada, 1977), 15; and Alisa Apostle, "Canada, Vacations Unlimited: The Canadian Government Tourism Industry, 1934–1959," unpublished PhD thesis, Queen's University, 2003.

42 Attorney-General, *Annual Report*, 1911–1931; and Williams interview. However, beginning in 1926, Williams' position was listed as "head clerk." There is indication that Williams was being squeezed out of the senior role in publicity work, and replaced by J.C. Campbell, who in the 1930s became Director of Publicity within the National Parks Branch. After a 1928 trip, Williams wrote her family that "They all seemed glad to see me back in the office. Mr. Harkin welcomed me with both hands and kept me for an hour talking. He wouldn't have done that if Mr. Campbell had been home for he would have had his head in the door on some pretense. He wants to be in on everything I suppose." Williams to "dear people," 11 May 1928, MB1931, file, Williams papers, LAC.

43 Bridgland and Douglas, *Description of and Guide to Jasper Park*, 13.

44 Williams, *Jasper National Park* (Ottawa: Department of the Interior, 1928), 1. Williams actually alters Carpenter's quote, which referred to "lands sacred," plural. As I.S. MacLaren notes, "Whether intentional or not, this alteration makes possible the reading of the

passage in her context as though 'land' and Canada were one and the same." See MacLaren, "Introduction," *Culturing Wilderness*, xl note 26.

45 RG 84, vol. 184, file U113-100, LAC; and RG 84, vol. 177, file PA113-200, LAC.

46 Williams, *The Banff-Windermere Highway* (Ottawa: Department of the Interior, 1923), 5 and 34–35.

47 Williams, *The Kicking Horse Trail* (Ottawa: Department of the Interior, 1927), 5.

48 Williams, *Through the Heart of the Rockies and Selkirks*, 4th ed. (Ottawa: Department of the Interior, 1929 [1921]), 7. Please note that in this instance, I did not have access to the first edition of the guide.

49 Williams, *Waterton Lakes National Park* (Ottawa: Department of the Interior, [1927?]), 6–7.

50 Bridgland and Douglas, *Description of and Guide to Jasper Park*, 33; and Williams, *Jasper National Park*, 133.

51 Harkin, *Annual Report*, 1922, 1; 1925, 66; and 1929–30, 99.

52 Harkin, *Annual Report*, 1916, 5.

53 Harkin, *Annual Report*, 1919, 4; and 1927–8, 77.

54 Williams, *Guardians of the Wild*, 127, and dedication page. The Carpenter quote also begins the foreword by "William Lyon Mackenzie King" in *Prince Albert National Park*.

55 On inviolability, see Taylor, "Legislating Nature"; and my *Natural Selections*, 175–83.

56 See Murphy, "'Following the Base of the Foothills'," 107.

57 *Crag and Canyon*, 24 September 1926.

58 Lothian, *History of Canada's National Parks*, 17; and C.J. Taylor, *Negotiating the Past: The Making of Canada's National Historic Parks and Sites* (Montreal: McGill-Queen's University Press, 1990), 110. The Parks Branch would have suffered some staff losses regardless, because in 1930, natural resources in the western provinces were transferred from federal to provincial responsibility, which reduced staffing across the federal Department of the Interior.

59 The system was not completely inactive in that period, of course. On the parks system during the 1930s and the war, see such works as Bill Waiser, *Park Prisoners: The Untold Story of Western Canada's National Parks, 1915–1946* (Saskatoon: Fifth House, 1995); Waiser, *Saskatchewan's Playground: A History of Prince Albert National Park* (Saskatoon: Fifth House, 1989); and my *Natural Selections*, chaps. 2–4.

60 Herridge had married William Thomas Herridge – a clergyman, and friend and advisor to William Lyon Mackenzie King – shortly before his death in 1929. Williams dedicated *Guardians of the Wild* to "M.B.H. Best of critics because she is so easily bored."

61 Williams letter, 10 October 1930, MB 1931, file, Williams papers, LAC.

62 Biography of M.B. and Ernie Williams, Williams papers, LAC. It should be noted, however, that she had thirty years in, and as such was eligible for an annual retirement allowance.

63 This was how she later characterized it. See J.C. Campbell, Parks Branch Publicity Director, to Williams, 20 March 1936, Grey Owl file, Williams papers,

LAC. From a twenty-first century perspective, it is tempting to read in the contours of Williams' life indications of homosexuality. But there is no suggestion of that in her correspondence, while there is evidence of a heterosexual relationship with journalist and parks staffer Alfred B. Buckley. See Buckley to Williams, 18 May 1935, and Williams to "Dearest," 8 June 1936, M.B. to A.B. Buckley 1935 file, Williams papers, LAC. I know nothing of Buckley, other than that he wrote the deservedly obscure *Choric Ode on the Opening of the Banff-Windermere Highway, June 30, 1923* (Ottawa: Department of the Interior, 1923).

64 Not that the texts ever much changed. In both the 1928 and 1948 editions of *Jasper National Park*, the Athabasca glacier is described as 4.5 miles long, but the glacier had in fact retreated almost half a mile in that period.

Nature's Playgrounds: The Parks Branch and Tourism Promotion in the National Parks, 1911–1929

𝔢

JOHN SANDLOS
DEPARTMENT OF HISTORY
MEMORIAL UNIVERSITY OF NEWFOUNDLAND

Every summer the migration begins. From the peaks of Rocky Mountains to the shores of the Bay of Fundy's intertidal zones, from the broad sand beaches of Vancouver Island's west coast to the deep inlets of Newfoundland's eastern shore, people by the thousands pack themselves into their cars or onto airplanes and travel to Canada's national parks. For many, the trip ends at a nearby park with a day trip or a weekend of camping. Others travel longer distances to more iconic wilderness or mountain parks, for experiences that range from a stay at a luxury hotel to a grueling multi-day hike through the backcountry. Regardless of the circumstances, all of these people encounter the national parks through the medium of commercial tourism, as sightseers, vacationers, day-trippers – as consumers of experience. Consider just a few of their options: the scenic highway loops, the ski resorts, the golf courses, the resort towns, the hotel lodges, the campgrounds (complete with electrical hookups for owners of luxury recreational vehicles), the beaches, the backcountry trails, the canoe routes, and the interpretive centres. In many national parks, particularly the older parks located near the more populated regions of southern regions of the country, private and public development schemes have dramatically shaped the landscape to meet the expectations of the visiting tourist.

Historians have spared little ink describing the influence of tourism development on the national parks in the mountainous west. In the United States, several books have recently challenged the prevailing idea that the preservationist ideal associated with John Muir was the founding principle of the western parks, instead arguing that the push to sell mountain landscapes to railway patrons, and later auto tourists, was a primary influence on the creation of iconic spaces such as Yellowstone, Olympic, and Mt. Rainier national parks.[1] In Canada, a similar idea emerged much earlier with Robert Craig Brown's foundational 1968 essay "The Doctrine of Usefulness," the first of many works that highlighted the impact of tourism on the development of the national parks in the Rocky Mountains.[2] In the public realm, the long-term ecological consequences of tourism developments have been a matter of intense debates over the past three decades. At Banff National Park, in particular, the realization that highway, railway, and townsite developments within the ecologically sensitive montane habitat of the Bow Valley were having severe impacts on some wildlife populations led to the implementation of a government task force and the eventual removal of some facilities, the construction of highway overpasses for wildlife, and the establishment of a strictly protected wildlife corridor at the edge of the Banff townsite.[3] In other national parks with a history of heavy tourism development, Parks Canada similarly must attempt to balance the recent legislative emphasis on maintaining ecological integrity in the parks with the more traditional goal of packing in as many visitors as possible to maintain gate revenues, but also, paradoxically, to nurture public support for the mission and ideals of the national parks.[4]

And yet, despite the evidence of a close marriage between tourism and national park promotion in North America, some park advocacy groups and wilderness activists have promoted the idea that the early national parks were founded wholly on principles of wilderness preservation. The naturalist and photographer Janet Foster served as a foundational author in this regard. Her *Working for Wildlife: The Beginnings of Preservation in Canada*, first published in 1978, is a hagiography of early Canadian conservationists that locates the origins of the wilderness movement in bureaucratic organizations such as the Parks Branch.[5] In the popular realm, the Canadian Parks and Wilderness Society has, as Alan MacEachern points out this volume's first chapter, publicly venerated the first parks commissioner James B. Harkin, as "the Father of National Parks, [who] developed the idea of conservation in Canada at a time when there was little precedent. Harkin created Canada's National Park system, the world's first park service. By establishing standards for their preservation, Harkin created a world class example of land conservation."[6] Such a portrait of Harkin as a conservation hero is deeply ironic, as we shall see, given his devotion to developing tourism in the parks. Nonetheless, the imperative to establish heroic historical antecedents for the contemporary wilderness movement tends to overshadow the contradictory goals of the early conservation movement. In his address to the Canadian Parks for Tomorrow: 40th Anniversary Conference, held at the University of Calgary in 2008, prominent wilderness activist Harvey Locke claimed that the historical argument for commercial concerns as a driving force behind Canada's national parks is misleading, primarily because it ignores the role of wilderness activists and conservation groups. It was these committed and public-spirited preservationists, Locke argued, who promoted national parks, not as tourist playgrounds, but as a means to protect wilderness and declining wildlife in the mountainous regions of western Canada.[7]

Undoubtedly, as Locke has suggested, civil society's emergent wilderness activism did play a role in the creation of the early national parks. Pearlann Reichwein's extensive work on the Alpine Club has argued convincingly that the efforts of this organization to work with the Dominion Parks Branch in the 1920s to oppose hydro and irrigation dams within the mountain national parks represented an early example of wilderness activism.[8] Writers, painters, and photographers immersed in the late nineteenth century's affection for sublime mountain wilderness also did much to promote the creation of national parks within the Rocky Mountains.[9] If commercialism was one important influence on the mountain national parks during this early period, it was not the only influence, as a few voices in defence of the wilderness idea began to make themselves heard.

Fig. 1. Clark's Beach in the 1940s, Riding Mountain National Park. [Courtesy of Riding Mountain National Park Photo Collection.]

But all of this focus on the mountain parks as historical exemplars of a public commitment to wilderness preservation may obscure as much as it reveals about the shifting purpose and origins of the national parks in Canada. For almost two decades (until the creation of St. Lawrence Islands National Park in 1904), the four mountain parks – Rocky Mountains (1885), Glacier (1886), Yoho (1886), and Waterton Lakes (1895) – represented the sum total of what can only loosely be described as a parks system. The haphazard early administration of these earliest parks does not tell us much about the policy agenda behind the creation of the much broader system of national parks that emerged in subsequent decades. Originally, there was no legislation or administrative body dedicated to the first three mountain parks, each of which was originally designated as a forest park under the broad authority of the *Dominion Lands Act*. When the first legislation specific to the parks, the *Rocky Mountains Park Act*, was finally passed in 1887, the result was not a well-defined policy regime governing the parks as wilderness, but a grab-bag of policies that included preserving land and wildlife, the issuing of permits for grazing and hay production, the leasing of land for residences and commercial development, and sanction for the development of mines within the parks. Although Howard Douglas's appointment as the first commissioner of Dominion Parks in 1908 suggests some development of a broader federal policy agenda for parks, several historians have outlined how the subsequent transfer of authority over parks to the Department of the Interior's Forestry Branch, an administrative body that devoted much of its attention to a burgeoning network of federal forest reserves, produced policy drift and confusion rather than systemic planning of a national park system during this early period.[10]

All of this changed in 1911, arguably the most important single turning point in the administration and development of national parks in Canada. In May, the first legislation dedicated to a truly national system of parks, the *Dominion Forest Reserves and Parks Act*, was granted royal assent. The new law provided for the first administrative body dedicated to the administration of national parks in this country – the Dominion Parks Branch – and for the appointment of a parks commissioner as its head. This position was filled by the energetic and decisive figure of James Bernard Harkin, a figure who, along with his secretary Mabel Williams (see the previous chapter), did more than anyone to promote the expansion of the national parks system and shape the individual parks that were established during his twenty-five years as head of the Branch. Under Harkin's direction, the first semblance of a national system of Dominion parks took shape, guided by his oft-stated goal of establishing at least one park in each province.[11] In this, he was extremely effective: between 1911 and 1930 the Parks Branch established twelve new Dominion Parks (see Appendix A), one of the most significant expansions of the system in its history, and extended the reach of the national parks beyond the mountainous west to the Prairies, the parkland regions of Manitoba and Saskatchewan, and the Carolinian forests and waterways of southern Ontario.

Remarkably, however, national park historians and activists have devoted far less attention to this crucial period of park development than to the era of mountain wilderness and luxury hotels associated with the early mountain parks. It was during this period, however, that we can most readily assess, on a national scale, the public, bureaucratic, and political influences that fostered the creation of national parks in Canada. Did preservationism or commercialism guide this first massive expansion of the parks system? Certainly, the government created several parks through the 1910s and 1920s where the explicit purpose was to protect wildlife, a resolute expression of preservationist sentiment within the parks bureaucracy. At the same time, the advent of automobile tourism led to local organizations clamouring for the creation of national parks to capture the increasing numbers of motorists, from urban Canada and the United States, searching for attractions along the highway networks that were expanding throughout North America. Civil society thus played a critical role in promoting and expanding the national parks system during this period, as Locke has argued. Typically, however, it was chambers of commerce, local governments, tourism promoters, and recreational groups rather than conservationists that campaigned for the creation of individual parks. In most cases these groups advocated commercial development as a stimulus to the local tourist industry, though in some instances they campaigned also for game sanctuaries to protect remnant populations of elk, antelope, or bison. The Parks Branch was only too happy to respond these local initiatives, simultaneously adopting preservationist *and* pro-development policies that seem so contradictory from a contemporary perspective.[12] If national parks have served recently as wild spaces upon which human beings projected the idealized forms of nature, Canada's park system was founded with a particularly strong emphasis on the parks as playgrounds, vacation destinations, and roadside attractions that might simultaneously preserve the fading scenic beauty and wildlife populations amid increasingly agricultural and industrial landscapes.

Building the Parks System

In 1911, Rocky Mountains National Park became the first in Canada open to the automobile when a crude highway was completed from Calgary to the Banff townsite.[13] Although it is coincidental that the Parks Branch was founded in the same year, the promotion of automobile tourism became one of the most important influences on the new administrative body. Indeed, highways and cars determined the location and type of many national parks as automobile ownership and travel became more commonplace. In the first two decades of its existence, the Parks Branch enthusiastically built roads and related tourist facilities such as scenic lookouts and golf courses and facilitated the private sector development of resort towns in many of the same national parks where the preservation of wildlife and scenery were also important objectives. Harkin played a central role pushing for this road development within the parks, advocating for the completion of scenic driving loops or highway linkages to expansive circular routes through the mountain ranges of western Canada. By the end of Harkin's career as parks commissioner, there were just over 609 miles of roads winding their way through Canada's national parks.[14] In many cases, the Parks Branch's efforts to create auto-accessible parks were a direct response to lobbying from local groups hoping to create a high profile attraction that would justify the extension or improvement of highways (at least partly at federal expense) while attracting four-wheeled visitors to their local region.

At Revelstoke, British Columbia, for example, the town's Progress Club spearheaded a campaign (apparently with widespread local support) calling for the simultaneous creation of a national park and completion of an existing road from the townsite to the summit of Mount Revelstoke.[15] The Parks Branch responded with great enthusiasm, establishing in 1914 a park that would, as the enabling Cabinet order suggested, "attract large numbers of tourists and make it adapted for the purposes of a scenic park."[16] Two years later, the Parks Branch, with Harkin's blessing, extended the park boundary southwards towards the townsite in 1920 so it could control and develop the entire length of the road.[17] Although the highway was not completed until 1928 due to the war and technical obstacles, one local newspaper declared effusively that the creation of the park would mean the "speedy completion of the automobile road to the summit of Mt. Revelstoke," and the "official recognition of the city as the great tourist capital of Canada."[18] The pronouncement proved prophetic: Revelstoke became an internationally renowned ski mecca, with the local ski club organizing high profile ski jumping competitions at a facility constructed in 1915, and improved to Olympic standards in 1933.[19]

An even more extreme example of a park organized around the spatial dimensions of a road can be found in Kootenay National Park. This mountain park was established in 1920 due in part to the lobbying efforts of R. Randolph Bruce, an engineer from Invermere who in 1916 convinced the Parks Branch and Department of the Interior to continue construction of a road from Banff to Windermere, British Columbia, that the provincial government had abandoned due to poor finances. As a condition of completing the highway, the federal government demanded that the province cede a strip of five miles on either side of the highway for park purposes.[20] The Banff-Windermere Highway, completed in 1923, provided the first road link across the central Canadian Rockies and a vital commercial route from Vancouver to Calgary, but the road and the park that envelopes it were also conceived as a means to draw tourists to the region. Writing to Harkin about the route in 1922, Bruce suggested that "It is purely a tourist road, and we have got to get out with a slogan that will draw the tourists. We have got to look to the United States for the bulk of these tourists…. We want their cars and their money and their business, and that is a good deal why we started it originally. I know because it was me who started it."[21] The Department of the Interior's reports echo this sentiment, stating in one case that "the completion of this highway will open up a spectacular scenic route through the Rocky Mountains and, it is considered, will serve to attract greater tourist traffic." A second proclaimed that "it will undoubtedly form one of the most spectacular motor drives in the world and will, in addition to connecting Calgary with Vancouver by automobile road, afford the opportunity to those desiring a round trip through the mountain to take a motor ride between Calgary and

Lethbridge, via Banff, Windermere, and the Crow's Nest Pass."[22] For the first time, the federal government had created a national park as a mere extension of a motor highway, a scenic shadow of an automobile route designed to filter tourists through the spectacular mountain landscape. Even the wildlife was thought of as a mere appendage to the view from the road. In 1922 Harkin asked Park Superintendant Howard Sibbald to place salt licks close to the highway so that game might frequent the area when the road was finally open to the public.[23]

This pattern of local lobbying for a federally funded tourist attraction was a major influence on the location and development of national parks established outside the Rocky Mountains. Prince Albert National Park, for example, was established in 1927 partly due to lobbying from politicians such as Saskatchewan's minister of Labour and Industry, T.C. Davis, and the rare personal involvement of Prime Minister William Lyon Mackenzie King, the sitting MP for the Prince Albert riding. These senior officials, however, were largely responding to active local lobbying from several sources: members of the local Liberal Riding Association (to whom King owed recompense, for granting him a nomination so he could gain a seat in Parliament the previous year), the Prince Albert Board of Trade, and an ad hoc national park committee in Prince Albert, all of whom were interested in developing automobile tourism in their region.[24] One of the ad hoc committee's reports did mention the scenic value of diverse wildlife population in the proposed park area, but it devoted the bulk of its attention to the development and tourist potential of the park, declaring that "we have the finest opportunity to develop a road system for this park," and "it is a well proven fact that the tourist business is one of the most important industries of Canada and we have not been getting it. The development of this park will attract swarms of people who are investing great amounts of capital in their pleasures."[25]

At almost the same time, local governments and citizens in Manitoba conducted a high profile campaign advocating the Riding Mountains northwest of Winnipeg as the most suitable site for a park (as opposed to a competing site in eastern Manitoba).[26] Two leading Dauphin residents, J.N. McFadden and D.D. McDonald, formed the Riding Mountain National Park Committee, a citizens' advocacy group that conducted letter-writing campaigns and published literature promoting the Riding Mountains area for its rugged scenery, its significance as a sanctuary for a threatened elk herd,

FIG. 2. CLARK'S BEACH IN THE 1940S, RIDING MOUNTAIN NATIONAL PARK. [COURTESY OF RIDING MOUNTAIN NATIONAL PARK PHOTO COLLECTION.]

and its promise as a draw for automobile travellers from the United States. They imagined "mile upon mile of the most tempting winding drives over hills and valleys beside deep ravines and glassy lakes with something new and unexpected at every turn."[27]

Local citizens and ratepayer groups afforded similar attention to the islands of southern Georgian Bay in the early 1920s.[28] The two men who spearheaded the initiative – cottage owner R.B. Orr and the local senator W.H. Bennett – urged Harkin to purchase Beausoleil Island (and other smaller islands) from the Department of Indian Affairs partly for its rumoured historical significance as a brief refuge for missionaries and native people after the Iroquois invasion of the seventeenth century, but primarily for its potential to attract tourist traffic as a playground for Torontonians and a terminus point for American boaters on the new Trent-Severn Canal system. Senator Bennett, in particular, envisioned a park where golf, horseback riding, and automobile travel along a specially constructed woodland road would create a playground paradise for tourists. None of these projects went

FIG. 3. INDIAN GRAVEYARD SHOWING FONT AT ENTRANCE, BEAUSOLEIL ISLAND, ONTARIO CA. 1940. [SOURCE: LIBRARY AND ARCHIVES CANADA/CREDIT: MOTION PICTURE BUREAU/ CANADIAN GOVERNMENT MOTION PICTURE BUREAU/C-021407.]

ahead due to low visitorship after the park was finally created in 1929, but Bennett was convinced that setting aside Beausoleil Island as a national playground was the best means to attract tourist dollars from the United States.[29]

Natural beauty, permanence, and scenic wonder: public advocacy and bureaucratic promotion of national parks in the 1910s and 1920s was infused with all these values, but only insofar as they could be sold to the expanding North America market. As parks commissioner, Harkin actively campaigned for parks as public goods that might simultaneously serve conservation and commercial objectives. He argued in a staff memo that "the commercial potentialities of tourist traffic are almost startling," even as he invoked John Muir in defence of the parks as sites of spiritual uplift and renewal through intimacy with the great outdoors. For Harkin, there was no contradiction between preservationist idealism and commercialism in the national parks. "To sum up then," he wrote in an oft-quoted statement, "Dominion Parks constitute a movement that means millions of dollars of revenue annually for the people of Canada; that means the preservation for their benefit, advantage and enjoyment forever, of that natural heritage of beauty."[30] In some of his writings, Harkin did argue for limits on tourism developments, particularly roads, within the national parks.[31] In practical terms, however, he worked tirelessly to promote the construction of roads and tourism amenities within the parks, especially those outside the mountainous areas that were conceived more as recreation areas.

He did this in large part because he felt that the public expected the government to implement a program of improvements that would transform the parks into viable hubs of regional tourist activity. In the case of Riding Mountain National Park, Harkin implemented an immediate and ambitious program of road and golf course construction, enlarging existing motor camps, and granting approvals for private sector development within the planned resort town of Wasagaming, which eventually included hotels, restaurants, a dance hall, gas stations, and other amenities of a modern tourist town. He was adamant that project funding should be approved quickly because the public was "looking forward to the various improvements to be made by the Department in Riding Mountain National Park," and local residents would tend to judge the park based on the development work completed in the first year.[32] At Prince Albert, the Parks Branch responded to a similar local push for quick development with the construction of a scenic highway, public campgrounds, cottage subdivisions, and the expansion of Wasekesiu as the main park resort town (developments that stirred controversy by the late 1950s, when the federal government proposed removing cottages and shack tents from the park, as Bill Waiser points out in the next chapter).[33] The development program at Georgian Bay Islands National Park was less ambitious, restricted mainly to the construction of a campground, beach, and playground area, as the island nature of the park likely made the construction of roads and townsites prohibitively expensive.[34] There is no doubt, however, that Branch officials supported the establishment of the park based on its tourism potential. Both the field agent A.A. Pinard and Harkin noted that Beausoleil Island's "bracing air, its remarkable beauty, its advantages in the way of boating and bathing and its easy access from Toronto and other points make its future as an important tourist centre certain."[35] By the 1920s, Harkin and the Parks Branch had created a constellation of national parks that were intended to pull vacationers within their sphere of influence, serving as regional epicentres for the development of modern tourism within rural and hinterland areas.

Public values other than tourism promotion did work their way into the process of establishing national parks during this period. Harkin was particularly concerned with regional equity and the development of a truly national system of parks. He was pleased that the establishment of Georgian Bay Islands and Riding Mountain National Parks in 1929 had helped to create a chain of parks running from the Rocky Mountains in the west to the St. Lawrence Islands in the east.[36] Even the focus on parks as public playgrounds was tinged with idealism, as Harkin argued that the national parks provided critical opportunities for outdoor recreation in popular vacation areas such as Georgian Bay and the St. Lawrence River, where would-be cottagers and hotel owners were snapping up Crown lands at a rapid pace.[37] If, with hindsight, we now recognize the negative ecological consequences of attracting hordes of visitors to the national parks, we must also acknowledge that the development of roads, campgrounds, and other low-cost visitor facilities embodied a democratic ideal that the national parks should not be the exclusive preserve of the wealthy, but remain as open to the Canadian public as possible.[38]

Such idealism for the recreational values of parks was generally not extended to their potential as wilderness preserves. Indeed, when I began archival research on the Parks Branch many years ago, I was surprised to find that the word "wilderness" is almost completely absent from correspondence justifying the creation of individual parks. It is clear that Parks Branch saw national parks, especially those outside of the mountainous west, primarily as public playgrounds.

In fact, the Branch hoped to designate the Riding Mountains as the first in a series of special national recreation areas, distinct from national parks (marked by their truly spectacular scenic value) until the public protested that this moniker would diminish the significance and appeal of the park.[39] After World War I, the Parks Branch vigorously promoted the tourism potential of the parks system as a whole, establishing a publicity division that produced and distributed promotional pamphlets, brochures, and advertisements. This included a steady stream of press releases to local newspapers that were only too eager to participate in the process of marketing the parks to tourists (sometimes reprinting government material word for word without listing any author). The resulting plethora of government literature and newspaper articles (which the Branch collected meticulously) solidified the

image of parks as playgrounds rather than wilderness areas within the public imagination.[40]

As within the Branch itself, not all discussion of the parks among Canadians more widely was oriented towards commercialism. By the 1920s, a small number of public figures and organizations had begun to elucidate the value of wilderness rather than the parks' commercial potential. These included the Alpine Club of Canada and the National Parks Association, as well as celebrity conservationists such as the popular nature writer Tony Lascelles (a.k.a. Herbert U. Green), a police officer who lived near Riding Mountain National Park, and Grey Owl (a.k.a. Archie Belaney), the native poseur who – ironically – the Parks Branch hired explicitly to serve as a tourist draw in Riding Mountain and Prince Albert National Parks.[41] Although these two men focused much of their writing on natural history rather than public policy, Green did express more overt preservationist politics in one article when he condemned the managers of Riding Mountain for allowing logging in the park and failing to protect game from poachers.[42] Yet if Canadian conservationists such as Green articulated objections to industrial activity or hunting in the parks, no evidence has emerged that they opposed the extension of roads and other tourist developments within the national parks prior to World War II. This is in sharp contrast to the United States, where historian Paul Sutter has argued that opposition to roads among such activists and public officials as Aldo Leopold, Benton MacKaye, Robert Sterling Yard, and Robert Marshall was a primary influence on the early development of the preservationist movement south of the border.[43] As I.S. MacLaren's chapter suggests later in this volume, the vast majority of public protest aimed at national parks policy in Canada during the 1910s and 1920s originated with local homesteaders who contested the restriction of hunting activities, the elimination of grazing rights, and the elimination of their homesteads and reserves within new national parks.[44]

What about the wildlife parks? Surely, the Parks Branch adopted a preservationist philosophy when it acted decisively in the 1910s and 1920s to protect species on the brink of extinction due to hunting excesses and habitat loss in the late nineteenth century. After all, the list of parks created with an explicit mandate for wildlife protection during this period is impressive and unprecedented. Between 1911 and 1922, the Department of the Interior established Buffalo, Elk Island, and Wood Buffalo national parks in Alberta to protect remnant and imported populations of wood and plains bison; Nemiskam, Wawaskesey and Menissawok national parks to preserve pronghorn antelope on the prairies; and Point Pelee National Park to protect an important stopover point for migratory birds.

These parks were never subject to development on the scale of the more tourist-oriented parks; none contained resorts towns, and, save for hotels at Point Pelee, other forms of intensive commercial tourism developments were generally absent. Nonetheless, the Parks Branch's utilitarian focus on tourism and commercial development remained a critical influence on even the parks designed for wildlife preservation. Buffalo National Park, for instance, contained two enclosures displaying elk, moose, antelope, bison, and imported yak as part of a visitors' wildlife menagerie and recreation area. Park staff also participated in cross-breeding experiments with domestic cattle and bison in order to produce a new type of optimal stock animal – the cattalo – for the ranching industry, and established a small public cottage industry in the sale of bison meat as they culled herds that had grown beyond the capacity of their fenced range.[45] Elk Island National Park was created to protect wapiti

Fig. 5. Extremity of Point Pelee, Ontario, 1918. [Source: Library and Archives Canada/Canada. Marine Aids Division Collection/pa-119818.]

herds, but over time the development of recreational facilities at Astotin Lake and the increasing identification of the imported buffalo herds as a tourist attraction (and a source of stock for commercial meat production) transformed the public perception of the park into that of a summer playground, complete with Sunday band concerts and golf tournaments.[46]

Perhaps the most visible manifestation of the Parks Branch's attitude toward wildlife preservation in this period is that many of these wildlife parks no longer exist. As the numbers of bison and antelope fell below critical levels of endangerment across Canada and the United States, and as range depletion and disease problems continued to plague fenced-in parks, the Branch was only too happy to delete protected areas from the system. Wawaskesey, Menissawok and Nemiskam were abolished in 1930, 1938, and 1947 respectively, while Buffalo National Park was designated as a military training ground in 1939 and officially removed from the parks system in 1947. Harkin was likely not distressed to see these parks disappear: he had always been uncomfortable with national park designation for what he thought were less than spectacular scenic landscapes, and he had hoped to define the wildlife parks as a separate category of game sanctuaries in early versions of the *National Parks Act*.[47]

Wood Buffalo National Park represents something of a historical anomaly among federal protected areas. When the park was created in 1922 to protect the remnant wood bison herds south of Great Slave Lake, the Northwest Territories and Yukon Branch of the Department of the Interior rather than the Parks Branch was granted control over the park for administrative convenience. Due to its remote location, there were no major tourism developments in the park, though the northern administration did propose the development of road access in the mid-1950s with traditional park amenities such as hotels, lunch stops, and golf courses.[48] When the Parks Branch was granted control over the park in the late 1960s, however, it is clear that older attitudes about tourism remained dominant. Parks officials constantly referred to Wood Buffalo as not a "real park" due to its lack of scenic values, and contemplated returning the Alberta portion of the park in exchange for areas in the southern part of the province more attractive to tourists. An agreement between the federal and Alberta governments was never completed, but the official disdain for Wood Buffalo National Park – until 2008, the world's largest protected area – suggests that concern for ecological integrity in national parks had not yet entered the Branch's policy framework. Even the imperative of preserving one of the world's last free roaming bison herds paled in comparison to acquiring other parcels of land that might serve as playgrounds for the nation.[49]

Perhaps no other national park embodies the contradictions of the early Parks Branch's management philosophy more than Point Pelee. The federal government created the park in 1918, partly in response to a report from National Museum of Canada naturalist Percy Taverner highlighting the significance of the area as a stopover for migrating birds, but also to fulfill obligations under the Migratory Birds Treaty with the United States.[50] Public pressure also played a significant role in convincing the Branch to establish Point Pelee as a federal protected area. Members of a local sport hunting group, the Essex County Wild Life Association, lobbied federal wildlife officials furiously for the protection of the Pelee marshes (at the same time, they managed to protect their own recreational interests, convincing Harkin that they ought to be allowed to hunt ducks seasonally within the park, a practice that continued until 1989).[51] This inconsistent approach to park management was not limited to wildlife issues: Point Pelee soon became the most highly developed tourism centre among national parks created with an explicit wildlife conservation mandate. By the 1930s, the construction of roads, campgrounds and two hotels within the park attracted large numbers of visitors to the park's popular beaches. The environmental impact of these developments was severe, particularly the loss of vegetation and habitat alterations associated with unregulated camping and the local tradition of driving automobiles along the beaches. Nonetheless, the Parks Branch continued to expand the network of roads and parking lots after World War II, as Point Pelee became Ontario's most popular destination among birdwatchers hoping to catch a glimpse of rare migratory songbirds in the Carolinian forest. Indeed, the efforts of the Branch and local promoters to market bird watching as an engine of tourism in the area were too successful: annual visitorship exceeded 700,000 people by the end of the 1960s, resulting in such a crush of car traffic along park roads that automobiles were banned from the tip area of the point after a park master plan recommended use of a shuttle bus in 1973.[52] Space for birdwatchers has been at a premium as well, with crowds of birders jostling for the best view of warblers and other rare species.[53] On this thin point jutting out into Lake Erie, non-human lives have been commercialized as much as they have been preserved for middle-class tourists seeking to reconnect with nature, a somewhat extreme manifestation of an impossibly paradoxical management philosophy – the integration of visitation and preservation – that continues to haunt the national parks to this very day.

Parks for the People

In a popular indictment of industrial tourism and its attendant development pressures in the United States national park system, the iconoclastic writer and wilderness activist Edward Abbey wrote, "the first thing that the superintendent of a new park can anticipate being asked, when he attends the first meeting of the area's Chamber of Commerce, is not 'Will roads be built?' but rather 'When does construction begin?' and 'Why the delay?'"[54] Clearly the same pattern holds true for national parks established in Canada during the first two decades of centralized administration under the Dominion Parks Branch. The public demanded that national parks be developed as playgrounds to attract tourists on an expanding highway network, bringing not only the roads themselves but also campgrounds, golf courses, hotels and townsites – all conveniently at the expense of the federal purse or private investors looking to profit from the influx of visitors. As tempting as it may be to establish an origin myth for the national parks grounded in a historical continuum of wilderness activism, both government officials and civil society in the 1910s and 1920s were much more focused on parks' commercial potential. By 1930, the contradictory philosophies of preservation and utilitarianism that governed individual national parks had been codified into law as the *National Parks Act*, which famously declared that "the National Parks of Canada are hereby dedicated to the people of Canada for their benefit, education and enjoyment, subject to this Act and the regulations, parks shall be maintained and made use of so as to leave them unimpaired for the enjoyment of future generations."[55] Though we may choose from a contemporary vantage point to emphasize the word "unimpaired," the legislation's emphasis on public use and enjoyment was generally interpreted through the lens of tourism development and promotion until the 1970s, when Parks Canada expanded the parks system into more remote and inaccessible areas. Preservationist sentiment – much of it flowing out of the popular back to nature movement of the 1910s and 1920s – did influence parks officials. But even in cases where the protection of wildlife or scenery were advanced as key arguments for national park establishment, advocates often suggested that the preservation of scenic beauty or rare animals would only enhance the appeal of a site for the visiting tourist. If national parks served as a counterpoint to increasingly urban and industrial landscapes during the 1910s and 1920s, ironically their primitive appeal was repackaged and sold to visitors as part of a much broader expansion of industrial tourism during this period.[56]

Given this dominant theme in the early history of the national parks, why then are some contemporary environmentalists so determined to establish an origin myth for the parks system grounded in grassroots and bureaucratic wilderness activism? One might reasonably argue that the early national parks laid the groundwork for the establishment of protected areas with a more ecological focus as the mandates and policy frameworks governing Parks Canada began to shift toward the maintenance of ecological integrity in the 1980s. There is also the very real fear that acknowledging the utilitarian focus of the early parks system will justify the ongoing attempts of tourism operators to promote development within the parks. By ignoring the close association of tourism and the early national parks, however, we fail to ask difficult questions about whether these types of protected areas represent the best means to preserve biodiversity and promote environmental sustainability. While park advocates tend to decry resource extraction activities such as mining, logging, and hydro-carbon development, they often fail to acknowledge that automobile tourism in the national parks can only be supported through dependence on these industrial processes. In broad terms, the historian Hal Rothman has argued that the popular conception of tourism as a post-industrial activity (focused, as it is, on the production of experience rather than material goods) masks a chain of development activity that leads from roads, airports, and hotels to oil fields and open pit mines.[57] The national parks in Canada, particularly those on major highway networks, have served – and continue to serve – as one important link in this chain of unsustainable economic activity. They are iconic attractions that draw tourists and their motor vehicles by the millions each summer, creations of North America's car culture and commercial sensibilities as much as they are emblems of our love for wild nature.

NOTES

1   For the birth of automobile tourism in the U.S. national parks, see David Louter, *Windshield Wilderness: Cars, Roads and Nature in Washington's National Parks* (Seattle: University of Washington Press, 2006); Paul Sutter, *Driven Wild: How the Fight against Automobiles Launched the Modern Wilderness Movement* (Seattle: University of Washington Press, 2002); Chris J. Magoc, *Yellowstone: The Creation and Selling of an American Landscape: 1870–1903* (Albuquerque: University of New Mexico Press, 1999); and Theodore Catton, *National Park; City Playground: Mt. Rainier in the Twentieth Century* (Seattle: University of Washington Press, 2006).

2   Robert Craig Brown, "The Doctrine of Usefulness: Natural Resources and National Parks Policy in Canada, 1887–1914," in *The Canadian National Parks: Today and Tomorrow*, ed. J.G. Nelson and R.C. Scace, 1: 94–110 (Calgary: National and Provincial Parks Association and the University of Calgary, 1969). See also Leslie Bella, *Parks for Profit* (Montreal: Harvest House, 1986); I.S. MacLaren, "Cultured Wilderness in Jasper National Park," *Journal of Canadian Studies* 34 (Fall 1999): 7–58; Gabrielle Zezulka-Mailloux, "Laying the Tracks for Tourism," in *Culturing Wilderness in Jasper National Park: Studies in Two Centuries of Human History in the Upper Athabasca River Watershed*, ed. I.S. MacLaren, 233–59 (Edmonton:

University of Alberta Press, 2007); and C.J. Taylor, "The Changing Habitat of Jasper Tourism," in *Culturing Wilderness in Jasper National Park*, 199–225. For the influence of tourism on the exclusion of Native people from Rocky Mountains Park, see Theodore Binnema and Melanie Niemi, "'Let the Line be Drawn Now:' Wilderness, Conservation and the Exclusion of Aboriginal People from Banff National Park in Canada," *Environmental History* 11 (2006): 724–50.

3   Banff–Bow Valley Task Force, *Banff–Bow Valley: At the Crossroads, Technical Report* (Ottawa: Minister of Supply and Services, 1996).

4   Panel on the Ecological Integrity of Canada's National Parks, *Unimpaired for Future Generations? Conserving Ecological Integrity within Canada's National Parks* (Ottawa: Minister of Supply and Services, 2000); Rick Searle, *Phantom Parks: the Struggle to Save Canada's National Parks* (Toronto: Key Porter, 2000).

5   Janet Foster, *Working for Wildlife: The Beginnings of Preservation in Canada*, 2nd ed. (Toronto: University of Toronto Press, 1998).

6   Canadian Parks and Wilderness Society, "Harkin Award," http://cpaws.org/about/harkin.php; accessed 29 July 2009.

7   Harvey Locke, "Civil Society and Protected Areas." Final version of paper presented at the Parks for Tomorrow Conference, 7 July 2008. Available at http://dspace.ucalgary.ca/bitstream/1880/46874/1/Locke.pdf; accessed 6 April 2009.

8   Pearlann Reichwein, "'Hands off our National Parks': The Alpine Club of Canada and Hydro-development Controversies in the Canadian Rockies, 1922–30," *Journal of the Canadian Historical Association*, New Series, 6 (1995): 129–55. For popular histories of the mountain parks that emphasize their wilderness character, see Eleanor G. Luxton, *Banff: Canada's First National Park, a History and a Memory of Rocky Mountains Park* (Banff: Summerthought, 1974); and Sid Marty, *A Grand a Fabulous Notion: The First Century of Canada's National Parks* (Toronto: NC Press, 1984).

9   For an overview of mountain aesthetics, see Marjorie Hope Nicolson, *Mountain Gloom and Mountain Glory: The Development of the Aesthetics of the Infinite* (Ithaca, NY: Cornell University Press, 1959); Simon Schama, *Landscape and Memory* (Toronto: Random House, 1996); and Christopher Armstrong and H.V. Nelles, *The Painted Valley: Artists along the Bow River, 1845–2000* (Calgary: University of Calgary Press, 2007). For collections of photographs, see Edward Cavell, *Legacy in Ice: The Vaux Family and the Canadian Alps* (Banff: Whyte Foundation, 1983); Bart Robinson, "A Biographical Portrait of Byron Harmon," in *Byron Harmon: Mountain Photographer*, ed. Carole Harmon, 5–14 (Banff: Altitude, 1992). Writers have produced a vast amount of material about the Rockies from the late nineteenth and early twentieth centuries. Representative examples may be found in Colleen Skidmore, ed. *This Wild Spirit: Women in the Rocky Mountains of Canada* (Edmonton: University of Alberta Press, 2006); Mary Schaeffer, *Old Indian Trails: Incidents of Camp and Trail Life, Covering Two Years' Exploration through the Rocky*

Mountains of Canada (New York: G. Putnam's Sons, 1911); and James Outram, *In the Heart of the Canadian Rockies* (London: Macmillan, 1905).

10 For an overview, see W.F Lothian, *A History of Canada's National Parks* (Ottawa: Parks Canada, 1976); 1:10–13; C.J. Taylor, "Legislating Nature: The National Parks Act of 1930," in *To See Ourselves / To Save Ourselves: Ecology and Culture in Canada*, ed. Rowland Lorimer and Michael M'Gonigle, Canadian Issues, vol. XII , Proceedings of the Annual Conference of the Association for Canadian Studies, University of Victoria, 31 May to 1 June 1990, 139–67 (Montreal: Association for Canadian Studies, 1991); Peter R. Gillis and Thomas R. Roach, "The American Influence on Conservation in Canada 1899–1911," *Journal of Forest and Conservation History* 30, no. 4 (October 1986): 160–74; and R.D. Turner and W.E. Rees, "A Comparative Study of Parks Policy in Canada and the United States," *Nature Canada* 2, no. 1 (1973): 31–36. See also MacEachern, this volume.

11 Taylor, "Legislating Nature," 134. E.J. Hart, *J.B. Harkin: Father of Canada's National Parks* (Edmonton: University of Alberta Press, 2010).

12 Alan MacEachern, *Natural Selections: National Parks in Atlantic Canada, 1935–1970* (Montreal: McGill-Queen's University Press, 2001).

13 W.F Lothian, *A History of Canada's National Park*, I:14.

14 Lucy Alderson and John Marsh. "J.B. Harkin, National Parks and Roads," *Park News* 15 (Summer 1979): 9–16

15 For a record of local influences on the creation of the park, see James Harkin to W.W. Cory, Deputy Minister of the Interior Library and Archives Canada (hereafter LAC), RG 84, vol. 1673, file MR2, pt. 1. See also "Revelstoke National Park Unanimously Approved as Most Suitable Name for New Park." *Revelstoke Mail Herald*, 5 February 1914. Clipping found in LAC, RG 84, vol. 1673, file MR2, pt. 1.

16 Order in Council P.C. 1125, 28 April 1914. A copy was found in LAC, RG 84, vol. 1673, file MR2, pt. 1.

17 Harkin to Cory, 28 April 1920. LAC, RG 84, vol. 1673, file MR2, pt. 1.

18 "Mount Revelstoke is National Park," *Revelstoke Mail Herald*, 5 February 1914. LAC, RG 84, vol. 1673, file MR2, pt. 1. Clipping found in LAC, RG 84, vol. 1673, file MR2, pt. 1.

19 Lothian, *A History of Canada's National Parks*, 58; "Mount Revelstoke National Park," no date, Clipping found in LAC, RG 84, vol. 16, file MR109, pt. 1.

20 For a summary of Bruce's role, see R. Randolph Bruce to Harkin, 22 June 1922. LAC, RG 84, vol. 1632, file K2, pt. 2. The Banff-Windermere Highway Agreement was established through Order in Council P.C. 827, published in the *Canada Gazette* 58, no. 47.

21 R. Randolph Bruce to Harkin, 22 June 1922. LAC, RG 84, vol. 1632, file K2, pt. 2.

22 Minister of the Interior to the Governor General in Council, 28 February 1919. LAC, RG 84, vol. 1631, file K2, pt. 1; "Banff-Windermere Road," undated memo. LAC, RG 84, vol. 1632, file K2, pt. 2.

23 Harkin to Sibbald, 12 December 1922. LAC, RG 84, vol. 477, file K210, pt. 1.

24 For a summary, see a memo on the historical development of the park, dated 25 November 1926. LAC, RG84, vol. 1726, file PA2, pt. 1. See also William Waiser, *Saskatchewan's Playground: A History of Prince Albert National Park* (Saskatoon: Fifth House, 1989).

25 The park committee report is quoted in full in a memo from W.W. Cory, Minister of the Interior to Harkin, 30 November 1926. LAC, RG 84, vol. 1726, file PA2, pt. 1.

26 See, for example, "Riding Mountains Favored as Site of Federal Park," *Brandon Sun*, 3 September 1927; W.W. Childe, "Defends Eastern Area for National Park," *Winnipeg Free Press*, 8 October 1927; "Want National Park at Riding Mountain," *Winnipeg Free Press*, 10 January 1927. All clippings were found in LAC, RG 84, vol. 1841, RM2, pt. 1.

27 D.D. McDonald and J.N McFadden, "The Advantages of the Riding Mountain Forest Reserve as a National Park for Manitoba," published by the Riding Mountain National Park Committee, 30 January 1928. LAC, RG 84, vol. 1841, RM2, pt. 2.

28 Public advocacy for a park in the nearby towns of Midland and Penetanguishene is discussed in an undated document titled "Position Paper on Beausoleil." LAC, RG 84, vol. 487, file GB2, pt. 3. Harkin mentions a pro-park resolution put forward by the Penetanguishene Ratepayer's Association in a letter to Cory, 5 January 1923. LAC, RG 84, vol. 488, file GB11325-9-6.

29 Orr described Beausoleil Island's potential as a historical park to Harkin in a letter dated 31 January 1921, and the tourist potential of the park in a letter to Harkin dated 22 September 1920. LAC, RG 84, vol. 487, GB2 (U325-9-9), pt. 2.

30 James Harkin, "Memorandum re. Dominion Parks, Their Values and Their Ideals," 20 March 1914. LAC, MG 30, E-69, vol. 2.

31 J.B. Harkin, *The Origin and Meaning of the National Parks of Canada, Extracts from the Papers of the Late Jas. B. Harkin, First Commissioner of the National Parks of Canada.* Compiled by Mabel B. Williams (Saskatoon: H.R. Larson, 1957).

32 Harkin to Cory, 28 April 1930. LAC, RG 84, vol. 1841, file RM2, pt. 2. For overviews of development within the park, see Lyle Dick, "Forgotten Roots: The Gardens of Wasagaming," *Newest Review* (November 1986): 10–11; Helen Bazillon, Connie Braun, and Richard C. Rounds, *Human Intervention in the Clear Lake Basin of Riding Mountain National Park: Land Use, Subdivision, and Development* (Brandon, MB: Brandon University, Rural Development Institute, 1992); W.F. Baird, "Clear Lake Waterfront Beach Study, Riding Mountain National Park." Unpublished report. Baird and Associates and Environment Canada, 1994.

33 Waiser, *Saskatchewan's Playground*, 37–46.

34 For details on construction in the park, see Arlene Yaworsky, "Preserving the History of Georgian Bay Islands National Park," Unpublished report, Georgian Bay Islands National Park (June 1976): 69–75, 332–35.

35 Hoyes Lloyd to F.H.H. Williamson, 7 August 1929. LAC, RG 84, vol. 487, file GB 2, pt. 3. A.A. Pinard to Harkin,

21 December 1922. LAC, RG 84, vol. 488, file GB1325-9-6. Harkin to Cory, 5 January 1925. LAC, RG 84, vol. 488, file GB1325-9-6.

36 Harkin to Cory, 5 January 1925. LAC, RG 84, vol. 488, file GB1325-9-6.

37 Harkin to Cory, 5 January 1925. LAC, RG 84, vol. 488, file GB1325-9-6.

38 For further discussion, see Paul Kopas, *Taking the Air: Ideas and Change in Canada's National Parks* (Vancouver: UBC Press, 2007), 3–4.

39 For objections to the national recreation area idea, see J.M. McFadden to the Minister of the Interior, 20 March 1929. LAC, RG 84, vol. 1841, file RM2, pt. 2. See also the editorial, "When is a Park not a Park?" *Winnipeg Tribune*, 31 August 1929 (clipping found in LAC, RG 84, vol. 1841, file RM2, pt. 2). For an overview of the National Recreation Area concept, see Taylor, "Legislating Nature," 133.

40 For background on the Publicity Division, see Lothian, *A History of the National Parks*, 2:15. Most of the archival collections for individual parks from this period included a file containing publicity material produced internally and in the public press. Representative publications that emphasize the public playground status of the parks include, "Discovering Clear Lake: Manitoba's New Playground is Sanctuary Where Denizens of Wild Live Free from Fear and Tourists Enjoy the Unspoiled Beauty of Life in the Open," *Winnipeg Tribune* 27 August 1932 (p. 1 of Magazine Section); "A Northern Playground," *Toronto Globe*, 8 January 1930 (p. 4 of Lifestyle section; reference is to Georgian Bay Islands National Park); and "Holiday Lake or Mountain – Canyons of

Kootenay Provide for Tourist Scenic Display of Unusual Beauty," *Calgary Herald*, 7 July 1939, clipping found in LAC, RG 84, vol. 15, file K109, pt. 1. See also "Visit Revelstoke: The Mountain Paradise," a pamphlet with text and photo spreads that emphasize the recreational and vacation potential of the park. LAC, RG 84, vol. 16, file MR109, pt. 1.

41 See Tony Lascelles and Grey Owl, "A Philosophy of the Wild," *Forest and Stream* (Dec. 1931): 15–16.

42 Tony Lascelles, "Politics and Our National Parks." Undated and unpublished manuscript, H.U. Green Papers, M2 43, Whyte Museum of the Canadian Rockies.

43 Paul Sutter, *Driven Wild: How the Fight against Automobiles Launched the Modern Wilderness Movement* (Seattle: University of Washington Press, 2002).

44 John Sandlos, "Federal Spaces, Local Conflicts: National Parks and the Exclusionary Politics of the Conservation Movement in Ontario, 1900–1935," *Journal of the Canadian Historical Association* 16 (2005): 293–318; John Sandlos, "Not Wanted in the Boundary: the Expulsion of the Keeseekoowenin Ojibway Band from Riding Mountain National Park," *Canadian Historical Review* 89 (2008): 189–221.

45 Jennifer Brower, *Lost Tracks: Buffalo National Park, 1909–1939* (Edmonton: AU Press, 2008).

46 The purpose of the original forest park as an elk preserve is outlined in a letter from James A. Smart to Clifford Sifton, Minister of the Interior, 21 June 1904. LAC, RG 84, vol. 479, file

E2, pt. 1. For an account of the park as a tourist draw, including laudatory comments on the golf course, see "Elk Island Park Draws Summer Vacationers," *Edmonton Journal*, 4 July 1942. For the band shows, see "Barrhead District Band to Play at Elk Island," *Edmonton Bulletin*, 17 August 1950. Clippings of both these articles were found in LAC, RG 84, vol. 9, file E109, pt. 1.

47 Taylor, "Legislating Nature," 134–35.

48 F.J.G. Cunningham, Director, Northern Administration Branch to the Deputy Minister, 3 October 1956. LAC, RG 85, accession 1997-98/076, box 73, file 406-13, pt. 5.

49 The recommendation to return portions of the park to Alberta is contained in a Northern Administration Branch Planning Division Report prepared by C.L. Merrill in Dec. 1963. LAC, RG 85, accession 1997-98/076, box 73, file 406-13, pt. 8.

50 For Taverner's report, see Commission of Conservation Canada, *Report of Sixth Annual Meeting* (Toronto: Bryant Press, 1915): 304–7.

51 A resolution that the Essex County Wildlife Association presented in favour of Point Pelee National Park is quoted at length in a letter from Dominion Entomologist C. Gordon Hewitt to W.W. Cory, 30 May 1917. LAC, RG 84, vol. 1700, file P2, pt. 1. For an overview of the duck hunting issue, see Sandlos "Federal Spaces; Local Conflicts."

52 J.G. Battin and J.G. Nelson, ""Recreation and Conservation: the Struggle

for Balance in Point Pelee," in *Recreational Land Use: Perspectives on Evolution in Canada*, ed. G. Wall and J. Marsh, 77–101 (Ottawa: Carleton University Press, 1982); J.G. Battin and J.G. Nelson, *Man's Impact on Point Pelee National Park* (National and Provincial Parks Association of Canada, 1978).

53 W.A. Martin, "Spring Fever: A Trip to Ontario's Point Pelee during the Height of Bird Migration Reveals that for Many Serious Birders the Name of the Game Is Not to See Their First Prairie Warbler of the Year but to Spot it before Anybody Else Does," *Globe and Mail* (8 April 1991): A14.

54 Edward Abbey, *Desert Solitaire: A Season in the Wilderness* (New York: Touchstone, 1968).

55 *National Parks Act*, Statutes of Canada 20–1 Geo. V, chap. 33.

56 The historians Henry Jackson Lears and Ian MacKay have argued that this process of commercializing antimodern sentiment was common in North America during this period. T.J. Jackson Lears, *No Place of Grace: Antimodernism and the Transformation of American Culture, 1880–1920* (New York: Pantheon, 1981); Ian McKay, *Quest of the Folk: Antimodernism and Cultural Selection in Twentieth Century Nova Scotia* (Montreal: McGill-Queen's University Press, 1994).

57 Hal K. Rothman, *Devil's Bargains: Tourism in the Twentieth-Century American West* (Lawrence: University of Kansas Press, 1998). See also, John Urry, *The Tourist Gaze* (London: Sage, 2002).

"A Questionable Basis for Establishing a Major Park": Politics, Roads, and the Failure of a National Park in British Columbia's Big Bend Country

᪣

BEN BRADLEY
DEPARTMENT OF HISTORY
QUEEN'S UNIVERSITY

In the history of Canada's national parks there needs to be a place for parks that never were, for parks that were proposed but failed. Areas that might have become national parks, but did not, deserve to be treated as integral to the larger history of the national parks system because they provide important context for the better-known success stories. The failures hidden in the history of Canada's national parks serve to illustrate the changing political, economic, and aesthetic criteria involved in constructing the present-day parks system. They also help denaturalize or demythologize the existing national parks by revealing the myriad actors and interests involved in determining which proposed parks went forward and which fell by the wayside.

National parks have been proposed by the federal government, provincial governments, regional boosters, tourism promoters, and environmental organizations. The proposals made by provincial governments are of particular interest because, without provincial cooperation, it has been effectively impossible to establish national parks in southern Canada since 1930, when the *Natural Resources Transfer Act* gave the prairie provinces control over their lands and returned the Dominion Railway Belt to British Columbia. As Alan MacEachern has shown in his study of national parks in the Atlantic provinces, the provincial governments' willingness to give land for new national parks usually depended on the federal government's willingness to invest in the development of regional infrastructure, most often in the form of roads.[1] Thus the history of Canada's national parks during the middle decades of the twentieth century – including both the success stories and the numerous parks that were proposed but never established – needs to be recognized as having been linked to intergovernmental politics and infrastructure priorities. This chapter examines the intertwined histories of parks and roads in British Columbia's Big Bend country. It tells the story of an area that could plausibly have become an important national park during the mid-1930s, and again in the early 1940s, but was rejected by the federal government and ended up becoming more of a national "sacrifice area," where irreparable damage was done to extensive swathes of land in the name of progress and the greater good.

Few people have heard of Hamber Park, but it is an especially noteworthy example of a failed national park. The government of British Columbia established Hamber Provincial Park in 1941 as part of a scheme to have the federal government incorporate it and several other provincial parks into the national parks system. This scheme was tied to a larger effort to get Ottawa to build, improve, and maintain automobile roads in B.C.'s rugged and sparsely populated Selkirk and Rocky mountains. Hamber's size and location make it particularly important: when it was established, Hamber was one of the largest parks in Canada, and was contiguous with Jasper, Banff, Yoho, Glacier, and Mount Robson parks. To understand why British Columbia created this enormous, strategically located park with the expectation that the federal government might have made it into a national park, it is necessary to go back to the late 1920s, when a network of automobile roads was taking shape in the mountains of western Canada.

*****

The completion of a road between Lake Louise and Golden in the summer of 1927 meant that the only gap in an interprovincial route between Vancouver and Calgary was located between Golden and the town of Revelstoke, a distance of less than one hundred kilometres as the crow flies. The road connecting Lake Louise and Golden had been built by the engineering service of the National Parks Branch and the B.C. Department of Public Works, and after it was completed, many expected those agencies' construction crews would move west and begin work on a link between Golden and Revelstoke.[2] However, the federal government was opposed to building a road through the Selkirks via the notorious, avalanche-plagued Rogers Pass, even though this would have made Glacier National Park accessible to tourists travelling by automobile.[3] Ottawa instead proposed that the two governments build a road *around* the Selkirks by following the horseshoe-shaped course of the Columbia River, known as the Big Bend.[4] An agreement was reached whereby the province would build the western section of the road – from Revelstoke to the site of Boat Encampment, an old fur trade rendezvous located at the apex of the Big Bend – while Ottawa would have the National Parks Branch build the eastern section, from the outskirts of Golden northwards to Boat Encampment.

The advantages Ottawa saw in the roundabout Big Bend route are difficult to discern. A road paralleling the Columbia River would be more than double the length of a road through the pass, and would traverse a veritable howling wilderness for more than three hundred kilometres. There were no farms, mines, or logging camps in the Big Bend country, only a few prospectors' cabins and half-obscured trails. True, it avoided the treacherous Rogers Pass, but the Big Bend country experienced heavy snowfall, especially on the western slope of the Selkirks where between five and ten metres fell annually. Dense forests with jungle-like undergrowth climbed high on the mountainsides, and the Columbia was un-navigable between Revelstoke and Golden, which meant that during the short construction season all supplies would need to be delivered by pack trains hacking their way through the forest. No one could have guessed it in the summer of 1929, but the two governments could not have chosen a worse moment to begin such an ambitious project.

Construction began in early 1930 but was slowed by the area's difficult terrain and inaccessibility. The downturn in the global economy also played a role. British Columbia's economy was based on primary resources, and

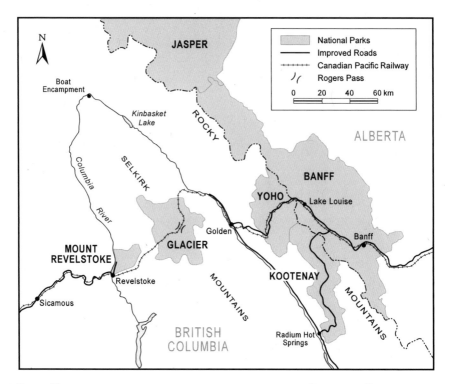

government revenues depended on fees collected on logging, milling, and mining activity. As a result, the province was hit particularly hard when commodity markets collapsed in late 1929. Simon Frasier Tolmie's government slashed spending on public works, but work proceeded on the Big Bend road because Victoria had made a commitment to Ottawa that it would complete its share of the project. However, fewer resources were put into the western section than originally planned.

By early 1931, British Columbia's unemployment rate hovered around 28 per cent, compelling the provincial government to provide relief employment on public works projects. The construction camps on the western half of the Big Bend project were converted into relief work camps, which further slowed progress on the road. The efficient construction techniques used by professional road building crews were rejected in the relief camps because they would reduce the total amount of work available; shovel brigades and horse-drawn scrapers became more common than caterpillar tractors and steam shovels. It is no surprise that the relief work camps made slow progress, for they were intended as much to prevent unemployed men from congregating in urban centres as they were to complete important infrastructure projects.[5]

British Columbia was effectively bankrupt by the summer of 1932 and unable to meet its public works commitments. Emergency federal funding helped keep the Big Bend relief work camps open until the Department of National Defence took control of relief camps nationwide the following year. This meant Ottawa was paying for construction of the entire Big Bend road project, with the National Parks Branch overseeing work on the eastern section and the Canadian Army on the western.[6] It was during the summer of 1932, when British Columbia was in its direst financial straits, that the National Parks Branch approached the provincial government about having forest scenery protected along the Big Bend road.

*****

J. M. Wardle was responsible for overseeing the Parks Branch's major construction projects in western Canada. In August 1932 he asked Tolmie's government to establish a quarter-mile-wide reserve along thirty kilometres of the surveyed right-of-way on the eastern section of the Big Bend road.[7] The tall ancient firs and cedars found between Kinbasket Lake and Boat Encampment were thought to be worth preserving as an attraction (or distraction) for motorists who one day would be driving through an unpopulated wilderness for many hours. As John Sandlos shows in his essay, encouraging auto tourism was one of the federal government's key priorities for the national parks in the interwar years. Wardle said nothing about a national park in the Columbia River valley, but provincial politicians may have interpreted his request for a scenic roadside timber reserve as an overture to a proposal for a new park. This is because the situation with the Big Bend road closely echoed their experience with Kootenay National Park a decade before, when Ottawa had agreed to complete B.C.'s section of the Banff-Windermere Highway project in exchange for three hundred and twenty thousand acres (twelve hundred square kilometres) of Crown land on which to establish a new national park.[8] Thus the idea of swapping park land for road development in the mountains of eastern B.C. was quite familiar to provincial leaders.

British Columbia's deputy minister of lands replied that the province was not opposed in principle to the preservation of tall, scenic timber along the Big Bend road but that implementation of such a reserve would be difficult.[9] Over the years many timber licences had been issued in the Big Bend country, including in the desired strip between Kinbasket Lake and Boat Encampment. No cutting had actually been done due to the area's inaccessibility, but logging companies and timber brokers held onto these licences as speculative investments. This made it impossible to say when the timber rights might revert to the province.

There the issue was left until early 1934, when Minister of the Interior Thomas G. Murphy wrote directly to T. D. "Duff" Pattullo, the new premier of British Columbia, to draw his personal attention to the National Parks Branch's desire for a roadside timber reserve.[10] "[T]his department is naturally interested in the scenic attractions of the Big Bend Highway," Murphy explained. He argued that the ancient forest that the Big Bend road would traverse between Kinbasket Lake and Boat Encampment deserved to be protected from unsightly resource exploitation because it was "the only stretch of virgin timber of fairly large size along the whole route of the Trans-Canada Highway from the Atlantic to the Pacific." Murphy urged Pattullo to act on the National Parks Branch's request and predicted a "storm of protest from the general public" if logging was allowed to mar roadside scenery along this section of the Big Bend Highway.

Pattullo agreed that a scenic timber reserve was a good idea. However, while it was fine for the National Parks Branch to desire unspoiled forest scenery along the new highway, the premier felt it was unfair to expect the impoverished province to bear the cost of acquiring it. He suggested that if the federal government truly believed the preservation of tall timber along the Big Bend Highway was a matter of national importance, then it should arrange to buy up all the valid timber licences in the area.[11] Pattullo had been B.C.'s minister of lands between 1919 and 1926, when the Banff-Windermere Highway agreement was negotiated and the land base for Kootenay National Park transferred to the federal government. By dragging his feet on the scenic timber reserve and coaxing the federal government to make

Fig. 2. New grade and big timber at Boulder Creek, Big Bend Highway. [Source: Library and Archives Canada, Parks Canada Collection/e010836790.]

further expenditures along the Big Bend road corridor, he may have hoped to manoeuvre it into proposing a new national park in the area.

Pattullo's reluctance to preserve the scenic roadside timber must have struck Thomas Murphy as rather ungrateful, given that Ottawa had been paying for all the work on the Big Bend road since 1933. Murphy reminded Pattullo that the Department of the Interior had agreed to participate in the project in 1929 on the basis that it was meant "primarily to increase the revenue from tourist traffic." It was therefore "of first importance that the scenic advantages of the road be duly capitalized."[12] If there were no scenic attractions to make driving between Golden and Revelstoke a pleasurable experience, then further federal involvement in the project would be called into question. If Murphy expected his veiled threat – to quit work on the Big Bend project – would convince Pattullo to protect the scenic timber desired by the Parks Branch, he must have been taken aback by the response he received. "The time has come," Pattullo's minister of public works asserted in November 1934, "when the Canadian National Parks [Branch] can advantageously assume the whole of the Columbia-Revelstoke Highway, *together with a strip of land ¼ mile wide on either side of the road which will be available for park purposes* [emphasis added]." The province took the position that the completed Big Bend road would form "an integral part of the National Parks System connecting [Mount] Revelstoke Park ... with the Rocky Mountain and Yoho parks to the east." Thus it was only logical that Ottawa should establish a national park or parkway along the road and assume permanent responsibility for its maintenance. Once Ottawa agreed to B.C.'s proposal for a new national park along the Big Bend road corridor, legislation would be passed along the lines of the 1919 bill that had transferred provincial Crown land to the federal government for the creation of Kootenay National Park.[13] Such an arrangement would permanently relieve British Columbia of the cost of maintaining almost all of the roads between Revelstoke and the B.C.–Alberta boundary. The province had little to lose by this proposal, for the forests of the rugged Big Bend country were of little value to timber companies in the days before long-haul truck logging.

For Thomas Murphy and the National Parks Branch, B.C.'s offer of land for a national park along the Big Bend road appears to have come out of the blue. No official reply was made to the province's proposal, but Pattullo was informed through political back channels that Ottawa was not interested in a new park if it meant being responsible for maintenance of the road.[14] This left the terms of the completion of the road project up in the air. As the Department of National Defence began preparing to return responsibility for relief work camps to the provinces, British Columbia pleaded for the National Parks Branch to take over the camps on the western section of the Big Bend. In the months before the 1935 construction season, Murphy delivered an ultimatum to Pattullo. The eastern section of the road between Golden and Boat Encampment was nearly finished, and, once it was, the federal government would be under no obligation to do further work on the project. Murphy was willing to have the National Parks Branch take over construction of the western section, but only after the two governments had reached a satisfactory agreement. He set out three key conditions. First, the province had to agree to maintain the completed road. Second, it had to "conserve in perpetuity" the desired strip of tall roadside timber between Kinbasket Lake and Boat Encampment. Third, Murphy wanted an agreement that "should the Dominion at some time in the future apply for Mount Assiniboine Park area, Mount Robson Park area, [...] or an area west of Waterton Lakes Park for an extension of [the] National Parks system, the Province will transfer same free of all encumbrance." The nationalization of Mount Robson and Mount Assiniboine provincial parks had been under discussion for several years, and Murphy no doubt saw the province's urgent desire to have the Big Bend road completed as a means of acquiring them – but not a new park in the Big Bend country itself – on favourable terms. Murphy concluded his ultimatum to Pattullo with a warning that "it is necessary that definite arrangements be made immediately."[15]

Pattullo agreed to maintain the completed highway and to preserve the strip of scenic roadside timber desired by the National Parks Branch. However, he equivocated on the question of turning over provincial parks and other land for national parks. His government would be "glad to cooperate" on this matter, but further discussion would be needed regarding the developments the federal government would undertake in exchange.[16] This was enough to satisfy Murphy, and he assigned the National Parks Branch the task of completing the western section of the Big Bend road. Discussions about parks and scenery along the Big Bend Highway disappear from Pattullo's correspondence with Ottawa after the Conservatives lost the October 1935 federal election and T.A. Crerar replaced Murphy as minister responsible for national parks. However, this was not the end of the idea of a national park in the Big Bend country.

*****

When the Big Bend Highway finally opened to the motoring public in June 1940, the provincial government made it the centrepiece of an elaborate publicity campaign to lure American tourists northwards. The road was described in brochures and magazine advertisements as "a splendid new highway extending for 200 miles through a scenic wonderland," providing motorists with "a thrilling travelogue of mountain peaks, glaciers, and entrancing views of the mighty Columbia River."[17] However, doubts quickly emerged about how splendid and thrilling the new highway really was. Driving around the Big Bend was a test of endurance, taking between five and seven hours. The gravel-surfaced road was narrow and twisting, and incredibly dusty in hot, dry weather. The dust made driving unpleasant and sometimes hazardous, and coated the roadside foliage, turning the immediate scenery drab and lifeless.[18] Promotional materials neglected to mention there was no food, gas, or lodging available in the "virgin territory" between Golden and Revelstoke.[19] A month after the highway opened, Revelstoke's board of trade reported that "not a day goes by that we do not have two or three accidents" but pinned the blame on Prairie drivers unaccustomed to mountain roads.[20] Furthermore, heavy winter snowfall meant the road was only open to traffic between May and October.

Soon first-hand reports began to demonstrate why the highway might fail to become popular with drivers. "I have just been over that stretch of road," one motorist wrote to Premier Pattullo, "and have been told that you have had the consummate nerve to spend money advertising the Big Bend road in American newspapers and magazines. You should be ashamed of yourself!"[21] Austin Cross, travel writer for the *Ottawa Citizen*, savaged the new road in an article on the nascent Trans-Canada Highway. "It is positively the loneliest road in North America," he complained, with "not a town, not a village, not a hamlet, not two houses together, not a suggestion of civilization." The road itself was "villainous," "built by people whose minds must be back in the 1920s." Even the tall timber along the highway failed to impress Cross, for there were few open vistas, and the dense, seemingly endless forest crowded claustrophobically close to the roadway. In terms of scenery, Cross concluded, "the much-touted Big Bend Highway could play second fiddle to many another British Columbia turnpike."[22]

Despite the early bad publicity for the Big Bend Highway – or perhaps because of it – Pattullo decided to take another shot at convincing Ottawa to assume responsibility for its maintenance and improvement. In an election campaign speech in Revelstoke in August 1941, he promised to press the federal government to pay the estimated $1 million cost of paving the road, because making it faster, safer, and more comfortable would help draw American tourists and bring in hard currency that was vitally important to Canada's war effort.[23] Pattullo recognized that the establishment of a national park in the Big Bend country remained the easiest way to get the federal government involved in the highway's upkeep, but convincing Ottawa to create such a park remained a tricky problem. While the province's 1934 proposal for a half-mile-wide park along the road corridor had been firmly rebuffed, Thomas Murphy's 1935 conditions for the National Parks Branch to complete the Big Bend road project had indicated a lingering interest in absorbing Mount Robson and Mount Assiniboine provincial parks into the national parks system. Previous discussions of this idea had foundered over disagreements about natural resources and a suggestion that the two parks were too small to become national parks in and of themselves. This could be read as implying that a larger area would be more acceptable. Thus one way to get the federal government involved in improving and maintaining the Big Bend Highway was to establish a very large new provincial park that would be made available for transfer to the national parks system.

The creation of provincial parks remained a cavalier process in British Columbia during the early 1940s, and Pattullo had the executive authority to establish a new park that might prove tempting to Ottawa. Abruptly and with little consultation, Pattullo issued an Order-in-Council on 16 September 1941, that created an enormous new park called Hamber.[24] Named after a former lieutenant-governor, Hamber Provincial Park was nearly 2.4 million acres (9,700 square kilometres) in size and consisted of archetypal British Columbia wilderness: mountainous, glaciated, heavily forested, cleft by icy watercourses, and almost completely uninhabited; large areas of the park had never been surveyed or accurately mapped. Hamber's boundaries encompassed the eastern slope of the Selkirks and the western slope of the

Fig. 3. Golden Revelstoke Highway, base sta 240 + 100 looking west, Big Bend Highway, August 1939. [Source: Library and Archives Canada, Parks Canada Collection/e010836789.]

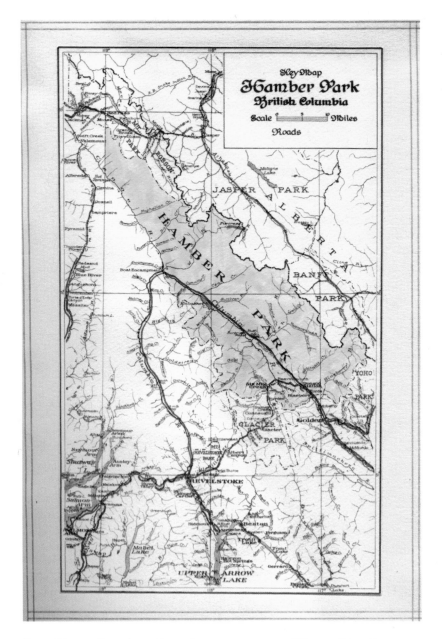

Fig. 4. Hamber Provincial Park. From the pamphlet "Hamber Park, British Columbia, Canada," 1942. [Courtesy of the British Columbia Ministry of Forests and Range.]

Rockies, from the main line of the Canadian Pacific Railway in the south to the Yellowhead Pass and the Canadian National Railway's main line in the north. The park's boundaries took in the eastern section of the Big Bend Highway, and had been carefully designed so that it would act as a kind of land bridge: Hamber bordered against Mount Robson Provincial Park in the north, Jasper and Banff national parks on the east, and Glacier and Yoho national parks in the south. Pattullo must have felt certain that this magnanimous and rather spontaneous gesture would finally convince Ottawa to take over British Columbia's provincial parks in the Rockies, for an unbroken chain of national parks covering both slopes of the Rockies from Mount Robson in the north to Radium Hot Springs in the south was bound to be a great tourist draw, even in wartime. Underlying it all was the expectation that if the federal government did agree to take over Hamber Park, it would be obliged to maintain and improve at least half of the Big Bend Highway, and to undertake other possible infrastructure developments.[25]

But this bold scheme quickly fell apart, for the federal government showed no interest in taking over Hamber or any other of B.C.'s provincial parks. The war effort was the main preoccupation for Canadian governments in 1941; moreover, the Mackenzie King administration had previously informed British Columbia of its desire to have national parks spread all around the country rather than concentrated in the mountainous west.[26] But probably the most important factor in Hamber's failure as a gambit towards a new national park was a lack of opportunity to discuss the subject. Pattullo was abruptly pushed out of the premiership by members of his own party on 3 December 1941, just weeks after he had won his third term as premier and less than three months after Hamber had been established. It is unclear whether a tentative proposal for Hamber to be incorporated into the national parks system had been made by then, but losing the man who had been the architect of the scheme to have a new national park in the Big Bend country would have scuttled any plans that had been discussed. Four days after Pattullo was forced out, Japan attacked the American Pacific fleet at Pearl Harbor. In September, when America had not been involved in the war, it might have seemed reasonable to gamble that the federal government would look favourably on the establishment of an enormous new national park along the route of the emergent Trans-Canada Highway. However, once the United States had been drawn into the war, American motorists' pleasure travel was sure to be curtailed, and thus the immediate rationale for establishing Hamber Park was lost.[27]

****

Four years later, as the end of the war neared, British Columbia found itself stuck with an enormous provincial park of questionable utility. Loggers and sawmill operators in Golden and Revelstoke complained that Hamber would stifle the region's postwar forest industry, prompting members of B.C.'s coalition government to ask difficult questions about the new park. In an attempt to salvage something from the situation, the Parks Branch of the B.C. Forest Service was dispatched to investigate possible developments in Hamber Park in the summer of 1945. The reconnaissance report was profoundly unenthusiastic about Hamber's value as a park, despite the fact that no attempt had been made to explore beyond the immediate right-of-way of the Big Bend Highway. In fact, dissatisfaction with the road was a key factor in the provincial Parks Branch's initial reluctance to retain the park. The Big Bend Highway was described as "well-built from a constructional point of view, but poorly located from the aesthetic point of view. In general, it is above and beyond view of the river and often separated by a narrow fringe of timber. There are many cases where a better location would have been possible so as to improve the view and break the monotony of the drive." Trees and underbrush crowded right up to the verges of the road, producing an uneasy sense of confinement. According to the B.C. Parks Branch, driving the Big Bend Highway had "a tendency to being monotonous, due primarily to the lack of cleared look-out points." Most of the interesting sights along its route were obscured by intervening forest; the Columbia River was hidden from view for long stretches, and motorists got only a few fleeting glimpses of glaciers and mountain peaks. The open vistas along the shores of icy Kinbasket Lake were deemed the only section of the drive that had high scenic value. The B.C. Parks Branch considered the Big Bend Highway a failure as a scenic drive, and Hamber's inadequacy as a park was an extension of this.[28]

In its reconnaissance report, the B.C. Parks Branch recommended that Hamber be cancelled and replaced by a handful of small roadside viewpoints and campgrounds. However, because some kind of mechanism for the management of land use was needed along the route of the Trans Canada Highway,

Hamber was instead downgraded from a class A to a class B provincial park.[29] This gave the provincial Parks Branch the power to permit mining and logging activity within Hamber's boundaries, for, whereas conservation principles were increasingly being incorporated into the management of the national parks, British Columbia was careful to avoid permanently locking up land and resources in its provincial parks.[30]

Hamber's story following its designation as a class B provincial park is one of neglect and drawn-out decline. The B.C. Parks Branch did nothing to develop, publicize, or indicate the existence of the park. No roadside signs were erected to inform motorists that they were traversing one of the largest parks in Canada when driving between Boat Encampment and the outskirts of Golden. No public campgrounds were developed along the highway, no scenic pullouts were cleared, no trails were developed, and no brochures or pamphlets were published. Tourist bureaus were dissuaded from mentioning Hamber Park in promotional material about the Trans-Canada Highway.[31] Even when effectively ignored by the B.C. Parks Branch, some staff still believed that Hamber represented "a needless burden to the provincial park system." They advocated a liberal approach to allowing logging within Hamber's boundaries, on the basis that it had been "set aside for a reason only remotely related to its recreational values" and "should not be a park to start with." Eventually it was decided that logging operations would be permitted anywhere inside the park, provided they were "not obvious from the highway." In 1950, Forest Service headquarters bypassed its own Parks Branch and began to sell timber licences inside Hamber Park just as they would anywhere else in the province. By the mid-1950s, provincial park planners were musing that Hamber should be deleted except for the area around Kinbasket Lake, deemed the "the scenic high point" of the Big Bend Highway.[32]

In the mid-1950s a consortium of municipal power companies from the American Pacific Northwest approached the B.C. government with a proposal to build a series of dams on the Columbia River, including a large impoundment dam one hundred and fifty kilometres north of Revelstoke at Mica Creek. This proposal fell through, but a dam at Mica was later incorporated into the international negotiations that led to the Columbia River Treaty.[33] The dam's reservoir was projected to inundate hundreds of square kilometres of the Columbia and Canoe river valleys, destroying Boat Encampment, Kinbasket Lake, and the eastern half of the Big Bend Highway. The proposed destruction of the Big Bend section of the Trans-Canada Highway was the most problematic aspect of this scheme until 1956, when the provincial and federal governments agreed to share the cost of replacing it with a modern, paved, all-season highway through the Selkirks via the Rogers Pass and Glacier National Park – the same route that Ottawa had rejected in the late 1920s. No one was likely to miss the lonely, roundabout Big Bend road, for Canadian motorists' perceptions of what constituted a proper highway had changed during the postwar years, and narrow, dusty, gravel-surfaced roads that were closed to traffic half the year were no longer considered up to date.[34] The *Vancouver Sun* welcomed the demise of the unpopular Big Bend Highway, which it called "the weak link" in an otherwise safe and scenic drive between Vancouver and Banff, "just a road through the trees and plainly boring."[35]

By the late 1950s work was underway on the new highway through the Rogers Pass, and the future construction of the Mica Dam was all but assured. In anticipation of the Big Bend country being flooded out, the province threw Hamber Park wide open to logging, even in scenic areas that were visible from the highway. Portable sawmills were set up inside the park, and in February 1959 the reserve over the tall, ancient roadside timber between Kinbasket Lake and Boat Encampment – which in 1935 Pattullo had assured Murphy would be conserved in perpetuity – was cancelled so that the timber could be made available for logging. As completion of the new highway through the Rogers Pass approached, the impending relegation of the Big Bend Highway to the status of a back road removed the last reason for maintaining the charade that Hamber Provincial Park had become. In late 1960 B.C. Parks Branch staff were circulating confidential memos about how to proceed with its cancellation.[36]

In the briefing document that recommended Hamber's deletion to the minister responsible for provincial parks, the director of the Parks Branch was at a loss to explain why it had been created in the first place. "There is no report, even a general analysis, on the park potential of the area which would outline the purpose of its dedication," he complained. Scrutiny of the files revealed only that Hamber had been established in a vague hope that the federal government could be induced to take it and Mount Robson over as national parks. "This," he concluded, "would seem to be a questionable basis for establishing a major park." Nothing was remembered about the province's 1934 proposal for a national park along the Big Bend road, or about Hamber's complicated relationship with the completed highway. In the spring of 1961 almost the entire park was deleted, with only a sixty thousand acre (240 square kilometre) rump retained around Fortress Lake, isolated high in the Rockies and accessible only by floatplane. Hamber's evisceration drew nary a whimper from the public, for few realized it had ever been there.[37]

Construction of the Mica Dam began in the mid-1960s. When the dam became operational in 1973, it gradually inundated hundreds of square kilometres of the Columbia and Canoe river valleys that had formerly been located within the boundaries of Hamber Park. The province had tried to clear huge amounts of timber from the reservoir area, but extensive forested areas ended up being submerged. The Kinbasket Reservoir, as it is known today, took three years to fill to capacity, destroying in slow motion the remnants of the old Big Bend Highway, the small roadside service centres that had been developed at Boat Encampment and Kinbasket Lake, and the habitat of grizzly bears, mountain caribou, and Columbia River sturgeon.

*****

If few people were aware of Hamber Park's existence between 1941 and 1961, even fewer have heard of it today. Its story – like those of most failed, deleted, and unrealized parks – has escaped the attention of Canadian historians and parks supporters.[38] On the rare occasion Hamber is mentioned, the focus is on its unfortunate history after 1945, with its origins in the intertwined politics of roads and national parks going overlooked.[39] Yet Hamber's deletion in 1961 takes on a new significance in light of the fact that the provincial government had created the park in the hope of giving it away: Hamber had been a gambit, meant to convince the federal government to incorporate it and B.C.'s other provincial parks in the Rockies into the national parks system. In retrospect this may seem "a questionable basis" for establishing such an enormous park, but it made perfect sense in the context of the province's sustained campaign to get Ottawa to build, improve, and maintain automobile roads in the rugged terrain of the Selkirk and Rocky mountains. After Pattullo's 1934 proposal for a linear national park along the Big Bend road had failed and the highway had been completed (albeit to a not very high standard), British Columbia could only hope to tempt the federal government into such a scheme by offering up a much larger block of park land.

In addition to shedding light on some of the political, economic, and aesthetic criteria that have shaped proposals for new national parks, the intertwined histories of roads and parks in B.C.'s Big Bend country invite speculation about how things might have turned out differently. For example, how might a park in the Big Bend country have fit into the larger national parks system? Could it have proven popular with North American tourists, who were fast becoming accustomed to open vistas, modern roads, and a growing number of roadside services in their national parks? How might a national park along the Columbia have affected plans to dam the river at Mica Creek? How would a large park on the western slope of the Rockies have affected the ecological integrity of the mountain parks as a block? These kinds of questions show how examining failed park proposals can encourage us to think differently about the present-day park system. Failed parks' stories remind us that there was nothing natural or inevitable about decisions to accept or reject areas for national parks. What happened in the Big Bend country is particularly noteworthy because of the great size of Hamber Provincial Park and the fact that the forests drowned beneath the surface of the Kinbasket Reservoir are located so close to the 'crown jewels' of Canada's national parks system. However, many other never-realized national parks need to have their histories told so that we can have a fuller understanding of the threshold between success and failure.

NOTES

1 Alan MacEachern, *Natural Selections: National Parks in Atlantic Canada, 1935–1970* (Montreal: McGill-Queen's University Press, 2001).

2 R.G. Harvey, *Carving the Western Path: By River, Rail, and Road through BC's Southern Mountains* (Surrey, BC: Heritage House, 1998), 86.

3 R.G. Harvey suggests that political pressure from the Canadian Pacific Railway was behind the federal government's reluctance to build an automobile road through the Rogers Pass. *Carving the Western Path*, 89–91.

4 Charles Stewart, Minister of the Interior telegram to Nelson Lougheed, Minister of Public Works, 4 October 1929, cited in Harvey, *Carving the Western Path*, 87–89.

5 See University of British Columbia Special Collections, Simon Fraser Tolmie papers, box 8, file 19, Minister of Public Works R.W. Bruhn to Premier Tolmie, 17 June 1931. The cynicism that 'make work' projects engendered amongst Canadian relief camp workers is touched on in James Struthers, *No Fault of Their Own: Unemployment and the Canadian Welfare State, 1914–1941* (Toronto: University of Toronto Press, 1983), 133–34; and John Herd Thompson and Allen Seager, *Canada, 1922–1939: Decades of Discord* (Toronto: McClelland & Stewart, 1985), 268–69. Also see Bill Waiser, *Park Prisoners: The Untold Story of Western Canada's National Parks, 1915–1946* (Saskatoon: Fifth House, 1995), chaps. 2–3.

6 See Thomas William Tanner, "Microcosms of Misfortune: Canada's Unemployment Relief Camps Administered by the Department of National Defence, 1932–1936." MA thesis, University of Western Ontario, 1965; Lorne Alvin Brown, "The Bennett Government, Political Stability, and the Politics of the Unemployment Relief Camps, 1930–1935." PhD dissertation, Queen's University, 1983.

7 British Columbia Archives (hereafter BCA), GR-1222 Premier's Papers, box 97, file 2, J.M. Wardle, Chief Engineer to H. Cathcart, Deputy Minister of Lands, 31 August 1932, cited in Cathcart to Wardle, 10 April 1933. Also see box 15, file 7, Cathcart to Pattullo, 4 June 1935.

8 On the Banff-Windermere Highway and the origins of Kootenay National Park, see John Sandlos's chapter in this book and W.F. Lothian, *A History of Canada's National Parks*, vol. 1 (Ottawa: Parks Canada, 1976), 58–60.

9 BCA, GR-1222, box 97, file 2, [H. Cathcart] Deputy Minister [of Lands] to Wardle, 10 April 1933. The province only responded to Wardle's request after the B.C. Forest Service reported that the feasibility of profitable logging in the desired area was uncertain. British Columbia Ministry of Forests Library, W.A. Johnston, "Big Bend, Columbia River Reconnaissance" (Victoria, 1932).

10 BCA, GR-1222, box 97, file 2, Thomas G. Murphy to Pattullo, 26 January 1934 and 9 June 1934.

11 BCA, GR-1222, box 97, file 2, Pattullo to Murphy, 15 February 1934, forwarding A. Wells Gray, Minister of Lands, memo for Pattullo, 13 Feb 1934.

12   BCA, GR-1222, box 97, file 2, Murphy to Pattullo, 8 September 1934.

13   BCA, GR-1222, box 15, file 7, [Frank M.] MacPherson [Minister of Public Works] to Murphy, 10 November 1934, attached to Department of Public Works to Pattullo, 30 May 1935.

14   BCA, GR-1222, box 15, file 7, E.A. Boyle, Secretary, Big Bend Highway Committee to Pattullo, 27 April 1935; W.A. Gordon, City Clerk, City of Revelstoke to MacPherson, 11 May 1935.

15   BCA, GR-1222, box 15, file 7, Murphy, telegram to Pattullo, 28 May 1935; Pattullo to Murphy, 30 May 1935; Murphy telegram to Pattullo, 1 June 1935.

16   BCA, GR-1222, box 15, file 7, Pattullo telegram to Murphy, 4 June 1935. Also see Murphy to Pattullo, 19 June 1935; Pattullo to Murphy, 10 July 1935. Due to the need to acquire the remaining valid timber licenses, the tall roadside timber between Kinbasket Lake and Boat Encampment was not formally put under the protection of a provincial Crown reserve until April 1936.

17   University of British Columbia Special Collections, British Columbia Government Travel Bureau, *Advertising Campaign for Promotion of Tourist Travel, 1940* (Victoria, 1940). On the strategic importance of encouraging American tourists to visit B.C. during the early war years, see Michael Dawson, *Selling British Columbia: Tourism and Consumer Culture, 1890–1970* (Vancouver: UBC Press, 2004), chap. 4.

18   Driving conditions on the Big Bend Highway are recalled in Bob Metcalfe, "Goodbye to the Big Bend," *Imperial Oil Review* 46, no. 4 (August 1962): 16–19; Donovan Clemson, "Goodbye to the Big Bend," *BC Motorist* 9, no. 1 (January–February 1970): 4; and Tom Parkin, "Disappearing Highway," *British Columbia Historical News* 28, no. 4 (1995): 31.

19   In May 1940 the B.C. Ministry of Lands had identified Kinbasket Lake, Downie Creek, and Boat Encampment as locations along the Big Bend Highway that were suitable for gas stations and other roadside services. However, it was several years before any such operation opened. BCA, GR-1222, box 34, file 5, Minister of Lands, memo to Pattullo, 30 May 1940.

20   BCA, GR-1222, box 34, file 5, Revelstoke Board of Trade to Pattullo, 21 July 1940.

21   BCA, GR-1222, box 34, file 5, W.B. Hill to Pattullo, 31 August 1941. Stories about unsafe and un-scenic conditions along the Big Bend road can also be found in the pages of the *Revelstoke Review* throughout the summer and fall of 1941.

22   Austin Cross, "The Big Bend Highway," *Ottawa Citizen*, 20 December 1942.

23   *Revelstoke Review*, 7 August 1941. Also see Dawson, *Selling British Columbia*, 120–26.

24   Hamber Park was created by an Order-in-Council (#1305) because the Legislature had been dissolved in preparation for an October election. The fact that Pattullo waited until after the dissolution of the Legislature to create such an important provincial park suggests that he may have been involved in backroom negotiations with the federal government regarding

its possible incorporation into the national parks system.

25 An automobile road through the Yellowhead Pass is one development that the province may have expected in exchange for Hamber and Mount Robson parks. It had also been suggested that a road from Boat Encampment to the Yellowhead Pass via the Canoe River valley might form a leaping off point for a future road to Alaska, which was one of Pattullo's pet projects. "Big Bend Road Looms Large in Alaska Highway Plan," *Revelstoke Review*, 27 April 1939; Robin Fisher, "T.D. Pattullo and the British Columbia to Alaska Highway," in *The Alaska Highway: Papers of the 40th Anniversary Symposium*, ed. Ken Coates, 9–24 (Vancouver: UBC Press, 1985).

26 In 1938 T.A. Crerar informed the provincial Minister of Lands that funds were unlikely to be found for more national parks in B.C. due to the federal government's focus on establishing parks in the east. BCA, GR-1991 Parks and Outdoor Recreation, reel 1754, Crerar to A. Wells Gray, 25 August 1938, cited in H. Cathcart, Deputy Minister of Lands memo to Premier John Hart, 1 December 1944. Also see C.J. Taylor, *Negotiating the Past: The Making of Canada's National Historic Parks and Sites* (Montreal: McGill-Queen's University Press, 1990), 109–11; MacEachern, *Natural Selections*, 45, 52–53.

27 Dawson, *Selling British Columbia*, 120–26. When Pattullo visited Revelstoke in August 1941, he had been approached with complaints about the need to make the Big Bend Highway more attractive to auto tourists. *Revelstoke Review*, 7 August 1941.

28 British Columbia Ministry of Forests Library, C.P. Lyons and D.M. Trew, "Reconnaissance of Hamber Park and Big Bend Highway" (Victoria: B.C. Forest Service, Forest Economics Division, Parks Section, 1945), 13, 11.

29 Ibid., 6; BCA, GR-1991, reel 1754, Percy [illegible] to [Premier] John Hart, 19 March 1945; Thomas King, MLA (Golden) to E.T. Kenney, Minister of Lands, 6 April 1945.

30 On B.C.'s classification system for its provincial parks in the postwar years, see Jeremy Wilson, *Talk and Log: Wilderness Politics in British Columbia, 1961–1996* (Vancouver: UBC Press, 1998), 93–98.

31 For example, see BCA, GR-1991, reel 1754, E.G. Oldham to Ontario Government Department of Travel and Publicity, 17 May 1950.

32 BCA, GR-1991, reel 1754, C.P. Lyons memo to F.S. McKinnon, 15 July 1946; D.M. Trew to E.G. Oldham, 25 May 1949; G.A. Wood, report, 1954. The oral agreement whereby the Forest Service bypassed the Parks Branch regarding timber sales in Hamber is described in Minister of Lands and Forests to Earle C. Westwood, Minister of Recreation and Conservation, 3 February 1961.

33 Neil Swainson, *Conflict Over the Columbia: The Canadian Background to an Historic Treaty* (Montreal: McGill-Queen's University Press for the Institute of Public Administration of Canada, 1979), 54–56.

34 See David W. Monaghan, *Canada's 'New Main Street': The Trans-Canada Highway as Idea and Reality, 1912–1956* (Ottawa: Canadian Science and Technology Museum, 2002), 23–24.

On the enthusiastic reception that the opening of the highway through the Rogers Pass received from the motoring public, see Daniel Francis, *A Road for Canada: An Illustrated History of the Trans-Canada Highway* (Vancouver: Stanton, Atkins, and Dosil, 2006), 1–5.

35   "Reporter Finds Vancouver-Banff Highway Good and Getting Better," *Vancouver Sun*, 22 July 1959.

36   BCA, GR-1991, reel 1754, R.H. Ahrens, Reconnaissance Section [Parks Branch] to Forester-in-Charge, Parks and Recreation Division, 14 November 1956; H.G. McWilliams, Director, Provincial Parks Branch to C.T.W. Hyslop, Superintendant of Lands, 6 January 1959; E.W. Bassett, Deputy Minister of Lands, "Notice of Cancellation and Establishment of Reserve" pursuant to Order in Council #213, 6 February 1959; Director, Provincial Parks Branch to W.H. Hepper, 30 September 1960.

37   BCA, GR-1991, reel 1754, H.G. McWilliams, Director, Provincial Parks Branch to D.B. Turner, Deputy Minister, Department of Recreation and Conservation, 25 April 1961.

38   An important exception to this is Jennifer Brower's history of Buffalo National Park, which was located in eastern Alberta prior to being deleted and turned into present-day Canadian Forces Base Wainwright. Brower, *Lost Tracks: Buffalo National Park, 1909–1939* (Edmonton: AU Press, 2008).

39   See, for example, Wilson, *Talk and Log*, 95; Robert William Sandford, *Ecology and Wonder in the Canadian Rocky Mountain Parks World Heritage Site* (Edmonton: AU Press, 2010), 201–2.

"A Case of Special Privilege and Fancied Right": The Shack Tent Controversy in Prince Albert National Park

Bill Waiser
Department of History
University of Saskatchewan

Former Liberal prime minister Jean Chrétien had the reputation as a street fighter, someone known for his steely resolve in advancing the government's agenda, even in the face of fierce opposition from both the right and the left. In fact, during his lengthy parliamentary career, he is probably remembered for retreating only once, when as a young minister of Indian Affairs and Northern Development in 1970, he publicly withdrew the Trudeau government's controversial White Paper on Indian Policy. It was not the only time, though, that Chrétien backed down during his early ministerial career. That same year, he met face-to-face with representatives of the Waskesiu Tent Cabin and Portable Cabin Association in an effort to defuse a growing local protest over a development plan to eliminate these semi-permanent structures from the Prince Albert National Park [PANP] townsite campground. But instead of holding to the federal plan that had been a decade in the making, Chrétien offered to review the attrition policy in light of the local situation. The National Parks Branch never regained the initiative.

This debate over the existence of shack tents and portable cabins in Saskatchewan's first national park might seem puzzling, if not confusing, in that most Canadians readily assume that national parks exist for the benefit and pleasure of all visitors, not just a select few. But private cottages have always been one of the defining features of the Waskesiu townsite. Indeed, Canada's national parks have struggled for the better part of their existence with a dual identity as both nature preserves and recreational playgrounds. This double purpose, a common theme in Canadian national park literature,[1] has often pushed and pulled national parks in two different directions. One author has even claimed that the two-sided mandate has been "the constant, unresolved problem at the heart of park history."[2] But for the generations of people who made Waskesiu their summer home, there was no such "unresolved problem." With many of the same visitors returning season after season, there developed a strong sense of community, especially among the shack tenters who came to identify their interests and desires with those of the park. This attitude not only applied to summer campground policy, but also to what actually went on in the larger townsite – to the point where recreational interests triumphed over any sense of ecological integrity. Any attempt by Ottawa to challenge this situation was regarded as gross interference by a distant bureaucracy which, in the words of one long-time park resident, "did not appreciate the needs or wishes of the people who use the park the most."[3]

Saskatchewan's Playground

Private dwellings have existed in Canada's national parks since the late nineteenth century. The 1887 legislation that set aside Rocky Mountains (later Banff) Park allowed for villa or cottage lots that, in the words of Conservative Prime Minister Sir John A. Macdonald, would be "leased out to people of wealth, who will erect handsome buildings on them."[4] The prime minister also insisted that park tenants be granted long-term, minimal-payment leases, or, at the very least, first right of renewal; otherwise, without something approximating security of tenure, Macdonald maintained that people would be reluctant to invest money in suitable dwellings and probably visit the park less frequently.[5] So began the policy of allowing private cottages in national parks, and they became thereafter a regular fixture in most townsites. Those in Prince Albert National Park had been erected even before the park was created. In 1914, in an effort to protect the timber and water resources of the boreal forest immediately north of Prince Albert, the federal government set aside the present-day southern half of the park as the Sturgeon River Forest Reserve.[6] The regulations allowed for the recreational use of the reserve in specially designated resort areas, where summer lots would be made available for an annual fee of five dollars. It was not until 1924, though, that a summer cottage subdivision was established at the Big Beach area (also known as Primeau's Landing) along the southeast shore of Red Deer (later Waskesiu) Lake. Even then, access to the site was difficult, and the few cottagers were lucky if they could travel the 100 kilometres from Prince Albert to Waskesiu in one day.

A solution soon presented itself in the form of a defeated prime minister.[7] When Liberal leader William Lyon Mackenzie King lost his seat in the October 1925 general election, Charles McDonald, the newly elected MP for Prince Albert, offered to step aside.[8] But the safe seat came at a price. The local Liberal riding association, which included members of the Prince Albert Board of Trade, wanted a national park established around Waskesiu Lake. It was a logical request for the city that billed itself as the gateway to Saskatchewan's north,[9] but there were also personal interests involved. Several prominent citizens held permits for summer lots at Waskesiu and believed that the area would receive the needed improvements, in particular a good road, only after it had achieved national park status. What really clinched the deal, though, was the prime minister's belief that a national park would enhance his popularity in the riding and guarantee his continued support at the polls.[10] Once King had handily won the February 1926 by-election, it was time for him to honour his side of the bargain. The Prince Albert people were not disappointed. They not only got a national park in the area they wanted, but had the deciding say in size (1,377 square miles) and name (Prince Albert) of the park, established by Order-in-Council on 24 March 1927. From the outset, Tommy Davis, the provincial MLA for the area, boldly predicted that "The Park is going to be a grand thing for Prince Albert.… It is going to preserve in perpetuity a great playground … a playground which is totally different from the prairie area of our province."[11] But there was much to be done to bring these words to fruition – from laying out a park townsite and building an all-weather road to advertising the new park and getting ready for visitors (typical of the era, as John Sandlos shows). In particular, the Parks Branch decided to reserve the so-called Big Beach area for campers, now occupied by Forest Reserve lots, and create a new summer cottage site at Prospect Point, a height of land immediately to the west. The subdivision offered an unrivalled view of the lake and it was not every day that someone had the chance to live next door to the prime minister (King had been given a cottage for his role in creating the park). But the high costs of construction, particularly when a cottage could be occupied for only a few months each summer,[12] meant that most park visitors had to make do with the 150 public campsites that had been underbrushed and cleared at Big Beach for the 1928 summer season. Even then, the campground proved too small, and over the next few years the area was gradually enlarged to accommodate several hundred cars.[13]

A Tent, a Car, and Some Elbow Space

The creation of Prince Albert National Park was followed three years later by the passage of the *National Parks Act* (1930). Whereas earlier legislation had allowed resource development within park boundaries, national parks were now defined as inviolable spaces of nature "dedicated to the people of Canada for their benefit, education, and enjoyment" and to "be maintained and made use of so as to leave them unimpaired for the enjoyment of future generations."[14] This wording in the 1930 act has been hailed as "the foundation upon which all subsequent ecological protection [in national parks] has been based."[15] But the legislation also confirmed the traditional role of parks as serviced recreation areas. In fact, despite this new emphasis on park ecology, the priority in Prince Albert National Park in the early 1930s continued to be the development of the townsite and the provision of visitor accommodation. By the end of 1932, only eight cottages had been built in the Prospect Point subdivision because of the building requirements. The Waskesiu campground, on the other hand, was severely overtaxed. At one point in July 1931, there were 3,800 people under canvas trying to share the 480 camping lots. Park Superintendent James Wood described the scene in a letter to Harkin later that fall: "tents were jammed so closely together that at times it was impossible to get between them."[16] One solution to the problem, put forward by the Prince Albert Board of Trade, was to set aside an area in the townsite where cheaper cottages could be erected. Ottawa was cool to the idea as long as lots were still available at Prospect Point. As a compromise, though, a number of people were allowed to erect tent houses, or "shack tents" as they were popularly known, in a designated area of the main campground. These were knock-down structures with sectional wooden floors and walls that were hinged or bolted together, and a canvas-covered frame roof.[17]

In 1932, the campground was still congested – "just big enough," in the words of one visitor, "for a tent and a car and some elbow space."[18] One of the reasons for the popularity of the Waskesiu campground was that the only highway to the park ended there; it literally was the end of the road. The townsite was also something of an oasis in the northern wilderness, where families of modest means could forget about the outside world and enjoy a few carefree weeks; it was as if the Depression and the deteriorating economic situation did not exist. But the park was also relatively difficult to reach during the early years of its existence. Unlike the mountain parks, which were served by the railways, there were no direct highways from neighbouring provinces or from the international boundary to the park. Those who visited the park consequently came largely from central Saskatchewan, from within a 150-mile radius that included Prince Albert and to a lesser extent Saskatoon.[19]

That Prince Albert National Park served essentially a local clientele had a profound impact on park development. The National Parks Branch had anticipated from the beginning that canoe tripping on the park's many lakes and rivers would be the major recreational activity and that the townsite would serve as a starting point and supply base. But most visitors to the park in the 1930s and 1940s were families who spent their entire vacation in and around Waskesiu. And because of the relatively short summer season and the prohibition against staying in the park during the winter, it made little sense to expend money on a more substantial cottage when a shack tent would do. It really did not matter if the structures were draughty or unsteady, or that the furniture was crude or unstable; all these families wanted was a cheap place to stay for the summer season. Over time, shack tents led to a sense of community. Segregated on a row of blocks that had specifically been set aside for them in the campground, the shack tents essentially comprised a

Fig. 1. Shack tents in the Waskesiu townsite campground offered an affordable family summer holiday. [Courtesy of Prince Albert National Park Collection, Parks Canada.]

small town within the larger townsite. People came to know one another as neighbours on a first-name basis, particularly since they were allowed to occupy the same lot summer after summer. This sense that Waskesiu was a perfect place for an affordable, family-oriented holiday was captured by a local reporter who visited the campground in 1938. One man roused from his hammock described Prince Albert as "the best damn playground between the Great Lakes and the Rockies."[20]

Not everyone was pleased, however, with the cottage situation at Waskesiu. The Prince Albert Board of Trade, which had always taken a lively interest in the park, believed that the national park building regulations were encouraging people to build cottages elsewhere in the province and hence losing business for the city.[21] The board of trade consequently decided in 1936 to push again for a new subdivision for cheaper cottages. The Parks Branch remained opposed to the idea. In an internal memorandum on the topic, National Parks Commissioner James B. Harkin insisted that conditions at Waskesiu did not warrant special treatment. "If any cheaper type of cottage were allowed," he noted, "the character of the park area would be no better than that of areas where no Park Regulations are in effect and the whole advantage of development under National Parks supervision would be lost."[22]

The Prince Albert situation was different, though, in that it was the prime minister's riding. And so, instead of turning down the proposal, Thomas Crerar, the Minister of the Interior, instructed his department to come up with a solution. Two years later, the Lakeview subdivision, an area for cheaper cottages along the lakeshore, was carved out of four existing blocks of the main campground. Superintendent Wood, for his part, hoped the Parks Branch would not stop there and suggested that it was also an opportune time to remove all shack tents from the campground over the next few years. "Personally I would be glad to see them done away with," he advised Ottawa. "A camping ground with numerous tent houses is far from attractive."[23] But federal officials, sensitized to the Prince Albert situation, were not foolish enough to resolve one contentious issue only to create another. Besides, it was assumed that people occupying shack tents would probably opt for a small cottage lot.

A Park Institution

The coming of the Second World War temporarily eased the demand for accommodation in Waskesiu, as park attendance fell by two-thirds from its pre-war high of 30,000 visitors. But once the war was over, Saskatchewan people flocked to the park in unprecedented numbers. By 1949, attendance at Prince Albert exceeded 50,000 and then steadily climbed through the decade. The average daily townsite population during the 1958 season was 5,200 people – more than the total attendance in 1928. Although Waskesiu had always figured largely in park development, it never dominated it to the extent that it did in the 1950s and 1960s. The large influx of visitors placed a severe strain on accommodation facilities and ultimately led to crowded conditions at Waskesiu that were clearly at odds with the values and purposes commonly identified with national parks.

The Parks Branch responded to the explosion in park visitation by creating two new subdivisions for moderately priced cottages in the townsite: Lakeview 2 in 1946 and Lakeview 3 in 1951. But the real problem area remained the crowded campground. As park attendance started to rebound in the late 1940s, eighty new lots were added to the campground. This was followed in 1953 by the commencement of work on a seventy-two-lot trailer area that was intended to free up more space in the campground. What was completely unanticipated, however, was the phenomenal expansion in the number of shack tents. By the summer of 1950, there were 412 shack tents in the Waskesiu campground, a 25 per cent increase from the previous year. A small number had also popped up in the campground at the Waskeiu Narrows. National Parks Controller James Smart did not even like their name, let along their use, and instructed the new park superintendent, B.I.M. Strong, to employ a more dignified term such as "cabins" or "house tent" when referring to them.[24]

Ottawa soon had a more serious challenge on its hands. In early July 1950, R.D. Kerr, secretary of the new Prince Albert National Park Shack Tent Owners' Association, presented Strong with a 274-name petition requesting that shack tents be allowed to remain on their campground lots year-round. The petition noted that the existing storage facilities could not handle the steadily growing volume of shack tents, that the structures and their contents were often damaged during their removal from the campground, and

FIG. 2. BY THE 1940S, THE SHACK TENT COMMUNITY HAD BECOME A PARK INSTITUTION.
[COURTESY OF PRINCE ALBERT NATIONAL PARK COLLECTION, PARKS CANADA.]

that the owners would take better care of them if they could be left standing year-round.[25] It was not the first time the question of leaving shack tents on the campground had been raised; the issue had come up every few years. But the sharp rise in their numbers, together with the problem of dismantling, storing, and then erecting them all each year, however, forced the shack tenters to take concerted action. They formed themselves into an association, drew up and circulated the petition, and solicited the support of both the Prince Albert and Saskatoon boards of trade. They also had an unlikely ally in Superintendent Strong. Whereas his predecessors would have been happy to rid the park of the structures, Strong believed that the Waskesiu shack tenters were "an institution" in the park and that the owners had "a legitimate complaint." He suggested to Ottawa that the shack tents be converted into what he called "portable cabins" with permanent walls and roofs and skid foundations for towing.[26]

The National Parks Branch's initial reaction to the petition was to say no. Controller James Smart was worried on two counts: that the public campground would be taken over by permanent cabins, and that allowing the owners to occupy the same lots year-round might give them some preemptory right to the property. But upon reflection – and the application of some political pressure from the town of Prince Albert[27] – Ottawa softened its stand. It still refused to allow shack tents to remain on the campground year-round but, at the same time, proposed the creation of a separate "tourist camp" where private families could erect small inexpensive cottages[28] – exactly what Harkin, now long retired, had fought against in the early 1930s.

This portable cabin scheme seemed to please all concerned parties and, over the next year, the details were worked out. Two blocks in the campground on the east side of Waskesiu Drive were set aside for the erection of small (fourteen feet by twenty feet), single-storey cabins to be based on one of five government-approved plans. These structures could be left on the same site year-round but had to be built on skids so that they could be moved if necessary. The lots themselves (forty feet by fifty feet) were to be awarded on a draw system and occupied on the basis of a twenty-dollar seasonal camping permit. No individual was allowed to hold both a portable cabin and a shack tent lot. In an attempt to reduce the number of shack tents, preference was given to existing shack tent owners in the awarding of portable cabin lots

– their names were drawn first. The Parks Branch was also willing to allow shack tents to be converted to portable cabins.[29]

The first draw for portable cabins was made on 28 March 1951. The scheme proved an immediate success – there were more applicants than available lots – and within three years, a further five new blocks had to be added. The portable cabin development, however, had no impact on the number of shack tents. As families moved from the shack tent area into portable cabins, their places were simply taken up by others. What this meant by the summer of 1956 is that the number of spaces specifically set aside for tents in the Waskesiu campground dropped to a mere fifty-eight sites. Shack tents and portables, in the meantime, occupied 616 lots, or more than two-thirds of the available campground space, including the trailer park.[30] It appeared that the weekend camper might have to be placed on the endangered species list.

J.R.B. Coleman, the new national parks director, wanted shack tents – what he derisively described as eyesores – to be phased out completely at Prince Albert. But the question of what to do about the Waskesiu campground could not be handled so easily, or so brusquely for that matter. During a visit to Saskatoon on 30 June 1956, a parks official was privately warned that "changes in the shack tent arrangement ... could only result in wide scale trouble."[31] The new Prince Albert superintendent, Harry Dempster, concurred. Asked to study the "camping problem" at Waskesiu over the summer of 1956, Dempster prepared a comprehensive, thoughtful memorandum in which he repeatedly advised against any action against the shack tents if Ottawa wanted to avoid an emotional, acrimonious public battle. "It seems to me that the shack tent problem is one that we are stuck with," he mused, "and the main thing to be done is to make up our minds that they will be with us at the Waskesiu campground and how best to control them with the least amount of trouble to ourselves and to the occupants."[32] What Dempster had in mind was placing an absolute limit on the number of shack tent lots, as well as warning the owners that the structures could not be rented. Beyond that, he believed that the best alternative was to find a new location for (regular) tenters on the outskirts of the townsite and, ironically, away from the lake.

But the National Parks Branch's new planning section,[33] intent on keeping Canada's so-called special places special, was not prepared to be so understanding. In an internal 1958 report on future planning considerations for

Prince Albert National Park, Chief Planner Lloyd Brooks identified several "problem" areas. He argued that Prince Albert's principal use as a kind of regional holiday resort was not in keeping with its status as a national park. He also warned that the number of short-term visitors to the park, and hence the demand for camping spaces, would sharply rise over the next few years. Brooks' most damning remarks, however, were reserved for the private structures in the townsite. "The present spectacle which confronts the visitor is not a pleasant one," he seethed, "this is a misuse of a national park, a misuse at the expense of the more legitimate short-stay visitor whose tax dollars have made possible through subsidization, the present favoured position of the shack tenter, portable cabin owner, and summer home owner at Waskesiu."[34] Brooks' solution was a complete redevelopment of the townsite to provide for more, cheaper accommodation and day-use facilities – minus the shack tents and portable cabins.

These comments marked a shift in Ottawa's opposition to Prince Albert's shack tents and portable cabins. Whereas the semi-permanent structures were usually criticized for monopolizing the Waskesiu campground at the expense of other park visitors, they were now being portrayed as a special privilege in a place that had been formally set aside for the benefit and enjoyment of all Canadians. But before attempting to do away with them, Gordon Robertson, the deputy minister of the Department of Northern Affairs and National Resources, decided to visit the park to assess the situation firsthand. The senior bureaucrat was pleasantly surprised by what he found at Waskesiu, even going as far as to report that the shack tents and portable cabins "look thoroughly respectable and undoubtedly are providing a great many people with a cheap and healthful holiday."[35] But he too questioned whether individuals should be allowed to benefit from what appeared to be semi-proprietary rights in a national park on the basis of a seasonal camping permit. Robertson consequently called on the Parks Branch's planning section to give the matter "a good deal of attention ... so that we can work out a suitable policy."[36]

The planning section was ready with an answer by early 1960. Its document put into words the sense of frustration that the National Parks Branch had felt about the issue for the past few years. On the opening page, it described the situation as "a case of special privilege and fancied right ... unjust to other citizens and taxpayers ... and a contradiction of national park purpose."[37] The report then went on to argue that the structures, although important in the early years of park development, not only dominated the Waskesiu campground at the expense of the growing number of short-term visitors, but also interfered with the orderly development of the park by occupying areas that were better suited for public day-use facilities. In short, the structures had no place in a national park: "The settled pattern must be undone."[38]

Like Deputy Minister Robertson, however, the planning section realized that shack tents, and to a lesser extent portable cabins, were an entrenched tradition at Waskesiu – an undeniable part of Prince Albert National Park's history. So any new program of redevelopment would require "enlisting the understanding and cooperation of the present occupants."[39] The report therefore recommended that the elimination of shack tents and portable cabins should proceed in stages over a five-year period with as little disruption as possible. It also advised that alternative forms of accommodation, attractive to local long-term visitors and yet still in line with national park purposes, should be in place before any redevelopment got underway. The ultimate aim was to turn the Waskesiu townsite into a visitor service centre.

The shack tent/portable cabin report was delivered to Robertson in February 1960 and approved in principle three months later by Alvin Hamilton, minister of Northern Affairs and National Resources in the Diefenbaker government.[40] Parks Branch Director Coleman then ordered the planning department to work up a preliminary redevelopment plan for the Waskesiu townsite.[41] In the meantime, he urged that construction start immediately on 105 low-rental cabins at Waskesiu that in turn would allow the department to establish new day-use in facilities in the campground area now occupied by shack tents (between the main beach and Waskesiu Drive). "The time has arrived," Coleman announced, "to provide facilities for all park visitors which are more in line with today's and tomorrow's needs and demands, and more in accordance with national park purposes."[42] Hamilton's successor, Walter Dinsdale, however, was in no hurry to proceed with these changes, particularly since the Prince Albert riding had been represented by Prime Minister Diefenbaker since 1953.[43] Instead, he decided to visit the park personally during the summer of 1961. There, Dinsdale was clearly made aware of the sensitivity of the issue, for it was subsequently decided that local individuals and groups should be advised and consulted about any long-term development plans for the park.[44] One summer park resident sensed victory and in an act of defiance attached a fixed roof to a shack tent. When this violation of campground policy was ignored, several shack tents began being stored over the winter as whole units.

Public Land for Private Individuals?

The question of private residences in a national park setting soon spread beyond the boundaries of Prince Albert National Park. Residential areas for regular park visitors had been allowed to take root in a number of other national parks. The Banff and Jasper townsites, for example, had become just like any other small town (as C.J. Taylor shows in the next essay); while Riding Mountain had shack tents too. By the mid-1950s, though, the Parks Branch finally began to question the wisdom of this policy when measured against the spirit and intent of the 1930 *National Parks Act*.[45] Liberal Northern Affairs and National Resources Minister Jean Lesage, for example, reminded Parliament in August 1956 that "parks are preserved for the people of Canada as a whole for very special purposes, not for the inhabitants of one area."[46] This sentiment was evidently shared by the new Progressive Conservative government, which prohibited the establishment of any new lots or residential subdivisions in national parks as of July 1959. Walter Dinsdale, in fact, was moving towards a wholesale review of national parks and their role in meeting the growing recreational needs of Canadians just before the Conservatives were bounced from office in 1963.[47]

The matter was taken up, though, by his Liberal successor, Arthur Laing. The new minister of Northern Affairs and National Resources was disturbed by the fact that park lease holders paid ridiculously low rents yet made huge profits when the property changed hands. He also believed that it was improper for individuals, who were fortunate enough to live near a national park, to enjoy these special privileges.[48] "It is not the purpose of the national parks," he lectured the House of Commons in June 1963, "to provide summer residential subdivisions, cottage lots or shack tent areas for the exclusive use and possession of private individuals." A little more than a year later, the Liberal government gave substance to Laing's words in a new *National Parks Policy* statement. Under the new policy, all private residential occupation of national parks was to be gradually eliminated; only those persons who worked for the park or provided an essential service would be allowed to stay. "National Park land is public land," Laing stated in September 1964. "It must be used in a way that clearly contributes to public enjoyment and service, not for the private benefit and convenience of individuals."[49]

The minister's stand was favourably received across the country, especially by wildlife groups and park organizations that were worried about the disappearance of Canada's wilderness heritage. Perhaps his staunchest supporter was *The Globe and Mail*. In a strongly worded editorial, entitled "Render to Canada ...," the newspaper argued that "the parks belong to all Canadians, here, now, and yet to come.... No individual should be allowed to stake claims in them for their private enjoyment or their private profit. Mr. Laing should have the support of every Canadian in reclaiming this vital heritage."[50] Residents and business people in western parks, on the other hand, mounted a determined campaign to derail the program with the aid of their parliamentary representatives. Laing refused to back down in the face of this criticism and, in an August 1965 letter to all holders of residential leases in western parks, repeated his department's objective to acquire gradually all existing private summer homes.[51]

It was against this background that the redevelopment plans for Waskesiu were finally completed in 1967. Given the flak that the Branch and the Department had taken over the past two years, park officials knew that the proposed changes, particularly the decision to do away with shack tents, portable cabins, and cottages, were certain to generate controversy. But they were more concerned that park attendance would more than double over the next fifteen years – as it had already between 1950 and 1965 – and that the strain on the Waskesiu campground would only get worse until steps were taken to provide new facilities. In fact, steps had already been taken to ease the congestion by clearing a new 100-site campground, known as Beaver Glen, just northeast of the townsite in 1964. The planners were also privately confident that any protest could be kept to a minimum if the proposed changes were carefully explained to those affected; it was all a matter of how the issue was handled.[52] It would certainly be a test of the National Park Branch's new policy about citizen involvement through public consultations and hearings.[53]

The Waskesiu redevelopment plan was formally presented by Alex Reeve, National Parks Assistant Director, at a public meeting in the townsite theatre on 12 August 1967. Reading from a prepared text, Reeve first outlined how park use had changed over the past decade: more people were visiting but for shorter periods of time. He then went on to argue that new facilities were required in areas that were currently being used for other purposes. The first of these targeted areas was the row of shack tents on the lakeshore side of Waskesiu Drive. To free up this part of the Waskesiu campground for new day-use facilities, Reeve announced that only those shack tenters or their spouses who held a valid camping permit at the end of the 1967 camping season would be allowed to occupy a campground lot in subsequent years, provided they continually renewed their camping permit each spring. Those shack tenters who failed to keep their camping permit in good standing or decided to sell or otherwise dispose of their shack tent would no longer be eligible for a lot. This attrition scheme was expected to lead to the eventual relocation and consolidation of the remaining shack tents to the east side of Waskesiu Drive on blocks *L* to *Q*, and thereby enable the park to go ahead with the redevelopment of the immediate lakeshore area. A similar policy would then be applied to portable cabin owners, effective 30 September 1970. In the long run, it was expected that these structures, like shack tents, would gradually disappear from the Waskesiu campground and be replaced by new trailer sites and additional campground facilities. Curiously, the idea of building rows of cheap rental cabins – something that planners had earlier deemed essential to townsite redevelopment – was shelved until it could be proven that there was a definite need for such accommodation. As for the more substantial cottages in the Prospect Point and Lakeview subdivisions, they were to be acquired by the government in the distant future upon the expiration of the leases.

The initial reaction to the Waskesiu redevelopment plan was one of shock and dismay. Many shack tenters feared that they were about to be summarily evicted and, over the next few days, Prince Albert National Park Superintendent John Malfair was kept busy explaining to permit holders that they would not be forced to give up their privilege of occupying a camp-ground lot. Despite his assurances, the mood quickly turned to anger. Many of the owners of shack tents and portable cabins had been patronizing the park for decades – in a few cases, generations – and had come to regard themselves as the backbone of Waskesiu. They had seen the park evolve from its simple beginnings, had invested considerable time and energy in building

FIG. 3. PORTABLE CABIN OWNERS WERE PREPARED TO FIGHT THE NATIONAL PARKS
BUREAUCRACY TO KEEP THEIR SPECIAL ACCOMMODATION PRIVILEGES IN THE PARK.
[COURTESY OF PRINCE ALBERT NATIONAL PARK COLLECTION, PARKS CANADA.]

and maintaining their summer homes, and had deep-felt memories of their holidays at Saskatchewan's "poor man's paradise." Going to Waskesiu each summer had become part of the natural rhythm of their lives. The shack tenters and portable cabin owners were therefore outraged by the suggestion that their long and intimate association with the park no longer mattered and was, in fact, detrimental. There were also upset by the apparent inequality of the scheme: cottage owners would not only be left alone for several years but also receive financial compensation.

The Waskesiu Tent Cabin and Portable Cabin Association lost little time organizing a campaign to stop the redevelopment plan. It lobbied Saskatchewan's members of Parliament and the provincial Legislature for assistance. It flooded the park superintendent with written objections to the plan. And it drew up a petition, which argued that shack tents and portable cabins were entirely in keeping with Prime Minister Mackenzie King's 1928 dedication of Prince Albert National Park to "the average man." As far as the Association was concerned, "we [should] be permitted to continue as we have done in the past and that additional space, as and when necessary, be developed elsewhere in the 1500-odd square miles of park property to accommodate future day and week-campers in increasing numbers."[54] The thought of eliminating shack tents to make space for expensive trailers and motor homes seemed a contradiction, if not a betrayal, of the reason for the park's creation.

The petition was formally presented to Arthur Laing on 17 November 1967 by Association President Mrs. Mary Jackson. As the diminutive homemaker left for Ottawa armed with hundreds of signatures, her departure was depicted in the *Prince Albert Daily Herald* as a kind of David-and-Goliath encounter. Laing, for his part, refused to be drawn into a public spat and simply reiterated his ministry's determination to proceed with the redevelopment plan. The stalemate continued until the following summer when the young, promising Jean Chrétien took over the portfolio in the new Liberal government of Pierre Trudeau. Seizing upon Laing's departure and Trudeau's emphasis on participatory democracy, Mrs. Jackson immediately wrote to Chrétien and urged him to reconsider the redevelopment plan. "Our aim," she told him, "is to achieve a development of Waskesiu townsite ... that is for all Canadians and equitable to the pioneers of the Park and their successors." She also complained that the association was particularly upset over the former minister's repeated refusal to discuss the matter and called on Chrétien to visit Waskesiu. Was it not, she asked coyly, "Prime Minister Trudeau's wish that Cabinet Ministers of his Government ... learn first hand the problems that face local groups?"[55]

But any hope Jackson might have had that Chrétien might be persuaded to rescind the attrition policy for shack tents and portable cabins was quickly dashed. In a revised policy statement, issued shortly following his appointment, he made it quite clear that the private use of public lands was at odds with the purpose of national parks and that he was intent on pursuing the policy of his predecessor. "We are trying to improve the park experience of all visitors," he wrote former Prime Minister Diefenbaker in October 1968 about the plans for Waskesiu.[56] By January 1970, however, Chrétien's attempt to revise national park leasing regulations through a new Leaseholds Corporation bill was being successfully challenged in the courts.[57] He consequently began to have second thoughts about the wisdom of implementing the second phase of the Waskesiu plan: the portable cabin provisions. This seeming change of heart made National and Historic Parks Director John Nicol apoplectic. In a heated memo to Chrétien's senior assistant deputy minister, Nicol pointed out that after answering "almost 150 Ministers' letters as well as telegrams and petitions on the topic … the portable cabin owners appear to have finally accepted our point of view. If we are to back down now, we will undoubtedly cause more of a furor than when the 1967 announcement was made."[58] In fact, a number of portable cabin owners had already sold their structures on the assumption that their days in the park were numbered. He also warned that failure to proceed with the portable cabin policy would provoke a storm of protest from shack tent owners. Since 1967, the number of shack tents had dropped from 375 to 305, and it would not be fair to these former park residents to discontinue the policy. For Nicol, then, it was not a time to have doubts.

Chrétien, on the other hand, decided to try to assuage local concerns and finally accepted Mrs. Jackson's invitation to meet with the Tent Cabin and Portable Cabin Association in Prince Albert. The association used the February 1970 visit to present Chrétien with a lengthy brief that essentially argued that, despite the National Parks Branch's forecast of a tourist boom, Prince Albert remained a regional national park serving a regular group of local visitors. Chrétien, in response, told Mrs. Jackson that the policy would remain unchanged. "The purpose of the redevelopment plan of 1967," he reminded her, "was to make all land in the National Park available to visitors rather than have any park land alienated for a select group of people."[59] He also took issue with her suggestion that his department was forcing residents out of the park and stressed that park redevelopment would take place over several years as visitation increased. He did, nonetheless, concede that the new policy might leave portable cabin owners at a disadvantage because they had made a greater investment in their structures than shack tenters. He consequently promised that his ministry would take "another look at the situation."[60]

What People Really Want

The review of the Waskesiu redevelopment plan led to a number of changes. During the summer of 1970, the department decided to delay the implementation of the portable cabin restrictions – originally to start on 30 September 1970 – for another year. This one year's reprieve was designed to defuse some of the anger over the policy. In order to mitigate the potential financial loss to portable cabin owners, the Department of Indian Affairs and Northern Development also agreed to purchase at market value any structure that became available after the policy went into effect. Otherwise, the same regulations that had applied to shack tents since 1967 were to be in force. Finally, in an effort to forestall any future charge that portable cabin owners had received preferential treatment, the department decided in January 1971 that shack tents could be left standing on-site year-round, as well as serviced with electricity at the owner's expense. With these changes, the metamorphosis was complete. Structures that were initially intended to serve as temporary campground lodging now took on all the trappings of a permanent cabin, albeit on a smaller, cheaper scale.

These various concessions were intended by the department to be a kind of olive branch. Henceforth, it expected to be able to proceed with the phasing out of the shack tents and portable cabins with little protest.[61] The strategy quickly came undone, however, with the spring 1971 release of the Prince Albert National Park Provisional Master Plan. Based on the assumption that there were already a number of purely recreational areas already in existence in Saskatchewan, the management scheme suggested that Prince Albert National Park's future was as a "national wildland park."[62] The three major park biomes – boreal forest, aspen parkland, and southern grasslands – would be set aside for wilderness hiking, canoeing, and camping, while roads and activity centres would be located to facilitate access to these areas. By the early 1970s the Parks Branch increasingly was using such ecological characterizations for national parks across the country (as Taylor, George Colpitts, and Olivier Craig-Dupont note in their essays).

Although the plan for Prince Albert did not make any specific references to the redevelopment of the Waskesiu townsite, it inadvertently helped the cause of the Tent Cabin and Portable Cabin Association. Since 1967, the association had been complaining that "their park" was under attack by

Ottawa bureaucrats who had no understanding of Prince Albert's uniqueness (a similar complaint was made by residents of Kouchibouguac, as Ronald Rudin shows). The Provisional Master Plan now appeared to be further evidence of this insensitivity, particularly the proposal that motor boats be banned from Kingsmere Lake, one of the more popular fishing lakes in the park. The association had also been clamouring for a chance to voice its opposition to the attrition policy at some kind of public forum. That opportunity was now made possible thanks to the two days of public hearings on the Provisional Master Plan that were scheduled for late June in Regina and Prince Albert. Whether Ottawa realized it or not, the issue was far from settled.

Saskatchewan political leaders were the first to castigate the Provisional Master Plan. "It is a place for the people … not a playground for bureaucrats in Ottawa," a sanctimonious John Diefenbaker thundered a few days after the plan was unveiled. "These people are trying to tell us out here in the west what we want."[63] Saskatchewan deputy premier Davey Steuart said much the same thing, calling the proposals "another example of their stupidity and lack of concern for what people really want in this area."[64] This criticism was carried over into the public hearings. The plan did have its supporters, but these individuals and organizations, such as the Saskatchewan Natural History Society and Saskatchewan Wildlife Federation, were dismissed as misguided tree-huggers who did not appreciate Prince Albert's importance as a family park. Some briefs argued that the proposed plan did not take into account the regional nature of the park, a fact ironically confirmed by Ottawa's own statistic that 86 per cent of all visitors to the park were from Saskatchewan. Others, conveniently forgetting their own privileged position, complained that the plan catered to a small minority of wilderness enthusiasts and was prejudiced against those who used their leisure time to pursue other, more sedate activities. The Tent Cabin and Portable Cabin Association ridiculed the idea that only 5.2 square miles of the total 1,496-square-mile park area were to be reserved for intensive use. It seemed as though the plan was another step in an attempt to take the park away from the people. As one woman sarcastically observed, Ottawa was spending $5 million "to make a wilderness area into a wilderness area."[65]

The federal government's response to the public hearings on the Prince Albert National Park Provisional Master Plan was not announced until four years later. Although the shack tent and portable cabin attrition policy remained in place during this period, the delay was probably not deliberate. Park planners not only had to rethink the Prince Albert proposals in light of the public reaction but were also busy preparing management plans for a number of other parks at this time. The uncertainty as to what might be the outcome of the hearings, however, did not help the strained relations between long-time park residents and park officials. Nor did the government response once it became public in the spring of 1975. Parks Canada had now decided that new low-rental accommodation would be developed as shack tents and portable cabins disappeared.[66]

The dispute was far from over. Still smarting from the reception of the Provisional Master Plan, Parks Canada pledged that there would be further public consultation regarding the future development of Waskesiu. This process started in June 1975, and the long-expected showdown between the two sides occurred two months later during an August meeting in the former Terrace Gardens Dance Hall in Waskesiu. Parks officials knew beforehand that the meeting might not be a friendly one. But little did they expect that the meeting hall would be packed to capacity and that those who were unable to get in would be lined up outside anxiously waiting for their turn to speak to the planning team. The meeting was intended to initiate public discussion on a wide range of planning issues affecting the townsite. From the outset, however, the speakers maintained that the attrition policy was the only issue and refused to discuss anything else. "We get the impression ... these hearings are just a sham," said Mrs. Jackson. "Are you really going to listen this time or once again just go through the motions?"[67] Another portable cabin owner suggested that the attrition program "amounts to public harassment of the people who built the park." This feeling was echoed by another speaker who warned, "If there have been decisions made ... which affect our livelihood and they aren't what we want they will ... be changed."[68] One parks planner who had been on the job for only six weeks probably wondered whether things could get any worse.

This emotionally charged meeting finally prompted Parks Canada to forsake its attrition program for shack tents and portable cabins. Over the next few months, the park superintendent, the executive of the Tent Cabin Association, and park planners met on a regular basis to devise an alternative concept for the townsite. It was eventually decided in early 1977 that a fixed number of seasonal permits (448 in total) would be made available for these structures. The planning team justified this retreat from the 1967 Waskesiu redevelopment policy by noting that shack tents and portable cabins "have a longstanding tradition in Waskesiu and are acceptable to the majority of park users." Equally significant was the admission that "no 'higher use' was required of the lands" at that time.[69] This was largely because attendance had not grown as expected. Fewer people visited the park in 1976 than had nine years earlier when the attrition policy was announced. Most remarkable, however, was Parks Canada's willingness to bend the principle that private use of park land was wrong in favour of giving into local opinion.

Conclusion

In 1988, the *National Parks Act* was amended to provide for the better administration and operation of Canada's special places. "Ecological integrity" now became the watch phrase for park management and visitor use in the late twentieth century. But once again, the experience in Prince Albert National Park suggested that local entrenched interests trumped any new national parks legislation. Two recent examples will suffice. Although shack tents were converted to portable cabins and higher rents eventually introduced to better reflect market value,[70] running water and sewage were installed in the portable cabin area *before* an environmental impact assessment study was undertaken. These same cabin owners were also part of a larger Waskesiu group that successfully lobbied Parks Canada to spray the townsite with *Bacillus thuringis* to stave off a spruce budworm infestation – against the wishes of the park superintendent, who resigned over the issue. That these summer cottagers have become so powerful, so influential, in deciding park policy in the townsite is largely a consequence of the circumstances behind the creation of Prince Albert National Park and its popular use over the decades as a regional summer playground. Perhaps the local newspaper put it best: "The PANP – which originated and was promoted by Prince Albert citizens – is … 'our' park."[71]

Notes

1 See, for example, Leslie Bella, *Parks for Profit* (Montreal, Harvest House, 1987), and, most recently, Paul Kopas, *Taking the Air: Ideas and Change in Canada's National Parks* (Vancouver: UBC Press, 2007).

2 Alan MacEachern, *Natural Selections: National Parks in Atlantic Canada* (Montreal: McGill-Queen's University Press, 2001), 15. MacEachern calls this double purpose, "preservation and use," and suggests that it is more useful to look at both aspects in terms of "intervention" (156).

3 Quoted in *Prince Albert Daily Herald*, 2 July 1971, 3.

4 Canada, House of Commons *Debates*, 3 May 1887, 245.

5 Liberal John Platt took issue with Banff becoming "a very nice health resort of the wealthy people of this country" and insisted that other Canadians "ought to receive an equal benefit with those who have influence." Ibid., 246. See also Bella, *Parks for Profit*, 114.

6 The 729-square-mile Sturgeon River Forest Reserve stretched from the Sturgeon River Valley on the west to the third meridian on the east and from the line between townships 57 and 58 (taking in most of Red Deer or Waskesiu Lake) on the north and a slightly irregular line between townships 52 and 53 (that excluded all possible agricultural lands) on the south. Established under the provisions of the *Dominion Forest Reserves and Parks Act* (1911), it was one of fifteen reserves that the federal government set aside in Saskatchewan.

7 For the full story behind the creation of Prince Albert National Park and the role played by Mackenzie King, see B. Waiser, *Saskatchewan's Playground: A History of Prince Albert National Park* (Saskatoon, 1989), chap. 4.

8 Mackenzie King never forgot McDonald's generosity and appointed him to the Senate in 1935. But the Prince Albert pharmacist was too ill to take his place. McDonald has the dubious distinction of being elected to the House of Commons and appointed to the Senate and never having uttered a single word in either chamber.

9 G.W.P. Abrams, *Prince Albert: The First Century, 1866–1966* (Saskatoon: Modern Press, 1966), 245.

10 LAC, Manuscript Division, William Lyon Mackenzie King papers, Diaries, 20 April 1926.

11 LAC, Manuscript Division, William Lyon Mackenzie King papers, vol. 167, 121011, T.C. Davis to W.L.M. King, 28 April 1927.

12 Thirty-eight lots in Prospect Point were made available in June 1928. Each applicant was required to erect a cottage with a minimum value of $1,000 within one year. Before construction could commence, however, the plans and specifications had to be approved by the Parks Branch. Upon the satisfactory completion of the structure, the lot holder was issued a standard forty-two-year lease with the option of renewal. The seasonal rental fee was $10 for the period from April 1 to October 30. For the balance of the year, the structure could not be occupied.

13 This work was plagued by a large patch of muskeg just back from the beach. Indeed, future prime minister

John Diefenbaker was well within the truth when he referred to Waskesiu as "that mosquito park offered to Prince Albert as a reward for the election of Mackenzie King." Quoted in *Saskatoon Star-Phoenix*, 19 August 1949.

14 D. DeBrou and B. Waiser, eds., *Documenting Canada: A History of Modern Canada in Documents* (Saskatoon: Fifth House, 1992), 299.

15 Kopas, *Taking the Air*, 33.

16 RG 84, vol. 587, file PA36, J. Wood to J.B Harkin, 15 October 1931.

17 Shack tents could remain on the same spot in the campground for the summer on the basis of a seasonal camping permit. This privilege cost a mere two dollars per month in 1935, the equivalent of the daily rate at one of the park hotels. By 1937, the shack tent fee had doubled, but it was still an incredible bargain.

18 University of Alberta Archives, Karl Clark papers, K. Clark to no name, 16 November 1932.

19 Despite a concerted effort to advertise the park in the United States and the larger Canadian market, in particular Alberta, 92 per cent of the visitors in 1950 came from Saskatchewan.

20 Quoted in RG 84, vol. 18, PA109, pt. 3.

21 On 15 December 1933, the Prince Albert Board of Trade reviewed the matter of park residences with J.M. Wardle, supervisor of western parks. *Prince Albert Daily Herald*, 16 December 1933.

22 RG 84, vol. 1744, file PA25, J.B. Harkin to J.M. Wardle, 20 March 1936.

23 Ibid., J. Wood to Controller, 18 November 1937.

24 Ibid., vol. 1751, file PA36-1, pt. 1, J. Smart to B.I.M. Strong, 25 July 1950.

25 Ibid., PANP Shack Tent Owners' Association to B.I.M. Strong, 30 June 1950.

26 Ibid., B.I.M. Strong to J. Smart, 25 July 1950.

27 Ibid., J. Smart to B.I.M. Strong, 1 December 1950.

28 Ibid., 5 September 1950.

29 Ibid., "Conditions Governing Portable Cabin Lots on Campgrounds at Waskesiu," 1 March 1952.

30 Ibid., vol. 1750, file PA36, pt. 4, G.H.L. Dempster, "Report on Control of Camping Facilities, Prince Albert National Park," 7 November 1956.

31 W84-85/407, box 16, f. PA36-2, "Matters Taken up with Director Hutchinson in Saskatoon on June 30, 1956."

32 RG 84, vol. 1750, file PA36, pt. 4, G.H.L. Dempster to J.R.B. Coleman, 21 August 1956.

33 In 1957, a new planning section was created within the national parks service. This move was part of a general trend within the Canadian federal service towards greater professionalization and specialization. It was also a recognition of the increasingly important role that planning had assumed in the operation of the national parks system.

34 *Planning Considerations-Prince Albert National Park*, report n. 7, Planning Section, National Parks Branch, 15 December 1958, 2–3.

35 RG 84, vol. 1749, file PA28, pt. 2, R.G. Robertson to J.R.B. Coleman, 11 August 1959.

36 Ibid.

37 L. Brooks; J.C. Jackson; H.K. Eidsvik, *Shack Tents and Portable Cabins Proposed Program*, report n. 1, National Parks Branch, 1959, 1.

38 Ibid., 5.

39 Ibid.

40 RG 84, vol. 1749, file PA28, pt. 3, J.R.B. Coleman to R.G. Robertson, 11 August 1959.

41 The planning section initially contempated eliminating all private residences in the park, including those in Prospect Point and Lakeview (1–3), in favour of a variety of rental structures.

42 RG 84, vol. 1749, file PA28, pt. 3, J.R.B. Coleman to R.G. Robertson, 21 December 1960.

43 Prince Albert has the distinction of being represented by three prime ministers. Sir Wilfrid Laurier won election in Quebec East and Saskatchewan (Prince Albert) in 1896 when it was possible to run in more than one riding; Laurier chose to represent Quebec East. William Lyon Mackenzie King held the riding from 1926 to 1945, while John Diefenbaker represented Prince Albert from 1953 until his death in 1979.

44 RG 84, vol. 1749, file PA28, pt. 3, J.R.B. Coleman to R.G. Robertson, 29 December 1961.

45 Kopas, *Taking the Air*, 37–38.

46 Canada, House of Commons *Debates*, 2 August 1956, 6884.

47 Bella, *Parks for Profit*, 114–15. A 1962 planning section document proposed that park residences be restricted to those serving the visiting public.

48 *Debates*, 26 June 1963, 1618.

49 *Debates*, 18 September, 1964, 8194.

50 *Globe and Mail*, 2 August 1965, 6.

51 W84-85/496, box 2, form letter from A. Laing, 25 August 1965.

52 RG 84, vol. 1750, file PA28, pt. 5, A.J. Reeve to J.H. Gordon, 12 July 1967.

53 Kopas, *Taking the Air*, 67–72.

54 Ibid., vol. 1753, file PA36-1, "Petition Regarding the Proposed Waskesiu Redevelopment Plan, Prince Albert National Park," 2 September 1967.

55 W84-85/496, box 2, M. Jackson to J. Chrétien, 15 July 1968.

56 Ibid., J. Chrétien to J.G. Diefenbaker, 30 October 1968.

57 Bella, *Parks for Profit*, 117–18.

58 W84-85/405, box 17, J.I. Nicol to J.H. Gordon, 17 February 1970.

59 Ibid., J. Chrétien to M. Jackson, 13 May 1970.

60 Ibid.

61 Ibid., box 18, J. Rae to D. Clark, 22 January 1971; J.I. Nicol to R.P. Malis, 9 February 1971.

62 *Prince Albert National Park Provisional Master Plan* (Ottawa 1971), 11.

63 Quoted in *Saskatoon Star-Phoenix*, 5 May 1971.

64 Quoted in *Prince Albert Daily Herald*, 5 May 1971.

65 Ibid., 2 July 1971.

66 *Decisions Resulting from the Public Hearing on the Provisional Master Plan for Prince Albert National Park* (Ottawa: Parks Canada, 1975).

67 Quoted in *Prince Albert Daily Herald*, 18 August 1975.

68 Ibid.

69 *Waskesiu Visitor Services Plan, Prince Albert National Park* (Winnipeg: Parks Canada, 1977), 133.

70 Up to 2007, owners of portable cabins paid $350 per year for a twenty-four-week camping permit. Effective 1 April 2007, portable cabin owners were given a forty-two year, seven-month residential lease (April to October). The leaseholders pay rent based on the appraised value of the land (not the cabin and/or any improvements). T. Schneider to B. Waiser, e-mail communication, 11 March 2009.

71 *Prince Albert Daily Herald*, 30 April 1971.

Banff in the 1960s: Divergent Views of the National Park Ideal

ᐁ

C.J. Taylor

During the 1960s Banff National Park was at the epicentre of a revolution in thinking about what national parks should or should not be.[1] The National Parks Branch and others in the federal government sought to come to terms with the conflicting aims of a national park as they had been established: as both a protected natural area and a recreation area for public benefit. This dilemma or contradiction had been recognized by the first commissioner of national parks, James B. Harkin, who wrote: "'Use without abuse' – how can it be attained? That is the problem which must confront everyone who is responsible for the protection and development of our national parks."[2] Harkin believed that a middle road could be charted, permitting increased development while protecting those values that make the parks special places. With some variations, this has continued to be the creed of Parks Canada through to the present. At times, however, this balancing act has been difficult to achieve, and one of the most difficult cases occurred at Banff in the 1960s, when overdevelopment threatened the mountain scenery that attracted tourists in the first place.

The number of visitors had been rising through the 1950s, but the pace quickened in the 1960s. Banff had had a half million visitors in 1950; this doubled by 1960 and doubled again, to two million, by 1966. This rapid growth was due to a number of factors: the post-war boom, growing young families, and the increasing popularity of motor tourism. During the 1950s the provinces of British Columbia and Alberta greatly expanded and upgraded their highway systems, making travel by car easier and faster. This was matched by highway improvements through the mountain parks, including the completion of the Trans-Canada Highway through Banff and Yoho and the opening of the improved Icefields Parkway in 1961. Highway tourism changed the way people experienced the mountain parks. As roads brought more visitors, the visitors demanded more facilities: accommodation, gas stations, and then more roads. Here, more than ever before, Harkin's warning from a previous era was in danger of being realized: that development was in danger of destroying "the very thing that distinguished [parks] from the outside world."[3]

But Banff also revealed that increased tourist traffic was not the only reason for the reassessment of the national park ideal. The growing influence of universities on shaping government policy, vested local interests, the increased complexity and size of the Parks Branch and the federal bureaucracy, a more affluent population, and a more critical mindset about environmental issues all shaped approaches to the management of the park. Before the 1960s Banff National Park was managed fairly simply, by an engineering service that managed front-country development and a warden service that looked after the backcountry, while a few commercial resorts such as the Canadian Pacific Railway's Banff Springs Hotel looked after tourist services. During the 1960s this system began to change, as planners and interpretive specialists were added to the mix, affecting the mindset and practices of the larger organization. At the same time academic and environmental interest groups lobbied for what they considered to be more appropriate use in the park. The debate that emerged around Banff National Park in the 1960s would shape the outlook toward all national parks for a generation or more.

When Jim Thorsell came to Banff as a seasonal park interpreter in the summer of 1962, change was in the air. Looking back on that time forty-five years later, he pointed to three milestones that had occurred that year: the completion of the Trans-Canada Highway opened the floodgates to massive tourist growth, the publication of Rachel Carson's *Silent Spring* helped inspire the emergence of a North American movement concerned with environmental issues, and the death of Banff pioneer Norman Luxton underlined the significance of a local community with deep cultural ties to the park.[4] A fourth milestone may have been the presence of Mr. Thorsell himself. A recent graduate of the University of Alberta, he was a keen backcountry enthusiast, on the forefront of a resurging interest in wilderness recreation. He also presaged the growing number of youthful idealists who would take up the cause of protecting Banff from the philistines. Amid the massive increase in tourist numbers, an emerging sense of social activism coupled with a strong appreciation of wilderness values, together with a strong sense of community in the town of Banff itself, roiled around the park during the 1960s. Significantly, the participants in much of this drama – the National Parks Branch, the town of Banff, and environmental activists – would themselves be influenced by events of the 1960s.

These were indeed "interesting times." When Arthur Laing became minister of Northern Affairs and Natural Resources in 1963, he assumed control of a department profoundly invested in the economic boom of the postwar years. Not only was it responsible for overseeing a new interest in the opening of the north and the exploitation of mineral and other resources, but the boom in the tourist industry was bringing visitors to national parks in ever-increasing numbers. National parks, which formed a third component of Laing's department, were likewise seen as a national asset, with great potential value but requiring careful management.

At the same time, the organization that Laing inherited to manage the national parks was itself experiencing change. Professional services such as engineering, architecture, and planning had grown in the late 1950s, reflecting an increased reliance on technical expertise and the growing complexity of the work. Biologists, however, were generally situated in a parallel organization, the Canadian Wildlife Service, so that scientists remained largely outside the park management structure. Influenced by both its own internal studies as well as the 1962 report of the Royal Commission on Government Organization (known as the Glassco Report), the Parks Branch became a somewhat more decentralized organization with powers delegated to a series of regional offices, even as more sophisticated mechanisms for planning and development were implemented at the national level.[5] It was this upgraded organization that would face the challenges of growth and change in the national parks in the 1960s.

Laing and his staff were confronted with a rising tide of tourist numbers threatening to engulf an already significant building program. The policy then, as now, was for public enterprise to develop hotel and motel units at Lake Louise and Banff, while the Parks Branch undertook the establishment and management of the automobile campgrounds. In 1963 the Banff *Crag and Canyon* announced that two new motels were planned for Banff Avenue, while the Rimrock Hotel (now the Juniper) opened in July of that year. Meanwhile, the park embarked on a bold plan to expand and upgrade its campgrounds. At first park planners aimed to phase out the large and unsightly Tunnel Mountain Campground in the town of Banff and replace it with a series of medium-sized, attractively landscaped campgrounds ringing the town. To this end, Two Jack and Johnston Canyon Campgrounds added 400 new units to the Banff area between 1960 and 1965.[6] Even this wasn't enough, and the old Tunnel Mountain campground remained in use, attracting numerous complaints. One visitor wrote: "The crowded, squalid, and unsanitary conditions of the camp are truly beyond belief."[7] At Lake Louise, the old campground was closed without regret and a new one was built between 1963 and 1965, providing space for 221 tents and 189 trailers.[8]

Growth in the tourist industry and the expansion of the park organization also increased the populations of the urban communities within the mountain parks, especially the town of Banff and the village of Lake Louise. While many of the residents of Banff were park employees, some with deep roots in the area, many were also private businessmen, with names like the Brewsters, Harmons, Luxtons, and Whytes – families that went back generations. The Canadian Pacific Railway was also an important component of the park, and its Banff Springs Hotel and Chateau Lake Louise were major tourist centres in themselves. During the 1960s these established forces were joined by new faces relocating to Banff to open motels and restaurants. At the other end of the social spectrum, Banff became a magnet for travelling youth who camped by the museum, sometimes climbed the mountains, or just hung out. While not large, the town was well off and had the amenities of any other prosperous town in Canada: schools, churches, a hospital, department stores, and a supermarket. Residents, however, lacked many of the rights that other municipal citizens took for granted. Properties were owned through government leases instead of through freehold tenure, so while there were no property taxes, Ottawa decided the rate of land rents. There were no elected municipal officials; the town was run as part of the larger park, and many of the decisions regarding its administration seemed arbitrary and unfair. Some local representation was delegated to the Banff Advisory Council but, as its name implied, it had no real powers. Civic opinion was expressed through the Banff Chamber of Commerce and the *Crag and Canyon*. Naturally enough, much of this opinion was directed against the dictatorial rule of Ottawa. But at the same time, the remoteness of this authority encouraged a certain amount of local autonomy. For Banff, the old Chinese aphorism seemed particularly apt: "The mountains are high and the emperor is far away."

The National Parks Branch was moving toward asserting greater authority over the town's direction even before Laing assumed office. A central planning division, created in 1957, was tasked with establishing policies and guidelines for future development in all the national parks. Park planners were helped by the work of consultants. Two studies of townsite issues in Banff, in 1960 and 1961, had made some wide-ranging recommendations, although very little from these reports had been acted upon.[9] Laing presided over a reorganization of the Branch that devolved much of the routine decisions and research agendas to regional directors,[10] establishing the western regional office in Calgary in 1963. Soon after, the appointment of a Banff townsite manager eased the administration of municipal affairs. But a conflict was brewing between the town and Ottawa over the future identity of the town; a conflict spurred by this bureaucratic reorganization, which generated new discussion within the federal government about the nature of parks management.

The new minister and the freshly reorganized Parks Branch would have collaborated to provide the new national parks policy that Laing presented to Parliament in September 1964. Referring to a "quiet crisis" in the national parks, he articulated broad guidelines for their future development.[11] Since much of this development was occurring in Banff National Park, his remarks had particular significance for that place. Laing proposed regulations to safeguard against unsuitable development, to restrict use to appropriate activities related to outdoor recreation and sightseeing, and to rein in some of the quasi-municipal status accorded to the townsites. In many ways Laing's statements echoed the earlier sentiments articulated by Harkin in the 1930s: a middle ground would be sought between the extremes of wide-open development and complete protection from use.[12] Approved park plans would guide parks to this middle route, and Laing made reference in his speech to land-zoning systems and design guidelines. But he departed from earlier precedents in his wish to *diminish* the status of the park towns. Townsites with distinctive identities were to be strongly discouraged within the parks, and places like the town of Banff or the village of Lake Louise were described as merely large convenience stores. "In terms of this policy," Laing told the House of Commons, "the present park townsites can be considered only as visitor services centres. Their only reason for being is that they provide essential services to visitors or services to the national parks and its staff."[13] He added that his intention was to "eventually exclude private residential occupation."[14] The debate over seasonal residences had been simmering in other national parks, as Bill Waiser's chapter on Prince Albert demonstrates, but had slightly different implications at Banff, where many lived year-round.

At first, the town of Banff was inclined to support the minister. After all, his "middle path" merely controlled development; it did not deter it. A year before tabling the national parks policy in Parliament, Laing had travelled to Banff to sound out local opinion. At his meeting with the Banff Advisory Council, the minister struck a reassuring tone: he was not against new development, just unplanned and unregulated growth. "Banff," he said, "will have controlled expansion." Regarding the townsite in particular, he added: "there will be reasonable control, but I want to be sure there is not overprotectionism."[15] He promised that plans for a shopping mall would proceed – with adequate parking, of course. Following this meeting, new lots were opened for residences on Cougar Street and development permits issued for several new commercial ventures in the town. Meanwhile, a complete overhaul of the Lake Louise area provided new sewer and water systems, a large new campground, a shopping centre, and staff residences.

While Minister Laing and his staff were prepared to authorize substantial levels of new development, there was still considerable discomfort within the Branch with the notion of permanent settlement within the park boundaries. In calling them "service centres," as opposed to towns or villages, the government betrayed a tendency to view them as utilitarian concessions set up to serve park visitors rather than as communities with separate identities and interests. By 1967 businessmen in Banff began to feel the cold wind of the new policy. In November of that year, a writer for the nationally distributed *Weekend Magazine* wrote an article, reprinted in the *Crag and Canyon*, that would have sent a chill down the spines of the members of the Chamber of Commerce. Titled "Battle for our national parkland," it took aim at urban development in Banff and Jasper. The Banff businessmen would have been further disheartened to see the hand of senior government officials behind the article, which stated that the town of Banff has been allowed to grow too big, citing "government experts" who "hold that the saturation point has been reached." The article then quoted senior assistant deputy minister John MacDonald as describing the lease question in the townsites as "a cancer at the breast of the National Parks Service."[16] Despite his conciliatory message earlier in the decade, it seemed as if the minister was finally taking up the cudgel against private ownership in Banff.

The issue came down to the definition of the leases. Because leases were granted in perpetuity, it was the custom that property could be bought and sold as if they were freehold. Now Laing was trying to impose a system in which leases might not be automatically renewed, so improvements could revert to the crown. Any lease coming up for renewal would have the "in perpetuity" clause removed. Furthermore, only those people who actually worked in the park and their families would be permitted to reside in the town, now known as a service centre (a term chosen in part to undermine claims to municipal status). For the government, this meant that it could assert greater control over towns as components of national park development. For the businessmen, some of whom had spent millions in new building, it boded disaster. They were fearful of the restrictive covenants being placed on what they viewed as their property. The issue was particularly significant at Lake Louise, where the government was trying to attract new investment to develop the new service centre there. This uneasy relationship between Parks Canada and the community of Banff would continue until that community was granted limited municipal status in 1990. Lake Louise, however, has remained as a service centre within Laing's original definition.

Ironically, one area of particular agreement between the minister and the Banff Advisory Council involved ski hills. Since 1960, there had been considerable new development at Norquay, Sunshine, and Lake Louise to accommodate the new craze in downhill skiing that had been precipitated by the Winter Olympic Games of 1960, held in Squaw Valley, California. Skiing enthusiasts from both Banff and Calgary paid close attention to this event, and representatives from Alberta travelled there to tour the facilities and consult with the organizers. This led to the formation of the Calgary Olympic Development Association (CODA), to organize a proposal for the 1968 games to be held in Banff. At his first meeting with the Banff Advisory Council, Art Laing promised his full support for the idea, suggesting that the Olympic village could be developed beside the Banff School of Fine Arts. When the Games were awarded to Grenoble in 1964, attention refocused on the 1972 Olympics, but the government continued to publicly support developing world-class skiing destinations in Banff. In March Laing told a Calgary audience that he forecast the development of Banff National Park as a year-round resort, adding that "emphasis will be on ski facilities."[17]

The Parks Branch did not just support ski hill development: for a while it led the way. In 1964 Banff National Park engaged an American ski resort consultant to study the park's three ski facilities. Based on this report and other internal studies, in 1965 the Branch prepared a document entitled "Winter Recreation and the National Parks: A Management Policy and Development Program." This report began by acknowledging that ski hills were not always seen as being compatible with the principle of use without impairment (which was the case in the United States national parks system, for example). That said, the report then advanced a position that presumably had the approval and perhaps even the direction of the minister: "A middle course and the one decided upon was to define certain areas of high potential for ski development but of limited scenic value, and, in effect, zone these for intensive development of skiing facilities." The document formed the basis of a policy that countenanced capital-intensive infrastructure such as chair lifts and lodges and encouraged related resort development such as overnight accommodation and "evening entertainment facilities generally associated with a holiday ski centre."[18] Subsequently the Branch began preparing development plans for the three sanctioned ski areas – Norquay, Sunshine, and Lake Louise – as well expensive road construction to provide better automobile access to the sites.

The park planners proposed other developments to improve visitor facilities in the park. Recognizing that demand for outdoor recreation could rapidly outstrip the supply of suitable wilderness areas, they believed that, given sufficient information, rational choices could be made to satisfy all of these demands. In particular, they felt the adverse effects of more building in the parks could be mitigated if it was confined to specific areas or development zones. In the 1960s, zoning became the cornerstone of the planning process in parks across North America. Planners surveyed each national park and laid out a system of zones that prescribed an authorized level of development for each. Specific projects were assigned to the appropriate zone, and the scheme was then enshrined in the management or master plan. The advantage of the approach, at least in theory, was that it kept development from sprawling throughout the park and limited the blight of unplanned building along the highway corridors. The first provisional master plans completed by the Branch's planning division in 1967, including the one for Banff, were approved in the spring of 1968 – just after the arrival of Laing's replacement as minister of Indian Affairs and Northern Develoment, Jean Chrétien.

The first Banff provisional master plan delineated five management zones. Two were tagged as wilderness areas; one was a transition zone, allowing limited development but accessible by road; another permitted developed outdoor recreation areas, such as ski hills; and the fifth was for intensive use areas such as a townsite or service centre. While the plan promised to balance protection with visitor use, it was clearly preoccupied with managing more development, not managing natural areas. The planners' creed seemed to be "predict and provide," emphasizing the value of visitor statistics in order to better prepare for future demand. The plan for Banff explained: "This is the start of a systems planning approach. Where possible accent is on long range view of problems such as information management or the saturation of a park's known camping facility."[19]

Also indicative of its concern for accommodating increasing numbers of tourists was the master plan's ambitious program of new construction, especially of scenic roads. It proposed enlarging the old Cascade fire road through wilderness zones north of the town of Banff, as well as extending Alberta's David Thompson Highway west across the Rockies through the Howse Pass wilderness area to connect with the British Columbia highway system. The plan also proposed expanding winter use beyond ski hills, suggesting "[t] hat winter use be further encouraged by allowing over snow vehicles to use selected and marked trails within the park."[20] While these plans called for further study, they meant further social science research to identify future tourist trends. There was no mention of environmental impact studies.

This proposed development in Banff, from highways to ski hills, became a rallying point for environmental groups in the 1960s, which would argue for curbing growth and focusing on protecting wilderness areas. This emerging environmental lobby, called the second conservation movement by Leslie Bella (to distinguish it from the conservation movement of the early twentieth century[21]), had its roots in a reaction to the pace and scale of postwar development and a growing sense of public advocacy in the universities, themselves infused with a climate of protest by the later 1960s. But this movement shared many ideals of earlier conservationists, including a belief in the importance of preserving wilderness or pristine ecological reserves as protected areas. Roderick Nash's 1967 book *Wilderness and the American Mind* was a landmark articulation of this idea. If national parks might be seen as important islands of wilderness in North America, some people now feared that they were in danger of being paved over. This perception was particularly strong in the United States, where opposition to the National Parks Service's Mission 66 building program became a rallying point for American environmentalists. Many people questioned the need for so much highway building in the American parks, and some even argued that access to parks needed to be restricted if wilderness ideals were to be protected.[22]

Expression of this new awareness in Canada can be traced to the Resources for Tomorrow Conference held in Montreal in 1961, which in turn led to the formation of the National and Provincial Parks Association (later the Canadian Parks and Wilderness Society) in 1963. At first, the NPPA (along with similar organizations such as the Canadian Audubon Society) acted almost as the formal constituency of the national parks, advocating greater support from Parliament and encouraging the expansion of the national park system. As the decade progressed, though, it became more radical, becoming at times a fierce critic of park management. Meanwhile, universities began offering courses in aspects of what would later become known as environmental studies; interdisciplinary programs such as the University of British Columbia's School of Community and Regional Planning and the University of Calgary's Department of Geography were prototypes for later programs. At the University of Calgary, an energetic young professor of geography named Gordon Nelson attracted a small group of graduate

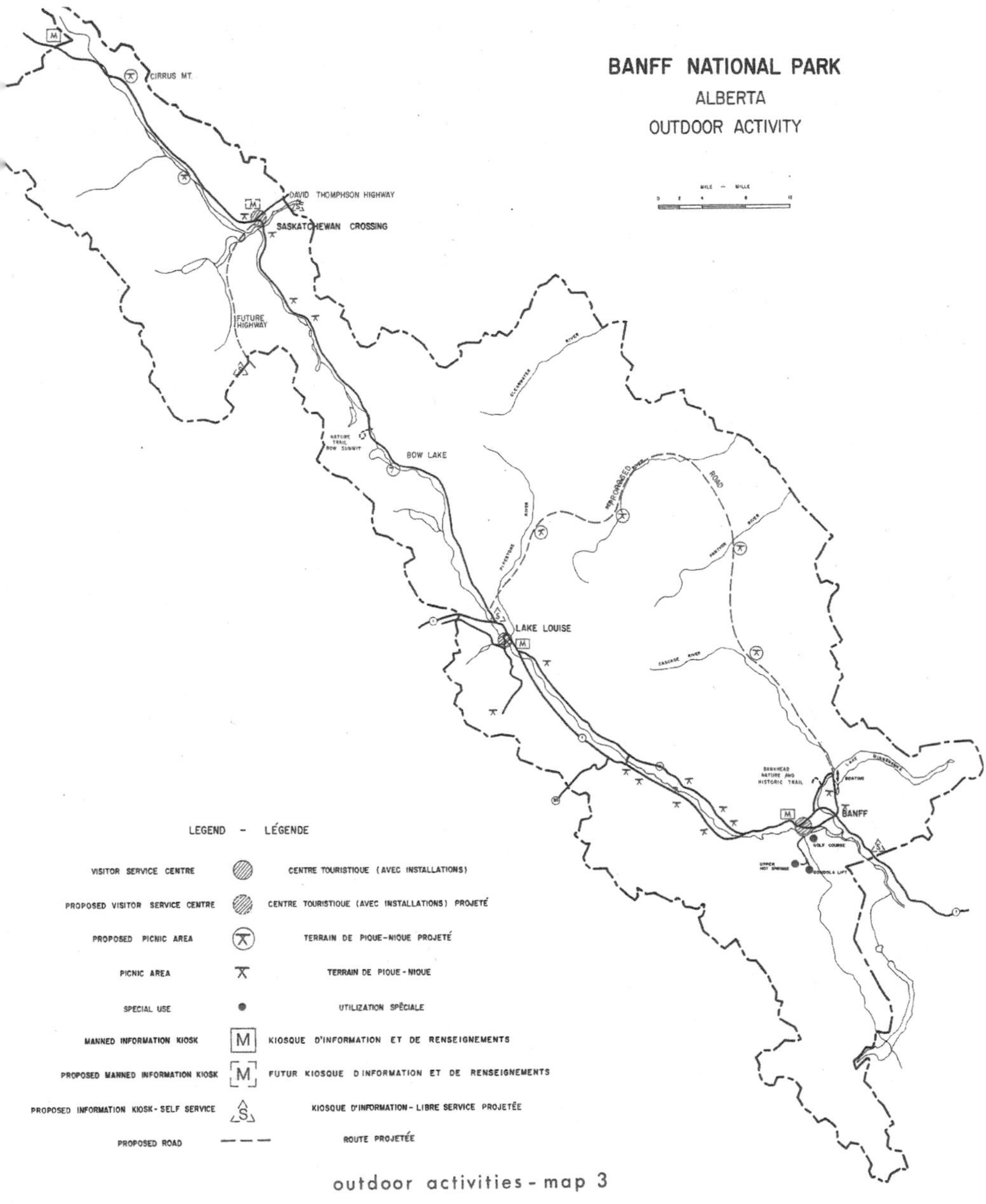

FIG. 1. *Banff National Park, Alberta, Outdoor Activity Map,* BANFF NATIONAL PARK PROVISIONAL MASTER PLAN/PLAN DIRECTEUR PROVISIOIRE. [OTTAWA: NATIONAL PARKS SERVICE, PLANNING, 1968, 61.]

students studying national park topics, who clearly possessed a sense of political engagement in parks questions. One of Nelson's graduate students, Bob Scace, helped form the Calgary-Banff chapter of the National and Provincial Parks Association.[23] There was also an emerging group of university scientists interested in ecological studies such as Ian McTaggart-Cowan at UBC, who likewise became engaged in public issues and occasionally advised on government policy. It was this growing interest in national parks as a means of protecting the environment that led the National and Provincial and Parks Association and the University of Calgary to organize the first "Canadian National Parks: Today and Tomorrow" conference in 1968, with Nelson as the principal agent.

Not surprisingly, the Banff provisional master plan became a hot button topic for much of the conference. Many of the plan's proposals for park development were attacked by Nelson in his paper, "Man and Landscape Change in Banff National Park: A National Park Problem in Perspective." He focused his criticism on the proposed scenic roads: "These roads seem to be intended to provide access by auto, rather than by foot or horse, to areas of outstanding beauty as well as to ease heavy automobile tourist pressure in Banff Townsite and other congested areas by spreading traffic and visitors over large 'undeveloped' areas of the park."[24] Nelson also attacked the planning process that produced the master plan itself. In a few instances he referred to the lack of public consultation that excluded outside expert views, and he objected to the lack of balance that favoured automobile tourists over the protection of wilderness areas. But he saved his harshest comments about planners for later in the conference. Adopting a deliberately combative tone, Nelson said: "I have been appalled at the way in which planning has been carried out in the past few years. I would hesitate to use the word 'planning' in any sense for what has been done as far as Banff National Park is concerned."[25]

Another articulate critic at the conference was McTaggart-Cowan, one of the first trained ecologists in Canada, then professor of zoology and dean of Graduate Studies at UBC. He had a very good knowledge of both Banff and Jasper, having carried out or directed several research projects in the mountain parks during the 1940s, and having provided occasional advice to the program's headquarters. His paper, entitled "The Role of Ecology in the National Parks," was also harshly critical of the national parks' existing development and any proposals for further development. But whereas Nelson had focused on social issues, McTaggart-Cowan emphasized the lack of scientific understanding behind the proposed projects. His paper began with the blunt statement that "ecological considerations had almost no part in the establishment or design of any of the Canadian National Parks."[26] He went on to make a number of observations that, while they may seem commonplace now, were highly original at the time. By focusing on ecological zones rather than scenery or bits of wilderness, he revealed a fundamental flaw in the planners' approach: that the parks' high use or frontcountry zones often occupied river valleys or montane areas that were also important habitat for wildlife. McTaggart-Cowan made a number of other important new observations: the protection of forests from fire was allowing forests to spread into natural grassland, and increased public use of sensitive grazing areas was further threatening the environmental health of the parks. While not directly critical of park planners, he did take aim at the engineering culture present in the Parks Branch, saying: "After thirty-eight years spent in our parks I have become progressively depressed by the complete failure of the highway engineers to respond to the unique demands inherent in the national park roadways." Like Nelson, McTaggart-Cowan decried the proposals for scenic roads, asking rhetorically, "is this any longer the best way of taking people quietly into the right environment to see the things we want them to see?"[27] Such a scientifically informed, ecological perspective was still rare at this time. Most advocates for saving "wilderness" were really arguing for the protection of scenic or aesthetic values, as had Harkin some decades before, or were simply taking a moral stand against automobiles in natural areas. But McTaggart-Cowan's views suggested the new thinking that would begin to reinterpret national park values in an ecological context – a way of thinking recognized by the Parks Branch in its National Park Systems Plan two years later, as Olivier Craig-Dupont discusses in his essay.

Perhaps surprisingly, given the nature of the conference, the Banff Advisory Council also made a presentation here. But the Council saw which way the wind was blowing and adapted to the tenor of the times. G.A. Leroy, Council chairman, argued that by calling Banff a "service centre" and imposing strictly utilitarian guidelines for development, the government was encouraging unattractive development. Besides reiterating the long-standing complaints about lack of municipal status and the lease arrangements, Leroy made a telling argument against the service centre planning: "The proposed asphalt-concrete jungle, with buildings designed for maximum use during the period of a short lease, seems a tragic incongruity in a natural setting such as the Banff area presents."[28]

The Parks Branch could not fail to take notice of the mood of the conference; after all, both Minister Chrétien and his senior managers were in attendance. Moreover, profound changes in attitude were underway within the Branch itself. Two examples serve to indicate the changing climate of opinion in the 1960s: the creation of a reinvigorated Interpretive Service in the mid-1960s and new attitudes toward predator control. When Jim Thorsell was hired as a seasonal park naturalist at Lake Louise in 1962, he was one of the very few working in that role in Canada's national parks. The park naturalist program really only became recognized as a dedicated function in the 1950s and even then was fairly rudimentary, with only three or four employees. But within a decade, park naturalists were being recognized as a formal component in all national parks. Much of the credit for legitimizing and expanding the role of the park naturalist rests with Winston Mair, who became director of the national parks interpretive division in 1964. A biologist by training, Mair had been chief of the Canadian Wildlife Service; articulate and energetic, he referred to natural history interpretation as the "key to the future of national parks."[29] Like Harkin before him, Mair argued that a better understanding of the ideals of national parks would foster greater support for their preservation. He saw young, idealistic, university-trained naturalists as an important strategy in countering the malignant effects of commercial development in the parks. Echoing American John Muir from the turn of the century, Mair believed that, if people could see the spiritual importance of nature and backcountry, they would be less inclined to want to pave over it. He saw the park naturalists as missionaries of this philosophy, and, as the largest park, Banff soon possessed a large and influential interpretive service. Many of its members further influenced the growth of local organizations such as the Bow Valley Naturalists, and while many of these young people, like Jim Thorsell, went on to other things, the "University of Banff" continued to influence their future outlook and nurture an abiding interest in the park.

In March 1968 the *Crag and Canyon* printed a frontpage article describing – in a humorous tone – how twenty coyotes had been killed by local park wardens, in response to that newspaper's campaign to eliminate nuisance animals in the town.[30] Although the animals had evidently been dispatched with community support, the response to the article indicates the growing environmental awareness within both the Parks Branch and the town of Banff. Local response came in the form of a letter to the editor from the Bow Valley Naturalists. It began by saying: "Your front page article entitled 'Carolling Coyotes Kapowed' in the March 20 edition of the Crag was nothing less than disgusting," and closed with the reprimand that "We sincerely hope that your attitude does not reflect that of the warden service."[31] In fact, the coyote cull *did* reflect the position of park wardens at that time: all wardens had the authority to shoot predators on sight and were happy to oblige calls from residents to dispose of nuisance animals. (Chief Park Warden Bob Hand was "old school," and would retire later that year.) But in Ottawa, park officials were disturbed by the *Crag and Canyon* article and its implication that the wardens were complicit in the destruction of these indigenous animals. Park planner Gerry Lee wrote: "If the Warden's Service, Banff, gave their consent or approval to this article on the coyotes ... then it would seem that we're further in the woods than ever before."[32] Lee's memo prompted queries from Ottawa to the regional director in Calgary and the park superintendent, and, following some discussion, the regional directive authorizing the shooting of predators was rescinded.[33] As George Colpitts's chapter demonstrates, revising public attitudes toward wildlife in the mountain parks became a major preoccupation for the Branch in this period.

While the end of the 1960s ushered in a new outlook in national parks generally, and Banff in particular, there was by no means consensus about the ideal way that a national park should be maintained or developed. Despite the new interest in ecology and wildlife, the scales were still tipped in favour of more rather than less development. As late as 1971 there were still no scientists officially working within the Parks Branch. The head of resource conservation in the western regional office was a former park warden with only a high school diploma. The head of engineering, by contrast, was a university-trained professional.

This imbalance in outlook was one reason that the organization was ambushed by the negative public reaction to the Lake Louise ski hill plan. The plan, which followed established policy and had been further approved by the regional office, proposed accommodation and venues for evening entertainment, creating the same kind of atmosphere that had been developed at Aspen, Colorado, and would later occur at Whistler, British Columbia. The new Lake Louise proposal gathered steam after 1969 when it got approval from the Parks Branch and backing from Imperial Oil in Toronto. However, when taken to public hearings in 1971, the plan attracted widespread criticism.[34] Ski hill development had long evoked criticism from the environmental lobby; for instance, the *Crag and Canyon* had blamed environmentalists for derailing the 1968 Olympic proposal.[35] But in 1971 the response from environmentalists was especially fierce, both locally in Calgary and across the country. Not only were the promoters roundly criticized for wanting to overdevelop a wilderness setting, but the Branch itself was vilified for allowing the plan to proceed as far as it had. The environmentalists won the day: the next year, Minister Chrétien stepped in and overturned the project's approval. As a result of this debacle, the western regional office hired its first university-trained ecologist.[36]

Incremental as it may have been, and as incomplete as some argue it still is, the National Parks Branch underwent a sea change in attitude over the course of the 1960s. At the second Canadian National Parks Conference held in Banff in 1978, the head of the national parks program, Al Davidson, summed up the changes of the past decade:

> In 1968, we were about to start the public hearings programme on park master plans. That programme had a profound impact on our planning emphasis and public participation leading to decision making. Look back at some of the provisional master plans, at the emphasis on road building, at the catering to the *arm chair* tourists, and compare them with our present emphasis on programmes which will provide park experiences uniquely attuned to the natural environment.[37]

Although Davidson's comments are still oriented toward public use rather than ecological suitability, acknowledging the role of public participation and the importance of "park experiences" in a natural setting would not be out of place in Parks Canada materials today. Indeed, the degree to which this new way of thinking affected development in the mountain parks can be seen in the next two management plans, produced almost twenty years later. *In Trust for Tomorrow: A Management Framework for Four Mountain Parks* (1986) was the culmination of five years of research and consultation. Recognizing that park ecosystems ranged beyond park boundaries, the plan attempted to engage larger issues by looking at the four-park block of Banff, Jasper, Yoho, and Kootenay as a single entity. Though it sought to reconcile the two opposing objectives of national parks of preservation and use, it too proposed a "middle path." Given the vocal opposition to earlier park development, it was remarkably sanguine on the subject. There was no attempt to limit visitor numbers; indeed, the plan encouraged the improvement of visitor services and transportation networks, though it did recommend keeping these confined to existing corridors in the parks, and not expanding development outward.

However, even the durable concept of the middle path was about to be profoundly altered. In 1988, the same year that a new *National Parks Act* established ecological integrity as the paramount value guiding park management, Parks Canada approved a new management plan for Banff, which articulated this new philosophy of national parks:

> Resource protection will take precedence over visitor use and facility development where conflicts occur. Visitor use will be managed to safeguard natural and cultural resources, as well as the aesthetics of the park. Park resources will be managed on an ecological basis; cooperating and coordinating resource management with the other parks in the four mountain park block, and with provincial and private interests managing adjacent lands.[38]

The document retained the planners' optimism about the ability of planning to adequately deal with threats caused by overuse, but for the first time a national parks document indicated that ecological principles would direct parks management.

The issues fomenting in Banff in the 1960s influenced a subsequent generation of managers, planners, and environmental activists. The culture of the National Parks Branch shifted away from an engineer-dominated ethos to one that gave greater voice to biologists. The degree to which this shift is reflected within the agency is still contentious. Rick Searle, for example, has concluded that national park policy is still governed by a development mentality.[39] Still, there was a paradigm shift in thinking about national park ideals in the 1960s. While the Branch continued to heed the needs and objectives of sophisticated business interests in Banff, a democratization of the decision-making process caused it to pay attention to other sectors of the Canadian public, including an increasingly militant environmental movement. Planners tried to reconcile these varying viewpoints in drafting their management plans, but the decision to incorporate public consultation was itself a result of the debates of the 1960s. The controversy over development at Banff energized the crusading mission of organizations such as the Canadian Parks and Wilderness Society, and they inspired people like Jim Thorsell to pursue careers advocating the benefits of protected heritage areas around the world.

NOTES

1   An earlier version of this paper was presented to the 40th anniversary of the Canadian National Parks: Today and Tomorrow conference, University of Calgary, June 2008. The author is indebted to the advice of Dr. Robert Scace, one of the organizers of the earlier conference, for his account of the outlook of that time.

2   J.B. Harkin, *The Origin and Meaning of the National Parks of Canada* (Ottawa: National Parks Branch, 1957), 12.

3   Ibid.

4   "Jim Thorsell Speaks at Banff Centre, May 2007," http://www.banffcommunityfoundation.org.

5   Walter Hildebrandt, "Historical Analysis of Parks Canada and Banff National Park 1968–1995," unpublished report prepared for the Banff–Bow Valley Study, Dec. 1995, Parks Canada library, Calgary, 40–41; Paul Kopas,

Taking the Air: Ideas and Change in Canada's National Parks (Vancouver: UBC Press, 2007), 46–47.

6   C.J. Taylor, "A History of Automobile Campgrounds in the Mountain National Parks of Canada," unpublished report, Calgary, Parks Canada, 2001, 62.

7   LAC, RG 84, vol. 538, B36 Tunnel Mountain, Herman Edelberg M.D. to National Parks Branch, 5 July 1964.

8   C.J. Taylor, "A History of Automobile Campgrounds," 62–63.

9   K.G. Crawford et al., *Banff, Jasper and Waterton Lakes National Parks: A Report prepared for the Department of Northern Affairs and National Resources respecting certain aspects of the operation of these National Parks and the Townsites therein* (Kingston: Institute of Local Government, Queen's University, 1960); Peter H. Oberlander, *Urban*

development plan: Banff, Alberta (Ottawa: National Parks Branch, Dept. of Northern Affairs and National Resources, 1961); Walter Hildebrandt, "Historical Analysis of Parks Canada and Banff National Park 1968–1995," unpublished report prepared for the Banff–Bow Valley Study, Dec. 1995, Parks Canada library, Calgary, 47.

10 Kopas, *Taking the Air*, 47.

11 Canada. House of Commons, *Debates*, Session 1964, vol. VIII, 8192.

12 "The objectives of national park policy must be to help Canadians gain the greatest long term recreational benefits from their national parks and at the same time provided safeguards against excessive or unsuitable types of development and use." Ibid., 8192.

13 Ibid., 8193.

14 Canada. House of Commons, *Debates*, Session 1964, vol. VIII, 8194.

15 *Banff Crag and Canyon*, 25 September 1963, 1.

16 Robert McKeown, "Battle for our National Parkland," *Banff Crag and Canyon*, 1 Nov. 1967, 11.

17 "All National Parks in Nation Encouraged to Boost Skiing," *Banff Crag and Canyon*, 17 March 1965, 1.

18 Department of Northern Affairs and National Resources, National Parks Branch, "Winter Recreation and the National Parks: A Management Policy and a Development Program," unpublished manuscript, March 1965.

19 Canada. National Parks Service. "Banff National Park Provisional Master Plan" 1967, 3.

20 Ibid., 4.

21 Leslie Bella, *Parks for Profit* (Montreal: Harvest House, 1987), 110–12.

22 Richard West Sellars, *Preserving Nature in the National Parks* (New Haven, CT: Yale University Press, 1997), describes the Mission 66 building program and the reaction it sparked. Paul S. Sutter, *Driven Wild: How the Fight Against Automobiles Launched the Modern Wilderness Movement* (Vancouver: UBC Press, 2002), argues that highway building programs in U.S. national parks stimulated the organization of the modern wilderness movement to curtail what it saw as inappropriate development.

23 Bob Scace, personal communication, 24 April 2008.

24 J.G. Nelson, "Man and Landscape Change in Banff National Park: A National Park Problem in Perspective," in *The Canadian National Parks; today and tomorrow, proceedings of a conference organized by the National and Provincial Parks Association of Canada and the University of Calgary October 9–15, 1968*, ed. J.G. Nelson and R.C. Scace, vol. 1, 138 (Calgary: University of Calgary, 1969).

25 "Summaries and Discussion," in *The Canadian National Parks*, ed. Nelson and Scace, vol. II, 969.

26 Ian McTaggart Cowan, "The Role of Ecology in the National Park," in *The Canadian National Parks*, ed. Nelson and Scace, II:931.

27 "Summaries and Discussion," in *The Canadian National Parks*, ed. Nelson and Scace, II:976.

28 G.A. Leroy, "A Paper Submitted by Banff Advisory Council," in *The Canadian National Parks*, ed. Nelson and Scace, II:801.

29   W.W. Mair, "Natural History Inter-
     pretation: Key to the Future of the
     National Parks," in "Fifth Annual
     Naturalists Workshop: Palisades Na-
     tional Parks Training Centre, Jasper
     National Park, Jasper, Alberta, July 3,
     4, 5 1964." Unpublished manuscript,
     Parks Canada library, Calgary.

30   "Carolling Coyotes Ka-Powed," *Banff
     Crag and Canyon*, 20 March 1968, 1.

31   Letter to the editor, *Banff Crag and
     Canyon*, 3 April 1968, 4.

32   Library and Archives Canada, RG 84,
     vol. 974, file B262, pt.1, Gerry Lee to
     L. Brooks, 27 March 1968.

33   Ibid., B.I.M. Strong to superintendent,
     Banff, 8 Dec. 1959.

34   Rodney Touche, *Brown Cows, Sacred
     Cows: A True Story of Lake Louise*
     (Hanna, AB: Gorman and Gorman,
     1990), 131–47; Chic Scott, *Powder
     Pioneers: Ski Stories from the Canadian
     Rockies and Columbia Mountains*

     (Calgary: Rocky Mountain Books,
     2005), 109.

35   *Banff Crag and Canyon*, editorial, 4.

36   Dr. Bruce Leeson, personal communi-
     cation, May 2008.

37   A.T. Davidson, "Canada's National
     Parks: Past and Future," in *The Can-
     adian National Parks: Today and
     Tomorrow Conference II* (Waterloo:
     University of Waterloo, 1979), 1:23.

38   Canadian Parks Service, *Banff National
     Park Management Plan, 1988* (Ottawa:
     Environment Canada, 1988), 16.

39   "Part of the problem is that the dom-
     inant culture of Parks Canada does
     not consider itself science based. The
     tendency is to place a low priority on
     ecological research and a higher prior-
     ity on the provision of facilities for the
     benefit and safety of visitors." Rick
     Searle, *Phantom Parks: The Struggle
     to Save Canada's National Parks* (To-
     ronto: Key Porter, 2000), 128.

Films, Tourists, and Bears in the National Parks: Managing Park Use and the Problematic "Highway Bum" Bear in the 1970s

༈

GEORGE COLPITTS[1]
DEPARTMENT OF HISTORY
UNIVERSITY OF CALGARY

In the 1960s and 1970s, Canada's national parks system was the closest it had ever been to fulfilling its earlier promoters' wildest dreams, and their nightmares. North American automobile culture joined with a popularized wilderness movement to expand park use to unprecedented levels. Every year, Canadians and Americans by the tens of thousands drove over improved highway systems, taking advantage of a federally managed network of camp and picnic grounds within the parks. Roads offered "drive-in" convenience in nature. Camping, barely contained within crowded, centralized sites with biffies, water pumps, and standardized outdoor film screens and auditoriums, now replicated the very suburbs from which parks visitors had hoped to escape.[2] All the while, parks were more effectively colonized by tourists using a variety of newfangled "leave-no-trace" consumer tent and hiking products that could support mass back-to-nature tourism and even greater visitor numbers.[3] To say the least, meeting the needs and expectations of car-driving urbanites presented enormous challenges for Canada's National Parks Branch dealing with what Turner has termed "the paradoxes of popular wilderness."[4]

C.J. Taylor, in this volume, describes the surging "second wave" of wilderness preservationism gaining force by the 1970s. Many of the movement's adherents were young activists with ties to universities and civil society wilderness advocacy groups who were reacting against the perceived overuse and development in the parks. Often overlooked, but indicative of the growing pressures on park managers in this period, was one of the most innovative wildlife films in Canada's government film history. Funded by Parks Canada and produced by the National Film Board, the twenty-five-minute *Bears and Man* was filmed as debate around use-versus-preservation grew in national parks across Canada, and indeed, North America.[5] This chapter, examining *Bears and Man* and other films of the era, suggests that their significance can be better understood in a longer history of visual representations of parks landscapes and of the animals and humans within them. After World War I, infrastructure and road-building projects had done more than engineer parks space to better exploit its tourist potential. Rather, these roads and automobile technology began influencing animal-human relationships whereby humans and wildlife in these "wilderness" settings evinced a host of mutualistic and rewarding behaviours. One involved the long-standing and enormously popular pastime of tourists feeding bears along roadsides and photographing themselves doing so.[6]

When *Bears and Man* appeared in 1978, it reached expanded audiences through movie theatres and television and presented a radically different portrait of human-animal relationships in the parks system.[7] Cinematographer Bill Schmalz, with parks officials and other individuals working in the context of their times,[8] used the film to rearrange elements of North American popular culture according to the growing ethic of wilderness preservation and the emerging science of bear ecology. The final product was far more comprehensive than the original project first discussed by the Parks Branch in 1967, which had been to create a "training film" for visitors encountering bears in the parks.[9] The 1978 film offers insights into how independent film-making, bear behavioural science, and the wilderness movement were coalescing in new ideas about nature itself. *Bears and Man* redefined space between wild animals and park visitors in a new "hybrid landscape," and in an ideal that, arguably, remains influential to the present day.[10]

Almost from the moments of their technological birth moving and still photo cameras complemented conservation efforts in North America.[11] American conservationists such as Henry Fairfield Osborn had long understood how wildlife films, in particular, could spread and shape conservation messages to wide audiences and gather public support for the further establishment of American parks.[12] Given the malleability of images in film and photographic media, film-makers could blur reality and recreate Nature itself by depicting wild animals in a variety of ways.[13] In one popular medium, that of very cheap and mass-produced postcards, the wild in Canada's mountain parks – what Keri Cronin termed "National Park Nature" – was profoundly shaped by the depiction of its animal life, especially of black bears.[14] Bears eating at hotel tables, wandering around on Banff's golf course, chained to poles, sniffing for food along park roadways, or sitting behind steering wheels of automobiles were not only popular in the interwar years, they were important in defining through "photographic clichés" park wilderness for larger numbers of tourists using roads and automobiles.[15]

These postcards were made locally for the mountain parks and sold en masse in tourist shops. A "Black Bears" postcard taken in the 1940s, one of many based on a photograph by Byron Harmon, suggests how autotourism and bears joined in a wilderness ideal: it shows a mother and her cubs crossing a highway in Banff, undoubtedly looking for handouts. In turn, the postcard was purchased by an autotourist from Minburn, Alberta and posted home with the note: "Here is a picture of the bears we keep watching for but haven't seen yet. We'll be at Banff tonight so I'm sure we'll see some there. We've had a fine time. Love, Auntie."[16] As tourists chugged through mountain parks in their new technological monstrosities – as some at first had viewed automobiles within parks – their visits were necessarily mediated in the landscape through graded roadways, roadside stops, and scenic loops and views cut through forest screens to best facilitate sight-seeing, often at a rapid pace.[17] Meanwhile, wildlife finding reward by frequenting roadways and auto stops to mooch for food were quickly conditioned to tourist traffic. Both parties seem to have enjoyed their encounters. The love-at-first-sight between wildlife and automobilists was romanticized further in tourist promotion.

FIG. 1. A QUITE TYPICAL BANFF POSTCARD CA. 1920S. "TOURISTS' CARS ARE SUBJECT TO INSPECTION BY WILD GAME ON THE AUTO ROAD NEAR BANFF, ALBERTA." POSTCARDS LIKE THESE WERE SOLD IN TOURIST SHOPS WELL INTO THE 1960S. [GLENBOW ARCHIVES, NA-4334-25.]

... ubject to inspection by wild game ———
... ad near Banff. Alberta.———

Habituated wildlife was featured feeding along the roadsides of some of the earliest automobile road films to thrill theatre audiences in the 1920s.[18] As Alan MacEachern and John Sandlos have noted in this volume, the Parks Branch was already skilled at tourism promotion. The promotion-savvy parks commissioner James B. Harkin knew how to please automobilists by suggesting that salt licks be put out beside the newly built Banff highway system in 1922.[19] Mabel B. Williams' own promotions of the new "auto parks" in Western Canada celebrated the ways that wild animals seemed "tamed" along roadways, in effect sharing the road with drivers. Park drivers, she promised, would encounter animals that innately understood that "within these boundaries" humans had "laid aside" their "ancient enmity." Animals, in return, were "quick to offer in return the gift of equal friendship."[20] She did not mention that, really, most of the animals were there for the free lunch. The pandering elk, mooching squirrels, and cheeky bears in park picnic areas and driveways had conditioned themselves to the handouts and very quickly confirmed expectations of drivers and auto passengers around ideas of wilderness itself: part of a larger intellectual complex that David Louter has termed "windshield wilderness."[21]

Bear ecology and behaviour reinforced its central presence in that conceptualization. Camera-toting visitors could snap photos of many compliant park animals, from the reintroduced elk species to deer. But it was the Black Bear (*Ursus americanus*) that became something of a "keystone" species in road landscapes. It adapted quickly to the rising numbers of tourists and the habitat changes within park areas in Canada and parts of the United States by the mid-twentieth century. Its remarkable adaptation in turn contributed to the growing popularity in bear-feeding. Research in the United States at Yellowstone and Great Smoky Mountains and in Canada's mountain parks would later show that bears displayed a manifestly "tolerant" behaviour. Once rolling in their vehicles into the confines of park boundaries, tourists could usually find a bear that had learned to "beg" along roadsides in order to elicit handouts. Many showed remarkable talent in "dancing," performing or aping gestures to please drivers and passengers. Some learned to aggress without inflicting injury in order to bully picnic tourists to share their food. Stephen Herrero found that, although the Black Bear did aggress tourists, it (unlike the Grizzly, *Ursus arctos*) did so in much lower numbers in proportion to the numbers of encounters, and inflicted comparatively minor injuries.

Fig. 2. Black bears became "keystone" species in tourist understandings of parks roads landscapes. This bear is crossing a park road in Alberta or British Columbia before 1942. [Whyte Museum of the Canadian Rockies; v263/na-2862, Byron Harmon.]

Animal behaviour, then, contributed to a cultured space between animal and human, with bears learning strategies that, for the most part, rewarded them.[22] Before the truly dangerous congestion of the 1960s – a decade also fraught with debate about the corruption of the wilderness by over-development and tourist use – bears and humans complemented each others' behaviours and bears themselves gained prominence in tourist-animal landscapes.

All the same, for parks staff the convergence of roads, automobilists, and bears was inviting a head-on collision of unintended outcomes, to say the least. In the United States, the bear problem loomed with increasing urgency, accelerated by greater numbers of tourists and, by the 1960s, ecologists suggesting a variety of controversial remedies.[23] Canada, of course, saw its own rapid increase in vehicular traffic in the post-war period. Vehicle passenger numbers at Banff's East Gate rose from around 300,000 in 1947 to 800,000 in 1957, and to almost 2.4 million by 1970.[24] Despite increased efforts to discourage highway liaisons, National Parks Branch officials were dismayed to find bear-feeding postcards still selling in Banff townsite tourist shops in 1959, the very year when the first conviction for the practice occurred.[25] Many of the maulings, as reported to wardens, often occurred at roadside lookouts, suggesting drive-in tourists had unrolled windows, much like they would have in a hamburger joint, to bear moochers in return for a photograph. Such exchanges, always loaded with misunderstandings, sometimes went very badly.[26] As J.R.B. Coleman, a senior Branch official, pointed out in one memorandum in 1965, "postcards depicting bears in the driver's seat of cars are on sale in various U.S. and Canadian National Park tourist shops and they encourage some foolish people in the belief that such a photographic set-up is easy and safe to arrange." He referred to the case of one Banff visitor who was observed *pushing* a "large black bear behind the steering wheel of his car so that he could take an unusual photograph."[27] The problem was that tourists simply saw the interaction as an integral element of a parks experience. Even the *Kingston Whig Standard* could find the Parks Branch's pamphlets that year reminding tourists "of the dangers of feeding and molesting bears" worthy of a comical editorial cartoon.[28]

With tourist expectations so dependent on such practices, it is interesting to see the somewhat mixed messages arising in a film produced in 1959 by the Branch entitled *Wildlife of the Rockies* (tellingly, originally titled "Zoo of the Mountains"). This film represented an effort by the Branch to both promote the parks system and remedy a problematic scarcity of Canadian national parks films available in the post-war period. What films it did have were perhaps informative but had all of the interest of high school biology lectures. Canadian and American audiences demanding films of Canadian mountain parks for Rotary Club dinners and bridge nights found the official selection of 16-mm films wanting, to say the least. By the late 1950s, documentary selections produced earlier by the federal government's film bureau were hopelessly bogged down in natural history detail, out of date, or simply too tattered from repetitive viewings for continued use.[29] After assessing the comparatively more exciting films promoting U.S. national parks, the Canadian Parks Branch liaised with the National Film Board to produce something, in the parlance of the times, hipper, and used wildlife to do so.

The decision was made to let a Banff cinematographer film what he could from a list of preferred mammals found in the parks system. The list ranged from moose to mountain goat and mountain sheep, to black and grizzly bear, deer, elk, and buffalo.[30] A storyline, it was thought, could be built up later. This approach was later defended in departmental memos as the project's costs began to balloon with few results to show. Given the difficult challenges of wildlife cinematography, the film-maker spent a year filming what amounted to Dall sheep.[31] The Branch realized that nothing new was being added to its existing stock and appointed cinematographer Dick Bird, a Regina-based film-maker with a "good reputation in North America" in wildlife cinematography and a number of park film projects under his belt, to take up the project.[32] The main contract, however, went to Bill Carrick, promised a per-season wage and contacts with park wardens to compile footage of animals. Carrack had already worked for the Parks Branch filming Point Pelee and had other credits with the Canadian Wildlife Service. A "highly skilled man in this field," with experience working with Walt Disney Productions, Carrick seemed right for the job. Still, the storyline was left to emerge from whatever animals proved "co-operative."[33]

The sheer difficulty of filming wildlife, the problem of scene composition, and the need to create an appealing and interesting script decisively influenced the film emerging from initial footage. An editor worked to make sense of what was coming in from Carrick, who managed to shoot ptarmigan, deer, bear, and the like; a biologist was appointed to make sense of it all, and to work with the editor who eventually added a storyline. By the end, both the "longshot" landscape scenes introducing the film and the original title were determined too uninteresting and were dropped. Television audiences, it was thought, "would likely turn off their sets" otherwise. The opening shot was changed and the title "Wildlife in the Rockies" was adopted instead.[34]

Perhaps planning the production had left little room for innovation, but the end product worked within the expectations of tourists of the time. *Wildlife of the Rockies* introduces a hypothetical "mammalogist resident" who encouraged autotourists to stop their cars and take a moment to look at park wildlife. The film opens with a family pausing impatiently on the side of the road, having vacated their car, and, "seeing nothing," as narrator Budd Knapp tells the audience, "piling into their car, this family concludes that the woods and mountains are deserted."[35] He goes on to say, however, that the mammalogist knew better. As the family returns to its prominent 1950s American vehicle and roars off down the road, the narrator explains that had they known better or been willing to look beyond the roadside, there would be plenty of animals to view. Even when the family stops again to chat with a park warden – through a rolled-down window – they are evidently in too much of a hurry to listen to his advice. And leaving him and the viewer in the dust of their vehicle, the film then turns to the warden who scans through Alpine, sub-Alpine, and valley complexes where communities of animals awaited, very apparent to the eye but invisible to autotourists moving too quickly to pause and take a careful, studious glance at their surroundings.

Whatever the original intent of the production, the drafts of commentary, shortened and synced to film, ended up reinforcing tourist behaviour along park roadsides. Given that many of the shots were taken from roadside vantage points, this is not surprising. About 230 seconds into the film, the narrator says, "Finding most of the wildlife in Banff and Jasper requires some careful searching. But even the road home can bring its surprises. You don't need binoculars to spot a black bear. He moves where he wants, and the presence of a few human beings doesn't bother him at all."[36] The key objective of the film, i.e., to have tourists "spend a bit more time in the parks, instead of speeding through them in their cars,"[37] was then obscured in the very infrastructure and road amenities tourists were using. The framing of the film around autotourists, in the end, reinforced current expectations and affirmed Steve Jones's idea that "cinematic and touristic ways of seeing" complemented each other quite naturally in the post-war period.[38]

Wildlife of the Rockies was added to the roster of films being shown to audiences in campground amphitheatres across the Canadian parks system.[39] The Branch developed two more films by 1969 to encourage tourism – each, however, revealing the growing problem facing park managers who were tasked with promoting parks as much as preserving them. *Away from it all* (1961), featuring Terra Nova National Park, was a fifteen-minute short that juxtaposed urban life and its many "daily urban struggles" with that of wilderness parks and sanctuaries, "natural retreats for the worried man," as the outline narration read.[40] A more explicit celebration of wilderness – as opposed to tourist promotion – appeared in the Branch's award-winning *The Enduring Wilderness* (1963), directed by nature cinematographer Christopher Chapman. The film provided a montage of scenes from park spaces across Canada. It too reinforced a message of the need for parks in a society increasingly "feeling the impact of civilization" beyond roadways, the din of traffic, and technological amenities supplied for auto-driving tourists. But the film was organized around "the whole idea to provide the experience of natural beauty and the feeling for it,"[41] quite innovatively seeking to provide a "philosophy film on National Parks," one of the reasons why its initial title was planned as "The Meaning of Wilderness."[42]

In Chapman's case, however, the film's original purpose was at odds with the promotional mandate still being managed by the federal ministry overseeing the project – and paying its production costs. An initial script read by the Education and Interpretation Section and the deputy minister of the Department of Northern Affairs and National Resources – of which the Parks Branch was only a part – felt that Chapman had scripted a film that did not encourage the use of parks by visitors. "Nowhere in the script is there any direct identification of the wilderness with people," Chapman was told. "Could not some people be shown ...? I feel rather strongly that all parks, National or otherwise, are, and should be for people – for their recreation, their education, their appreciation of nature ... it is an obligation on the trustees [of a park] to allow it to be used appropriately by people."[43] Closer to the events unfolding around them and the pressures on the ground, parks officials backing these new films were already anxious to support such efforts and even present to the public the "use and preservation dilemma" confronting them. Winston W. Mair, the new director of the Branch, developed the extraordinary idea of a film relating "the use-conserve dilemma as experienced system-wide – perhaps putting across the idea of public understanding as the only real solution." Mair perhaps was voicing the concerns of his own officials in a parks system grappling with logistic issues of garbage, road-widening, ski hill development, and other uses. His idea of telling "the story of the wild lands, without too much concentration on the spectacular,"[44] however, was quashed at the ministerial level. The Parks Branch's most recent film, *The Enduring Wilderness*, had already gone far enough in giving "the 'soft sell' type" to the public. The minister felt that "it was *not* what he wanted. What we need is something more aggressive and spectacular to ensure his continued support for more films in the future."[45] Whatever "philosophy" of wilderness Chapman had wanted to explore in his film, the times were not best for expressing them. Chapman's original film title, indeed, had gone through its own considerable modification. From the proposed "the Meaning of Wilderness," expressing a philosophy of wilderness, the film's title was changed to the "Vanishing Wilderness." However, the Parks Branch understood even that term's problematic semantics and tweaked it to a more reassuring title: "The Enduring Wilderness." At least on film, the Parks Branch was still attempting to balance tourism and increased use with its mandate to preserve Canada's great wild lands.

Against this backdrop of massive development and increased tourism in the parks, a series of bear culls and highly publicized mauling incidents brought into stark view a number of now unsustainable traditions in parks tourism. As early as the 1940s, and certainly by 1959, western parks wardens were shooting bears in greater numbers in an effort to reduce animal-human conflicts. Superintendents explored numerous remedies to address the problems posed by these omnivore "highway bums,"[46] but, given the costs of bear-proof garbage disposal, the largely unsuccessful educational campaigns to tourists, and complicity among concession and tour bus operators who were still escorting tourists to road-side bear photo-ops, parks managers believed that only large-scale culling and even complete eradication were solutions for areas frequented by visitors.[47] By the early 1960s, with some 100,000 people camping in Jasper National Park alone,[48] it was evident that there was not enough room for habituated "campground" bears in the Canadian parks system. In 1962, for example, wardens trapped 146 black bears and destroyed 112 (compared to 75 and 38 respectively a year before).[49] The superintendent of Kootenay National Park, K.B. Mitchell, voiced concern over the "highly accelerated control of the bear population." But he had also seen, as had the superintendent at Jasper, habituation increase with these expanding visitor numbers. By then, bears along the highways had "availed themselves of the supply of food offered by the increased numbers of tourists using the roadways and picnic grounds."[50] In turn, heavy culling led to noticeable declines in bear numbers by the late 1960s and early 1970s, at least in terms of animals seen by visitors. Wardens doing most of the culling, and grimly clearing out roadsides with control methods, were telling tourists wanting to see bears that the animals had simply "gone off" into the backcountry.

There was certainly more urgency in the issue now. The case brought successfully by a bear maul victim in the United States against the U.S. Parks Service raised the worrisome possibility of legal liability arising from mauling incidents. In 1967, an Alberta man brought to the courts his own, ultimately unsuccessful, case, which had occurred in Jasper.[51] The Parks Branch now broached the possibility of having "a short film produced as a public service message in which we would attempt to explain to tourists the procedures they should follow to avoid being confronted by a wild animal or what to do in the case they are."[52] Branch director, J.R.B. Coleman, supported the idea, hoping that such could provide "a training film on bear behaviour and the results of human carelessness and lack of judgment in dealing with bears." An "invaluable aid to such a training program," he imagined the film being shown to "general park visitors and the public-at-large as well."[53]

However, a broader change was occurring in wildlife film-making beyond the Parks Branch. In 1971, broadcaster and public commentator Warner Troye completed *Where Has Sanctuary Gone?*, a twenty-three-minute film that showed, not only the rising tensions of "modern" urban life, but the contrived element of park management whereby autotourists lined up for hours to gain entrance into the national parks. The scene of traffic jams outside Banff's east gates reinforced Troye's larger message of the disappearing wilderness areas in Canada, even within the national parks. The film identified a problem of too many automobiles, too many roads, and too many campgrounds, which offered too little "wilderness" beyond that which could be found in a suburban backyard. Troye captured some of the unreasonable extremes of "use" in Canadian parks, especially that accessible by roadways and filled with family station-wagons.

Even as the wilderness movement affected film-makers and parks promoters, bear studies launched in the 1960s in Yellowstone, Alaska, Great Smoky Mountains, and Glacier National Parks were beginning to elucidate the nature and meaning of bear behaviour, migration, and habituation. These explored bear movement in park areas, surveyed bear-feeding tourists in American parks, studied habituation, and analyzed footpath encounters. Before 1970, very little scientific study of the kind on bears and their habituation had been undertaken, and parks officials had little means of understanding the behaviour or even of guessing the ratio of "campground" and "wilderness" bears in the parks system.[54] The science of bear-feeding, however,

Fig. 3. The 1950s saw larger numbers of tourists and greater bear habituation, some of it encouraged by tourist bus operators and concessionaires who often stopped their vehicles to let tourists get photos of bears along roadways. [Glenbow Archives, na-5611-81.]

changed rapidly in the early 1970s, when international conferences for bear biologists consistently featured sessions on human-animal interaction and the problematic outcomes of habituation.[55] This research led to new social and ecological understandings of animal behaviour and psychology. In Canada, sensibilities were shaped by Stephen Herrero, whose work on animal behaviour focussed on Canadian bears and followed up John and Frank Craigheads' research in Yellowstone.

Such streams of influence informed Parks Canada's decision to support a clearly different kind of bear film. In the early 1970s, wildlife cinematographer Bill Schmalz was returning to Western Canada from a stint of work with the National Film Board when he proposed a bear documentary to the agency's prairie regional office in Calgary. Schmalz had begun his career filming a fisheries research project in the Gulf of Alaska before studying biology at UBC for a year. He then went on to spend several years filming bighorn sheep and other wildlife in the mountain parks. While with the NFB, he finished shooting and directing *Bighorn*, a theatrical short that, like Chapman's wilderness film, had no narration and instead provided a montage of images of areas "still untouched by man."[56] His knowledge that bears were "systematically being shot and killed" along roadsides, including what he believed had been the unnecessary killing of two grizzly cubs by parks wardens, prompted Schmalz to propose *Bears and Man*.[57] His idea of a bear film found evident support in the NFB organization. For the next three years, Schmalz worked with wardens at Kootenay, Banff, Jasper, and Waterton. *Bears and Man* (in French titled *L'Ours mon Frère*) can be viewed as an emerging compilation of environmentalist concerns and scientific understanding of bear behaviour. In terms of the latter, Schmalz was well aware of current science through bear conferences. He consulted with Herrero on the project, and, indeed, Herrero provided advice to Parks Canada as the film took shape.

Schmalz's proposal moved beyond a merely informational production and employed state-of-the-art film editing, music, and narration that emotively disassembled the bear-automobile landscape that had been idealized and preserved in popular photography. His first report, dated December 1974, describes the film's planning process. Its major points were developed thematically on storyboard in consultation with Parks officials. Schmalz had already collected footage of bears in parks from previous work; during his first filming on contract, he witnessed a horrific mauling when the translocation of a drugged grizzly went wrong, and the bear attacked and killed Canadian Wildlife Service biologist Wilf Etherington.[58] Deeply traumatized, but encouraged to continue the project, Schmalz spent the 1974 season capturing sequences for the "Bears in Nature" section of the film, which included shots taken in the summer of two grizzly families (counting a sow with three yearling cubs) and of two lone cubs. During the filming, the warden service helped Schmalz find locations and provided carcasses of road-killed elk and moose to attract bears to open areas "suitable for filming."[59] Eventually, the film moved from "Bears in Nature" to "Bear-People Interaction" – which included the film's most dramatic moment, "bear-people highway feeding" – to "Bear immobilizing and translocation." The film adhered tightly to the eventual script storyboard, although Schmalz's initial hope to include shots showing the warden service shooting problem bears in the "Bear Confrontation Conduct" section were dashed when they were "deleted from scene" by parks officials despite his protests.[60]

Blocked in five sections, the final film went far beyond "instructional" fare; its overarching message promoted a negotiated space between humans and the national parks' now-declining black and grizzly bear populations. The editor eventually working on the project, Kalle Lasn, who had returned from a filming project in Japan with "avante-guard" editing techniques, changed the first editions of the film to be more effective in that respect. Chief Dan George was chosen as narrator for the opening sequences, using narration written by Schmalz and the film editor so that the famous Salish chief could very directly plead viewers to "respect the bear."[61] The original script called for "Old Indian" to say: "the ways of the city are lost in the wilderness. Here the spirit of the great bear fills the land. He was wilder and stronger than we are, we must learn to respect its ways."[62] Considering its long exclusion from national parks, the First Nations' voice was effective but also logical given the popularity of the idea of the "ecological Indian" in the North American environmental movement at the time.[63] The narrator in effect reconceptualized aboriginal history in saying that "at the time of my great grandfather the spirit of the bear filled our land." The native voice then drew bear behaviour around tourists in critical terms. Their feeding was not idealized but criticized as "spoiling" the animal:

DAN GEORGE – Man, once he is given power over the wilderness and its creatures, but he does not have the power to make a spoiled bear natural once more.

Here, the film's characterization of bear behaviour reflected current scientific behavioural research, effectively branded in the native voice. The leading narrator, Patricia Best, went on to further define the "spoiled" bear, the animal habituated around garbage cans and roadside feeds, killed by traffic, tranquillized, transported or destroyed by parks officials. In one scene, a mother black bear and two cubs converge upon a garbage dumpster in Jasper. Adroitly lifting the lid, the mother, then a cub, nose around and disappear into the receptacle. The mother bear's sudden charge from the dumpster suggests the violence and danger of such habituated animals. It provides the transition to footage of a vehicle completely destroyed by a bear attack, its side ripped out and interior plundered for food.

NARRATOR – They call them "spoiled" bears. They have given up their natural feeding habits and learned to survive on human garbage.

The film goes on to explicitly undermine linkages between complementary automobile culture and tourist bear-feeding and negotiated space for both in park recreation. In sequences played by actors, "Russ and Jenny" hike through a park to camp in the wild. They happen upon bear tracks along a stream:

RUSS – "Grizzly tracks."
JENNY – "Is it still around?"
RUSS – "Could be. We're not going to stick around to find out though. I know a better spot about a mile down the trail."

Russ and Jenny eventually locate their camp out of bear's way. They start a fire for cooking distanced at least a hundred yards from their tents. Russ pulverizes burnt cans and then elevates them and other food leftovers by a rope to a high tree limb beyond a bear's reach.

The film's most dramatic scene further defines animal-human parks space in a bear-feeding scene shot between Jasper and the Mile 45 warden station. Bear jams often formed there in a stretch of highway. The scene shows droves of camera-toting tourists converging on a mother with two cubs, which have appeared along the shoulder. Unlike earlier films showing tourists and bears sharing the photographic space, the camera trains attention mostly on the humans who appear as habituated to the bears as the animals to them. In the scene, one brazen youth is seen handing cherries to the mother, which nearly bites his hand.[64] A family passes a brown paper bag to the bears through a rolled down window. The mother is later seen climbing atop of a vehicle, its delighted owners laughing at the bear's pandering. Perhaps the most effective shot comes at the scene's conclusion, when one of the cubs traversing the highway is nearly killed by a motorist who drags it a few metres before its screeching tires; the cub runs to safety, apparently unharmed. Film-editing and another acted sequence shows a park warden arriving, radioing in a "244" bear-on-road call, and confronting the occupants of a car who had just fed the bears in question.

Bears and Man disassembled a terrifically popular, but problematic, photographic ideal that had linked humans and wildlife in North American national parks. This happened at an important moment in parks history, when the growing and increasingly heavy tourist use of national parks was animating anew the "use-versus-preservation" dilemma. It was not, however, a statist imposition into popular culture, or simply the tourist instruction film originally talked about by the Parks Branch. Herrero, indeed, remembered the film "was a celebration of the wild with suggestions on how to keep it that way."[65] Indeed, Parks Canada gave its blessing for the film project at a time when managers themselves were at something of a crossroads in solving the almost-century-old "bear problem." In the context of mauling incidents, heavy culling, and the possibility that victims of bear attacks might sue the government for "mismanaging" the bear problem, this type of popular tourist recreation was no longer tenable in the parks system. Challenges raised by mass tourism had gone beyond the mere question of distinguishing between and managing differently "campground" versus "wilderness" bears. The Parks Branch itself, contemplating a complete eradication of bears in tourist areas, was likely aware of at least a minority of scientific experts who advocated the ridding of the animals in parks in order to protect visitors.

The film represented, then, its endorsement of a management compromise, that of providing new scientific advice and more effective re-education to the public aimed to modify tourism and maintain space in parks for humans, black, and even grizzly bears.[66]

In reorganizing aspects of tourism, however, *Bears and Man* did as much to propose a new bear psychology as it did to delineate an ideal space between humans and these animals. Throughout Schmalz's production, viewers were asked to "respect the bear" as Chief Dan George stated in the film's opening and ending sequences, an admonition suggesting both the unknowable and frightening aspect of a bear's makeup, whatever it truly is. This did not mean that bears lost their keystone status in tourist landscapes. Hardly. If *Bears and Man* enjoyed any success in reshaping tourist behaviours, it was likely because it reassembled, rather than threw away, pieces of older, popular understandings of parks wilderness. The film reinforced the importance of bears in a wild space now understood as "bear country"; catching a larger shift, identified by Tina Loo, in wildlife conservation in Canada by the 1970s, whereby government acted to conserve wild areas and not merely wild animals within them.[67] In the new assemblage, hikers, drivers and sightseers could continue to find recreation in parks, but they did so upon a backdrop of a wilderness idealized by the bear's invisible presence, his "spirit," in Dan George's narration. The bear and its wilderness habitat is of such importance that the roadway is almost completely erased. Once used by visitors to experience and define nature in national parks, it now figured only as a backdrop element, but one now looming as another problem in parks' management of humans and wildlife.

1 The author wishes to thank Alan MacEachern and Jim Taylor for references to parks bear files, films, and photographs, André D'Ulisse and François Houle, National Film Board Archive, for documents; and Ted Hart and Stephen Herrero for reading and commenting on an early version of this paper. Thanks, too, must go to Pamela Banting for her initial suggestions. I am indebted, in particular, to Bill Schmalz for taking much time in recounting his experiences filming *Bears and Man*. The article is dedicated to my "little bear," Gabriel.

2 Richard Harris, *Creeping Conformity: How Canada became Suburban, 1900–1960* (Toronto: University of Toronto Press, 2004), 11–12, 130–32; Doug Owram, *Born at the Right Time: A History of the Baby Boom Generation* (Toronto: University of Toronto Press, 1999); on overall American trends and the development of a "Drive-In Society," see Kenneth Jackson, *Crabgrass Frontier: The Suburbanization of the United States* (New York: Oxford University Press, 1987); in Ontario, see Steve Penfold, "'Are we to go literally to the hot dogs?' Parking Lots, Drive-Ins, and the Critique of Progress in Toronto's Suburbs, 1965–1975," *Urban History Review* 33, no. 1 (2004): 8–23. James Morton Turner, "From Woodcraft to 'Leave no Trace': Wilderness, Consumerism, and Environmentalism in Twentieth-Century America," *Environmental History* 7, no. 3 (2002): 475–76; Alan MacEachern, *Natural Selections: National Parks in Atlantic Canada 1935–1970* (Montreal: McGill-Queen's University Press, 2001), 162–63, 224, 220–22; Gregg Mitman, *Reel Nature: America's Romance with Wildlife in Film* (Cambridge, MA: Harvard University Press, 1999), 105.

3 James Morton Turner, "From Woodcraft to 'Leave no Trace'," 467–68; Victor B. Scheffer, *The Shaping of Environmentalism in America* (Seattle: University of Washington Press, 1999), 41–42.

4 Turner, "From Woodcraft to 'Leave no Trace'," 468–69; see, also, *Reel Nature*, 91; PearlAnn Reichwein, "Holiday at the Banff School of Fine Arts: The Cinematic Production of Culture, Nature, and Nation in the Canadian Rockies, 1945–1952," *Journal of Canadian Studies* 39, no. 1 (2005): 56; Mark W.T. Harvey, *A Symbol of Wilderness: Echo Park and the American Conservation Movement* (Seattle: University of Washington Press, 2000), 57–63.

5 See "Of preservation and Use," in Alan MacEachern, *Natural Selections*, 14–19. In many ways, the period was marked by the growing stress of unresolved pre-war contradictions implicit in marketing "wilderness" to tourists, who in turn peopled these places. See Gabrielle Zezulka-Mailloux, "Laying the Tracks for Tourism: Paradoxical Promotions and the Development of Jasper National Park," in *Culturing Wilderness in Jasper National Park: Studies in Two Centuries of Human History in the Upper Athabasca River Watershed*, ed. I.S. MacLaren, 243–45 (Edmonton: University of Alberta Press, 2007); in the United States, see Paul Sutter, *Driven Wild: How the Fight against Automobiles Launched the Modern Wilderness Movement* (Seattle: University

of Washington Press, 2002), 30–35, 40–47.

6   Paul Schullery, *Searching for Yellowstone: Ecology and Wonder in the Last Wilderness* (Boston: Houghton Mifflin, 1997), 195–98.

7   National Film Board Archives, Montreal (hereafter "NFBA"). See overview of the film's potential television and theatrical audiences in Helène Dennie to Ken Preston, 4 May 1978, 'Bears and Man' correspondence file.

8   From his present home in Langley, BC, Schmalz acknowledged the important contribution of parks naturalist Larry Halverson, Jasper warden Gordon Anderson, and glaciologist Dr. Ronald Goodman. He singled out Mike Porter, then information officer, later a prominent director in national parks, as key to shepherding the earlier stages of the production and seeing it approved by government. He also acknowledged the invaluable contributions of Kalle Lasn and Barbara Baxendale. Telephone interview, Schmalz to author, 2 July 2010.

9   Library and Archives Canada, Ottawa [hereafter "LAC"] AC. J.R.B. Coleman used the term to describe the possible film project, 21 August 1967, RG 84, A-2-a, vol. 2130, file U212, pt. 5.

10 Richard White, "From Wilderness to Hybrid Landscapes: The Cultural Turn in Environmental History," *The Historian* 66 (2004): 558. Schullery describes "a widespread public consciousness" of such parks as Yellowstone as "part of a greater ecosystem," probably the most "important conceptual shift in public understanding." *Searching for Yellowstone*, 197.

11 See Mitman, *Reel Nature*, 85–87; D.B. Jones, *Movies and Memoranda: An Interpretive history of the National Film Board* (Toronto: Canadian Film Institute, 1981); Ted Magder, *Canada's Hollywood: The Canadian State and Feature Films* (Toronto: University of Toronto Press, 1993).

12 Mitman, *Reel Nature*, 90–91; on Henry Fairfield Osborn and films, see 101–2.

13 Cynthia Chris, *Watching Wildlife* (Minneapolis: University of Minnesota Press, 2006), x, 28–34. Ralph H. Lutts, "The Trouble with Bambi: Disney's 'Bambi' and the American Vision of Nature," *Forest and Conservation History* 36, no. 4 (1992): 160–71. In Canada, currents of post-war ideals in film are explored by PearlAnn Reichwein, "Holiday at the Banff School of Fine Arts: The Cinematic Production of Culture, Nature, and Nation in the Canadian Rockies, 1945–1952," *Journal of Canadian Studies* 39, no. 1 (2005): 37. Jennifer Cypher and Eric Higgs, "Colonizing the Imagination: Disney's Wilderness Lodge," *Capitalism, Nature, Socialism* 8, no. 4 (1997): 107–30; and Eric Higgs, *Nature by Design: People, Natural Process and Ecological Restoration* (Cambridge, MA: MIT Press, 2003).

14 Keri Cronin, "'The Bears are Plentiful and Frequently Good Camera Subjects': Postcards and the Framing of Interspecies Encounters in the Canadian Rockies," *Mosaic* 39, no. 4 (2006): 77–92. On the culturing of wilderness, see I.S. MacLaren, "Cultured Wilderness in Jasper National Park," *Journal of Canadian Studies* 34, no. 3 (1999): 7–58.

15 Almost with the very official opening of some park areas to autos – in Banff by 1910 – bear feeding followed. By 1921 the *Edmonton Journal* could report that "Feeding Bears is Popular Past Time in Jasper." The 1921 article is cited (n.d.) in "Evolution of Bear Management in the Mountain National Parks." Parks Canada, 2003.

16 Tourists were warned of the potential danger of feeding bears from the very first decades of the century; signs discouraged the practice and the parks superintendent proposed formal educational campaigns as early as 1939; the *National Park Game Act* explicitly prohibited feeding bears by 1951. "Evolution of Bear Management in the Mountain National Parks." Parks Canada, 2003. See the amendments to the regulations respecting game in the national parks of Canada, "to curb the dangerous practice of touching or feeding bears by making this practice an offence under the Game Regulations." LAC, Précis, Nov. 16, 1951; RG 84, a-2-a, vol. 2129, file u212, pt. 2.

17 David Louter, *Windshield Wilderness: Cars, Roads, and Nature in Washington's National Parks* (Seattle: University of Washington Press, 2006), 59–60.

18 Mitman, *Reel Nature*, 97. The tamed wild animal figures centrally in the 1919 film, "Back to God's Country," where a pet bear protects the heroine from villains. For analysis of the film, see Christopher E. Gittings, in, *Canadian National Cinema: Ideology, Difference and Representation* (London: Routledge, 2002), 21–25. Also, Pierre Berton, *Hollywood's Canada: The Americanization of our National Image* (Toronto: McClelland & Stewart, 1975), 27.

19 See, in this volume, John Sandlos, "Nature's Playgrounds: The Parks Branch and Tourism Promotion in the National Parks, 1911–1929."

20 Mabel B. Williams, *Kootenay National Park and the Banff-Windermere Highway* (Ottawa: Department of the Interior, 1928), 32, quoted in George Colpitts, *Game in the Garden: A Human History of Wildlife in Western Canada to 1940* (Vancouver: UBC Press, 2002), 160–63.

21 Louter, *Windshield Wilderness*, 3–4, 12–13, 37–39; the individualism of autotourism is suggested in Hall K. Rothman, *Devil's Bargains: Tourism in the Twentieth-Century American West* (Lawrence: University of Kansas Press, 1998), 146–47.

22 See Stephen Herrero's documentation of bear habituation along roadsides in *Bear Attacks: Their Causes and Avoidance* (Piscataway, NJ: Winchester Press, 1985), 52; and on the 'tolerant black bear,' 92–94.

23 In the U.S., parks officials were facing a similar problem on a much larger scale. Alice Wondrak Biel, *Do (Not) Feed the Bears: The Fitful History of Wildlife and Tourists in Yellowstone* (Lawrence: University of Kansas Press, 2006), 14–15, 21–23.

24 R.C. Scace, "Man and Grizzly Bear in Banff National Park, Alberta," MA thesis, University of Calgary, 1972, 86.

25 LAC. The postcards were "detrimental" to "any campaign we carry out against the feeding of bears," Superintendent of Banff National Park, D.B. Coombs, 15 May 1959, RG 84 A 2-a, vol. 229 K212, pt. 2.

26 LAC. "[D]rivers of sightseeing buses and taxis are among the worst offenders, in

that on sighting a bear they frequently stop and permit their passengers to alight from the vehicle for the purpose of taking pictures and feeding the bears." H.A. deVeber, 3 November 1951; RG 84, a-2-a, vol. 2129, file u212, pt. 2. For a good example of typical encounters, see "Bear clawing incident," 10 July 1962, RG 84, A-2-a, vol. 229, file K212, pt. 2.

27 LAC. J.R.B. Coleman to Johnson, 4 January 1965, RG 84, A-2-a, vol. 2130, file U212, pt. 5.

28 *Kingston Whig Standard*, 15 July 1959. The cartoon was sent on to the parks director. RG 84, A-2-a-, vol. 2130, file U212, pt. 4.

29 LAC. "Catalogue of Motion Picture Films Distributed by the National Parks Bureau," appearing in National Parks files in 1964, RG 84, A-2-a, vol. 2063, file U1117-56, pt. 5.

30 NFBA The first to take on the project was Harry Rowed. "Mammals of the Mountain Parks" Memorandum, National Film Board, 29 April 1955, 54–411.

31 NFBA Michael Spencer to Col. Homer S. Robinson, 4 May 1955, 54-411.

32 NFBA Spencer to Robinson, 5 July 1955, 54-411; David Bairstow in Memorandum, 4 June 1956. Ibid. Bird's qualifications are described in Spencer to J.R.B. Coleman, 27 July 1956, 54-411.

33 LAC. Carrack was retained for a summer contract, Spencer to Robinson, 11 June 1956.

34 NFBA, Proposed Title Slide, and Letter, Michael Spencer to H. S. Robinson, 28 May 1957. 54-411. By 12 June,

the title was changed to "Mammals of the Mountain Parks."

35 NFBA "Commentary," Wildlife in the Rockies, National Film Board Archives, 54-411.

36 The narrator added a cautionary note: "Visitors should avoid the temptation to make friends, or to feed the bears. They are unpredictable, and sometimes dangerous. Their diet ranges from ant eggs to small deer." NFBA "Commentary" Short Version, Wildlife in the Rockies, 54-411.

37 NFBA "Mammals of the Mountain Parks" objective and description, 54-411.

38 As quoted in Reichwein, "Holiday at the Banff School of Fine Arts," 57.

39 LAC. Robinson to Greenlee, 17 January 1961, NAC, RG 84, A-2-a, vol. 2062, file U117, pt. 46.

40 LAC. 4 July 1960, Outline, "Away from it all," RG 84, A-2-a, vol. 2063, file U117-56-19, pt. 1.

41 LAC. Marsha Porte, Review, 'The Enduring Wilderness,' *Film News*, October 1964, in RG 84, A-2-a, vol. 2064, file U117-56-20.

42 LAC. RG 84, A-2-a, vol. 2062, reel T-16023; See RG 84, A-2-a-, vol. 2063 U-117-56-20 for George Stirett to Coleman, 22 October 1962.

43 LAC. S.L. Roberts to Chapman, 28 June 1962, ibid.

44 LAC. Mair to Reeve, 24 December 1964. RG 84, A-2-a-, vol. 2063, file U117-56, pt. 5.

45 LAC. Alex Keen memo, same date, ibid.

46 LAC. The expression was made on 10 September 1958 by the superintendent

of Kootenay National Park, RG 84, A-2-a, vol. 2130, file U212, pt. 3.

47   LAC. Coleman admitted that culling was "one of our most effective measures of control" in a memorandum 22 October 1958, ibid., Supt. G.H.W. Ashley, at Prince Albert, 12 September 1958, was pessimistic: "If we must accept that bears are undesirable in areas of the Park frequented by visitors, it is my belief that the solution to the problem will depend on the application of all of the practical aspects of the suggestions mentioned, including the trapping and destruction of all bears entering such used areas. This will be a continuous seasonal operation, and will eventually result in a very drastic reduction in the bear populations in Parks."

48   LAC. RG 84, A-2-a, vol. 229, T-12954, J 36, Jasper National Park Campground Report, 1963–64.

49   LAC. Western national parks: Cumulative totals for season as at end of October 1962, RG 84, A-2-a, vol. 2130, file U212, pt. IV.

50   LAC. Mitchell memorandum, 6 September 1962, in RG 84, A-2-a, vol. 229. K.B. Mitchell, in Jasper, stated that "up until 1957 it was a rare occurrence to see a bear [in town] but last year for some unknown reason the bear population suddenly increased and the townsite was invaded by about a dozen bears at one time." 9 September 1958, RG 84, A-2-a, vol. 2130, file U212, pt. 3.

51   LAC. R.T. Flanagan, 14 September 1967, RG 84, A-2-a, vol. 2130, file U212, pt. V. It involved a parks worker, Frederick Sturdy, who was mauled at night near the Maligne Lake garbage dump in Jasper in 1965. See

Sid Marty, *The Black Grizzly of Whiskey Creek*, 30.

52   LAC. R.T. Flanagan, 14 September 1967, RG 84, A-2-a, vol. 2130, file U212, pt. V.

53   LAC. Coleman Letter, 21 August 1967, ibid.

54   LAC. "I am afraid there is no information on the ratio of 'wilderness' bears to 'campground' bears on which I can base a statement. Certainly there are sizeable wilderness areas in all the National Parks of the mountains but I do not know if bears living in these areas would not, on occasion, wander into visitor-use areas." J.R.B. Coleman to Johnson, 4 January 1965, RG 84, A-2-a-, vol. 2130, file U212, pt. 5.

55   Stephen Herrero, "Introduction to the Biology and Management of Bears," in *Bears: Their Biology and Management* (Papers of the International Conference on Bear Research and Management, Calgary, Canada, November 1970), (Morges: International Union, 1972), 11–12.

56   "Bighorn" Theatrical Release Publicity, NFB, 1970. National Film Board of Canada website, http://www.onf-nfb.gc.ca.

57   In a note to the author, Schmalz recounted that it "was the avoidable mishandling" of a situation involving a female grizzly and her two cubs by parks wardens that prompted him to propose the film. He had spent time observing and filming the cubs with their mother while they lived "undisturbed" by humans. A few months later, the trio was attracted to a nearby recently opened campground and its easily available food. Wardens then set up a single live trap in which only the

mother ended up being caught. This left two very upset 'orphaned' cubs to wander through the campground. The wardens then shot and killed the cubs. Instead of closing the campground when the grizzly family first appeared, "the campers were given priority and allowed to remain and the bears had to go." Wardens told Schmalz and the public that the cubs had been simply "tranquilized." "Apparently they were afraid of park visitor reaction to the killing. However, it was clear to me that … [o]nce educated, park visitors would understand and tolerate campgrounds or trails closures when bears were present. They would be motivated to be careful with keeping their food and other attractants from bears and to respect their wildness. I knew a good film would help do this." Personal communication, Schmalz to author, 7 July 2010.

58 Herrero described Wilf Ethrington's mauling in *Bear Attacks*, 45–47. The impact of Ethrington's death on parks wardens is well described by Sid Marty, *The Black Grizzly of Whiskey Creek*, 33.

59 NFBA, Schmalz, "Bears and Man Film Report, December 1974," *Bears and Man* correspondence file.

60 Telephone Interview with Bill Schmalz, 18 August 2008; in the rough cuts, Schmalz had included the shot because it showed what happened when tourists fed bears, "the consequences of their actions. But the park service did not want that in the film."

61 Schmalz interview, 18 August 2008: "We had to write for [Dan George]. He was getting on by then, maybe he was getting tired. He would fall asleep in his chair, and it took two or three or four sessions working with him, trying to get him to say his lines. Finally we had him read the script. We both worked on that (the lines that include the spirit of the great bear)."

62 NFBA *Bears and Man* script, undated.

63 Shepard Kretch III, *The Ecological Indian: Myth and History* (New York: W.W. Norton, 1999), 20–24.

64 Schmalz remembered that teenagers on the scene had initially feared the bears, but, after a half hour of watching other tourists feeding them, they gained their bravado to join in.

65 Communicated to the author, 15 June 2010.

66 Herrero disagreed with the view of those advocating eradication and supported the need for public education, "to be carried out by parks personnel, scientists and wildlife appreciators." Herrero, "Introduction to the Biology and Management of Bears," 13.

67 Tina Loo, "From Wildlife to Wild Places," *States of Nature: Conserving Canada's Widllife in the Twentieth Century* (Vancouver: UBC Press, 2006), 183–209.

Hunting, Timber Harvesting, and Precambrian Beauties: The Scientific Reinterpretation of La Mauricie National Park's Landscape History, 1969–1975

Olivier Craig-Dupont
Département d'aménagement
Université de Montréal

Introduction

The idea that national parks have a beneficial influence on the environment characterizes a dominant – although increasingly debated – trend in North American parks history.[1] Many historians have shared the conviction of the governmental agencies that they study: that national parks protect one of the fundamental dimensions of North American history in great unspoiled nature and true wilderness.[2] In that sense, those scholars followed the seminal claims of American historian Roderick Nash, who argued in 1970 that parks "reflect some of the central values and experiences in American culture."[3] From the Sierra Nevada to the Canadian Rocky Mountains, wilderness has effectively been the pride of North American political, intellectual, and artistic elites. This is evidenced by the famous naturalist John Muir (1838–1914) and the twenty-sixth president of the United States, Theodore Roosevelt (1858–1919), who both campaigned for the creation of the first national parks in the United States near the end of the nineteenth century; by transcendentalist poets Henry David Thoreau (1817–1862) and Ralph Waldo Emerson (1803–1882), who philosophized about the moral and spiritual virtues of wilderness; and by the Canadian painters of the Group of Seven, who illustrated the magnificent landscapes of Canada. All were sensitive to the sublime beauty of North American wilderness. Their masterworks, such as Muir's Yellowstone Park, Thoreau's *Walden; or, Life in the Woods*,[4] or Tom Thomson's (1877–1917) *The Jack Pine* have all contributed in shaping the idea of wilderness as a fundamental component of North American culture and national history.

But recent works in environmental history have criticized this concept of wilderness, especially that of national parks. A growing number of American and Canadian historians have demonstrated how national park wilderness is a powerful cultural product. Following William Cronon's myth-breaking essay on "The Trouble with Wilderness," they have shown how national parks served state initiatives to dispossess native inhabitants of hunting and living grounds, or to rework inhabited landscapes into human-free, "pristine" wilderness.[5] Although growing in number, those critical voices are still somewhat marginal, "voices crying in the wilderness" as described by historian Alan MacEachern,[6] compared to the strength of the image sanctioned by Parks Canada for the public imagination. Indeed, the wilderness ideal is still deeply ingrained in many laudatory representations of national parks. A careful look at this history shows that, since the very creation of the first national parks of Banff and Jasper in 1885 and 1907, Parks Canada has often used this idealized representation of wilderness to promote its parks.[7] Even today, its website reads that national parks:

> [...] celebrate the beauty and infinite variety of our country. Protected and preserved for all Canadians and for the world, each is a sanctuary in which nature is allowed to evolve in its

own way, as it has done since the dawn of time. Each provides a haven, not only for plants and animals, but also for the human spirit.[8]

As for the Parks Canada *Guiding Principles and Operational Policies* of 2008, they stipulate that the National Parks of Canada serve to "protect for all time representative natural areas of Canadian significance in a system of national parks, and to encourage public understanding, appreciation, and enjoyment of this natural heritage so as to leave it unimpaired for future generations."[9]

If this mandate appears today as self-evident, during its history Parks Canada has used a number of discourses – scientific, economic, political, and touristic – to promote its national parks. At different moments in the evolution of environmental thought in North America, Parks Canada has promoted its parks as resource reserves, as icons celebrating the picturesque landscapes of the country, or as natural areas protecting the dynamics of natural ecosystems in the Canadian environment. Canada initially created national parks at Banff and Jasper using the utilitarian logic of protecting resources for their eventual commercial uses. In these parks, the government of John A. Macdonald permitted the exploitation of resources such as timber, mines, or pasturing even as it encouraged the development of tourism.[10] Only at the end of the 1920s did certain civil servants of the agency begin questioning this approach. The first commissioner of the Dominion Parks Branch, James B. Harkin, contributed especially to changing the parks' industrial mandates. By 1927, Harkin was arguing that "areas deemed suitable for a National Park must possess scenic beauty and recreational qualities of a character so outstanding and unusual as to be properly classified National rather than merely local."[11] It was during Harkin's administration, which lasted from 1911 to 1936, that "scenic beauty" and the picturesque nature of Canadian landscapes became essential in justifying the protection of the already established parks, as well as in the selection of the sites of future national parks.[12]

The transformation of parks' mandates suggests that their "wilderness" state is, in fact, a social construct.[13] The protected environment of a national park is an amalgam of its natural environment's material dimensions and the multitude of its social representations. Different stakeholders, such as Parks Canada, industries, Aboriginal populations, or local inhabitants who use the territory for recreational purposes, articulate such different representations, and all have views on the territory being made into a park. This connection between environment and society creates those hybrid spaces, the parks, which consist equally of material and symbolic dimensions. La Mauricie National Park provides an exceptional field of investigation for understanding the social construct of this material and symbolic "double nature."[14] Established in 1970, this park is one of the first in Canada to preserve marsh ecosystems and other types of wetlands. But the great sub-boreal forests of the Canadian Shield, which make up the largest ecosystem of this park, have supported a thriving industrial activity for centuries in the Mauricie region. This is particularly the case for forestry, a true pillar of the local economy. This industrial presence also opened up the territory to hunters and fishermen, who exploited its game and fish resources from the beginning of the twentieth century. Although diminished by the end of the 1950s with a marked economic depression, these industrial and recreational activities were still well in place within the Mauricie landscape at the time the national park was established.

Considering these human-modified landscapes of the Mauricie region, this chapter analyzes how Parks Canada succeeded in creating here "a representative natural area of Canadian interest," where, according to the official history of the park, the visitor could find an "atmosphere of primitive wilderness …, much as it was when discovered by the early travelers and native Indians so many years ago."[15] In order to justify a national park in the hybrid landscapes of the Mauricie region, Parks Canada would have to transform local territory, with all its industrial and recreational imprints, to correspond to this wilderness ideal. To achieve this, the agency presented the natural and cultural history of the territory through concepts taken from the science of ecology, while at the same time erasing any contradictory human dimensions of the landscape. Instead of a socially neutral space preserved by a legal and scientific framework, La Mauricie National Park thus appears, in the course of this chapter, as a tool for structuring landscapes and for transforming local territorial characteristics in accordance with Parks Canada's wilderness ideal.

The "Natural Beauties" of Canada and the Project of a Park in the Mauricie

The idea of a recreational park in the Mauricie arose during a period of profound changes for this industrial region. In the early 1970s, the Mauricie, like other resource-based regions of Quebec such as the Gaspé and the Lower St. Lawrence, was having difficulty adapting an economy traditionally based on resource and manufacturing industries, such as mines, timber, or textiles, towards those of the tertiary sector or service activities.[16] Early on, both the federal and provincial governments recognized outdoor tourism as an activity likely to stimulate economic recovery for these regions.[17] Increase in outdoor activities in the 1960s, as well as interventions by the expanding Canadian welfare state, lead to the creation of numerous federal and provincial programs aimed at developing recreation and touristic projects in these parts of Quebec. For example, the Bureau d'aménagement de l'Est-du-Québec (BAEQ) supported a series of touristic initiatives in eastern Quebec, notably the creation of the first national park in Québec, at Forillon on the Gaspé in 1971.[18] Established by the province's Liberal government in 1963, the BAEQ enjoyed a significant input of funds from federal programs, such as those from the Canada Land Inventory (1961), the Fund for Rural Economic Development (FRED, 1966), and those originating from the *Agricultural Rehabilitation and Development Act* (ARDA, 1966), designed to introduce economic diversification into single-industry peripheral regions. But the federal and provincial governments were aware that national parks were enjoying greater popularity. In 1966, the Pearson government created a new Department of Indian Affairs and Northern Development to govern the management of "Indian affairs, Eskimo affairs, the Northwest Territories, the Yukon Territory, the national parks, the national battlegrounds, the historical sites and monuments, the migratory bird and wildlife."[19] In July 1968, the federal government entrusted this substantial mandate to a young minister from Shawinigan, also a Member of Parliament from the local riding of Saint-Maurice-Laflèche: the Honourable Jean Chrétien.

From the start, Chrétien indicated that he was a fervent promoter of national parks. During the "Canadian National Parks: Today and Tomorrow" conference held in Calgary in October 1968, Minister Chrétien outlined what he intended to do for the promotion and improvement of the Canadian parks system. He agreed with many at the conference about the pressures of popularity: too many visitors visiting too few parks were threatening the "natural heritage" that parks represented. Chrétien therefore proposed creating more national parks throughout Canada, with a minimum of one national park in each province. In his estimation, "to achieve an adequate representation of Canada's heritage at suitable scale, we would require forty to sixty new national parks in a complete system."[20] With a public commitment (formalized a year later in the parks policy of 1969) and equipped with a sizeable budget, Chrétien suggested the creation of a second national park for the province of Québec, in the Mauricie region.

Chrétien believed strongly that the landscapes of the Mauricie were particularly suited to the status of a national park. In a speech addressed to the committee for the national park in the Mauricie, he confirmed that:

> ... in a splendid region such as this one, I don't need to convince you of the merits of conservation and of the joys of outdoor recreation. The Mauricie region has just as many picturesque landscapes than the most beautiful national parks that I have visited. [There is] no need also to insist on the economic advantages that the whole Mauricie region would gain from the creation of a national park, as well as from its association with the system of Canadian National Parks.... As in the case of Kootenay, Kejimkujik, Yoho, Banff, Jasper and all the others, your national park will celebrate the beauty and grandeur of our country.[21]

If the landscapes of Western Canada sufficed to make Banff and Jasper parks popular, picturesque, and lucrative, then the "natural beauties" of the proposed La Mauricie Park could have the same effect on the Mauricie. As C.J. Taylor points out in his contribution to this book, Banff was effectively the flagship of the Canadian parks system in the 1960s. Accordingly, park committees in the Mauricie organized many field trips to Banff and other iconic parks between 1969 and 1971, in order to promote the project of a national park to the local population.[22] However, the National Parks Branch still faced the challenge of making a picturesque park out of an industrial landscape: a substantial and complex undertaking in a place that still bore the imprint of timber harvesting and fish and game exploitation. It is precisely these human dimensions that the Branch would try to erase from La Mauricie Park, as it attempted to turn a sow's ear into a "wild" silk purse.

Hunting and Timber Harvesting: The Industrial and Recreational Imprint in the Mauricie

The industrial and recreational dimensions of the proposed park were still alive and well in 1970. This was particularly the case with timber harvesting, one of the pillars of the regional economy since the construction of the first logging camp in 1830 by Edward Grieve.

One forest company in particular, Consolidated-Bathurst Limited, had exploited different forest concessions and private lands – which together made up almost the entirety of the site of the future park – until the end of the 1960s. In addition to concessions of Crown lands under provincial jurisdiction and a territory of 26 square kilometres obtained from the federal government as private lands, this company also managed an experimental forest of fifteen square kilometres, created in 1918 by the Canadian Forest Service, and a spruce plantation established by pulp and paper company La Laurentide in 1915. Consolidated-Bathurst used parts of the Mattawin and Saint-Maurice rivers (which were to form parts of the northeastern boundaries of the park) for stream driving and constructed dams to regulate the water level of certain lakes.[23] Meanwhile, another forest company, Domtar, was exploiting a forest concession in the southern part of the watershed of Lake Wapizagonke.

Signs of this forest exploitation were still clearly visible in the Mauricie at the end of the 1960s. Indeed, the first master plan of La Mauricie National Park cautioned in 1971 that "visitors strolling through paths might have the impression that the forest is considerably disturbed, even dilapidated, for he will have access only to the areas more recently affected by logging."[24] The imprint left by forest harvesting was particularly apparent because a vast logging road network ensured access to the territory. With the blessing of the forest companies, the local population used these roads to reach the interior of the forest to fish and hunt.

FIG. I. LA COUPE DU BOIS EN MAURICIE. 1921. [CENTRE INTERUNIVERSITAIRE D'ÉTUDES QUÉBÉCOISES, COLLECTION RENÉ HARDY, FONDS GROUPE DE RECHERCHE SUR LA MAURICIE, N60-365.]

Fishing and hunting was indeed a popular activity in the Mauricie. Since 1883, when the Shawinigan Club was established, numerous private hunting and fishing clubs had occupied vast stretches of territory. These were mainly owned by wealthy Canadian or American businessmen, but some of the smaller clubs were also frequented by the locals, who enjoyed the Mauricie's fish and game resources.[25] Among the 450 private clubs present in the region by the end of the 1960s, sixteen held lands designated for the future park.[26] The government of Quebec began nationalizing these private lands to create "controlled exploitation zones" (zones d'exploitation contrôlée, ZEC).[27]

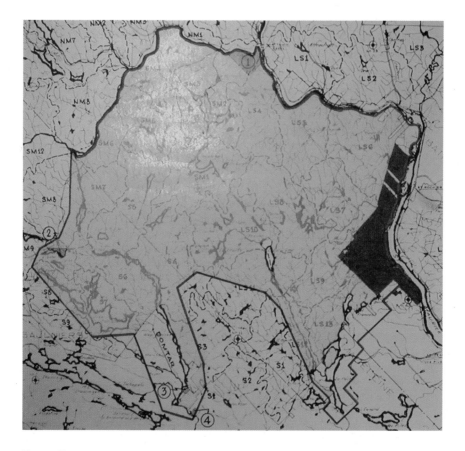

Fig. 2. Exploitations and land holdings before 1972 on the territory of
La Mauricie National Park, 1959–1972. In yellow, the provincial forest
concessions of Consolidated-Bathurst (CB); in brown, the private lands of CB
(Grand-Mère spruce plantation); in white, at the southwestern edge of the
park, the lands of Domtar. [Source: Consolidated-Bathurst Ltd, Exploitation
et tenure des terres avant 1972 sur le territoire du parc national de la
Mauricie, Université du Québec à Trois-Rivières, Map Library, +615.43gcrkin (q)
caqtu.]

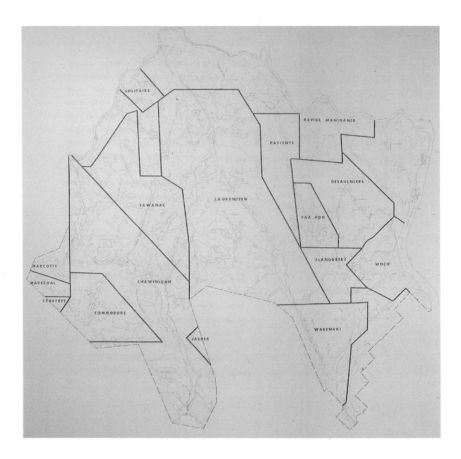

FIG. 3. Map of the hunting and fishing clubs that share the territory of the park before 1970. [Source: Aménagement et exploitation faunique antérieurs à la création du parc national de la Mauricie (1970), Service de la conservation et des ressources naturelles, 1979, 4–5. © Parks Canada Agency.]

But erasing their presence was more laborious, in part because these clubs had constructed numerous buildings and hunting camp facilities throughout the future park. Park superintendents' weekly reports indicate that ongoing cleanup work was aimed specifically at eliminating these structures. According to one of these reports, it is only in 1973 that:

> ... garbage was removed and the debris of an old saw mill were removed and burnt, and the dump sites of old clubs were cleaned up. In the Wapizagonke sector, the dump of the Shawinigan Club, where garbage had been accumulated for more than fifty years, has been completely emptied.... At Lake Wapizagonke, all the camps of the Shawinigan Club were demolished and burnt, except for one garage.... The five camps of the Désaulniers Club were demolished and burnt.... The camps at the western end of Lake Maréchal are demolished and burnt, and at Lake Waber, all that is left of the Consolidated-Bathurst camps is the section used for the construction site office.[28]

In addition to these buildings, and rather more seriously, the clubs had also undertaken substantial "improvements" to the local ecosystem in order to support their hunting and fishing activities. In 1969, for example, the Woco Club had a dam built at the outlet of Lake Bouchard to block the access to white suckers (*Catostomus commersonii*). As early as 1910, the Shawinigan Club introduced Atlantic salmon to the region, while other clubs experimented with speckled trout (*Salvelinus fontinalis*) and lake trout (*Salvelinus namaycush*); eventually these clubs introduced fish into more than twenty lakes within the future park. The Laurentian Club went so far as to fertilize two of its lakes in 1947 with seven tons of phosphate fertilizer in order to increase fish size. The same club also tried planting wild rice (*Zizania aquatica*) in three of its lakes to improve waterfowl production.[29] In short, a variety of local stakeholders had occupied and modified the territory of the future national park. Many of them, whether as employee, tourist, or resident, knew the Mauricie region and its resources well. In order to destabilize this industrial and recreational past and then reinvent it as wilderness, the Parks Branch would have to reinterpret the region's natural and cultural history.

The Scientific Reinterpretation of the Mauricie's Landscapes

Science played a key role in the establishment of the national park in the Mauricie region. By focusing on the natural environment, using data collected during inventories of its geology, fauna, and flora, federal scientists were able to construct a new and authoritative "natural history" for La Mauricie National Park. This official portrait of the park as wilderness erased certain dimensions of its industrial and recreational past. Maps of bioclimatic domains and ecosystem-based zoning plans presented the landscapes within park boundaries in an abstract and non-human way, simplifying any social complexity.[30] In the same way wildlife films funded by the agency sought to transform perceptions of the Rockies into wild "bear country" (as discussed by George Colpitts in this book), the Parks Branch used scientific abstractions to erase a human presence in favour of a boreal wilderness in the Mauricie.

During the 1970s, the biological and ecological sciences held an ambiguous status in the management of national parks in both Canada and the United States.[31] Scientists working for the Canadian government and the U.S. National Park Service had to deal with the traditional mandates for development or tourism, while producing new knowledge about ecological health (this growing tension between tourism and environmental protection is also discussed by C.J. Taylor). But what is surprising is that in the case of La Mauricie National Park, scientific findings were used *for* touristic imperatives instead of as "pure" research for the advancement of knowledge. For example, when the head of the Department of Chemistry and Biology of the Université du Québec à Trois-Rivières wrote to Chrétien in October 1970 to propose "the establishment of a biology station on or near the territory of the park, for purposes of monitoring, teaching and research,"[32] Chrétien referred to the parks policy of 1969 as a reason not to grant permission, arguing that "it goes without saying that national parks are not established mainly for scientific research." Research in the national parks was to be limited to "the observation of natural conditions, without taking any specimens and without any manipulation of the environment."[33] Indeed, the 1969 document specified that "the main goal of a national park is to resemble a museum or an art gallery."[34] The fauna inventory work compiled by the interpretation service at La Mauricie National Park confirms the Parks Branch's interest in using scientific findings to promote "spectacular" aspects of nature for tourism. In an internal memo in 1971, the park's head of natural resources, Pierre Desmeules, notified the Ottawa head office that "consideration should be given to attempting to re-establish populations of fur-bearers such as marten, otter and fisher. These species have decreased markedly and their re-establishment could be beneficial, although they are not as spectacular from a publicity point of view."[35] The subordination of ecology to the agency's traditional mandate of highlighting the "natural beauties" of the country is especially noticeable in the master plans produced during the establishment of the park. These were designed to provide a framework for the park's development and ensure its harmonious integration within the national parks system. They also served to render official and operational representations of nature – and representations of the park *as* natural.[36] In particular, the master plans achieved a scientific reinterpretation of the Mauricie landscape by characterizing the new national park as "The Laurentian Heritage."

From 5 to 15 June 1971, an "interpretive specialist" from the Branch, R.C. Gray, visited the territory of the future park with a working copy of the preliminary master plan drafted by the Société d'exploitation des ressources éducatives du Québec (SEREQ). SEREQ relied on the dominant landscape architecture practices of the time to make this plan, best represented by the ecological planning approaches developed by Scottish-American landscape architect Ian McHarg. In effect, using McHarg's system of transparent plastic coloured maps, SEREQ proposed a layered cartography of the multiple bio-geographical and human dimensions of the future park. With this proto-GIS cartography, SEREQ established different zones of activities (i.e., "special preservation areas," "Wilderness areas," "Natural environment areas," and "Outdoor recreational areas") based on the "ecological values" of the land.[37] Those four zones provided the basis of the future park's infrastructures, such as camping sites, roads, picnic areas, a "boating complex," and trails.

With this first plan in hand, Gray was to evaluate its quality with regard to the "interpretive possibilities" of the Mauricie territory. Although generally satisfied with the work of the SEREQ, he argued that the authors were unable to recognize "the primary values inherent to this landscape." He went on to say that:

La Mauricie National Park is, at present, almost completely unspoiled in terms of prime wilderness lake and forest land located very near industrial centers of the lower St. Maurice valley. Granted, there are forests areas that have been logged, areas where logging has only recently ceased and sites of major logging camps (Consolidated Bathurst) still within the Park area. Still, the Park contains clear, unpolluted lakes of varied dimensions, wide zones of mixed forests, pure stands of hardwood, swamps, fresh-water marshes, streams, cascades, waterfalls, beaches, bogs, valleys and rivers; all the components of the natural wilderness of the Laurentian Shield.

Gray continued by defining more clearly what he believes the authors of the SEREQ document have failed to recognize in this landscape. In his judgment,

… the outstanding feature of La Mauricie National Park is not its lakes and forests, or streams or waterfalls considered as separate land forms. The sum of these parts is more than their separate entities. It is the wilderness that makes La Mauricie National Park a vital addition to the system of National Parks in Canada. It is the wilderness that dictates the value system we must use when assessing priorities in this new National Park territory.

In short, he concluded that "La Mauricie National Park is nothing less than a true 'Laurentian Wilderness,'" confirming eloquently the Parks Branch's mission of recognizing true wild nature and promoting its good uses.[38] Gray disliked the overly utilitarian emphasis of the draft master plan, particularly its zoning arrangement. He proposed "radically" reducing the zones dedicated to intensive activities or moving them to more "appropriate" areas. For example, Gray suggested clustering campground development near the old Grand-Mère plantation in the southeastern part of the park, "since this is a completely artificial plant community." He also recommended changing the zoning of lakes Maréchal, Weber, and Atikamac, located in the western

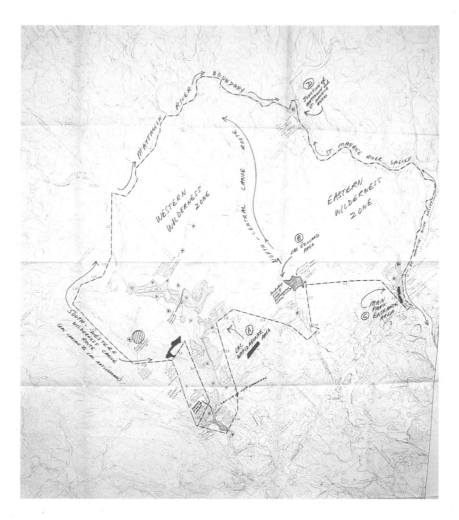

Fig. 4. Proposed zoning changes in La Mauricie National Park's backcountry by "interpretive specialist" R.C. Gray. [Source: Bureau central de classement, c8373/L1, Visit of interpretive specialist, R.C. Gray, 9–15 June 1971. © Parks Canada Agency.]

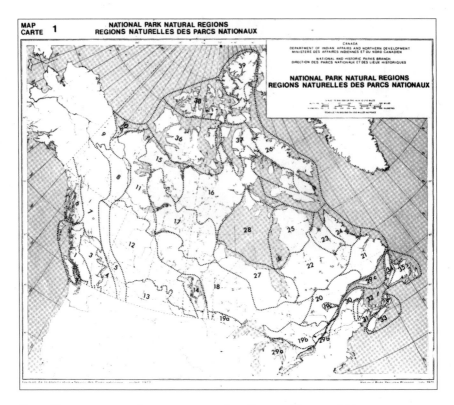

MAP 1
CARTE

NATIONAL PARK NATURAL REGIONS
REGIONS NATURELLES DES PARCS NATIONAUX

Fig. 5. The thirty-nine "natural regions" of Canada. [Source: Manuel de planification du réseau des parcs nationaux, 1972, 9. © Parks Canada Agency.]

part of the park, from type III, a "Natural Environment Area" (a type of buffer zone between areas of intensive recreational activities and the "back country") to type II, a "Wilderness Area" (which permitted only activities without significant impact on the environment, such as hiking, canoeing or camping). According to Gray, "only then will the lake country of the south-western portion of the Park be true wilderness and officially considered as such."[39] Parks Canada took Gray's recommendations into account and incorporated them into its second temporary master plan in 1975.[40]

Gray's comments give us some indication of the process by which a "true Laurentian Wilderness" was constructed in La Mauricie National Park. In order for visitors to be able to recognize the wilderness expected of national parks, official zoning plans had to initially circumscribe and label it as such. In the same way as the National Parks Branch was trying to contain long-established towns within or near Banff National Park by the 1960s (as C.J. Taylor discusses), this rezoning in La Mauricie National Park was meant to transform the forms and functions of the backcountry. As a tool for structuring the territory, the zoning plan materializes the abstract representation of different kinds of nature in national parks.

This new zoning representing the "wild" backcountry of La Mauricie National Park was only the first step necessary in reconstructing the history of the Mauricie landscape. Following the new policy of system planning after 1970, the Branch integrated La Mauricie National Park into the management plan laid out in the 1972 National Parks System's Planning Manual. This manual, largely inspired by a similar plan from the U.S. National Parks Service, aimed at "formulating a plan ensuring the creation of a network of National Parks that would be a judicious sample of the landscapes and natural attractions of Canada."[41] Equally important, this plan "must be objective and use criteria that all those interested can accept and understand" – so it is to be "based on the natural sciences and be free of all political or social impediments." This manual, then, was meant to integrate all of Canada's national parks into a scientific grid of land management and land categorization that largely excluded local cultural practices. In order to free it of "all political or social impediments," the Parks Branch adopted the maturing discourse of scientific ecology. The 1972 manual proposed a nation-wide territorial classification based on "natural regions" and "natural history themes worthy of representation." These themes were to be the "primary imperatives" in choosing the site of a future national park – *together with* the "outdoor recreation needs" of a given region. The manual also identified which geological and ecological features best conveyed "the essence of the natural regions."[42] The Systems Plan defined thirty-nine "natural regions" covering all of Canadian territory; these regions are still in use in the national parks system.

As a new park, La Mauricie was carefully positioned to exemplify this new approach to park planning. First, the 1972 Planning Manual designated La Mauricie Park as part of the "Canadian Shield" region, also identified as "19 b – Centre of the Precambrian region of the St. Lawrence and Great Lakes." Then, it identified the themes of "Precambrian," "the Age of primitive invertebrates," and the ecosystems typical of the "Great Lakes – St. Lawrence forest region, section 4a, Laurentians." Finally, in a stance that clearly showed the Parks Branch's new commitment to nation-building-through-science activity,[43] the manual specified which "natural values worthy of being represented"[44] would best illustrate these themes. For La Mauricie, this was the presence of the Canadian Shield, chains of lakes and rivers, the Great Lakes – St. Lawrence forest, and the "steep point of contact with the centre of the St. Lawrence lowlands."[45] In short, the manual clearly presented the "natural values" of the landscape as being the primary interest of national parks. It contained no mention of local uses or of the social and cultural history of the landscapes made into parks. In the specific case of La Mauricie, forest or fish and game exploitation were nowhere mentioned, although they had, as we have noted, an important role in shaping the region. By using concepts taken from geology and ecology, as well as maps that rendered these new scientific representations of the landscape concrete, Parks Canada generally succeeded in recreating its wilderness ideal on this territory.[46]

In such a wilderness, human activity is, by definition, absent.[47] Although the agency recognized the traces of a past human presence in La Mauricie National Park, the humanized characteristics of the newly protected ecosystems became, at best, artifacts of the "museum" of natural history that national parks were supposed to be.[48] An internal memo from the director of the Parks Branch in Ottawa illustrates very well this effacement of the social and cultural dimensions of the Mauricie landscape. This memo outlined choices by the head office regarding material presented at the official opening of the park's interpretation centre on 4 August 1972.[49] After a visit to Ottawa by Gilles Ouellette, who was in charge of the park's interpretation service, Branch Director John I. Nicol decided that the "natural history" of the park should be divided into four thematic sections: the "Laurentian Uplands," the "Diversity of Forest Types," the "Aquatic Environment," and "Human History." Nicol then selected a collection of objects that were characteristic of each theme: samples of gneiss and photos of taluses and eskers to represent the "Uplands"; approximately thirty samples of nuts, insects, and stuffed animals for the "Wildlife Mosaic"; and about twenty photos of fish and specimens of aquatic insects for the "Aquatic Web." For the last theme, "Human History," out of the ten or so objects proposed by the regional director, such as axes, logger cant hooks, and sculptures of a trapper and a logger, he retained only three photographs of a canoe, a logging camp, and stream driving and a few Aboriginal artifacts.[50] Compared to its geological, faunistic and floristic history, La Mauricie's human history was limited to a "folklorized" presence marked by the use of Aboriginal artifacts[51] and by photos of industrial and recreational activity that the Branch considered over and done with in this part of the Mauricie region. It would be indigenous peoples in the north who would more effectively challenge this selective exclusion of human practices – or *historical* practices – that has been part of the institutional culture of Parks Canada.

Without the scale and grandeur of the mountain parks, the agency nevertheless (re)created, through scientific representations, a significant wilderness in La Mauricie. This "scientification" of the landscape was evident by 1975, when Parks Canada presented a temporary master plan for the park:

> [...] an overview of the territory of the park allows one to observe a great homogeneity of the elements composing the biophysical environment. We observe a uniform distribution of interesting sites that can be retained as having potential for interpretation. This uniformity is also found at the level of the comparisons and evaluation among the components. The absence of large disparities among the elements composing this potential brings us to pay a particular attention to natural groupings that can occur at certain sites. Taken from a more general perspective, several isolated phenomena of moderate importance can create, in a given sector, as a set, a high interpretation potential.[52]

The plan encapsulates several elements of this essay. The search for "interesting sites that can be retained as having potential for interpretation" reveals the traditional sensitivity of Parks Canada for the picturesque in Canadian nature. The first Canadian parks established in the Rocky Mountains at the end of the nineteenth century, with their "large disparities" in geology, were the reference for deciding what is "interesting" in the Canadian landscape (and the plan asserts that the Mauricie territory is devoid of this type of "large disparities"). Taken separately, the biophysical characteristics of La Mauricie National Park, such as the marshes or great conifer forests, are phenomena of only "moderate importance." Seeking new arguments to justify the presence of a park, then, Parks Canada used the science and mapping of ecology to create a landscape that is scientifically significant, transforming the Mauricie territory into a new "representative natural area of Canadian interest."[53] The key moment of this scientific reinterpretation was the integration of the park into the 1972 planning manual's classification system, which was to be "based solely on natural sciences and thus detached from any political or social considerations" ("fondé sur les sciences naturelles et être dégagé de toute entrave politique ou sociale").[54] At that moment, the park, too, became a scientific object, completely detached from the social and cultural web that surrounds it and runs through it.

Conclusion

Far from being a natural area composed of biogeographical dimensions, La Mauricie National Park appears in this chapter as an object laden with interpretations of what wilderness should be, according to Parks Canada. In considering the natural and cultural history of landscapes, we can compare national parks to historical productions. They are the materialization of a discourse that has its roots in the history of human relations to the land. Indeed, in establishing La Mauricie National Park, Parks Canada joined an important current of environmental thought that contrasts the wild frontier of the North American west with the industrial landscapes of the East.[55] During its history, Parks Canada institutionalized this representation of wilderness, first through its iconic parks in the Canadian Rockies, and then sought to transpose it to the Mauricie territory. The area made into a park therefore bears the cultural stamp of the creator agency, in the same way that it bore the industrial and recreational territorial marks of the Mauricie's human presence.

This chapter also shows how scientific rationality is, like the environment, never neutral. Scientific discourse, especially that of ecology, has the power to "naturalize" the institutional culture of agencies in charge of national parks. When Parks Canada presents its ideals of wilderness through scientific discourse, and with material support such as maps and master plans, these ideals become a tangible reality. The materialized representations of the environment that are the national parks can then transform the territory and its uses, in relation to the political, economic, scientific, or cultural objectives of the institutions that promote the parks. The map of the thirty-nine "natural regions" of the 1972 Planning Manual speaks volumes in this respect. Through concepts taken from biology and geology, the federal agency presented Canada as a totally integrated geographical unit, where provincial political boundaries – as well as their associated social issues – disappear under the scientific lenses. Like Hamber Provincial Park served as a gambit to involve Ottawa in the development of the Canadian Selkirk region (as Ben Bradley discusses in this book), the science offered in the case of La Mauricie National Park contributed in strengthening federal power in Quebec.[56] This effaces local territoriality in favour of another promoted by a government agency in charge of the management and protection of the environment. In a radical way, this can be seen as a subtle form of cultural colonialism (a concept raised by Brad Martin in his essay here). The new scientifically informed parks of the 1970s, like the one in La Mauricie, effectively served to control local population activities in accordance with Parks Canada's idea of wilderness and to "educate" park visitors about the agency's preferred relationships with the environment.

More ethnological analysis of protected areas in Canada, of their social as well as ecological histories, would illuminate the multiple trajectories that have constructed these environments. Such an analysis would reveal the social complexity of contemporary Canadian landscapes and the issues at stake. As I. S. MacLaren critically demonstrates, even if not established in apparently humanized landscapes, as in Jasper's case, national parks now support – and always did – a rich and complex web of human practices and relationships to the land. Those relationships question the very notion of wilderness, especially, as we have seen, when parks are established in long-inhabited lands, such as in the Mauricie. More studies on the material and symbolic ties between local inhabitants and conservation areas might reveal the existence of territorial uses that are beneficial for the environment, or that support the sustainability of natural resources. Those studies in environmental history and cultural geography would surely help support Parks Canada's mandate of promoting protected areas that adequately reflect the biogeographical richness, as well as the social and cultural diversity, of the Canadian environment.

NOTES

1 This chapter is based on my master's thesis, *Idéal de nature sauvage et transformation des territorialités au parc national de la Mauricie, 1969–1977*, Université du Québec à Trois-Rivières, 2008, 130 pages. Many thanks to my supervisor, Professor Stéphane Castonguay, Chairholder of the Canada Research Chair in the Environmental History of Québec.

2 For examples of stories celebrating national parks, see: W.F. Lothian, *A Brief History of Canada's National Parks* (Ottawa: Parks Canada, 1987); Kevin McNamee, "From Wild Places to Endangered Places: A History of Canada's National Parks," in *Parks and Protected Areas in Canada: Planning and Management*, ed. Philip Dearden and Rick Rollins, 21–49 (New York: Oxford University Press, 2002); Kevin McNamee, "Preserving Canada's Wilderness Legacy: A Perspective on Protected Areas," in *Protected Areas and the Regional Planning Imperative in North America: Integrating Nature Conservation and Sustainable Development*, ed. J.G. Nelson et al., 25–44 (Calgary: University of Calgary Press, 2003); R.G. Wright and D.J. Mattson, "The Origins and Purposes of National Parks and Protected Areas," in *National Parks and Protected Areas: Their Role in Environmental Protection*, ed. R.G. Wright, 3–14 (Blackwell Science, 1996).

3 Roderick Nash, "The American Invention of National Parks," *American Quarterly* 22, no. 3 (1970): 726.

4 Henry-David Thoreau, *Walden: or, Life in the Woods ; and on the Duty of Civil Disobedience* (New York: Signet Classic, 1999).

5 William Cronon, "The Trouble with Wilderness: Or, Getting Back to the Wrong Nature," *Environmental History* 1, no. 1 (1996): 13; Karl Jacoby, *Crimes against Nature: Squatters, Poachers, Thieves, and the Hidden History of American Conservation* (Berkeley: University of California Press, 2003); John Sandlos, *Hunters at the Margin: Native People and Wildlife Conservation in the Northwest Territories* (Vancouver: UBC Press, 2007); Alan MacEachern, *Natural Selections: National Parks in Atlantic Canada, 1935–1970* (Montreal: McGill-Queen's University Press, 2001), 328; J. Keri Cronin, "Manufacturing National Park Nature: Photography, Ecology and the Wilderness Industry of Jasper National Park," (PhD dissertation, Kingston, Queen's University, 2004), 419.

6 Alan MacEachern, "Voices Crying in the Wilderness: Recent Works in Canadian Environmental History," *Acadiensis* 31, no. 2 (2002): 215–26.

7 The federal agency responsible for Canada's national parks changes names several times during its history. From 1966 to 1973, it is known as the National and Historic Parks Branch. From 1973 onwards, it is named Parks Canada. Much of the development of the park at La Mauricie occurs before 1973, so this essay accordingly uses both names.

8 http://www.pc.gc.ca/progs/np-pn/res-syst_e.asp [Consulted 31 August 2008].

9 *Parks Canada Guiding Principles and Operational Policies*. http://www.pc.gc.ca/eng/docs/pc/poli/princip/sec2/part2a/part2a2.aspx [21 July 2008].

10 Kevin McNamee, "Preserving Canada's Wilderness Legacy"; MacEachern, *Natural Selections*, 328; R.C. Brown, "The Doctrine of Usefulness: Natural Resources and National Policy in Canada", in *Canadian Parks in Perspective*, ed. J.G. Nelson and R.C. Scace, 46–62 (Montreal: Harvest House, 1970); C.J. Taylor, "Legislating Nature: The National Parks Act of 1930," *Canadian Issues* 13 (1991): 127; Janet Foster, *Working for Wildlife: The Beginning of Preservation in Canada* (Toronto: University of Toronto Press, 1978), 6.

11 Harkin to C.D. Richard, 13 June 1927, in Taylor, "Legislating Nature," 133.

12 Taylor, "Legislating Nature," 5; MacEachern, *Natural Selections*, 23ff.

13 A truism of the environmental historiography since Cronon's *Uncommon Ground: Rethinking the Human Place in Nature*, (New York: W.W. Norton, 1996), 561.

14 K. Olwig, "Reinventing Common Nature: Yosemite and Mount Rushmore – A Meandering Tale of a Double Nature," in *Uncommon Ground: Toward Reinventing Nature*, ed. W. Cronon, 379–408 (New York: W.W. Norton, 1995).

15 Lothian, *A Brief History of Canada's National Parks*, 144.

16 Patrick Moquay, "La référence régionale au Québec. Les visions étatiques de la région et leurs incarnations," in *L'institutionnalisation du territoire au Canada*, J.P. Augustin, 92ff. (Québec: Presses de l'Université Laval, 1996); René Hardy and Normand Séguin, eds., *Histoire de la Mauricie* (Québec:

Institut québécois de recherche sur la culture, 2004) 837ff.

17 M.S. Searle and R.E. Brayley, *Leisure Service in Canada: An Introduction* (Venture Publishing, 2000), 22ff.

18 Paul-Louis Martin, *La chasse au Québec* (Montréal: Éditions du Boréal, 1990), 162; Michel Bellefleur, *L'évolution du loisir au Québec: essai sociohistorique* (Québec: Presses de l'Université du Québec, 1997), 163–69; Canada Land Inventory, *Objectives, Scope and Organization, Report 1*, cited by C.S. Brown, "Federal-Rural Development Programs and Recreation Resources," in *Canadian Parks in Perspective*, ed. J.G. Nelson and R.C. Scace, 239 (Montreal: Harvest House, 1970); Bruno Jean, "La 'ruralité' bas-laurentienne: développement agricole et sous-développement rural," *Recherches sociographiques* 29, no. 2 (1998): 242; Bruno Jean, "Les études rurales québécoises entre les approches monographiques et typologiques," *Recherches sociographiques* 47, no. 3 (2006): 511; Moquay, "La référence régionale au Québec." For a critical history of the project of a park in the Gaspésie region, see J.M. Thibault, "La création d'un premier parc national au Québec: le parc Forillon, 1969–70." Master's thesis, Université de Sherbrooke, 1991.

19 Lothian, *A Brief History of Canada's National Parks*, 25.

20 Jean Chrétien, "Our Evolving National Parks System," in *The Canadian National Parks: Today and Tomorrow*, ed. Nelson and Scace, 10.

21 Parcs Canada – Centre de services du Québec (PC-CSQ), *L'aménagement d'un parc en Mauricie*, 24 March 1971, 5–6.

22 Parks Canada's economists referred heavily to Banff and Cape-Breton parks to estimate that 1 million visitors per year would visit the new park in the Mauricie (in Library and Archives Canada, RG22, 1229, 321-1, 3, *Prévisions sur l'effet économique d'un parc en Mauricie*, 26 février 1970). According to Parks Canada's Planning Division, touristic expenses for the region, based on a 1.5 million visitors per year projection, could also reach "a conservative estimate of $5.4 millions" (in Parks Canada, *Economic Aspects of the Proposed St. Maurice National Park, March 1970*, 1). Those numbers never came; the average for the ten first years of the park's activity topped 250,000 visitors per year (in Denis Pronovost, "Les retombées économiques du parc national: les meilleures années sont à venir!", *Le Nouvelliste*, 4 septembre 1981).

23 The spruce plantation established by La Laurentide became known as the "Grand-Mère plantation." Lothian, *A Brief History of Canada's National Parks*, 135–42.

24 SEREQ, *La Mauricie National Park*, 1971, 27.

25 Thierry Bouin, *Aménagement et exploitation faunique antérieurs à la création du parc national de la Mauricie (1970)*. (Ottawa: Service de la conservation et des ressources naturelles, 1979), 4–5; Martin, *La chasse au Québec*; Hardy and Séguin, *Histoire de la Mauricie*

26 SEREQ, *La Mauricie National Park*, 1971, 27; Jérémy Pringault, "Le parc national de la Mauricie: mise en valeur d'un espace protégé dans la perspective du développement durable" (master's thesis, Université de Caen, France, 1994) 67; Royal St-Arnaud, "La Mau-

ricie est la région la plus importante au domaine forestier," *Le Nouvelliste*, 17 September 1971; PC-CSQ, Bouin, *Aménagement et exploitation faunique*, vii.

27 Martin, *La chasse au Québec*, 170; Serge Gagnon, *L'échiquier touristique québécois* (Sainte-Foy: Presses de l'Université du Québec, 2003), 295.

28 Archives nationales du Canada (ANC), RG 84, 2344, C-1445-101/L1, 3, Rapports semi-annuels des surintendants, 24 May 1973.

29 Pringault, "Le parc national de la Mauricie," 67, Bouin, *Aménagement et exploitation faunique*, 36 and 47.

30 Paige West, James Ingoe, and Dan Brockington, "Parks and Peoples: The Social Impact of Protected Areas," *Annual Review of Anthropology* 35 (2006): 260ff.

31 Thomas R. Dunlap, "Wildlife, Science, and the National Parks, 1920–1940," *Pacific Historical Review* 59, no. 2 (1990): 187–202; Thomas R. Dunlap, "Ecology, Nature, and Canadian National Park Policy: Wolves, Elk, and Bison as a Case Study," in *To See Ourselves/to Save Ourselves: Ecology and Culture in Canada*, ed. Rowland Lorimer, 139–47 (Montreal: Association for Canadian Studies, 1990); Richard West Sellars, *Preserving Nature in the National Parks: A History* (New Haven, CT: Yale University Press, 1997); Gerald Killan and George Warecki, "J.R. Dymond and Frank A. Macdougall: Science and Government Policy in Algonquin Provincial Park, 1931–1954," *Scientia Canadensis* 22, no. 51 (1998): 131–56; Alan MacEachern, "Rationality and Rationalization in Canadian National Parks Policy," in *Consuming Canada:*

Readings in Environmental History, ed. Chad Gaffield and Pam Gaffield, 197–212 (Toronto: Copp Clark, 1995).

32 ANC, RG 22, 998, 321-10, 1, Lefebvre to Chrétien, 7 October 1970.

33 ANC, RG 22, 998, 321-10, 1, Chrétien to Lefebvre, 4 November 1970.

34 Article 9 of the National Parks Policy indicates that "no research, except that which is needed by the park itself, can be pursued within a park if an appropriate site for the research can be found elsewhere." Canada, Direction des parcs nationaux et des lieux historiques, *Politique des parcs nationaux* (Ottawa: Affaires indiennes et du Nord, Parcs Canada, 1969), 4, 6.

35 Parks Canada – Office national – Bureau central de classement (PC-ON-BCC), C-98103L1, Desmeules to Lesaux, 26 January 1971.

36 Louis Machabée, "La double nature de la nature: une analyse sociologique de la naturalisation des espaces verts en milieu urbain." Doctoral thesis, Université du Québec à Montréal, 2002, p. 26.

37 SEREQ, *La Mauricie National Park,* 1971, p. 60.

38 PC-ON-BCC, C-8320/L1, *La Mauricie National Park – Visit of the Interpretive Specialist R.C. Gray, June 9th to 15th, 1971,* 25 June 1971, 9–10.

39 Ibid.

40 PC-CSQ, Parcs Canada, *Plan directeur provisoire: parc national de la Mauricie,* 1975, p. 53.

41 PC-CSQ, Parcs Canada, *Manuel de planification du réseau des parcs nationaux,* 1972, p. 3–4.

42 Parcs Canada, *Manuel de planification,* 48.

43 Suzanne Zellers, *Inventing Canada: Early Victorian Science and the Idea of a Transcontinental Nation* (Toronto: University of Torono Press, 1988).

44 Parcs Canada, *Manuel de planification,* 107.

45 Parcs Canada, *Manuel de planification,* 115.

46 The annual report of fiscal year 1971–72 confirms this effacement of human dimensions of territories made into reserves. It indicates that the new scientific management of Canadian National Parks is inspired by "the principle that the natural park system must protect not only the unique and characteristic regions of the Canadian landscape, but also those that present physical and biological elements that are typically Canadian" (*in* Parcs Canada, *Rapport annuel: Année financière 1971/1972,* 1972, p. 9).

47 "The place where we are is the place where nature is not," in William Cronon, "The Trouble with Wilderness: Or, Getting Back to the Wrong Nature," *Environmental History* 1, no. 1 (1996): 17.

48 MacEachern, *Natural Selections,* 3-4.

49 Carole Pronovost, "Au parc national de la Mauricie: Inauguration d'un centre d'interprétation de la nature," *Le Nouvelliste,* 5 August 1972.

50 PC-ON-BCC, C-8333/L1, Nicol to the Regional Director (Central Region), 1 February 1972.

51 On the use of Aboriginal folklore by governmental agencies, see: Tina Loo, "Making a Modern Wilderness: Conserving Wildlife in Twentieth-Century

Canada," *Canadian Historical Review* 82, no. 1 (2001): 101–103; and Patricia Jasen, *Wild Things: Nature, Culture, and Tourism in Ontario, 1790–1914* (Toronto: University of Toronto Press, 1995), 13 and following.

52 PC-CSQ, Parcs Canada, *Plan directeur provisoire: parc national de la Mauricie* (1975) 31.

53 *Parks Canada Guiding Principles and Operational Policies.* http://www.pc.gc.ca/eng/docs/pc/poli/princip/sec2/part2a/part2a2.aspx [accessed 21 July 2008].

54 Parcs Canada, *Manuel de planification...*, 3.

55 Cronon, "The Trouble with Wilderness," *loc. cit.*; Eric Kaufmann, "Naturalizing the Nation: The Rise of Naturalistic Nationalism in the United States and Canada," *Comparative Studies in Society and History* 40, no. 4 (1998): 666–95.

56 For a recent discussion on this subject by one contributor of this book, see David Neufeld, "Indigenous peoples and protected heritage areas: Acknowledging cultural pluralism," in K. S. Hanna et al., ed., *Transforming Parks and Protected Areas: Policy Governance in a Changing World* (New York: Routledge, 2008), chap. 10.

Kouchibouguac: Representations of a Park in Acadian Popular Culture

RONALD RUDIN
DEPARTMENT OF HISTORY
CONCORDIA UNIVERSITY

A Walk in the Park

In July 2007, I visited Kouchibouguac National Park, on the east coast of New Brunswick, for the first time, although I already knew much of the story of how it had been created. In 1969 an agreement was reached between the governments of New Brunswick and Canada to create this park, but before it could begin to receive visitors, all of the residents of the territory had to be removed from their lands. This was standard operating procedure for the creation of national parks at the time.[1] However, while residents displaced in other such instances left with little sign of resistance, such was not the case at Kouchibouguac, where periodic instances of civil disobedience prevented the formal opening of the park until 1979 and continued for some time after that. In the end, however, the expropriations were carried out by

Fig. 1. Obliterating the park's name with those of the communities destroyed, 16 April 1980. [Centre d'études acadiennes, e-8364.]

the provincial government (responsible for this job in such agreements with Ottawa), resulting in the displacement of over 1,500 individuals, mostly Acadians, belonging to over 200 households.

In light of this background, I was surprised when I received a brochure at the Welcome Centre (staffed by some members of expropriated families), which noted that "Kouchibouguac holds souvenirs of more than 200 families who gave up their homeland so that Canadians today and future generations can benefit from this special protected area. Thank you for this legacy!" It was not as if the residents had willingly "given up their homeland," and so the remark was jarring to say the least.[2] The doublespeak then continued just outside the Centre, where a sculpture greeted visitors to the park: a picnic table around which there were bronzes representing individuals who had once lived here. Not far from the table, an explanatory panel rather blandly described the presence in the region of "descendants of three cultures [Mi'kmaqs, Acadians, and English-speakers] that have long shared this environment and left their mark in this area's beauty.... Today these people often share their table with a more recent arrival – you, the park visitor."

There was no reference near the picnic table as to what had happened to any of the people no longer present, but at least in the case of the aboriginal people interpretation could be found elsewhere in the park. For instance, the park's Migmag Cedar Trail allowed the First Nations people to be more than abstractions as it provided an opportunity for their story to be told; and upon leaving the trail, there was a message from elders of the nearby Elsipogtog First Nation, thanking the visitor for having come to the park. However, there was no such official recognition in terms of the Acadians. As the singer Zachary Richard, the narrator of a 2007 documentary about the creation of the park, observed, time had obliterated any traces of the Acadian communities that had once existed where the park now stood: "La documentation du parc ne parle pas des gens [acadiens] qui y vivaient: rien – pas un mot, pas une carte, pas un symbole; même pas une photo ou une petite plaque."[3]

There was, however, one exception to the removal of all signs that Acadians had once lived here. A bit off the beaten path for most visitors, there was a trailer where Jackie Vautour, the leading figure of the resistance to the creation of the park, and his family still lived. While the other residents of the territory ultimately left their properties, Vautour remained. In 1976, provincial authorities bulldozed his house to get him out, but in 1978 he returned to squat on his land and was still there thirty years later. Not far from this site, there was one further reminder of an Acadian presence, a cemetery, somehow a fitting metaphor for the communities that were obliterated so that the park might exist.

While there was no official indication in the park to indicate that longstanding Acadian communities had once existed there, the memory of the Kouchibouguac experience has been perpetuated over the past forty years through the artistic creations of Acadian musicians, filmmakers, artists, and writers. If Parks Canada has, until recently, refused to recognize officially that the Acadians once had a connection with this land, the story has nevertheless been a source of inspiration for Acadian creators working in a variety of media. This essay explores the changing contours of public representation of the Kouchibouguac story over this period. Far beyond its physical dimensions, this park became a landscape endowed with considerable cultural significance. In order to make sense of the various tellings of the Kouchibouguac tale, it is first necessary to understand exactly how these expropriations came about and how some Acadians resisted their dispossession. Then, in the last two sections of the essay, we will see the popular depictions of the story that emerged in the midst of the conflicts of the 1970s and how that story is being slowly transformed forty years after the creation of the park. As is often the case in terms of public memory, the changing contours of the Kouchibouguac story reflect some significant changes in society – in this case, Acadian society.

The Story[4]

There were numerous cases in post-war Canada of the use of the state to remove people from their homes, always in the name of "progress" or the "common good" and sometimes with claims that the expropriated would benefit in the process. To name only a few examples: both natives and non-natives were displaced from their homes in Ontario during the 1950s in order to construct the St. Lawrence Seaway; the African-Canadian residents of the Halifax community of Africville were sent packing during the 1960s so that they might be "liberated" from their homes, which were deemed unsuitable by the powers that be; and at the end of that decade the farmers of several communities to the north of Montreal lost their lands to permit the construction of Mirabel airport.[5]

In October 1969, seven months after the Mirabel announcement, the New Brunswick and Canadian governments signed the agreement that would lead to the expropriations needed to create Kouchibouguac National Park. In ordering the removal of everyone from the territory before the park could be developed, what happened in Kent County, New Brunswick, was consistent with federal policy, which had largely followed the "Yellowstone model" of park development. By insisting that a resident population could not coexist with "nature," Ottawa created a situation that led to numerous conflicts, some of which are chronicled in other essays in this volume.[6] However, while the federal government dictated national parks policy, it was the provinces that were given the responsibility for carrying out the evictions before turning over the land to Ottawa. Provinces, particularly poor ones such as New Brunswick, proved willing to do the job, believing that the fruits of

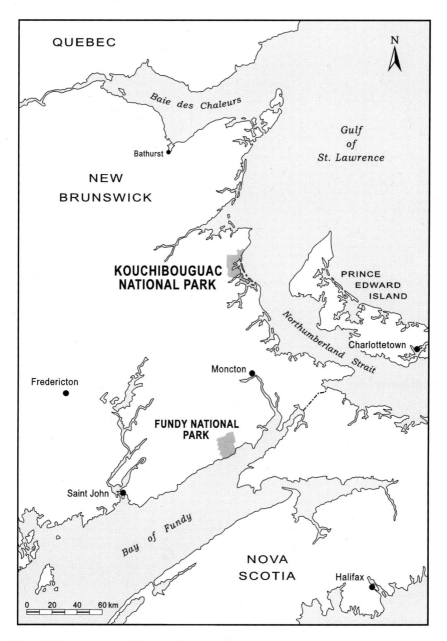

QUEBEC

N

Baie des Chaleurs

Gulf
of
St. Lawrence

Bathurst

NEW
BRUNSWICK

KOUCHIBOUGUAC
NATIONAL PARK

PRINCE
EDWARD
ISLAND

Northumberland Strait

Charlottetown

Moncton

Fredericton

FUNDY NATIONAL
PARK

Saint John

Bay of Fundy

NOVA
SCOTIA

Halifax

0   20   40   60 km

FIG. 2. KOUCHIBOUGUAC NATIONAL PARK.

Ronald Rudin   209 economic development via park-related tourism justified the inconvenience of some of their citizens, particularly since the federal government would be paying the bill, once the people were out of the way.[7]

On the face of it, the fate of the residents of Kouchibouguac was little different from that experienced by those displaced to create such parks as Cape Breton Highlands in Nova Scotia in the 1930s, Fundy in New Brunswick in the 1950s, or Forillon in the 1970s. As in these other cases in eastern Canada, certain natural features of the Kouchibouguac territory were deemed worthy of preservation, even if the way of life of a community would be destroyed in the process. In 1966, a joint federal-provincial survey of the New Brunswick shoreline with an eye towards creating a new national park concluded that Kouchibouguac Bay provided the ideal location, with "its 15 ½ mile sweep of sand bars which stretches across the entire ocean front.… Behind the bars, the quiet lagoons are the transitional basins from fresh to salt for the waters of the [local] rivers." The area also boasted a "major area of fresh-water bog which we wish to preserve and interpret. Its stunted trees, Labrador tea, blueberries and pitcher plants are representative of sphagnum bogs all along this lowland plain of New Brunswick. Within this general area, the higher, better-drained land has a cover of black spruce and some balsam fir, and is also a representative feature of the coastal plain."[8]

Quite aside from the physical attributes of the park, the New Brunswick government focused upon Kouchibouguac's potential for encouraging economic development, no small matter since Kent County was poor by almost any standard. A 1968 study carried out for Fredericton by Dollard Landry indicated that over two-thirds of the families in Kent County, and 80 per cent of those in the territory slated to become parkland, earned less than $3,000 per year. By contrast, only 39 per cent of New Brunswickers and 24 per cent of Canadians earned so little.[9] Accordingly, even before the agreement had been signed with Ottawa, the province produced a pamphlet touting the fact that "many new jobs will be created as a result of the park's establishment. Jobs will be available during construction of the park. Permanent jobs will be available for residents during the operation of the park. Other jobs will be created in motels and restaurants to serve visitors to the park."[10]

This use of the state to encourage economic development was typical of the sort of reforms that were introduced during the 1960s by the government of Louis Robichaud, New Brunswick's first elected Acadian premier

(1960–70). Given the later depiction of the Kouchibouguac expropriations as a specifically Acadian crisis, it is tempting to view Robichaud's role in the creation of the park as a special effort to improve the lot of Acadians, who made up roughly 85 per cent of those expropriated. However, most of Robichaud's efforts during his decade in power were designed to provide equal opportunities for all New Brunswickers, and so his creation, for instance, of an Acadian university, the Université de Moncton, in 1963, was only "part of a wider modernization of the province's postsecondary educational system."[11]

By and large, Robichaud and his federal partners were engaged in a process that could be found elsewhere in Canada, as the machinery of state expanded to take greater control over a wide array of concerns, sometimes uprooting people in the process. And so there was little out of the ordinary when residents started to be removed from their lands to create Kouchibouguac National Park in 1969. The provincial *Expropriation Act* allowed for the evictions to take place with little advanced warning, and most residents accepted the compensation that was offered, leaving quietly for nearby communities.[12] But here is where the Kouchibouguac story departed from the norm. In other situations, there had sometimes been isolated instances of resistance to expropriation, but never – at least in post-World War II Canada – was there widespread resistance accompanied by instances of violence and the destruction of property. In the end, the Kouchibouguac story has reverberated in Acadian popular culture over the past forty years thanks to the artistic creations inspired by the opportunity to depict this resistance.

Resistance

Provincial bureaucrats close to the Kouchibouguac dossier observed that there was something special here because "it was the first time a National Park would be developed involving so many people inside its boundaries."[13] In the end, however, resistance did not emerge in this case, as opposed to others, simply because of the size of the operation. In addition, insensitivity on the part of bureaucrats and their political masters (common enough in other contexts as well) coincided with the emergence of an unprecedented willingness on the part of Acadians to express their grievances on the public stage.[14] Students were taking to the streets to defend such causes as the right to an affordable education at the newly created Université de Moncton, and the right to use French in dealings with the municipal government of the largely English-speaking city of Moncton. They were joined by parents and teachers, who were upset over the administration of French-language schools in Moncton by a school board dominated by English-speakers.[15] While the Robichaud government attempted to improve the lot of Acadians by providing a higher level of services to all New Brunswickers, the protesters sought special recognition of the distinctive needs of Acadians.[16] The short-lived Parti acadien, for example, proposed dividing New Brunswick into two provinces in order to create one that would be largely populated by Acadians. The same willingness to stand up for specifically Acadian interests fuelled both the resistance that emerged to the expropriations at Kouchibouguac and the artistic creations inspired by the conflict.

The process by which residents were removed from their lands provided the raw material for those inclined to resist. Even though Premier Robichaud had indicated that $2.8 million would be needed to acquire the properties, only half that amount was actually made available. The residents were poorly informed about their options and were often confronted by an agent of the government who would scribble a price on a piece of paper, giving them the impression that this was a take-it-or-leave-it situation. Over time, even the provincial government recognized that the original compensation packages had been insufficient and in the end provided a total of $4.5 million to acquire the lands, not to mention a comparable amount "to deal with the social upheaval following the expropriation" and a further $2.2 million for the costs of relocation.[17] These offers were only made, however, after the expropriates (*expropriés*) organized and after some of them turned to confrontational tactics to advance their cause.

Resistance first surfaced in a significant way in June 1971, shortly after the federal government, which was responsible for providing compensation for the loss of income from commercial fishing, made an offer for the loss of an activity that was banned in national parks. Since fishing had been the main occupation of the former residents, it is not surprising that discontent on this score, when coupled with unhappiness about the paltry sums that had been provided to start their lives anew, boiled over into conflict. During the summer of 1971, several citizens' committees surfaced, one of which was headed by John L. (always called Jackie) Vautour.

Fig. 3. Jackie Vautour (on the right), 28 March 1980. [Centre d'études acadiennes, e-8377.]

Expropriated from his land and offered a sum that he would not accept, Vautour provided both leadership and a public face for the opposition to the park. While nearly all of his neighbours left when ordered to do so, Vautour remained. In 1976, at the time that his house was bulldozed by provincial authorities, there was only one couple left in the territory of the park, and they had been allowed to stay for "humanitarian reasons."[18] In 1978 Vautour returned to the park as a squatter and went to the courts to contest the legality of the expropriation process; even though he lost, Vautour remained in place. In the end, the Special Inquiry established to investigate the Kouchibouguac affair advised both levels of government to let Vautour stay on his land, with the understanding that he would be denied access to any services (including deliveries to his property), probably figuring that he would eventually tire of his situation and leave. Forty years after the creation of the park, Vautour was still on "his" property, a living symbol of a conflict that, for most people, had ended long ago.

Vautour and his more militant colleagues concluded early on that petitioning would never be enough to improve the lot of the *expropriés*, and so turned to more direct action. In the spring of 1972 they occupied park offices for two weeks to protest both the compensation being offered for the loss of fishing rights and the failure to hire a sufficient number of expropriated residents to work at Kouchibouguac.[19] Similar scenarios unfolded when park offices were barricaded from January to July 1973 and again briefly in November of the same year. On the second occasion, Jackie Vautour was arrested and found guilty of assault, following which his public statements became more extreme. Early in 1974, by which time most fishers had settled with the government, there were a number of cases of arson on park property, leading Vautour to remark: "Les citoyens du parc Kouchibouguac ont déjà fait brûler tout ce qu'ils étaient capables de faire brûler pour le moment. Le reste le sera lorsque le temps sera propice."[20] These incidents aside, a period of relative peace then returned to the park as most outstanding grievances had been resolved, largely through the government's willingness to spend far more than it had ever imagined in order to buy social peace.[21] As most residents were mollified by larger payments, the cause of the expropriates became increasingly that of Jackie Vautour, a shift that would have significant consequences for the public memory of the conflict.

Following the destruction of his home in 1976, Vautour moved to a nearby motel, but he was also evicted from that residence (when the government stopped paying his bills), resisting police in the process, which led to his arrest. Although the charges were dropped, Vautour by now had a following, and he played upon this public notoriety when in June 1978, just before his return to the park, he produced a petition that he claimed had the signatures of over 600 former residents – representing roughly 90 per cent of the expropriated families – who wanted to return. The timing of this petition was no accident: the provincial government had just handed over title to the property to the federal government, an act that anticipated the formal proclamation of the opening of the park early in 1979, nearly a decade after the signing of the original agreement for Kouchibouguac's creation. Although the extent to which the petitioners really wanted to return to the park could be questioned, Vautour used the document, along with his own return and a court challenge to the legality of the expropriations, to try to delay the inevitable.[22]

The legal route came to an end in March 1980 when the Supreme Court of Canada refused to hear an appeal of a lower court's ruling against Vautour's challenge to the expropriations, and in the months that followed sporadic instances of violence recurred. On the day following the Supreme Court's ruling, the *Globe and Mail* reported that "someone among the squatters living in the park here opened fire on a parks department building, blasting windows and barely missing a guard inside."[23] Later that same month, protesters barricaded the park, and, when park officials tried to reopen the closed offices a week later, tear gas had to be used to quell what the *Globe* described as a "melee." Late in April, one of Vautour's allies declared: "Let me say in plain words. We either get the land back or we destroy it completely. Fire in the woods, oil to pollute the rivers."[24]

These actions soon led the New Brunswick and Canadian governments to jointly establish a Special Inquiry so that all of the issues raised by the Kouchibouguac case might be aired. The report of the commission, issued in October 1981, recommended that Vautour be left alone, and when this suggestion was accepted the story slowly receded from public view. Vautour, however, has not entirely disappeared. In 1987, following defeat in the provincial election of that year and only hours before leaving office, Premier Richard Hatfield made Vautour an offer of over $275,000 plus 50 hectares of land in return for his departure from the park. On previous occasions when offers were made, Vautour refused them, but this time he accepted the payment – although he did not leave the park.[25] He returned to public view one more time late in 1998, when he and his wife were arrested for illegally digging for clams on park property, but his conviction was ultimately overturned because he had not been allowed to defend himself on the basis of his

Fig. 4. Barricading Offices, Kouchibouguac National Park, 28 March 1980.
[Centre d'études acadiennes, e-8367.]

aboriginal rights as a Métis. A retrial was ordered, but due to various delays the case remains before the courts as these lines are written.

Even before the Special Inquiry was created, however, the federal government had come (rather belatedly) to recognize that it was counter-productive to use expropriation as a means of creating new national parks. Quite aside from the insensitivity of uprooting people from lives they seemed to value, the point was often made during the Kouchibouguac crisis that tourists might have been attracted by the presence of "authentic" residents going about their lives within the park.[26] Accordingly, in 1979 Parks Canada announced that in establishing new national parks it would only remove people if they agreed to leave, making it highly unlikely that there would be another crisis such as the one provoked by the creation of Kouchibouguac National Park.[27]

Kouchibouguac Meets the Acadian Artistic Community

The story of the Kouchibouguac expropriations struck a chord among Acadian artists, sensitized by the ferment in their society during the 1960s and responsive to the story of yet another case of dispossession. Acadians had long been reluctant to make explicit public reference to the wrongs they had suffered at the time of their deportation by the British in the eighteenth century. Rather than point fingers at those responsible for this act of "ethnic cleansing," they preferred to view the deportation through the symbol of Evangeline, the creation of Henry Wadsworth Longfellow but one long assimilated by Acadians as the model deportee who had borne her suffering without either complaint or resistance.[28] In this context, the Kouchibouguac affair, a story of dispossession in its own right, offered an opportunity for Acadians to make public reference to the deportation, but without the baggage of Evangeline.

The link between the deportation and Kouchibouguac emerged quite clearly in the immediate aftermath of the destruction of Jackie Vautour's home in 1976, the most striking image of the heavy-handedness of the expropriation process. Numerous authors of letters to the editor of the Acadian daily *L'Évangéline* explicitly linked the two cases of expulsion, writing: "On revit en quelque sorte l'histoire de 1755"; or "Je suis convaincu que l'amertume ressentie par cette famille est aussi profonde que celle ressentie par leurs ancêtres en 1755." The same newspaper, which did not always support Vautour's actions, was moved nevertheless to editorialize that Kouchibouguac was "Le parc des déportés."[29]

Artistic creations also made the connection between the deportation and the story of the Kouchibouguac expropriations, frequently giving centre stage to Vautour, the assertive male, who seemed a more appropriate symbol than the submissive female, embodied by Evangeline. Jules Boudreau dedicated his 1979 play *Cochu et le Soleil*, which focuses on an Acadian family repeatedly uprooted by the *grand dérangement*, "À Jackie Vautour et aux déportés de Kouchibouguac, puissent-ils être les derniers."[30] Visual artist Claude Roussel created several works inspired by the Kouchibouguac affair, including one of molded plastic with the inscription, "Kouchibouguac: La nature sans

FIG. 5. Jackie Vautour holding "Kouchibouguac ou le grand déracinement." Epoxy resin work, created by the sculptor, Claude Roussel. [Courtesy of Claude Roussel.]

l'homme, c'est aussi triste que l'homme sans la nature"; this was followed by a second work, "Kouchibouguac ou le grand déracinement," which featured objects such as pieces of a small doll that he had found in the rubble of a house that had been demolished.[31]

These were only two of many cultural creations that made reference to Kouchibouguac during the 1970s, but some creators reached a larger audience than others. Cajun singer-songwriter Zachary Richard has probably done the most to advance the image of Vautour as the agent of resistance and has provided an account of his own discovery of the Kouchibouguac story in the 1970s:

> It was during one of [my first] visits to Acadie [in 1977] that I was asked to participate in a benefit concert, the proceeds of which were dedicated to helping the expropriates of Kouchibouguac. The creation of a National Park had provoked great turmoil in Acadian society. Many referred to it as a second Deportation.... When I learned of what had happened, I was outraged. The spokesman for the expropriates was John L. "Jackie" Vautour. This is how I came to learn the story of this otherwise ordinary man who, in spite of himself, has struggled against the governments of New Brunswick and of Canada for most of his life. I can't remember much about our first meeting. In the photos, Jackie is a small man, balding, smartly dressed with a Fu Manchu moustache. I can't remember anything about the speech he made during that concert. It must have inspired me, however, because, not too long thereafter, I wrote a song dedicated to him, *La Ballade de Jackie Vautour*.[32]

The song is written in the first person, with a menacing tone against a "you" representing the authorities, equipped with guns, that had driven Vautour from his home. Embracing the resistance of Vautour's actions, Richard wrote – in the first verse of the song – of someone who did not want to resort to violence, but who could be pushed in that direction if need be.[33]

O no, tu vas pas me grouiller.
c'est ma terre icitte,
c'est icitte que moi j'vas rester.
O no, tu me fais pas peur
avec ton fusil.
J'veux pas voir du sang couler,
mais c'est ma vie
que t'essaies d'arracher.

Born in Louisiana, Richard first came to *Acadie* in 1975 and has credited the people that he met upon his arrival with the "evolution of [his] militant French identity." He gave special credit to the Acadian poet Gérald Leblanc, who "was part of the Moncton counterculture which was shaking the cage of that mid sized small town with its reactionary English speaking anglo dominant style."[34] At the time that the two would have first met, Leblanc had already begun his own significant involvement with the Kouchibouguac story, finding himself as a researcher and scriptwriter for a National Film Board (NFB) project on the expropriation of Kouchibouguac Park.

> The project required considerable work, sifting through numerous documents and materials. I applied myself feverishly to the job. I was trying to stay objective and not to think too much about the way the population had been uprooted. These Acadians' ancestors had already lived through the Deportation of 1755 and were now going through something else not unlike that experience. I sorted through the documents and testimonies. I met with some of the people who had been expropriated, in order to familiarize myself with the facts of the crime.[35]

The film in question, *Kouchibouguac*, would appear in 1979 and would play a significant role in the public's understanding of the crisis. However, even before the completion of the film, Leblanc made his own personal contribution to the popular representation of the expropriation through his poem, *Complainte du parc Kouchibouguac*, written in 1978 and recorded by the band 1755, whose rendition of the piece figured prominently in the NFB production.[36]

Complainte was dedicated "aux expropriés du parc national Kouchibouguac," so as to make it appear less focused upon one individual than was the case in Richard's treatment. Nevertheless, there were elements of Leblanc's poem that paralleled the case of Vautour, who by 1978 was agitating for the return of the expropriates to their land, ultimately doing so himself in July of that year. The opening stanzas, written in the style of a fable, describe the general situation at the time of the creation of the park; the closing ones express the hope that Acadians would be able to get even for their mistreatment. By contrast, the central stanzas – with verbs written in an archaic form designed to make them appear more genuinely "Acadian" – describe a conversation between one individual and his neighbours. This character does not seem to have left his land, because some of his friends were telling him "Restez! Restez!" Still others express the hope that they might be able to return to their land, even if it was "Avec la vieille lampe pis le poêle plein de bois." A life of poverty at Kouchibouguac was preferable to the sterile lives they were enduring elsewhere.

The spirit of Leblanc's *Complainte* was reflected in the film *Kouchibouguac*.[37] Once again, the focus was not entirely upon Jackie Vautour. As David Lonergan has observed, "[il] y occupe une place importante, mais il n'est pas le pivot du documentaire." Indeed, the bulk of the film focused on the suffering of expropriates not as well known as Vautour. As Lonergan put it, the film "est essentiellement un film militant: on est dans l'action."[38] English-speakers (although they constituted about 15 per cent of the expropriates) are generally depicted in a negative light, so that they became the "other" to the dispossessed Acadians. One of the expropriates switches into English to recreate the offer made to him; and Richard Hatfield appears from time to time, speaking English and looking uncomfortable with his own role in a process that he had inherited from his Acadian predecessor. Hatfield's appearances, however, constituted one of the few moments when the focus was taken from those who had lost their land. That this was their film is reinforced by the absence of a narrator, so that the expropriated families, often standing where their homes had once been, do the talking without any intermediary. That this film had to do with a collectivity was further reinforced by the fact it was the work of a large group of people (26 participants, including Leblanc and the group 1755, are listed) functioning as one so that it did not belong to a single creator.

In the end, however, while Lonergan was correct in asserting that Vautour was not the "pivot" of *Kouchibouguac*, the fact remains that most of the final thirty minutes of the seventy-five-minute film focuses on him. It includes a series of interviews with people asking what they thought of Vautour, followed by footage of the major moments with which he was associated, especially the destruction of his home. Near the end of the film, the focus does return – albeit quickly – to the "other" expropriates, but *Kouchibouguac* closes with the following text running along the bottom of the screen, with storm clouds and thunder in the background: "En mai 1978, 577 expropriés de 213 familles signent une pétition réclamant des gouvernements de reprendre leurs terres et leurs droits." As we have seen, this petition was orchestrated by Vautour, only two months before his own return.

Now firmly installed, albeit illegally, on park property, a Vautour-like character made one further appearance during the 1970s in Jacques Savoie's novel *Raconte-moi Massabielle*, which was subsequently made into a film with a slightly different tale.[39] Savoie, himself a well-known member of the Acadian artistic community (having founded the band Beausoleil Broussard several years earlier), tells the story of Pacifique Haché, the sole remaining member of a community that had been expropriated by the Noranda Mining Company. Haché's neighbours are shown (in the novel but not in the film) living sad lives in Bathurst, "une ville d'Anglais," where the men pass their time hanging out in a bar. To the extent that Noranda (referred to as Panda Mining in the film) did have mining operations in the vicinity of Bathurst, Savoie's story about the challenges faced by Acadians was larger than that of Kouchibouguac. Indeed, some of the commentary on both the novel and the film has suggested little or no connection between Savoie's story and the Kouchibouguac crisis.[40] Nevertheless, it is hard to avoid seeing the sole remaining person on the land of an expropriated Acadian community of the 1970s as based upon anyone other than Vautour.

As his name suggests, Pacifique Haché is a complicated figure, depicted by Savoie as slightly (but not entirely) crazy in his insistence that he is "le roi de Massabielle," a place name that referred to the Grotto of Massabielle at Lourdes where Bernadette had seen visions of the Virgin Mary in the mid-nineteenth century. The religious allusion is appropriate since Haché has taken up residence in the parish church, the only structure still standing in the town, where he is courted by two very different forces. On the one hand, a lawyer from the mining company is trying to get him to leave his land, bringing gifts such as a television that was supposed to seduce him to accept modern society. Instead, Haché preaches to the lawyer from the pulpit of the church and eventually throws the television into the sea. The other suitor for Haché's attention is Stella, a woman presumably named after the Stella Maris, the star of the sea, a symbol of the Virgin Mary who has long played a central role in Acadian culture (the Stella Maris is the star on the Acadian flag and the Acadian national anthem is Ave Maris Stella). Unlike the lawyer, who was sent packing, Stella stays with Haché, although the consequences of their relationship differed in the novel and the film.

In his 1979 telling of the story, Savoie depicts Haché and Stella as living together detached from real time, so that Stella's diary ends with an entry on 51 September. Much like Vautour only months after he had repossessed his land, Haché and Stella live in "a form of escape or self-imposed exile."[41] By contrast, the film produced four years later had a much more positive ending that shows, during the credits, Haché and Stella with their ever-growing family. On one level, this reflected the changing circumstances for Acadians, who in 1981 saw the introduction of provincial legislation that established the equality of the two linguistic communities. This equality was enshrined in the Canadian constitution in 1983, providing Acadians with the sort of promise for a long-term existence that also now seems to lie ahead for Haché and Stella.

On another level, however, the "happy ending" for Haché reflects the fact that by 1983 Vautour had been accepted as a permanent, if bothersome, presence on park land; and in this regard the film *Massabielle* constituted both an end and a beginning in terms of popular representations of the Kouchibouguac affair. It constituted the last of a number of such representations that were produced by key members of the Acadian cultural community during the moments of greatest tension over the expropriations, only a few of which could be discussed here at any length, but all of which focused on the anger that came out of the 1970s version of the deportation. After the release of Savoie's production in 1983, it would be over twenty years until another version of the crisis would appear on film; and when the Kouchibouguac crisis returned to the screen it – along with other representations of the early twenty-first century – would pick up on the depiction in Savoie's film of people who had come, however difficult it may have been, to accept their lives after Kouchibouguac.

Acadians Return to Kouchibouguac

While Jacques Savoie's *Massabielle* suggested a new approach to depicting the Kouchibouguac affair, it stood as an exception to the norm during the 1970s and early 1980s when representations focused on the removal of the Acadians, leaving little room to consider what happened to the vast majority of expropriates who (unlike Jackie Vautour) went on to build new lives elsewhere. Indeed, one of the criticisms of the 1979 film *Kouchibouguac* was precisely its focus upon confrontation, without ample evidence that there was life, however difficult, after Kouchibouguac. Writing in *L'Évangéline*, Nelson Landry, who penned numerous pieces for the newspaper about the Kouchibouguac situation, published a pointed commentary in which he quite correctly observed that the film – and one could extend this to the other treatments from the 1970s – dealt with the victimization of the expropriates but had little to say about "l'avenir d'une population déracinée." While the film captured "le mode de vie de ces gens avant l'expropriation, [les réalisateurs] ont ignoré d'expliquer en profondeur le mode de vie actuel."[42] A similar critique was offered in the report of the Special Inquiry, which argued that the film had

> a powerful influence in shaping the perception that many people have of the park.... It is difficult to say that any particular event in the film is false, but the total impression is extremely misleading. The plight of the Park residents following the expropriation is rightly underlined. But life did not stop there. Much is made of the small amounts the expropriates received in compensation for their homes, and their consequent inability to find suitable homes outside the Park. But nothing is said of the relocation program under which the expropriates were able to get far better houses than most of them had before.[43]

The Inquiry looked forward to the day when the *expropriés* might see the park as theirs, and so, among its recommendations, called for Parks Canada "to involve the former residents in developments that directly affect them," and to "stress the history of the Acadian community in the development and promotion of the park."[44]

Fig. 6. Expropriated families return to Kouchibouguac, July 2008. [Photo: Ronald Rudin.]

While this sentiment was laudable, it was not realistic when proposed in 1981, given the focus at the time upon the conflicts, in general, and Jackie Vautour, in particular; and there was little evidence that anything had been done to act upon these recommendations when I visited the park more than a quarter century later. However, only weeks after that visit, an unprecedented event indicated that change was in the air. In late July 2007 Parks Canada organized a reunion in the park of those who had been expropriated, attended by over 500 people[45]; and following this event still other projects were put in place. By the fall, Parks Canada had established an advisory committee so as to "impliquer les anciens résidants expulsés, et trouver les façons de commémorer le passé. On souhaite ainsi que les expropriés puissent raconter leur histoire et en venir à se sentir chez eux dans le parc."[46] By early in 2008, the advisory committee was up and running, and its president, Linda Cormier, was hoping that there would soon be "quelque chose de permanent sur les sites pour identifier les anciens villages pour les générations futures. Les familles ont sacrifié leurs terres pour la création de ce parc. Mes enfants ne connaissent pas où j'ai été élevée.... Pendant longtemps, l'expropriation a été un sujet tabou. Au moins, si Parcs Canada veut travailler avec nous, cela facilitera le processus de guérison."[47]

So what had happened to make this possible? For new stories, not heard in the 1970s, to be told, for Parks Canada to welcome the expropriates back to "their" land, and for the expropriates to respond positively to the outstretched hand of the agency that had removed them? Obviously, time had healed some of the wounds from the 1970s, allowing both Parks Canada and the expropriates to look for common ground instead of dwelling on the conflicts of the past. Reflecting on the whole affair with the benefit of some distance, Zachary Richard remarked in 2006, "I understood much later that the situation was not as black and white as I had first imagined. The creation of the park was inspired by a sincere desire to improve the quality of life in the region."[48]

In addition, there had been some significant changes among New Brunswick's Acadians, who were feeling somewhat more confident about their prospects than had been the case in the 1970s. Acadians in the province still had some serious problems to confront at the start of the new century: their share of the New Brunswick population was in decline and the incomes of Acadians remained fixed at about 90 per cent of those earned by English-speakers. Nevertheless, while the Acadian population was in decline everywhere else in New Brunswick, the turn of the century saw the trend moving in the opposite direction in the vicinity of Moncton. This was particularly the case in the neighbouring, and largely Acadian, town of Dieppe, where such institutions as the Société nationale de l'Acadie (SNA), the leading organization representing Acadians, have their head offices.[49] It is worth remembering that Zachary Richard was introduced to the Kouchibouguac story (and to *Acadie* more generally) by such figures of the local arts community as Gérald Leblanc in the context of struggles between French and English-speakers in Moncton. By the turn of the century, these struggles, at least as far as Moncton was concerned, were things of the past, so that the city could be the site of a summit meeting of leaders of the *francophonie* in 1999. In this context, there was the possibility of developing a more relaxed, sometimes even optimistic, view of the prospects for Acadians, the expropriates included.

This upbeat view of both the past and present was evident in 2004, when the leaders of such organizations as the SNA invested considerable energy to celebrate the 400th anniversary of the founding of *Acadie*.[50] This was a self-conscious effort to move the start of the modern Acadian experience from the aftermath of the deportation to the arrival of the first French settlers in 1604. In the process, Acadian leaders were creating a story that did not dwell on suffering, but rather on the emergence of a people whose itinerary was like that of others (especially the *Québécois*) whose societies had taken root in North America in the seventeenth century. Starting from the same *point de départ* as other modern people, the president of the SNA could proclaim that Acadians on their 400th birthday constituted "a people who continue to shine through their dynamism, their cultural richness, and their unstoppable desire to affirm their existence."[51] Even in 2005, on the 250th anniversary of the deportation, Acadian leaders did not cultivate the image of a defeated people, but rather one which had resisted and now found itself ready to face new challenges. Recourse to the past was on the agenda in the early twenty-first century, but not simply as a tool to fuel grievances. The Kouchibouguac story could now be understood not simply as a second deportation, but also as a story that spoke to the Acadians' resilience.

This revisiting of the Acadian past facilitated the engagement of Parks Canada with the expropriates, but it also encouraged the creation of several new representations of the Kouchibouguac story, the first since the 1970s. A number of these efforts, including two plays and a novel, are at various stages of development as I write these lines.[52] However, a new documentary on Kouchibouguac had its première in 2007, only weeks after the expropriates had their reunion in the park. Jean Bourbonnais' *Kouchibouguac: L'histoire de Jackie Vautour et des expropriés* shares certain characteristics with the representations of the 1970s. First, it features Zachary Richard as narrator, along with his *Ballade de Jackie Vautour*; and closely connected to Richard's participation, the title emphasizes the role of Vautour, actually giving him even greater visibility than in the 1979 documentary *Kouchibouguac*. In this regard, writing in *Acadie nouvelle*, David Lonergan complained that the new documentary was wedded "aux canons d'aujourd'hui: une vedette populaire comme narrateur et intervieweur, [et] un personnage principal qui a valeur de mythe." While Lonergan did not contest the value of the film to educate a generation that would have no particular understanding of the expropriation, he did find that the film constituted an opportunity lost since there still remained, as in the depictions of the 1970s, an emphasis entirely "tourné vers le passé: les expropriés se souviennent et on ne saura rien de leur vie d'aujourd'hui même si cet aspect était un des objectifs du film. Unique exception, la famille Vautour qui continue sa lutte…. Vautour a choisi de consacrer sa vie à son expropriation, mais les autres où en sont-ils?"[53]

Indeed, there are relatively few interviews with people who had been expropriated, a much larger place being reserved for individuals who had been connected with the crisis (leaders of the citizens' committees, government officials, etc.), and of course there was the very large place accorded to Jackie Vautour who provided the focus for the second half of the film, not unlike the situation in the documentary from the 1970s. By and large, Bourbonnais' film dwelled on the same issues that had been touched on in the documentary made thirty years earlier; all that had really changed was that the park lands visited were now overgrown, providing little sense that anyone had ever lived there. If other stories were not told, this was – at least in part – because many of those who were contacted refused to speak, a point made in Richard's narration and by Bourbonnais in an interview about the documentary. On the subject of Vautour, the director observed: "Il est glorifié de la part des gens dans le film, mais les gens qui avaient quelque chose contre lui n'ont pas voulu venir témoigner devant la caméra. On a invité beaucoup de personnes, mais elles n'ont pas voulu venir."[54]

In spite of the focus on Vautour, however, there were moments when the film did provide some access to what had happened to the former residents in the nearly forty years since their expropriation. In this regard, the most touching moment in the film came with the interview of the family of Aurèle Arsenault. Arsenault had kind words for Vautour, viewing him as a hero who had stood up for the expropriated when no one else would. By contrast, his daughter, Doris Guimond thought that her father "était plus qu'un héros que Jackie" for all that he had done during the years since the expropriation – having moved his family to build a new life, all without the glare of television cameras. As for Jackie Vautour, who had received his considerable payment from the Hatfield government since the filming of the previous documentary, she had nothing but scorn, calling the payment "un cadeau avec nos taxes." While one can wish that the film had had more such stories, Doris Guimond's testimony – much like the stories that can now be told by the expropriates working with Parks Canada – offers the possibility of constructing a very different version of the Kouchibouguac story: one that reflects *Acadie* in the early twenty-first century, as much as those of the 1970s reflected that time of confrontation.

NOTES

1 In this regard, see Alan MacEachern, *Natural Selections: National Parks in Atlantic Canada, 1935–70* (Montreal: McGill-Queen's University Press, 2001).

2 In a similar case of whitewashing the past, the Historic Sites and Monuments Board of Canada put up a plaque in 2004 to tell the story of the Melanson settlement, just outside Annapolis Royal, Nova Scotia, to mark a site where an Acadian community had existed prior to the deportation. Oddly, the plaque indicated that the Melansons had "abandoned" the settlement in 1755, as if they had had a choice.

3 Jean Bourbonnais, *Kouchibouguac: L'histoire de Jackie Vautour et des expropriés* (Moncton: Bellefeuille Production et Productions Vic Pelletier, 2007).

4 This is a rather cursory description of the Kouchibouguac story. A more complete chronicle can be found in *Report of the Special Inquiry on Kouchibouguac National Park* (Gérard La Forest, Chairman; Muriel Kent-Roy, Commissioner), October 1981; hereafter referred to as La Forest/Kent-Roy.

5 Joy Parr, *Sensing Changes: Technologies, Environments, and the Everyday, 1954–2003* (Vancouver: UBC Press, 2010); Jennifer Nelson, *Razing Africville: A Geography of Racism* (Toronto: University of Toronto Press, 2008); Jean-Paul Raymond, *La Mémoire de Mirabel: le président des expropriés, Jean-Paul Raymond, se raconte à Gilles Boileau* (Montréal: Méridien, 1988). There were many other such examples, all cases of what James C. Scott has called "high modernism," which found the state imposing its will in the name of "progress" with scant regard for the interests of those already resident on the land, often viewing their displacement as in their own interest. For Scott's classic statement of the dangers of high modernism, see his *Seeing Like a State: How Certain Schemes to Improve the Human Condition Have Failed* (New Haven, CT: Yale University Press, 1998).

6 See, in particular, the essays by Bill Waiser, David Neufeld, Brad Martin, and I.S. MacLaren.

7 MacEachern, *Natural Selections*, 42.

8 Archives du Centre d'études acadiennes, Université de Moncton (hereafter CEA), Fonds Muriel-Kent-Roy,

188–119: "Proposed Kouchibouguac National Park: Preliminary Report, March 16, 1967." The La Forest/Kent-Roy commission observed that in the park territory "are found many different kinds of animals, fish, birds and plants ... [including] seals at play on the offshore islands, and 27 specific species of orchids including one hybrid believed to be unique" (5).

9   Provincial Archives of New Brunswick (PANB), RS106. 16/6, Dollard Landry, "Report on Survey of Kent County National Park: A Study of Its People and Their Relocation," 16 September 1968.

10 *New Brunswick's New National Park: What does it mean for the residents of Kent County?* (Fredericton: Government of New Brunswick, 1968).

11 Joel Belliveau, "Acadian New Brunswick's Ambivalent Leap into the Canadian Liberal Order," in *Creating Postwar Canada: Community, Diversity, and Dissent 1945–75*, ed. Magda Fahrni and Robert Rutherdale, 69 (Vancouver: UBC Press, 2008). Belliveau provides an excellent overview of changes in *Acadie* during the 1960s and 1970s that are pertinent to the Kouchibouguac story.

12 La Forest/Kent-Roy, 26.

13 PANB, RS639: C7, statement of R.S. MacLaggan to Interdepartmental Committee, 26 November 1968.

14 For the disinclination of Acadians to express their grievances on a public stage, see my *Remembering and Forgetting in Acadie: A Historian's Journey through Public Memory* (Toronto: University of Toronto Press, 2009).

15 Moncton, in particular, was a site of protest, represented as it was by the infamous Mayor Leonard Jones (1964–73), who preferred the deferential Acadians of the 1950s. An interesting view of the Université de Moncton students can be found in the documentary film, *L'Acadie l'Acadie?!?*, ONF, 1971.

16 Belliveau, "Acadian New Brunswick," 76; Belliveau has also dealt with the student movement of the time in "Contributions estudiantines à la Révolution tranquille acadienne," in *Regards croisés sur l'histoire et la littérature acadiennes*, ed. Madeleine Frédéric and Serge Jaumin, 169–90 (Brussels: Peter Lang, 2006).

17 La Forest/Kent-Roy, 12.

18 Ibid., 74.

19 *Globe and Mail*, 5 June 1972.

20 *L'Évangéline*, 28 March 1974.

21 La Forest/Kent-Roy, 12. In addition to the skyrocketing costs needed to resolve questions of property rights, the original estimate of $300,000 to extinguish fishing rights ended up at a final price of $2.2 million, and that did not even entirely do the job.

22 On the subject of the petition, see La Forest/Kent-Roy, 88.

23 *Globe and Mail*, 19 March 1980.

24 Ibid., 4 April 1980, 26 April 1980.

25 *Ottawa Citizen*, 29 October 1987.

26 Of course, the notion that the residents of Kouchibouguac might have been allowed to remain to play the roles of characters in a theme park has problems of its own.

27 MacEachern, *Natural Selections*, 238; Kopas, *Taking the Air: Ideas and Change in Canada's National Parks* (Vancouver: UBC Press, 2007), 88;

A.T. Davidson, "Canada's National Parks: Past and Future," in *The Canadian National Parks: Today and Tomorrow Conference II: Ten Years Later,* ed. J.G. Nelson et al., 26 (Waterloo: University of Waterloo, Faculty of Environmental Studies, 1979).

28 See, for instance, Robert Viau, *Les visages d'Évangeline: Du poème au mythe* (Beauport: MNH, 1998); I also discuss such issues in *Remembering and Forgetting in Acadie.* The reference to the Acadian deportation as an act of "ethnic cleansing" comes from John Mack Faragher, *A Great and Noble Scheme* (New York: W.W. Norton, 2005), 469.

29 *L'Évangéline,* 12 November 1976; 23 November 1976; 19 November 1976.

30 Jules Boudreau, *Cochu et le Soleil* (Moncton: Éditions d'Acadie, 1979), n.p.

31 The first of these works can be seen at: http://web.umoncton.ca/gaum/roussel/en_relief/en_relief9.html. Roussel gave the second work to Vautour in recognition of his resistance (e-mail correspondence with the artist, 13 March 2008).

32 http://zacharyrichard.com/english/reports2006.html.

33 Zachary Richard, *La Ballade de Jackie Vautour* (1978); Richard's English translation of the lyrics is available at: http://zacharyrichard.com/francais/parolesetpoesie.html. In some versions of the lyrics, there is a short poem that was not recorded and which refers directly to Vautour's removal from his land:

Exproprié de Kouchibouguac le 5 novembre, 1976.

Tous nos affaires étaient mis dans un truck.

Pis, ils sont rentré dedans avec un bulldozer.

Ils ont cassé toute la maison et le trailer à côté.

Ils ont rien laissé du tout

(http://www.lyricsmania.com)

Richard returned to the same representation of Vautour twenty years later when he recorded a song that had already achieved some success for the Acadian band, Zéro Celsius. *Petit Codiac* (written by the band's Yves Chiasson) has in its refrain a tribute to various "freedom fighters," including Crazy Horse, Beausoleil [Broussard], Louis Riel, and Jackie Vautour.

34 Zachary Richard, blog posted, 5 July 2006, http://zacharyrichard.com/english/reports2006.html; blog posted, 1 June 2005, http://zacharyrichard.com/english/reports2005.html.

35 Gérald Leblanc. *Moncton Mantra,* trans. Jo-Anne Elder (Toronto: Guernica Editions, 2001), 86. Leblanc billed this work as an autobiographical novel.

36 Gérald Leblanc, *L'extrême frontière. Poèmes : 1972–1988* (Moncton: Éditions d'Acadie, 1988), 57–58; 1755, *Kouchibouguac,* in album *Vivre à la Baie,* 1979. Leblanc wrote many of the lyrics for 1755. This particular poem/song, however, was sufficiently important in defining Leblanc's career that in the film *L'extrême frontière* (NFB, 2006) dedicated to his life (he died in 2005) it was played from time to time, leading up to a short rendition performed by Zachary Richard near the close.

37 The role of the NFB in representing a Canadian national park is also the subject of George Colpitts's essay in this volume. While *Kouchibouguac* was in opposition to the creation of the park, the film discussed by Colpitts, *Bears and Man* (1978), was funded by Parks Canada, which wanted to stop visitors from feeding the animals. The films were both produced in the late 1970s and dealt with similar issues in the sense that *Bears and Man* advocated separating humans from animals within the parks, and in that regard echoed the problem at the core of the Kouchibouguac crisis, namely that residents could not live within a park.

38 David Lonergan, "La mémoire nécessaire," *Acadie nouvelle*, 29 September 2007.

39 Jacques Savoie, *Raconte-moi Massabielle* (Moncton: Éditions d'Acadie, 1979); *Massabielle* (NFB, 1983). While most of the elements of the novel were carried over to the film (directed and with a screenplay by Savoie), it was very short (only 25 minutes) and some elements of the novel were purged, so as to keep the focus on Haché, the lawyer, and Stella.

40 See, for instance, Tony Simons, "'Raconte-moi Acadie': The Competing Voices of Acadia in Jacques Savoie's Novel *Raconte-Moi Massabielle* and his film *Massabielle*," in *Francophone Post-Colonial Cultures: Critical Essays*, ed. Kamal Salhi, 251–61 (Lanham, MD: Lexington, 2003).

41 Simons, "'Raconte-moi Acadie'," 255.

42 Nelson Landry, "'Kouchibouguac' la nostalgie," *L'Évangéline*, 26 March 1979.

43 Special Inquiry, 75; 83. After having viewed the film, Gérard La Forest wrote that the film makers did "not mind twisting reality a bit to convince people" (CEA, 188-1114).

44 Ibid., 110.

45 *Acadie nouvelle*, 30 July 2007. Interestingly, Parks Canada had a similar reunion only a week later for those who had been expropriated from Parc Forillon in Quebec, which was created in 1970. Radio-Canada (Est du Québec), "Parc Forillon: Retour émouvant des expropriés," http://www.radio-canada.ca/regions/est-quebec/2007/08/03/005-forillon-expropriation.asp?ref=rss. Further reunions, both of which I had the good fortune to attend, took place at Kouchibouguac during the summers of 2008 and 2009.

46 "Parcs Canada tend un rameau d'olivier aux expropriés de Kouchibouguac," radioacif.com, 30 September 2007, http://www.radioactif.com/nouvelles/imprime-32082-2.html.

47 *Acadie nouvelle*, 12 January 2008. A visitor's centre, providing significant attention to the lives of the families that had been removed, is slated to open in 2011.

48 http://zacharyrichard.com/english/reports2006.html.

49 While the population of New Brunswick declined between 1996 and 2001, Dieppe's increased by nearly 20 per cent. Moreover, while Acadian incomes lagged behind those of English-speakers everywhere else in the province, in Dieppe the Acadians had average incomes higher than those

of their English-speaking counterparts. Gilles Grenier, "Linguistic and Economic Characteristics of Francophone Minorities in Canada: A Comparison of Ontario and Quebec," *Journal of Multilingual and Multicultural Development* 18 (1997): 297; *Census of Canada*, 1996; 2001.

50 These celebrations are discussed in my *Remembering and Forgetting in Acadie*, but also in the documentary film that I produced and Leo Aristimuño directed: *Life After Île Ste-Croix* (Montreal: NFB, 2006).

51 Speech by Michel Cyr, 26 June 2004.

52 The plays are by Emma Haché, (*Wolfe*) and Marcel-Romain Thériault (*La persistance du sable*); the novel is by Jean Babineau (*Infini*).

53 David Lonergan, "La mémoire nécessaire," *Acadie nouvelle*, 29 September 2007.

54 Sylvie Mousseau, "Le combat de Jackie Vautour sur grand écran," *Acadie nouvelle*, 20 September 2007.

Kluane National Park Reserve, 1923–1974: Modernity and Pluralism

ॐ

DAVID NEUFELD[1]
PARKS CANADA/YUKON COLLEGE

Introduction

An aggressive and extensive transformation of Canadian heritage protected areas took place from the late 1960s through the 1970s. Jean Chrétien, the minister responsible for much of this activity, later wrote about his proudest moment, 22 February 1972:

> when I was able to announce the expansion of Canada's na-
> tional park system to northern Canada and the creation of the
> first three national parks north of the 60th parallel – Kluane
> in the Yukon, and Nahanni and Baffin Island (Auyuittuq) in
> the Northwest Territories. It was at this moment, as Minister
> responsible for National Parks, that I was able to ensure that
> thousands of square kilometres of unique Canadian wilder-
> ness will be preserved in their natural state in perpetuity for

FIG. 1. THE MOUNTAIN VASTNESS OF KLUANE NATIONAL PARK AND RESERVE. [D. NEUFELD, JUNE 2002, #023.]

the enjoyment of future generations of Canadians and indeed for all mankind.... [O]ne of my greatest satisfactions comes from the creation of 10 new national parks, the expansion of the area dedicated to national parks by almost 50 percent, and the extension of the National Parks system to every province and both territories.[2]

However, achieving such a monumental set of national parks was neither quick nor easy. The idea for a protected area in the southwest Yukon dates back to the 1920s, and, through the course of its establishment as Kluane National Park Reserve (Kluane NPR) in 1974, it was fraught with difficulties.

In 1978, John Theberge described the complicated and generally confrontational pathway to protection that led to the establishment of "Kluane National Park."[3] He outlined the interests and interactions of the prominent players who promoted or resisted state protection for Kluane over a span of nearly three decades. He also noted how a scientific definition of national park values and roles, consultation with interest groups, and internal coherence amongst the responsible government departments affected Parks Canada's understanding of the meaning of a national park, and how the agency's changing definition assisted, or limited, the development of the park. There is, however, an assumption in Theberge's account that the different participating groups shared a commensurate knowledge base and that, within a rational planning framework, all perspectives and interests could be accommodated. If we reconsider the establishment of Kluane NPR now, thirty-five years on, we may question the efficacy of such a process of consultation and accommodation. Can Western modernist thought,[4] with its assumption of shared knowledge, with the implication of culture as unimportant, realistically address a culturally pluralistic situation? Will such an analysis meaningfully present interests forwarded from a Yukon Athapaskan cultural perspective? Can it even imagine their existence?[5]

The challenges of presenting the history of northern national parks such as Kluane National Park and Reserve are perhaps best addressed by stepping away from the usual contest between development and preservation. In his statement above, Chrétien went on to identify himself with the Canadian mainstream, as "a strong believer in the philosophy of balanced development. Northern Canada is large enough to accommodate both the resource development that is essential for the economic well-being of all Canadians and the need for conservation of our natural heritage, which is just as essential for the quality of life of a society."[6] Describing the establishment of Kluane NPR as a confrontation between different facets of Western culture – between the betterment of the human condition through the conquest of nature for greater wealth and preserved areas illustrating a romantic idyll of God's handiwork or the base line of the continent which their civilization has successfully transformed from wilderness – holds limited value for gaining an understanding of the Aboriginal interests and connections to place within this debate.

In considering the national purposing of a part of the southwest Yukon between 1923 and 1974, this chapter sets aside the Western national discourse of protection or development, already identified as flip sides of the same coin in John Sandlos's chapter. Instead, this purposing process is viewed through the late twentieth century lens of northern cultural contact. This approach highlights the consequences of a Western rational vision of a highest or best use determined through universalistic scientific principles and considers how an engagement with Aboriginal people, using local contextually set knowledge, might be possible. Against such a backdrop, it examines the changing conceptions of a national park and the responsibilities it has, both to the nation and to the community hosting it.

Meeting Newcomers in the Southwest Yukon

The Southern Tutchone of the southwest Yukon[7] did not live in an isolated mountain Arcadia. Extensive trade and travel networks connected them to peoples both near and far away. Tanned hides and finished clothing were exchanged for fish oil and shells with the Tlingit on the nearby Pacific coast, while the precious obsidian in the mountains was traded into Alaska and south and east far into the interior. The long presence of the Southern Tutchone generated a detailed experiential knowledge of the local geography, seasons, and resources, allowing both a rich subsistence lifeway and a civilized discourse between peoples.[8] In the nineteenth century, though, newcomers with quite different appetites and values arrived. Russian, and later British, Canadian, and American traders probed the Pacific coast seeking furs to feed into their global trade networks. During the Klondike rush, miners moved through the region looking for gold and introducing new trade goods and animals. Although the southwest Yukon was isolated from much of the new traffic, some trading posts, prospectors, and game-hunting outfits moved into the area.[9] While these early developments had only limited effects on the Southern Tutchone, the newcomers anticipated more significant changes to the land and its residents. J.D. McLean, the assistant deputy and secretary of Indian Affairs, instructing the Yukon's first Indian Agent on his duties in the spring of 1914, wrote:

... you should endeavour by all means to gain the confidence of the Indians, who should be treated with considerate patience and who should learn that they have in yourself as an official of this department, an officer whose sole interest it is to protect them in the enjoyment of their rights, to improve their condition and to assist them in their progress towards civilization."[10]

In addition to civilizing Indians, the newcomers also grappled with the task of civilizing the land: making its resources more tractable to the creation of wealth in their vision of the world. The transformation of wild, unknown lands required the restructuring of human relationships with it. For the expanding and impatient Euro-Canadian state, this precluded any detailed study of place. Rather it applied an abstract, universalistic, scientific system of management to impose a more easily understood and administered order, an order reflecting their cultural values and interests. In the gold fields, the introduction of the Free Entry system of mining law addressed investment risks, limited the friction of speculation, and promoted the efficient exploitation of a targeted resource. The success of this approach, as in the amount of gold extracted, is evidenced by the rapid replacement of haphazard hand mining by well-organized corporate entities capable of fielding industrial scale dredges powered by centralized power plants and directing their activities through a scientific prospect drilling program.

After two decades of intensive gold production, however, the conditions supporting this infrastructure had changed and the Yukon mining industry was moribund by the 1920s. In response, the federally appointed administration of the Yukon Territory, directed to make the territory fiscally self-sufficient, was forced to consider new strategies for economic development. Up to this point wildlife had been largely unregulated; Aboriginal peoples enjoyed unconstrained hunting and fishing opportunities, only rarely subjected to local restrictions.[11] There was an implicit recognition of Aboriginal interests and the capacity of their traditional management practices.[12] However, the collapse of the mining industry led the territorial administration to reconsider this approach. In the early 1920s game regulations were revised, resulting in the commodification of animals as an economic resource. Rather than acknowledging Aboriginal social and subsistence reliance upon hunting,

FIG. 2. JACQUOT TRADING POST ON KLUANE LAKE, 1922. [YUKON ARCHIVES, CLAUDE AND MARY TIDD FONDS, #7206.]

FIG. 3. VILLAGE OF BURWASH LANDING, 1942. [YUKON ARCHIVES, R.A. CARTTER FONDS, #1515.]

regulations now considered their harvest as an administrative method of reducing the cash costs of relief. This change in attitude allowed the expansion
of trapping, big game outfitting, and the development of a fur farming industry, each taking a growing piece out of subsistence hunting by the 1940s.
With the revival of mining in the 1930s, Aboriginal subsistence lifeways were
further limited.

The Canadian state carried a broad vision of what constituted development. While economic exploitation was generally the first consideration,
rational thinking on best use sometimes suggested improvements to place.[13]
In the early 1920s, federal wildlife scientists proposed game reserves to ensure the future of wildlife populations both endemic and imported, including an Indian trapping area in the Peel River area – a proposal opposed by
the Yukon Council – and a national park buffalo reserve to be operated by
the Canadian Parks Branch, akin to those prairie parks noted by Sandlos
but in the southwestern Yukon.[14] However, as game appeared abundant and
importing buffalo proved costly, no action followed. H.A. Jeckell, Comptrol-
ler and head of the Yukon administration, was adamant about the importance of economic development and argued against any land withdrawals:
"I would not recommend the creation of special reserves in this territory
for the Indians for hunting and trapping," he wrote, "as such action would

greatly hamper the exploration and development of the mineral resources of the Territory."[15] The industrial strategy of purposing lands and resources was comprehensive and intrusive. Its totalizing, modernist narrative denied the existence of both local knowledge and regional interests, assuming as universal its own, imposed, knowledge and values. But over the next half century it generated a powerful response from Yukon Aboriginal people who felt they were being shouldered out of their own country.

Visions of a Northern National Park

Despite the early interest in a Yukon national park, nothing further happened until the Alaska Highway arrived in the Yukon in 1942. The presence of large numbers of foreign soldiers and construction workers in the previously isolated region appeared to threaten wildlife populations. The presence of the road also opened up new areas for prospecting and prompted thoughts of an expanded post-war tourism industry. The United States government moved quickly in Alaska, slapping down a twenty-mile-wide restrictive corridor on both sides of the highway in July 1942. Harold Ickes, the American Secretary of the Interior, noting the wilderness area between Kluane Lake and the Alaska boundary, suggested Canada consider similar restrictions to protect its interests.[16] Five months later, the Canadian government withdrew all unalienated lands within one mile on either side of the highway corridor, and set aside "an area of 10,130 square miles in the south western part of the Territory in order that it may be available in its present condition for establishment as a national park."[17]

Federal officials, having earlier and unsuccessfully pressured the Territorial Council for game preserves, moved quickly. Already fearing major losses in wildlife populations, R.A. Gibson, Director of Lands for the Canadian Department of Mines and Resources, noted the need "to save the game [in the Kluane area] from serious depletion and to provide breeding stock which, if protected adequately, would restore the game to its former numbers." He acknowledged that this "would deprive the Indians of some of their former hunting ground but it was considered that if a game sanctuary had not been created and sound conservation practices started there soon would have been little game for the Indians or hunters."[18] In the spring of 1943, the Territorial

Council agreed and created the Kluane Game Preserve, where all hunting would be forbidden. But while game animals were temporarily protected, their habitat remained vulnerable. In response to pressure from mining interests, the sanctuary was opened for prospecting, staking, and mining in December 1944. Prospectors were also allowed to hunt without restriction.[19]

Meanwhile, the Northern Administration Branch dispatched several teams of biologists to the Yukon "to inquire into the existence of [scenic and recreational areas] ... in their primeval condition."[20] C.H.D. Clark, assigned to the "Kluane Reserve" in 1943, reported:

> There can be no question that it is of superlative quality. It contains the highest mountains in Canada, the most extensive glaciers on the Canadian mainland, and scenery of remarkable grandeur. In so far as wildlife is concerned, it contains an excellent representation of the species of the region. Some, such as martin and beaver, are extremely rare, and the park can make a great contribution towards the rehabilitation of these and other fur-bearers.
>
> The proposed park would protect game animals, such as Dall's sheep and Osborn's caribou, which have never previously enjoyed the protection of a permanent reserve in Canada.... [N]umbers will be such (under protection) as to arouse the enthusiasm of tourists.

In addition to endorsing its "grandeur" as befitting a national park, Clark also recommended the introduction of both buffalo and mule deer as valuable resources. He noted that "The area of the Yukon suitable for buffalo is much more vast than any potential farm or stock land, and it would be desirable to have it producing something." Aboriginal settlements on the fringes of the reserve were deemed "unnecessary and undesirable to interfere with" if they were outside the boundary, like Klukshu; or if unfortunately within, as was Dalton Post, then destined to disappear, as the activities sustaining them, "hunting, fishing, and trapping," were now excluded by the sanctuary regulations.[21] Clark noted other disadvantages suffered by aboriginal trappers: although no method existed to grant exclusive trapping rights (thereby keeping newcomer trappers from entering areas trapped by Aboriginal families), regulations did allow a trapper to sell a trapline – something only white trappers did. As the natives were unlikely to adopt a practice they considered anti-social, Clark recommended the registration of traplines, bringing trappers within the state's model of order.[22]

The popular understanding of national parks in the middle part of the twentieth century centred on three main expectations.[23] Scenic beauty was paramount. Public perceptions focused upon mountains and waterfalls as icons of the untrammelled character of the natural world. In his report on Kluane, Clark differentiated between Kathleen Lake, with its mountainous viewscape, and nearby "bush lakes," with limited tourist appeal. With the soul-restoring beauty came opportunities for recreation. Camping in the forest, surrounded by an abundance of large mammals, national parks provided a tourist "playground," a playground that made money. Many stories, especially those anticipating the boom of the post-war economy, included promises of employment coming with a national park and the tourist horde that would migrate up the Alaska Highway. In the summer of 1941, the *Dawson News* reminded Yukoners that "The wisdom of … a system of national playgrounds dedicated to the people of Canada for their benefit, education and enjoyment has never been more apparent."[24] Finally, and in Kluane the original spark for action, there was the necessity of preserving wildlife, both as a tourist attraction[25] and as a sanctuary to breed animals for hunting in surrounding areas.[26] To fulfill this multiplicity of tasks, national parks needed an ordered regime following scientific principles of management and people on the ground to enforce such a regime. Aboriginal peoples, who would not get the vote until 1960, were not yet fully Canadians.

High Modernism Arrives in the Yukon

To be Canadian in the post-war period was to be modern, and federal policy in the north reflected the belief that the North needed help to catch up with the rest of Canada. This period accordingly saw huge changes in the Canadian north. The completion of the Alaska Highway in 1943, followed by the CANOL [Canadian Oil] Road and the expansion of the road network after the war – to Dawson in 1955 and the start of the Dempster Highway a few years later – connected the Yukon to the outside world, and opportunities for more intensive mineral prospecting and other forms of resource development grew exponentially. In addition to huge investments in northern access, the federal government greatly expanded the social safety net for Canadians. The state's position on the North was summed up by Gordon Robertson, deputy minister of Northern Affairs and Natural Resources, in 1960: "We own the north.... It belongs to us. Canadians for this reason, must look to the north to see what it is good for, to see how to use it."[27] Such attitudes would have important effects upon the planning and development of Kluane National Park, and on the Aboriginal people living around it.

Mining activity in the Yukon accelerated through the 1950s. Production of copper restarted at the Whitehorse mines after World War II, a large asbestos mine opened near Dawson, and the short-lived Johobo copper mine began operations within the Kluane Game Sanctuary in 1959. In the mid-1960s, the huge Cyprus Anvil lead/zinc open pit mine started operation, resulting in the new town of Faro. Even grander visions were spawned by the almost unimaginably large hydro-electric power generation opportunities in the Yukon. As early as 1946, the Aluminum Company of America proposed a large hydro project in the upper Yukon basin to support aluminum production in southeast Alaska. Variations on this idea continue to the present, the most extensive suggesting the reversal of the entire upper watershed of the Yukon River to flow though hydro-electric plants on the Taku and Alsek rivers: the latter in the heart of the land reserved for the national park. In 1949 the U.S. Bureau of Reclamation suggested the scale of such a project might require the town of Whitehorse to be moved and while "local residents ... would resist such a move ... [this] should not influence the planning of the project for the national good of both Canada and the United States."[28] The sense of excitement and national prosperity generated by the mining industry were celebrated and reinforced by the Government of Canada. Under the direction of Prime Minister John Diefenbaker's "Northern Vision" of development and progress, the National Parks Branch planned a network of national historic sites commemorating the Klondike gold rush. The sites spoke to their time: the nation glowed in the fulfillment of history.[29] Kluane National Park would reflect the same spirit of accomplishment.

These new developments also affected the relationship between Aboriginal people and the natural world. Demands for wildlife as part of the Territory's economic development and the extension of both government regulation and services had catastrophic effects upon Yukon First Nations people.[30] The Territorial Council made a major revision to the Yukon Game Ordinance in 1947 to address the interests of the recently established Yukon Fish and Game Association (1945),[31] and to broaden access to wildlife for both tourism development and big game outfitters. The desire to maximize the economic value of wildlife resulted in much stricter controls on access to the land – though the new regulations applied to *all* hunters and trappers, both native and newcomer. Percy Henry, a Tr'ondëk Hwëch'in elder in Dawson, described this separation from their land as, "Regulation, regulation, regulation, halfway to Heaven."[32] Meanwhile, the Yukon Council believed that, with the expansion of the federal social safety net, subsistence needs were now part of the past.[33] Waged jobs were available for the progressive, while welfare was provided for the reluctant. Them Kjar, the first director of the Yukon's Game and Publicity Department, wrote with satisfaction about these changes in 1954:

> If we look back only five or six years we find the times in the Yukon have changed greatly due to the many new mining, prospecting, and building enterprises which suddenly have been established, as well as improved road and air transportation, thereby enabling trappers (Indian and White) to occupy themselves elsewhere at a much higher profit than trapping or hunting could give, leaving obsolete the old way of living off the country as well as nullifying the use of dogs.[34]

But not everything was quite as neat and tidy on the fringes of the future national park. In the original boundaries of the game sanctuary, a ten-mile set-back had been allowed along the Alaska Highway near Burwash Landing for an outfitting business and as a local hunting and trapping area for the Burwash Indian Band. The Yukon Fish and Game Association and the Royal Canadian Mounted Police requested the boundary be brought up to the road to enhance the recovery of wildlife populations and facilitate the enforcement of game laws, and the Yukon Council obliged in April 1946. Having been denied access to their former ground, "most abundant in game,"[35] by the establishment of the sanctuary in 1943, the Burwash people were outraged by the closure of this last piece of their hunting ground south of Kluane

FIG. 4. RCMP OFFICER AT KLUANE LAKE DETACHMENT, 1943. [YUKON ARCHIVES, JAMES PHILLIPS FONDS, 93/93, #80.]

Lake. Before the start of the summer, the community wrote to J.E. Gibbon, the Yukon Indian Agent, noting the worsening of their situation due to:

... game laws in the great part of our territory called "Proposed Kluane Park" or again the "Kluane Sanctuary."

As you are aware, those who have proposed this park or sanctuary have taken with its limits all of our village as well as the part of our territory more easily reached and where the game is more abundant.... Up to the last spring we were given a certain freedom around our village and in the above mentioned territory. But we are now prohibited by federal and territorial laws, to hunt or trap there – fishing only is allowed, and that for how long?

We most firmly protest against these conditions forced upon us. For we are thus deprived of our means of subsistence and development; we, the natives of this country, are being driven away like a pack of useless dogs.

In the portion of our territory not included in the limits of the park or sanctuary, it may be possible to live for a time without starving; but on considering the difficulty of transportation in some seasons, the scarcity of game in that district, and also the distance from the village, the store, the mission and the school for our children, one must admit that such a solution would be disastrous for us.

It is not the Indians that are a threat to the game and fur trade of the country, but it is them that are punished. Before the whites came into this country, game and fur were abundant although the Indians were in much greater numbers than they are today. Hunting and trapping are our only resources – the whites have a thousand ways of earning money for a living....

Now prospectors arrive in great numbers each year, and they are allowed to hunt anywhere, even in the park, for their meat when they are "in dire condition." The government even makes them roads to make their work easier. We all know that they hardly bring any meat with them and can always easily claim to be "in dire condition." Having thus a sort of exclusive right on the game, they are in abundance, while we who cannot make money like they do, are prohibited this meat of which we have more need to live than the whites do.

We beseech you therefore to help us, to protect us in these conditions in which we have been placed by the development of the country and the new invasion of the whites [who] can work on the highway, look for gold and earn money in a thousand ways, why should we not be reserved, we the natives of this country, the exclusive right to hunt and trap in our territory either in the park or out.

We are not asking a favor, but the right to live and develop. The whites are always favored to our detriment. We are simply forgotten and set aside. After all we are human beings like they and in this country we have a right prior to theirs.

We have no objection to the development of the country, on the condition however that we be left free to live and develop ourselves also.[36]

The letter stirred up a hornet's nest. Government officials moved quickly to defend their programs and explain away the Burwash complaints. F.H.R. Jackson, the National Parks Branch superintendent in Whitehorse, reported in September 1946 that "no direct complaint has been [previously] received … from any Indian regarding the curtailment of their hunting activities in their favoured hunting area [now well within the Sanctuary]."[37] Two months later, Hugh Bostock, a geologist with the Department of Mines and Resources, submitted a frank appraisal of the situation based on his conversations with Eugene Jacquot, one of the two brothers who had established the trading post at Burwash Landing in 1910. According to Bostock, "before Jacquot came Indians seldom hunted in the park area south of the Highway so that its establishment does not deprive them of a main hunting ground," and that the area "is not particularly good game country, particularly now."[38] Subsequent investigations by the Fur Supervisor and the Indian Agent agreed that it was the arrival of the Jacquot brothers that had spoiled the Indians by luring them across the lake from their "ancestral home." They asserted the Indians had plenty of "good game country" on the north side of the lake,

Fig. 5. Jessie Joe, Mary Jacquot and Mrs. Jimmie of Burwash Landing, 1948. Jessie and Mrs. Jimmie were among the signers of the 1946 petition. [Yukon Archives, Elmer Harp Jr. fonds, 2006/2, #237.]

and, besides, other alternatives had been available to them: the Jacquots had offered the Indians boats to go fishing, which met with little interest, and there were no signs of any gardening in the village "despite the fact that sufficient seed has been sent annually to this group to satisfy their needs." The two men felt that "the close association of whites and Indians is a great detriment to the welfare of this Band of some 32 or 33 souls" and recommended their removal from the community to a more remote site.[39]

In 1946, and again in 1950, Father Morrisset in Burwash Landing and Bishop J.L. Coudert in Whitehorse suggested that, as the Burwash Indians had hunted previously in the sanctuary area, perhaps a special reserve for Indian hunting and trapping might be arranged, referring to the special situation in Wood Buffalo National Park.[40] There were immediate objections from both those advocating the rebuilding of wildlife stocks and the

Fig. 6. Canadian
government
geologist Hugh
Bostock. [Yukon
Archives, Bill Hare
fonds, #6985.]

National Parks Branch. In 1942, C.K. Le Capelain, one of the first to promote the idea of a Kluane National Park, and H.F. Lewis, Chief of the Canadian Wildlife Service, both wrote to the deputy minister: "It would be very undesirable to give the Indians a formal claim of this kind to any part of the National Parks reserve."[41] When Yukon Commissioner A.H. Gibson weighed in on the matter, he noted that Them Kjar, his assistant G.I. Cameron, and Superintendant Jackson supported "rigid enforcement of the preserve regulations." Gibson also reported the opinion of the local Indian Agent:

(a) he observes the scarcity of game and realizes the desirability of protecting it

(b) he is impatient with this particular band of Indians because they are not energetic or progressive

(c) it would simplify contact with the Indians if they were removed from this settlement and it must be admitted that if the Indians were forced to rely more on themselves, it would likely have good results.

They have obviously, to some extent, been pauperized and are more inclined to rely on maintenance from the church and the Indian Agent, then to bestir themselves to improve their conditions.

To address the immediate situation, Gibson offered a special one-time hunting permit for the sanctuary and requested "a careful survey ... of the game populations of the preserve by a competent wildlife observer" to determine both the economic value and best use for this resource.[42] The following summer, A.W.F. Banfield arrived to make the survey. He agreed that there was employment "available for Indians willing to work" and that there was an "unutilized opportunity for a fishery on Kluane Lake." He also

... found no signs of hardship among the Burwash Indians, all the men who had an inclination for work were employed by outfitters or service stations or on highway maintenance. Work in cutting wood, restaurants, etc., was available for women. Unemployed widows were receiving full rations from the Indian Agent. I received no complaints of destitution or unfairness with respect to trapping and hunting privileges from anyone except Father Morrisset.... There are good opportunities for fishing and gardening at Burwash Landing, but they are not utilized.[43]

According to government reports, then, the Indians would be fine, by either accepting wage labour or relocating to more remote territory; they did not need anything from the national park reserve.

Aboriginal Challenges to Modernism

From the late 1940s into the early 1950s, territorial and federal officials worked with industry to impose their vision of the modern world upon the Yukon. Any Aboriginal challenges to this colonialist regime were met with force, as the Indians of Burwash Landing discovered. While it appears Bostock had a relatively accurate understanding of the movement of the Kluane Lake Indians in the twentieth century, his (and others') conclusions about the centrality of contact in despoiling Indigenous peoples convinced him against any possibilities of Aboriginal adaption. Government officials preferred to think of Aboriginal peoples as either untouched, invisible, and thus safely out of the way, or defiled by contact with modernity, visible, and therefore unwanted.[44] In refusing to accept the community's claims, territorial officials, prodded by both the National Parks Branch and Indian Affairs, denied traditional aboriginal knowledge of place and even the existence of their culture. And to quell any continuing difficulties, they threatened to remove them altogether, thus completing the process of making the Indian invisible. Their approach to "best use" relied upon universalistic principles of scientific knowledge, still scanty on the specifics of the region, to manage the land, its people, and resources. In the enthusiasm for doing the right thing, the territorial and federal governments denied, not only the validity, but even the existence of the long tradition of deep local contextual knowledge shaping Southern Tutchone values, land use practices and their relationships with the Newcomers.

FIG. 7. RUPE CHAMBERS, PARK WARDEN, KLUANE GAME SANCTUARY, 1949. [YUKON ARCHIVES, RICHARD HARRINGTON FONDS, 79/27, #333.]

David Neufeld   255

The government, however, was not insensitive to the loss that the sanctuary regulations visited upon the Aboriginal peoples in the southwest Yukon. When the sanctuary boundaries were extended north to the Alaska Highway in October 1949, closing off the last part of country open to Aboriginal subsistence hunting, Indian Agent R.J. Meek proposed a muskrat trapping project as an alternative form of livelihood.[45] After surveys of the proposed area by the Regional Fur Supervisor and a biologist with the Canadian Wildlife Service, the Koidern River area of the sanctuary was chosen as a suitable site.[46] The muskrat project exhibited, on a small scale, the modernist traits active in shaping protected area management relations with Aboriginal peoples. In addition to subsuming the original subsistence hunting activities into a cash-driven trapping program that "best suit our ends in promoting the economy of the Indian people,"[47] the project also worked to "improve" the local environment. An active program designed to improve muskrat habitats, and thus it was hoped trapping success, included managing water levels and introducing alien species as a food supply.[48] But by the early 1960s the project lost any lingering Aboriginal connotation of trapping when it became known as the "muskrat farm."[49] This also reflected the denial of local contextual knowledge. A Canadian Wildlife Service biologist reviewing the farm operation in 1963 reported that he could not "raise any positive objection to [the Burwash families] trapping the area – *under proper control.*" Such supervision was necessary because "The Indians in the area have forgotten all their native management sense."[50] A.E. Fry, the new Indian Agent agreed, adding that

> It is possible that ultimately, out of the [Indian people trapping here], some might receive very useful training in this phase of wildlife management. We must recognize, of course, that at this stage we are dealing with a native lacking sufficient formal education to appreciate the completely scientific approach to fur management. Along with a competence in woodcraft, often walks a surprising ignorance of the true characteristics of specific populations in their environment. And our Indian people are no exception. In this way our fur project could be eminently useful as an instrument of education.[51]

The muskrat project did provide a number of Burwash Indian families with a modest livelihood, access to a part of their traditional hunting grounds and some grounds for hope in expanding their interests there.[52] However, attempts to establish a permanent access to this ground for trapping were stonewalled by National Parks officials. The Branch wished to avoid any commitments on possible park lands before a formal boundary was established.[53]

In the spring of 1958, W.A. Fuller of the Canadian Wildlife Service completed a report for the National Parks Branch on wildlife in the Yukon. He detailed its commercial, recreational, aesthetic, and scientific value, noting the small and rapidly diminishing number of Aboriginal people still relying upon subsistence hunting. While Fuller calculated the substantial cash worth of these different values, he suggested their non-monetary values were still greater.

> Wildlife is a part of our Canadian heritage which we have a right to expect and a duty to hand down unimpaired.... In the face of an expanding population and shrinking wilderness, the remaining wilderness assumes an every increasing importance. It seems self-evident that the highest use to which much of the Yukon could be put is the preservation of a part of our wilderness and wildlife heritage.[54]

The modern national park ideal of a land free of human beings was manifest – but it would not be long before a series of challenges by Aboriginal people eroded this confidence.

While the boundaries of the proposed national park might have remained undefined, the Parks Branch was actively developing its sense of what the park should be and attempting to negotiate its establishment through the thickets of local opinion. Yukon mining interests raised fierce resistance to the limitations associated with national parks, suggesting a special class of multiple-use national parks be created for the north.[55] The Branch, anxious to avoid any dilution of the *National Park Act*, answered with a compromise: the designation of a core protected area, considered inviolable, surrounded by a park *reserve*, whose boundaries might be altered if valuable resources were discovered. The reserve idea was outlined by the minister of Northern

Affairs and National Resources, Walter Dinsdale, in a letter to Yukon MP
Erik Nielsen in November 1961:

> I would ... withdraw the area in question from disposition.
> We would establish regulations permitting ... exploration for
> and development of minerals. I think the reservation might
> continue for a stated period – perhaps two years.... If no sub-
> stantial mineral development is proved up in the reservation
> period, the park would be established and we would go ahead
> with the construction and development needed to make it a
> National Park in all the senses of the word. If some part of
> the reservation area proves to have substantial mineralization
> within the reservation period it is *possible* that there could be
> some alteration in the boundaries of the proposed national
> park.... I certainly would not want to commit myself to the
> exclusion of areas or to the authorization of expenditures to
> create a National Park in too small or in an inappropriate
> area.[56]

Even as the future Kluane National Park was becoming more clearly defined,
the erasure of the Indian presence in the area of the national park reserve was
nearly complete. Mary Jane Johnson, a Kluane First Nation citizen and long-
time interpreter for Kluane NP&R, once illustrated this process by holding
her left hand palm up, saying "this was our land and our stories" and then,
pressing down with her right hand, adding "and then your stories came and
covered them all up."[57]

By the late 1960s, the creation of a Yukon national park appeared to be
imminent. The federal government was committed to an expansion of the
national park system, there was growing public support in the Yukon and
across Canada for new protected areas, and the core and reserve idea had, if
not quieted miners, hydro-electric planners, and outfitters, effectively marginalized them. In a 1969 background report on the Yukon park proposal,
planners with the National Parks Branch outlined the themes of human
history in the area: the Klondike gold rush, the Kluane gold rush and the
Mounted Police presence, the construction of the Alaska Highway, and the
commemorative naming of a Kluane mountain after the assassinated United

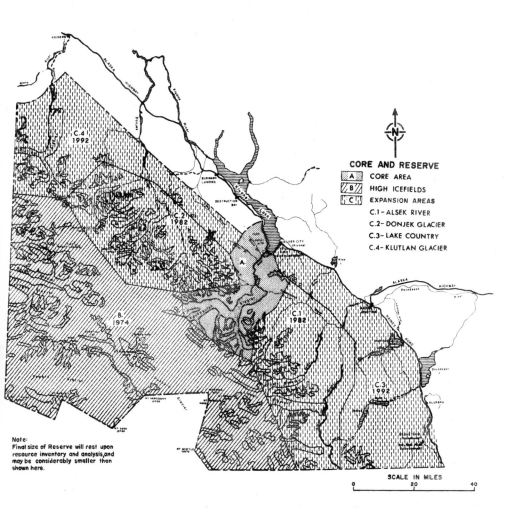

Fig. 8. Kluane core and reserve proposal. Canada, National Parks Service –
Planning, Yukon National Park Proposal: Background Data Report, Planning
Report 72, Ottawa, Oct. 1969, facing p. 15.

J.R.B. Coleman described his vision of how the reserve would work early in 1967:

I recommend that the Federal Government prepare to move unilaterally in the national interest and
establish a "core area" or National Park plus a National Park Reserve compromising lands which
might logically be added to the Park eventually if no significant mineral resource develops.

The "core area" or National Park should be substantial and be capable of standing by itself as a
national park, even if there is never any extension. The Donjek-Dezadeash area is still the choice...
our park planners consider that we could define an area of 750 – 1000 sq. Miles which would be
reasonably satisfactory. About fifty percent of this would be ice fields and perhaps 500 sq. miles
explorable territory. Incidentally, of the 8750 sq. Miles originally suggested much of it is so ice
covered or inaccessible as to protect itself.

[From: NAC RG84, A-2-A, vol. 11983, f.U2-20, pt.2 (1962–68) memo Feb. 22, 1967.]

States president John Kennedy.[58] The absence of any mention of Aboriginal peoples in this and most other contemporary reports indicated it lay beyond the realm of western thought. This notion was not isolated to the Yukon but reflected a broad international consensus amongst protected area professionals that people did not belong in parks.[59]

The disappearance of the Indian in protected areas was done as part of a liberal belief that rights, and thus identity, should be vested in the individual, rather than the group. Rationalism and democracy, the two highest achievements of western Enlightenment thought, were understood as the product of the individual mind and the individual citizen. In Canada, Prime Minister Trudeau pursued this ideal as a way of creating a "just society" and bringing unity to a country riven by the English-French linguistic divide. And he pursued it with consistency and vigour. He fully supported the 1969 policy document (the "White Paper") from the Department of Indian Affairs and Northern Development, which called upon Indian people in Canada to change "the course of history.... To be an Indian must be to be free – free to develop Indian cultures in an environment of legal, social and economic equality with other Canadians."[60] Aboriginal peoples disagreed with Canada's desire to slip away from the treaty obligations and responded by organizing in unprecedented ways. The Yukon Native Brotherhood was formed during consultations about the *Indian Act* and the draft policy in October 1968. It had three objectives: to oppose the White Paper, to draw down Indian Affairs programs to individual bands, and, most importantly, to seek negotiations for a comprehensive claim against Canada. In 1972 the Yukon Native Brotherhood prepared a statement of its position entitled *Together Today for Our Children Tomorrow: A Statement of Grievances and an Approach to the Settlement by the Yukon Indian People.*[61] This document laid out a plan for a settlement to recognize Indians as equal partners in the development of a shared future for the Yukon. On 14 February 1973, Trudeau met with Yukon Native Brotherhood representatives and accepted their submission as the basis for negotiations of a settlement.[62] The complete reversal by the federal government on its earlier rejection of Aboriginal status as "citizens plus" was no doubt influenced by the Supreme Court's mixed decision on the validity of the Nishga land claim.[63] The first demand by Yukon First Nations was a "freeze on development of all unoccupied crown land"[64]: including the Yukon national park.

FIG. 9. THE YUKON FIRST NATION LEADERS WHO TRAVELLED TO OTTAWA IN FEBRUARY, 1973 TO PRESENT *Together Today for Our Children Tomorrow* TO PRIME MINISTER TRUDEAU. [YUKON ARCHIVES, JUDY GINGELL COLLECTION, 98/74, #1.]

In December 1973 the Council for Yukon Indians, an umbrella organization established earlier that year to negotiate a settlement for both status and non-status Indians in the Yukon, presented a brief to a visiting Parliamentary Standing Committee. The brief strongly objected to the establishment of Kluane National Park, arguing that the federal government was acting in bad faith even before negotiations were fairly started, and asked the committee to get the minister to "back off from this land-grab policy." Flora MacDonald, a Conservative committee member, noted that the brief,

> has given me … serious cause for concern because it has pointed up a conflict between two legislative actions undertaken by the federal government. As the committee we are studying Bill S-4, An Act to Amend the National Parks Act which … outlines the boundaries of the proposed Kluane National Park.
>
> At the same time, the government has given a firm commitment … to negotiate the land claims of the Indian people in the Yukon. The extent of those land claims has yet to be determined…. If the establishment of the park were to be finalised before the negotiations concerning land claims were completed – that is, if a large area of Crown land were to be excluded from the negotiations – … the government could be accused of not acting in good faith in seeking a settlement concerning aboriginal title.

MacDonald went on to propose an amendment to the bill:

> (3) Any land so set aside as a national park shall not in any manner prejudice any right, title or interest of the people of native Indian origin of the Yukon should such a right, title or interest be eventually established.[65]

Kluane National Park Reserve was duly established in 1976. However, it represented a critical departure from the original intention of the core and reserve proposal, which was to allow time to assess the "best and highest use" for the land in the Kluane game sanctuary: that is, allowing time for economic interests to be fully explored and developed before committing the land to national park status. Miners were allowed a few summer seasons for assessment, but the "rational" park issue – western protection versus western exploitation – which had dominated the discussions of the park in Kluane through the three decades was abruptly closed off. There would be no "full National Park ... until the Native Claim issue in the Yukon was settled."[66] The new issue shaping the national park (and subsequent northern national parks, as Brad Martin shows elsewhere in this volume) was the negotiation of a diplomatic and cultural relationship between the Aboriginal peoples of the Yukon and the largely Euro-Canadian society, which had arrived in stages through the twentieth century.

A settlement with the Champagne and Aishihik First Nations in 1995 allowed the establishment of Kluane National Park on that portion of the lands within the Champagne and Aishihik traditional territory. However, the remainder of the reserved lands remains Kluane National Park Reserve, pending the implementation of agreements with both the Kluane First Nations (signed in 2003) and the White River First Nation (negotiations continue). Questions relating to the role, character, management, and direction of the national park remain subjects of continuing negotiation and debate between Parks Canada and all three First Nations.[67]

Conclusion

The story of Kluane between 1923 and 1974 – from the Yukon bison preserve to the Kluane Game Sanctuary, the national park reserve, and today's Kluane National Park and Kluane National Park Reserve – highlights a transition in the role of national parks in modern Canada. As powerful icons of the nation-state, national parks took on a triad of responsibilities, encapsulating a western aesthetic sensibility of nature's beauty, the importance of recreation for an urbanizing society, and the protection and management of wildlife. For the park proposed in the southwest Yukon, these values faced off against a related agenda of material well-being through economic development as the colonial state approached the supposedly empty land of northern Canada, bringing with it both benefits and threats. Then quite suddenly in the early 1970s, this closed discourse of "protection or production" was smashed open by the previously disenfranchised Aboriginal people of northern Canada, giving them a chance to participate in … what? In Canada, or in making a different kind of Canada? Perhaps Canadians have begun to escape the "abyssal thinking" that has long divided imperial powers from their colonized Aboriginal peoples. The opening of a cross-cultural dialogue through negotiated agreements such as those in Kluane offers a chance to think in new ways about our country. Perhaps we should be grateful for the robust quality of our liberal democratic institutions that eventually forced, at least in some small ways, mainstream society to acknowledge and respect the cultural plurality that makes up our country. We must also acknowledge the tenacity, resilience, and wit of northern First Nations in both forwarding their principles and forcing us to recognize and act upon our own.[68]

NOTES

1   I must acknowledge the citizens of Haines Junction and Burwash Landing for their continuing interest in what happens in Kluane National Park and Reserve. Both the Champagne and Aishihik First Nations and Kluane First Nation are active players in shaping the future of the national park and this can only be done through a sound understanding of the past. Their keen public interest in the national park was one of the primary reasons for the preparation of this chapter.

Parks Canada provides a supportive environment for thoughtful reflection upon its work. Colleagues within the Agency remain interested in reviewing, and often challenging, my work to make it better. In this regard I especially note Mary Jane Johnson, Anne Chilibeck, Laura Gorecki, Ron Chambers, Duane West, and Anne Landry, who involved me in their discussions and work on the park, responded to my calls for help, and supported this research. Gail Lotenberg's contracted research on the history of wildlife management in the south west Yukon is also a valued supporting piece for this chapter.

In the academy I remain indebted to Dr. Julie Cruikshank, University of British Columbia, who has guided me with kind and sage advice since I arrived in the Yukon in 1986. Dr. Glen Coulthard, University of British Columbia, introduced me to the literature on Indigenous resistance and resilience, which led me to rethink approaches to national park history. I also appreciate the care and skill that Dr. Paul Nadasdy, Cornell University, exercised in suggesting both additional research sources and corrections to an earlier draft paper. I also learned much from working collaboratively with Brad Martin, PhD candidate, Northwestern University, on our chapters. I would also like to thank the anonymous reviewers for the University of

Calgary Press for their comments. Dr. Claire Campbell, Dalhousie University, remained, always, a friendly, skilled, and patient editor, encouraging all of the book's authors to share and exchange ideas and making this book a pleasure to contribute to.

2   Jean Chrétien, Foreword to John B. Theberge, ed., *Kluane: Pinnacle of the Yukon* (Toronto: Doubleday Canada, 1980), vii–viii. Theberge, a wildlife ecologist at the University of Waterloo – a hot bed of protected area studies in the 1970s – began biological research in the southwest Yukon in 1970. He was an active and effective proponent of national park status for Kluane.

3   John B. Theberge, "Kluane National Park," in *Northern Transitions*, vol. 1, *Northern Resource and Land Use Policy Study*, ed. E.B. Peterson and J.B. Wright, 153–89 (Ottawa: Canadian Arctic Resources Committee, 1978).

4   James C. Scott, *Seeing Like a State: How Certain Schemes to Improve the Human Condition Have Failed* (New Haven, CT: Yale University Press, 1998), highlights four elements, all present in the Kluane story, leading to "tragic episodes of state-initiated social engineering." These are: 1) the administrative ordering of nature and society, 2) high modernist ideology, described as "a strong ... self-confidence about scientific and technical progress, ... [and] the mastery of nature (including human nature)," 3) "an authoritarian state," and 4) "a prostrate society that lacks the capacity to resist these plans."

5   Theberge expresses some surprise at the sudden appearance of the Indigenous voice at the national park discussions in the early 1970s. "Native people did not express concern over the an-

nouncement of Kluane National Park, nor were their interests represented or discussed by the Senate committee. Either the native people were not initially concerned, or they did not know how or where to express their viewpoint.... In summary, the native people entered the conflict late." Theberge, "Kluane National Park," 178–79.

6   Chrétien, Foreword in Theberge, *Kluane*, vii.

7   Southern Tutchone is a linguistic designation of the Athapaskan subgroup living in the southwestern Yukon Territory. Contemporary political groupings include the Champagne and Aishihik, Kluane and White River First Nations. M. Krause and V. Golla, *Northern Athapaskan Languages*; J. Helm, ed., *Handbook of Northern American Indians*, vol. 6, *Subarctic* (Washington: Smithsonian Institution, 1981), 70.

8   D. Neufeld, "Imposed by the Current: The Yukon River as a Cultural Route," *Momentum* 10, no. 1 (2002): 34–39.

9   Paul Nadasdy, *Hunters and Bureaucrats: Power, Knowledge, and Aboriginal-State Relations in the Southwest Yukon* (Vancouver: UBC Press, 2003), chap. 1: Aboriginal-State Relations in Kluane Country: An Overview.

10   Yukon Archives, YRG1, Series 2, vol. 23, file 29299, letter J.D. McLean to John Hawksley, 4 March 1914.

11   Gail Lotenberg, *Recognizing Diversity: An Historical Context for Co-managing Wildlife in the Kluane Region, 1890 – Present*, Parks Canada research manuscript, March, 1998.

12   Harvey A. Feit, "Re-cognizing Co-management as Co-governance:

Visions and Histories of Conservation at James Bay," *Anthropologica* 47, no. 2 (2005): 267, suggests this point.

13   John Muir's promotion of the wonders of nearby Glacier Bay spawned scientific interest in the recession of glaciers. In response, the U.S. National Park Service established Glacier Bay National Monument in 1925. Theodore Catton, *Inhabited Wilderness: Indians, Eskimos and National Parks in Alaska* (Albuquerque: University of New Mexico Press, 1997), chap. 1.

14   NAC, RG 85, vol. 666 file 3968, R. Lowe to C. Stewart, Minister of the Interior, Ap10/23 and Yukon Council Resolution of 15 June 1923. The first two decades of the twentieth century witnessed a fevered attempt to restore, or at least maintain small herds of, the buffalo on the plains. It was from the preserved remnants managed by the national parks in western Canada that Lowe hoped to draw from for the Yukon herd. See Andrew Isenberg, *The Destruction of the Bison: An Environmental History, 1750–1920* (Cambridge: Cambridge University Press, 2000), especially chap. 6. Brad Martin's chapter in this volume notes similar proposals by the Muries for protecting caribou in northeastern Alaska in the 1930s.

15   NAC, RG 85, vol. 1193 file 400-2-8 vol. 1-A, GA Jeckell to HE Hume, 21 November 1932. This item is only one example of this oft-repeated refrain in correspondence.

16   Theberge provides details on the contents of Ickes letter and the discussion between federal and territorial officials that led to the initial land withdrawal ("Kluane National Park," 158–59).

17   Canada, Order in Council, P.C. 11142, 8 December 1942, referenced in NAC, RG 85, vol. 1390, file 406-11, letter 5 October 1944, T.A. Crear to H. Ickes.

18   YA, YRG1, Series 3, vol. 11, file 12-23B, letter R.A. Gibson to A. Simmons, 22 April 1950. Gibson was reviewing the history of the Territorial game sanctuary legislation in this letter to the Yukon MP.

19   Privy Council Resolution C 9030, noted in Theberge, "Kluane National Park," 161–62.

20   NAC, RG 85, vol. 1191, file 400-2, pts. 1 & 2, C.H.D. Clark, "Extracts from: Biological Reconnaissance of Lands Adjacent to the Alaska Highway in Northern British Columbia and the Yukon Territory," 18 June 1945, 5. Clark specifically noted the Pan-American Union Convention on Nature Protection and Wildlife Preservation in the western Hemisphere (1940) and its definition of a national park as a guide for his assessment of the Kluane area. "Areas established for the protection and preservation of superlative scenery, flora and fauna of national significance which the general public may enjoy and from which it may benefit when placed under public control." The text quote is from p. 7 of the extracts. The *Shorter Oxford English Dictionary*, 5th ed. (Oxford: Oxford University Press, 2002), defines primeval from its Latin origins as first age, that is, the first age of the world from Creation, a Garden of Eden untainted by the knowledge of good and evil.

21   Clark extracts, pp. 1, 4, and 10.

22   Clark extracts, p. 3. Additional details in Lotenberg, *Recognizing Diversity*,

45, and Catharine McClellan, *Part of the Land, Part of the Water: A History of the Yukon Indians* (Vancouver: Douglas & McIntyre, 1987), 278. Paul Nadasdy notes that Burwash Landing people "spoke of trap line registration as a very positive development, one that allowed them to protect their interests vis-à-vis Euro-Canadian trappers." Personal communication, 23 November 2009. This point is more fully presented in chapter 5 of his *Hunters and Bureaucrats*, 239–41, and in Robert McCandless, *Yukon Wildlife: A Social History* (Edmonton: University of Alberta Press, 1985).

23   This section draws from a selection of almost sixty newspaper articles and editorials on the proposed national park published in the *Dawson Daily News* and the *Whitehorse Star* between 1940 and 1960. Jody Cox, *Newspaper Survey of Parks Canada Presence in Southern Yukon 1940–1980*, Parks Canada research mss., Whitehorse, 1995.

24   "National Parks a Perpetual Asset," *Dawson News*, 26 July 1941. The *Dawson News*, 15 July 1941 also noted that "by taking time off to relax and restore their energy [at national parks, Canadians] will be better equipped to carry on the nation's war effort." Most of the pieces that appeared in Yukon newspapers were likely the product of Robert Stead's office, produced personally or under his direct supervision. Stead started as director of publicity for the Dominion government in 1918. In 1936, he picked up M.B. William's mantle when he was appointed as Superintendent of Publicity and Information for the National Parks Bureau, authoring *Canada's Mountain Playgrounds – Banff, Jasper, Waterton*

Lakes, Yoho, Kootenay, Glacier, and Mt. Revelstoke National Parks (Department of Mines and Resources, National Parks Bureau, 1941). http://www.cartwrightmb.ca/rjstead/the-poet.htm; accessed 24 June 2010.

25   "Natural Museums of Wildlife," *Dawson News*, 4 April 1946.

26   NAC, RG 85, vols. 1193 & 1194, file 400-2-8, pts. 1, 1A, 2 & 2AJ. Smart, Controller, Mines and Resources to RA Gibson, 24 December 1946, notes that the "full protection" extended to the animals "create[s] a reservoir for wildlife which will spread to other areas and eventually improve conditions in the adjacent area where hunting can be enjoyed during the shooting season."

27   G. Robertson, *Administration for Development in Northern Canada: The Growth and Evolution of Government, Journal of the Institute of Public Administration in Canada* 3, no. 4 (1960): 362. A few years later, Lester Pearson voiced similar sentiments with the reorganization of the Department in 1966: "the joining of Indian Affairs and Northern Development is a national step which cannot but strengthen both the well being of Canada's indigenous peoples and the cause of northern expansion and development" from Lothian, *Canada's National Parks*, 2:23, via David Neufeld, "Parks Canada and the Commemoration of the North: History and Heritage," in *Northern Visions: New Perspectives on the North in Canadian History*, ed. Kerry Abel and Ken S. Coates, 190n14 (Peterborough, ON: Broadview, 2001).

28   UAF Archives, Earnest Gruening Papers, Governor's Alaska file, 1948–53, box 1, Confidential memo, Acting

Chief, Bureau of Reclamation to Commissioner, Jy23/49, via Claus M. Naske, "The Taiya Project," *BC Studies* 91–92 (1991–92): 20. At least some Whitehorse residents looked forward to abandoning their town to a reservoir and moving into modern new houses with plumbing and electricity up the hill. Ione Christenson, personal communication, Fall, 1995.

29 Neufeld, "Parks Canada and the Commemoration of the North," in Abel and Coates, *Northern Visions*, 59.

30 Yukon Native Brotherhood, *Together Today for Our Children Tomorrow: A Statement of Grievances and an Approach to the Settlement by the Yukon Indian People* (Brampton: Charters Publishing, 1973), 11. http://www.eco.gov.yk.ca/pdf/together_today_for_our_children_tomorrow.pdf; accessed 5 August 2010.

31 Lotenberg, *Recognizing Diversity*, 44.

32 Personal communication, Spring, 1996.

33 McClellan, *Part of the Land*, 94.

34 YA, YRG1, Series 9, vol. 3, file10, Kjar to Brown, 19 May 19 1954, via Lotenberg, *Recognizing Diversity*, 30.

35 NAC, RG 85, vol. 1390, file 406-11, letter FHR Jackson, Forest Engineer and Park Superintendent to RA Gibson Director Lands, Parks and Forests Branch, Mines and Resources, 12 September 1946.

36 NAC, RG 85, vol. 1390, file 406-11, letter Jimmy Johnson – Chief and 15 others to JE Gibbon, 23 June 23 1946. The letter was "fully endorsed" and appears to have been prepared for the community by Father Eusebe

Morisset, the Catholic missionary in Burwash Landing.

37 NAC, RG 85, vol. 1390, file 406-11, letter Jackson, to Gibson, 12 September 1946, describes this area as "west of the Donjek River between Wolverine, St Clair and Harris Creeks." Hugh Bostock described "Rex Jackson [as] a sort of 'jack of all trades' as far as the civil administration went for the Yukon." H.S. Bostock, *Pack Horse Tracks: Recollections of a Geologists Life in British Columbia and the Yukon, 1924–1954* (Whitehorse: Geoscience Forum, 1990), 211.

38 NAC, RG 85, vol.1191, file 400-2, pts. 1–2, letter H. Bostock (Geologist, Mines and Resources) to R.A. Gibson (Director, Lands, Parks and Forests) No28, 1946. NAC, RG 85, vols. 1193 & 1194, file 400-2-8, pts. 1, 1A, 2 & 2A. Bostock spent June, 1945, doing a field reconnaissance of the northern and western shores of Kluane Lake. Douglas Leechman, an archaeologist with the National Museum worked out of the same camp with Bostock and shared his findings which Bostock visited. Bostock, *Pack Horse Trails*, 211–20, notes his conversation with Eugene Jacquot. On "old Indian camps" see 216–17.

The cited letter appears to be the first and main source of information describing Indians as being in the wrong place and running counter to their history. Bostock had close relations with other "old Yukon hands" in Ottawa and was clearly in contact with the "intelligent men" of the Fish and Game Association in Whitehorse. J. Smart, Controller, Mines and Resources to RA Gibson, directly references this report to support his own thoughts on wildlife management in southwestern Yukon in December, 1946.

Elmer Harp, Jr., an archaeologist with the 1948 Andover-Harvard expedition, spent the summer doing a site survey north of Kluane Lake: *North to the Yukon Territory via the Alaska Highway in 1948: Field Notes of the Andover-Harvard Expedition* (Whitehorse: Yukon Tourism and Culture, 2005). His horses and guides all came from Burwash Landing and his field notes are rich in both field observations of camps and cabins and oral testimony from the men guiding him, several of whom were among those who signed the petition in 1946. It is clear many Burwash Landing families travelled and hunted north of Kluane Lake in the past (p.39) and that they had generally moved to the village that grew up around the Jacquots' trading post some twenty to twenty-five years earlier (pp. 26 and 49). Interestingly, Harp used a sketch map prepared by Bostock to figure out his party's route (p. 25).

39 NAC (Burnaby Branch), RG 10 DIAND, vol. 801/20-4, pts. 1–2. Letter R. Kendall Fur Supervisor for BC and Yukon and R.J. Meek, Superintendent, Indian Agency to H.R. Conn, Fur Supervisor, Indian Affairs, 20 June 1950. In August, 1948, after several perilous trips across Kluane Lake, Harp, who had served on the tiny PT boats during the war, observed, "Headed directly across in a slight quartering sea but the *Josephine* rolled & pitched as if we were in a gale. No wonder these people are afraid of the lake – they haven't got a decent boat to put on it." Harp, *North to the Yukon*, 84.

40 NAC, RG 85, vol. 1390, file 406-11, Note for file, 3 November 1950, by CK Le Capelain, Chief, Yukon-Mackenzie River Division.

41 NAC, RG 85, vol. 1390, file 406-11, Memo for deputy minister, 5 December 1950, from CK Le Capelain, Chief, Yukon-Mackenzie River Division and HF Lewis, Chief CWS.

42 NAC, RG 85, vol. 1390, file 406-11, Burwash Landing Indian Band, 5 January 1951, by AH Gibson, Yukon Commissioner. Cameron, a longtime RCMP constable/officer in Yukon, was the local "guide" for Kjar, whereas Kjar was an import from Alberta bringing with him new ideas of game management. Cameron's opinion was more informed by experience in the north, and this is why Gibson cited him specifically.

43 NAC, RG 85, vol. 1390, file 406-11, A.W.F. Banfield, Investigation of wildlife conditions, Kluane Game Sanctuary, Y.T., 1951.

44 The interpretation of this prevailing attitude relies upon Tim Ingold, *The Perception of the Environment: Essays in Livelihood, Dwelling and Skill* (London: Routledge, 2000). J. Igoe, "Global Indigenism and Spaceship Earth: Convergence, Space, and Re-Entry Friction." *Globalizations* 2 (2005): 1–13, offers a survey of the troubled contemporary relationships between Indigenous peoples and conservation organizations, while Mark Dowie, "Conservation Refugees When Protecting Nature Means Kicking People Out," *Orion Magazine* (Nov.–Dec. 2005), available at http://www.orionmagazine.org/index.php/articles/article/161/ (accessed 23 July 2010),

describes the contemporary application of this continuing process.

45 NAC, RG 85, vol. 1390, file 406-11, vol. 1-A, RA Gibson to A. Simmons (MP) 22 April 1950; NAC, RG 10, vol. 6761, file 420-12-2-RT-1, RJ Meek to Indian Affairs Branch, 15 March 1950.

46 Kendall's investigation in 1950, NAC, RG 10, vol. 6761, file 420-12-2-RT-1; AWF Banfield's report and related correspondence, NAC, RG 85, vol. 1390, file 406-11, vol. 1-A, HF Lewis to Smart, 13 November 1951.

47 NAC, RG 10, vol. 801/20-9, pts. 2-3, letter AE Fry, Indian Agent to Indian Commissioner BC, 22 February 1963.

48 Cattails and phragmites were thought to improve the habitat and increase muskrat production. NAC (Burnaby Branch), RG 10, vol. 801/20-1, pt. 1, DJ McIntosh to Indian Commissioner for BC, 11 February 1965.

49 NAC, RG 10, vol. 801/20-9, pts. 2-3, letter AE Fry, Indian Agent to Commissioner GR Cameron, 23 July 1963.

50 NAC, RG 84, A-2-a, vol. 1985, file U2-21-1 pt. 3, letter AM Pearson to Regional Superintendent CWS, 10 July 1963, emphasis in original.

51 NAC, RG 10, vol. 801/20-9, pts. 2-3, letter AE Fry, Indian Agent to Indian Commissioner BC, 22 February 1963.

52 NAC, RG10, vol. 801/20-9, pts. 2-3, Minutes, Meeting held at Burwash Indian Village, 30 October 1961.

53 NAC, RG 84, A-2-a, vol. 1985, file U2-21-1 pt. 3, letter JRB Coleman to JH Gordon, Indian Affairs, 4 September 1963.

54 NAC, RG 109 CWS, WLYT (Wild Life Yukon Territory), vol. 300 W.A.

Fuller, Mammalogist to F.H. Collins, 4 March 1958.

55 Paul Kopas, *Taking the Air: Ideas and Change in Canada's National Parks* (Vancouver: UBC Press, 2007), 48–50. There was increasing pressure through the late 1950s for the establishment of multi-use parks. Alvin Hamilton, Diefenbaker's minister responsible for national parks, viewed conservation as "using our resources as rationally as we can [and,] … whenever possible, a multiple use of our resources." In addition to developing the reserve idea to forestall such a development, the Parks Branch also worked actively to develop public support for parks. Their efforts, and direct investment, resulted in the establishment of the National and Provincial Parks Association of Canada (NPPAC) in 1963, which subsequently evolved into the Canadian Parks and Wilderness Society (CPAWS). William Baker, a key figure in the establishment of the NPPAC, was contracted by the Parks Branch to prepare a survey of potential northern national parks. His 1963 report characterized the North as "The Frontier Recreation Region." NAC, RG 84, A-2-A, vol. 11983, file U2-20, pt. 2 (1962–68).

56 NAC, RG 84, A-2-A, vol. 11983, file U2-20, pt. 2 (1962–68), emphasis in original.

57 Personal communication, summer, 1992.

58 Canada, National Parks Service – Planning, *Yukon National Park Proposal: Background Data Report, Planning Report 72*, Ottawa, October, 1969.

59 The 1969 IUCN General Assembly in New Delhi passed a resolution defining a national park as: "a relatively

large area 1) where one or several ecosystems are not materially altered by-human [*sic*] exploitation or occupation, where plant and animal species, geomorphological sites and habitats are of special scientific, educative and *recreative* interest or *which contains a natural landscape of great beauty* and 2) where the central authority of the country has taken steps to prevent or eliminate as soon as *possible exploitation or occupation in the whole area* and to enforce effectively the respect of ecological, geomorphological or aesthetic features which have led to its establishment and 3) where visitors are allowed to enter under special conditions for inspiratio al, [*sic*] educative, cultural and recreative purposes." Emphasis in original. NAC, RG 84, vol. 2294, file C-1070-112, pt. 1-4.

60   The White Paper is formally known as Statement of the Government of Canada on Indian Policy, 1969, presented to the first session of the twenty-eighth Parliament by the Honourable Jean Chrétien, Minister of Indian Affairs and Northern Development, Early Canadiana Online, http://www.canadiana.org/ECO/ItemRecord/9_07786; accessed 24 September 2009.

61   Yukon Native Brotherhood, *Together Today for Our Children Tomorrow.*

62   Catherine McClellan, *Part of the Land*, 99–104, summarizes the history of Indian organizations in the Yukon.

63   "Citizens Plus" was first suggested in *A Survey of the Contemporary Indians of Canada*, vols. I and II, ed. H.B. Hawthorn (Ottawa, Indian Affairs Branch, 1966–67). The Indian Association of Alberta subsequently promoted the idea in their response to the 1969

White Paper as *Citizens Plus* in June 1970.

64   *Whitehorse Star*, "Nishga Land Claim Rejected," 31 January 1973, and "Indian Land Claim Revealed: They want land control and money," 14 February 1973.

65   "C.Y.I. Opposes Park and Power Line …," *Whitehorse Star*, 12 December 1973, "land-grab policy" from Chief Elijah Smith, House of Commons, Issue No. 29, 12 December 1973, *Minutes of Proceedings and Evidence of the Standing Committee on Indian Affairs and Northern Development*, p. 29:132 and "(3) Any land …" from Miss Flora MacDonald, MP, ibid., p. 29:133. Theberge, however, demonstrates that it was the NDP that ultimately proposed the amendment to the Act at its third reading in April, 1974, p. 182.

66   NAC (Burnaby Branch) RG 10, vol. 801/1-19-11, pt. 1, Minutes, Meeting of the Kluane Native Liaison Committee, 29 May 1975. item (6).

67   Thanks to Anne Landry, Parks Canada, for her explanation of the complicated circumstances of national park designation in the southwest Yukon Territory. Final Agreement between the Government of Canada, the Champagne and Aishihik First Nations and the Government of the Yukon, 1993. http://www.eco.gov.yk.ca/pdf/champagne_aishihik_fa.pdf; and Final Agreement among the Government of Canada and Kluane First Nation and the Government of the Yukon, 2003 http://www.eco.gov.yk.ca/pdf/kluane_final_agreement.pdf; both accessed 22 June 2010.

The White River First Nation also has interests in those western portions of the game sanctuary not included in Kluane National Park Reserve.

CBC News, 24 April 2008, *Kluane Park may open up to First Nations hunters*, http://www.cbc.ca/canada/north/story/2008/04/23/kluane-park.html; accessed 25 April 2008.

A description of the post-1974 Parks Canada approach to Indigenous issues at Kluane National Park and Reserve is included in D. Neufeld, "Indigenous Peoples and Protected Heritage Areas: Acknowledging Cultural Pluralism," chap. 10 in *Transforming Parks: Protected Areas Policy and Governance in a Changing World*, ed. Kevin Hannah,

Douglas Clark and Scott Slocombe (London: Routledge, 2007).

68 Boaventura de Sousa Santos, "Beyond Abyssal Thinking: From Global Lines to Ecologies of Knowledges," *Eurozine*, 29 June 2007, and Scott, *Seeing Like a State*. James Tully suggests the acceptance of cultural pluralism means a state with distinct cultural groupings constantly negotiating with each other on the basis of mutual recognition, respecting the continuity of group traditions with governance rising from consent. James Tully, *Strange Multiplicity: Constitutionalism in an Age of Diversity* (Cambridge: Cambridge University Press, 1995), 116.

Negotiating a Partnership of Interests: Inuvialuit Land Claims and the Establishment of Northern Yukon (Ivvavik) National Park

BRAD MARTIN
DEPARTMENT OF HISTORY
NORTHWESTERN UNIVERSITY

If the essays in this collection provide a single key lesson, it is perhaps that Parks Canada has wrestled with the issue of human presence in the national parks from its very inception. First entrenched under the direction of James B. Harkin, as demonstrated by Alan MacEachern in his contribution to the volume, the mandate of the agency to couple preservation with use has often created complex management dilemmas requiring administrators to reconcile the competing expectations of sightseers, industrial developers, scientists, wilderness advocates, aboriginal peoples, and others. Yet, as John Sandlos argues (both in his essay here and in his wider body of work), the National Parks Branch has often privileged the interests of tourists and other short-term visitors over those of local residents.[1] Indeed, the contributions by Bill Waiser, Ronald Rudin, David Neufeld, and I.S. MacLaren in this volume confirm that officials have frequently, sometimes forcibly, opposed human habitation and local resource use in the parks. These essays support a growing international body of scholarship that documents the removal of local peoples from protected areas in which sustained human presence has been regarded as a threat to the protection of wildlife or the preservation of pristine nature.[2] While some scholars have questioned the effect of wilderness values on the early development of the national parks system in Canada (including Sandlos, earlier in this book), there can be little doubt that park officials in this country, to paraphrase Lyle Dick in the epilogue that follows, have often viewed people – especially local people – as a 'problem.'[3]

When senior park planners began to contemplate the expansion of the national parks system into the Canadian North in the decades following the Second World War, they exhibited the same sort of biases against human settlement and local resource use that officials before them had demonstrated. These views were consistent with the rise in rationalism, scientific management, and high modernist planning in the Parks Branch that political scientist Paul Kopas has recently described, and which Neufeld and Olivier Craig-Dupont address in this volume.[4] In the early 1960s administrators in the recently created Planning Division were determined to establish a great chain of wilderness reserves stretching from the Yukon-Alaska border to Labrador for the benefit of the increasingly affluent and mobile Canadian population (also described by George Colpitts and Jim Taylor here). Yet as critics of both the Canadian and American national parks systems have often noted, an avowed commitment to wilderness preservation by government administrators has not always prevented intensive development and environmental modifications in the national parks.[5] Not surprisingly, then, the new northern reserves were planned as automobile-friendly vacation destinations connected by new roads to nearby communities, dotted with visitor facilities, and justified by their role in boosting the northern tourist economy. While the exceptionally large size of the proposed parks appealed to the scientific community and to a Canadian public gripped with nationalistic concerns about the fragility of the northern environment, plans to establish a new recreational frontier in the North were tailored to the expectations of southern visitors and presaged for local aboriginal peoples the sort of dispossession and disruption that had accompanied the creation of Banff and other national parks decades earlier.[6]

A central theme in this collection involves the influence of wider social, political, and intellectual developments on national parks policy and management in Canada. It is critical to understand that efforts to establish new national parks in the North during the second half of the twentieth century took place within a context of growing native political power and evolving federal land claims policy, both of which dramatically shaped how the new parks operated and the philosophy that underpinned them. These parks were fundamentally different from most of their southern counterparts because they were created through a process of negotiation with indigenous leaders. As a result, they reflected local ideas about land and wildlife and facilitated the involvement of Inuit and First Nations peoples in conservation planning. While some scholars have argued that co-management arrangements with Aboriginal peoples have merely reinforced colonial relationships and subordinated local concerns, it is important to understand that land claim negotiations were an effective way for northern leaders to 'talk back' to the state, as Peter Kulchyski and Frank Tester have put it in their recent history of game management in the Northwest Territories.[7] Such an appreciation for aboriginal agency resonates with scholarship in subaltern studies and the recent work of Sherrill Grace and Julie Cruikshank, who have demonstrated how native and non-native northerners continue to oppose colonial incursions through various means, including art, literature, and storytelling.[8]

This paper examines the history of Northern Yukon National Park (later renamed Ivvavik National Park) in order to highlight how northern indigenous peoples have challenged and helped transform the practice of conservation in Canada. As the first national park in the country established as part of a comprehensive land claim settlement, Northern Yukon National Park set important precedents for future conservation planning both inside and outside the North and provided a stage for the Inuvialuit of the western Arctic to oppose the ideal of 'uninhabited wilderness' that historians Theodore Catton and Mark Spence have argued is at the root of the national park movement in North America.[9] However, in addition to exploring the details of an influential episode in the history of the national parks system, this paper provides ways to explore several critical themes that knit the essays in this collection together. First, it highlights how national park establishment in Canada has often been characterized by social and political conflict rooted in different cultural understandings of nature. Second, it reveals how recent

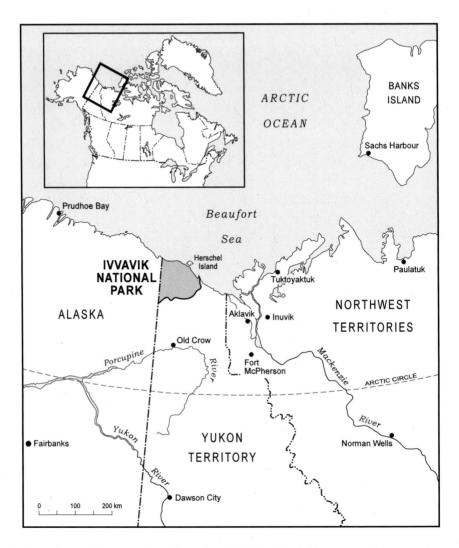

FIG. 1. IVVAVIK NATIONAL PARK. FROM *Ivvavik National Park Management Plan* (OTTAWA: CANADIAN HERITAGE, PARKS CANADA, 1994), VI.

engagements between indigenous peoples and national park officials, while unique in important respects, can be understood as part of a longstanding discussion in Parks Canada over the proper place of humans in the natural world. Third, it underlines how indigenous peoples and local communities have succeeded in raising issues of social and environmental justice in conflicts over protected areas, thereby introducing moral questions into conservation debates traditionally dominated by scientific, economic, and aesthetic considerations. Finally, the history of Northern Yukon National Park must be understood as part of a broader international movement toward managing national parks and other protected areas as cultural landscapes.[10] Studying it helps us illuminate key aspects of this important trend.

Conservation and Development in the Western Arctic

At the beginning of the 1970s, the northern Yukon was a hornet's nest of competing industrial interests, clashing government agendas, and conflicting environmental values. Following the rapid expansion of oil exploration in the western Arctic after the discovery of rich deposits off the coast of Alaska in 1968, the region became a hotbed of political controversy, garnering national headlines in Canada and attracting attention across the continent and overseas. Concerned about the fate of wildlife and unique tundra and taiga ecosystems in the area, environmentalists, the National Parks Branch, and the Canadian Wildlife Service (CWS) strongly condemned the growth of industrial activities along the Beaufort Sea coast. By contrast, federal officials in the Department of Indian Affairs and Northern Development (DIAND) – encouraged by the governments of the Yukon and Northwest Territories – generally supported the operations of oil and gas companies in the region, routinely granting permits for exploration on the mainland, offshore, and on the arctic islands. Furthermore, indigenous groups had deep cultural attachments to the rugged foothills, deeply etched valleys, and coastal flats of the Yukon North Slope. Both Gwich'in and Inuvialuit peoples had, at various points in their histories, used the region for hunting, trapping, and trading. Therefore, whether it was viewed as a storehouse of valuable natural resources, a wilderness in need of safeguarding, or a source of cultural and nutritional sustenance, these various groups valued the northern Yukon in

distinctive ways, ensuring that debates over its future were contentious affairs.[11]

When Northern Yukon National Park was created in this contested region as part of a negotiated land claim settlement between the government of
Canada and the Inuvialuit in 1984, calls for environmental protection in the
hinterlands of the Canadian northwest were not new. Indeed, the interest of
conservationists in the area date back to the 1940s, when American biologist
Olaus Murie and his wife Mardy first considered lobbying the governments
of Canada and the United States for the protection of wildlife in the Yukon-
Alaska borderlands. The Muries were primarily concerned with the welfare
of the Porcupine caribou herd, which wintered in the boreal forests of the
Yukon interior but travelled annually to critical calving grounds in coastal
regions on both sides of the international border (Fig. 1). Through their
connections to the powerful Wilderness Society, Olaus and Mardy helped
generate widespread support for protection of the northern caribou, culminating in the establishment of the Arctic National Wildlife Range in 1960
(Fig. 2).[12] A decade later, spurred to action by increasing oil exploration in
the Beaufort Sea, a group of eminent Canadian biologists formed the Arctic
International Wildlife Range Society (AIWRS) and called for the creation of
a large reservation to protect the Yukon portion of the caribou range.[13] Still
another call for protection came from the small community of Old Crow on
the Porcupine River, where Gwich'in residents demanded an end to oil and
gas activity on their nearby trapping grounds in 1968.[14] Faced with such stiff
resistance to industrial growth in the northern Yukon, Canadian officials
imposed a moratorium on development in the winter range of the Porcupine
caribou herd in 1970.

Later in the decade, federal authorities were forced to make additional
concessions on the coastal plains of the northern Yukon. As plans for the construction of pipelines and transportation corridors across the calving grounds
of the iconic caribou herd proceeded, the government of Canada established
the Mackenzie Valley Pipeline Inquiry in 1974 to assess the potential social
and environmental impacts of industrial development in the region. Three
years later, Mr. Justice Thomas Berger recommended in his final report,
Northern Frontier, Northern Homeland, that the construction of a pipeline
along the shores of the Beaufort Sea should be delayed pending the settlement
of Aboriginal land claims and that a vast park should be established to protect

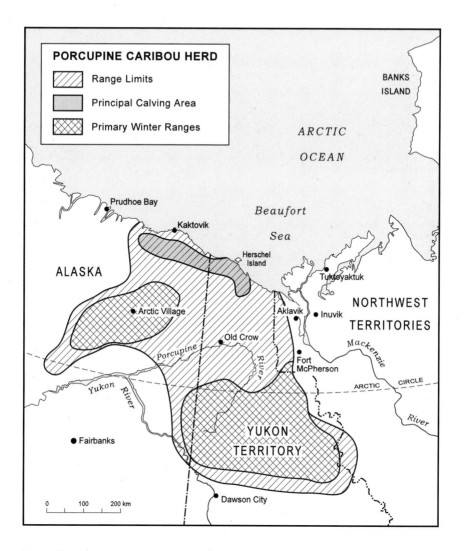

Fig. 2. Coastal calving grounds and winter ranges of the Porcupine caribou herd in the northern Yukon and Alaska, 1971–78. From *A National Wildlife Area in the Northern Yukon and Northwest Territories* (Ottawa: Canadian Wildlife Service, 1979), 6.

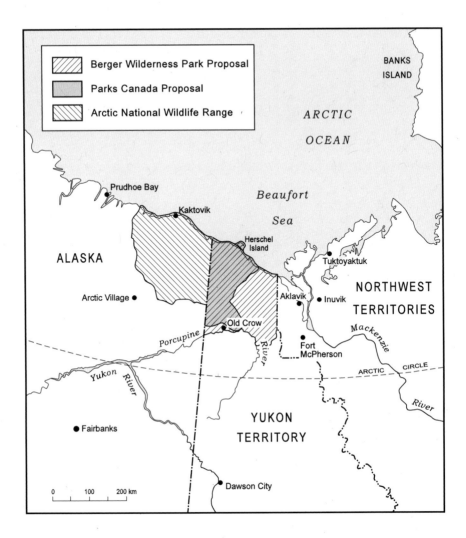

FIG. 3. THE YUKON-ALASKA BORDERLANDS, SHOWING THE ARCTIC NATIONAL WILDLIFE
RANGE, THE BERGER WILDERNESS PARK PROPOSAL, AND THE 1977 PARKS CANADA
PROPOSAL FOR A NATIONAL PARK IN THE NORTHERN YUKON. FROM CONSTANCE HUNT,
RUSTY MILLER, AND DONNA TINGLEY. *Wilderness Area: Legislative Alternatives for
the Establishment of a Wilderness Area in the Northern Yukon* (OTTAWA: CANADIAN
ARCTIC RESOURCES COMMITTEE, 1979); AND *Northern Yukon – A Natural Area of
Canadian Significance* (OTTAWA: PARKS CANADA, 1978), 5.

wildlife in the region (Fig. 3).[15] This popular publication secured Berger's reputation as a defender of indigenous rights and environmental protection in Canada, but it drew heavily on the ideas of residents and outside experts far more familiar with the complex realities of northern society than the judge himself. In 1972, as part of ongoing efforts to expand the national parks system into the Arctic and sub-Arctic, Parks Branch officials identified the northern Yukon as a region rich in natural values and recreational opportunities and subsequently touted its wilderness qualities before the Berger inquiry.[16] For their part, northern indigenous peoples made it abundantly clear in testimony at local hearings that their relationship to the land was critical for the survival of their communities and that they viewed their hunting lifestyles as an inherent right.[17] With the help of his staff, Berger amassed these submissions and crafted their essential points into a blunt and principled work that resonated deeply with Canadians. While it is justly regarded as a landmark study in the history of the environmental and native rights movements in Canada, his report is best viewed as a synthesis of grassroots sentiment and technical expertise, rather than as an expression of personal political philosophy.

Still, while *Northern Frontier, Northern Homeland* may not merit the label of individual genius and inspiration that some have bestowed upon it, the publication was crucial in shaping the political context of national park establishment in the northern Yukon. In addition to providing legitimacy and moral impetus to the emerging northern land claims movement, it drew on powerful and sentimental links between 'the North' and Canadian national identity to call for the protection of arctic ecosystems.[18] Within months of its publication, the National Energy Board rejected the proposal by Canadian Arctic Gas Limited to build a pipeline along the Beaufort Sea coast and down the Mackenzie Valley. This decision was roundly applauded by environmental organizations across the country which, in turn, used the Berger report as a launching pad for campaigns against what they viewed as destructive and irresponsible northern resource development. For its part, the Parks Branch drew on the rising tide of environmental discontent to generate support for its plans to expand the parks system into the northern territories. This effort had been prompted years earlier by the development in 1970 of the National Parks System Plan, an agency-wide initiative to create national parks in thirty-nine natural regions across the country, and which yielded proposals for new reserves in the southwest Yukon, along the Nahanni River, on Baffin Island, and in the western Arctic by 1977.[19] In response to the environmental activism triggered by the Berger report and the lobbying of northern park planners, the federal government withdrew fifteen thousand square miles in the northern Yukon from industrial development in 1978 with the intention of creating of a national park and other conservation lands.[20] Six years later, Northern Yukon National Park was established in the westernmost corner of the withdrawn area.

Negotiating the National Park

As the oil companies, public interest groups, and federal and territorial agencies were debating the future of the arctic environment in the early 1970s, northern indigenous peoples were finding their political voice. Following the controversy sparked by the publication of the 1969 White Paper and the conclusion of the 1973 *Calder* case, which established a basis in Canadian law for a concept of Aboriginal title, the federal government made new commitments to address all unresolved land claims in dialogue with native leaders. Formal discussions were required to follow a prescribed format and were intended to facilitate the exchange of land, cash, and economic benefits for the extinguishment of certain Aboriginal rights.[21] The announcement of the new federal policy resulted in an explosion of grassroots organizing in the North, as native groups prepared to take their grievances to the negotiating table.[22] In the western Arctic, community leaders formed the Committee for Original Peoples' Entitlement (COPE) and began meeting with federal authorities.[23] The need for a grassroots political organization in the region had become apparent in 1970 during bitter conflicts between Inuvialuit hunters on Banks Island and oil companies operating in the Beaufort Sea. Island residents complained that seismic surveys were endangering caribou populations and interfering with traplines near their communities, and they threatened to take DIAND to court to halt exploration activities.[24] Once COPE was established, its leaders represented the Inuvialuit in a wide range of dealings with government and industry and joined the Inuit Tapirisat of Canada (ITC) in launching the Nunavut land claim proposal. However, when ITC withdrew this proposal in 1976 in order to revise its negotiating strategy, COPE officials pushed ahead with a separate Inuvialuit land claim.

An early task for the new political leadership in the western Arctic involved organizing a Land Use and Occupancy Study, the standard legal vehicle for establishing Aboriginal title to territory in the new federal land claim process. When completed in 1976, the western Arctic study provided documentation on historic Inuvialuit land uses along the coast of the Northwest Territories and on Banks and Victoria Islands in the Arctic archipelago. The study also claimed traditional Inuvialuit use of the North Slope of the Yukon by documenting how the Inuvialuit had hunted caribou, whales, and other wildlife in the region for years and had established settlements along the coast.[25] When Inuvialuit negotiators submitted their land claim proposal, *Inuvialuit Nunangat*, to the federal government in 1977, they drew heavily on evidence from the western Arctic study to justify their demands for land ownership in the northern Yukon and their rejection of government proposals for protected areas in the region.

The Inuvialuit were not alone among indigenous groups in opposing the use of their traditional territories for state-run environmental protection. As Neufeld demonstrates in this volume, Aboriginal peoples in the southwest Yukon have protested the creation of the Kluane Game Sanctuary and Kluane National Park since the 1940s. Similarly, Sandlos has documented how native hunters and trappers resisted the establishment and thwarted the regulations of the Thelon Game Sanctuary and Wood Buffalo National Park in the Northwest Territories.[26] Indeed, by the time Inuvialuit negotiators submitted their land claim proposal, Inuit and First Nations people in many parts of the Canadian North had developed a suspicion of government conservation programs and a distrust of the National Parks Branch in particular. These apprehensions were often based on the knowledge of a long history of native displacement and exclusion at the hands of park managers, wildlife enforcement officers, and other conservation officials, in the North and beyond. The most common criticism leveled by native leaders was that park management interfered with Aboriginal harvesting activities. These leaders argued that a wide range of restrictions on hunting and trapping, the construction of settlements and camps, and modes of transport undermined the fundamental reliance of Aboriginal peoples on local wildlife. In addition, northern Aboriginal groups commonly objected to the tourist orientation of national parks. They insisted that the construction of visitor facilities and the provision of recreational opportunities for southern wilderness enthusiasts caused disruptive social change in remote northern communities and generated tensions between local resource users and outsiders. As a means of addressing these problems, during the 1970s and 1980s Aboriginal organizations often demanded changes in park policies. While many of these organizations were not opposed in every respect to the creation of national parks, their demands were part of a larger effort by Inuit and First Nations leaders to make conservation officials respect the unique realities of local harvesting economies and lifestyles.[27]

Faced with this resistance from indigenous groups, Parks Canada was forced to revise its traditional approach to managing protected areas under its jurisdiction. The process was tentative at first and (as MacLaren argues in the penultimate chapter in this collection) it applied primarily to new northern parks rather than pre-existing southern ones. But a confluence of developments in different parts of the country made it difficult for officials to forestall. In 1973, northern First Nations voiced concerns before committees of the House of Commons and the Senate that the creation of national parks outside the framework of land claim negotiations amounted to the denial of Aboriginal title. As a result, Parks Canada created a new legal designation known as a "national park reserve," which set aside land for national park purposes but did not finalize boundaries or management arrangements pending the settlement of native claims.[28] In addition, the final report of the Mackenzie Valley Pipeline Inquiry forced federal officials to change their approach to northern conservation. Building on key inquiry recommendations, Parks Canada established a Northern Parks Working Group in 1979 to develop policy guidelines for reconciling the interests of wilderness preservationists, resource developers, and Aboriginal communities, and to examine the viability of "joint management regimes" involving these groups.[29] So, too, events in southern Canada reinforced policy changes in the North. For instance, after families removed from Kouchibouguac National Park in New Brunswick protested their expulsion with civil disobedience in the 1970s, park officials abandoned the use of expropriation as a tool for land acquisition (see Rudin, this volume).[30] Therefore, by the end of the decade, Parks Canada was in the midst of making fundamental procedural and policy changes precisely as the controversy over Northern Yukon National Park was unfolding. It is telling that when a revised edition of the *Parks Canada Policy* was approved by the federal Cabinet in 1979 it included provisions permitting subsistence activities in national parks and establishing more inclusive mechanisms for sharing management authority with local communities. In particular, the following statement, included in a background section of the document, was clearly written to address the concerns of Aboriginal northerners:

> Not all national parks are the same. In remote or northern areas, potential national parks may be identified which are the homeland of people who have traditionally depended on the land and its resources for their survival. Their culture reflects this fundamental relationship. In certain cases, lands which have been traditionally used by native people are the subject of unresolved native land claims. If such areas are to be protected within the national parks system, they must be planned and managed in a way that reflects these special circumstances.[31]

In regular contact with DIAND officials as a result of their land claim negotiations, Inuvialuit leaders would have been well aware of the changes taking place in Parks Canada during these years, and they took advantage of them to influence conservation plans in the northern Yukon. A close examination of Inuvialuit land claim documents reveals that, as negotiations began, COPE officials were deeply distrustful of federal conservation practices, yet remained committed to the principle of conservation itself, as long as they could define it on their own terms. For instance, the opening pages of *Inuvialuit Nunangat* list the four overarching goals of Inuvialuit negotiators. The fourth goal describes the "[p]rotection and preservation of the Arctic wildlife, environment, and biological productivity" as a priority.[32] Not surprisingly, Inuvialuit negotiators were determined to prevent the destruction of key subsistence resources on their traditional territories in the face of increasing industrial activity in the western Arctic. Certain features of the land claim proposal confirm this, most notably provisions for the creation of new protected areas on Inuvialuit-owned lands and an ecological preserve in the Beaufort Sea. Yet in other ways *Inuvialuit Nunangat* suggests that the Inuvialuit themselves required protection from government conservationists. For example, several sections demand guarantees of Inuvialuit access to large tracts of land in the Mackenzie Delta as a means of guarding against the exclusion of local people by federal agencies. Another section calls for an end to the prosecution of Inuvialuit hunters under the *Migratory Birds Convention Act*. And still other sections demand Inuvialuit ownership of key wildlife areas (including the northern Yukon), a clear indication that negotiators did not trust federal authorities to care for important resources.[33]

When read in conjunction with other aspects of the land claim proposal, these sections suggest that Inuvialuit leaders felt a profound ambivalence about state conservation in the mid-1970s. On the one hand, they recognized its potential benefits, yet on the other, they objected to the way it was practised. As historian Paul Sabin has argued in his analysis of the Mackenzie Valley Pipeline Inquiry, local control over resources and government programs was a key political objective for northern native peoples in the 1970s.[34] Indeed, Inuvialuit land claim documents demonstrate how the COPE negotiating team was motivated by an overarching goal of ensuring meaningful participation in Canadian society for the Inuvialuit, while simultaneously preserving their cultural identity and protecting the northern environment.[35] The efforts of negotiators to secure greater control for the Inuvialuit over the establishment and management of protected areas on their traditional territories were part of a larger strategy to reconcile these basic objectives.

Shortly after COPE leaders submitted their land claim proposal in the spring of 1977, they were told by government officials that their demand for land ownership in the northern Yukon was unacceptable to the Crown. The DIAND minister, Warren Allmand, explained that the Yukon territorial government claimed jurisdiction over the entire area and was vehemently opposed to the surrender of any of it to a First Nation whose members lived primarily in the Northwest Territories. This impasse prompted the first major compromise in the western Arctic negotiations.[36] Drawing on the final report of the Mackenzie Valley Pipeline Inquiry, federal officials suggested that a wilderness park of no less than five thousand square miles stretching across the Yukon coastal plain should be considered as an alternative to fee simple ownership by the Inuvialuit. The proposal provided for the continuation of Inuvialuit hunting and trapping within park boundaries and included guarantees that lands surrounding traditional fishing camps would revert to Inuvialuit ownership if they were withdrawn from the public dedication.[37] After some deliberate consideration, COPE negotiators agreed to this proposal because it afforded them the opportunity to select other lands in the western Arctic as part of their settlement package while ensuring a certain degree of protection for valued wildlife in the northern Yukon.

The Inuvialuit Land Rights Settlement Agreement-in-Principle (AIP) signed between COPE and federal officials in October 1978 reflected the fact that Inuvialuit leaders felt by this point that any final settlement was likely to confirm the government of Canada as the owner of most of the land in the western Arctic. Consequently, they decided to focus their negotiating efforts on gaining control over the management of natural resources on Crown lands. In particular, the AIP included several provisions intended to protect Inuvialuit access to wildlife within the proposed park, to increase their influence over park planning, and to accommodate their cultural values in policy decisions. Perhaps the most significant of these provisions gave expression to Inuvialuit desires to maintain their hunting and trapping lifestyles in the face of rapid social and economic change in their communities. These provisions granted the Inuvialuit exclusive rights to hunt and trap within park boundaries, to construct temporary facilities and use motorized transport in the park, and to trade, barter, and sell animal products procured on the Yukon North Slope. They were designed to protect longstanding Inuvialuit harvesting activities by guaranteeing access to park lands and by permitting the use of late-twentieth-century technologies, rights negotiators intended to secure by employing the tools of the modern bureaucratic state. Furthermore, COPE leaders insisted that Inuvialuit beneficiaries should play significant roles in the management of any permanent conservation regime established in the northern Yukon. This demand resulted in the creation of the National Wilderness Park Steering Committee (NWPSC), a joint management board charged with the task of defining the purpose and functions of the proposed park and developing management guidelines for its operation. The new board included two Inuvialuit members, two members from Old Crow, and representatives from the Department of the Environment and the Department of Fisheries and Oceans. Lastly, COPE officials demanded employment opportunities in the park for beneficiaries of the final land claim settlement.[38]

When the AIP was signed, all of these issues remained to be negotiated in detail and there was no guarantee that federal authorities would ultimately accede to COPE demands. Nonetheless, the document contains valuable information on Inuvialuit perceptions of national parks in the late

1970s and provides a useful benchmark for assessing how debates over the northern Yukon unfolded in subsequent years. Two features of the agreement seem particularly worthy of emphasis. First, the document makes plain the importance that the Inuvialuit attached to wildlife and habitat conservation in their land claim negotiations. The fact that environmental protection featured so prominently in discussions between COPE and the federal government reflects both the desire of the Inuvialuit to safeguard wildlife resources on their traditional territories and their pragmatic understanding that protected areas could serve their larger social and cultural needs. Second, the AIP demonstrates the determination of the Inuvialuit to ensure that conservation was practised according to a new set of rules in the western Arctic. Many residents of the region were suspicious of how national parks had been run in the past, and felt that Aboriginal people themselves should be responsible for managing local land and wildlife. They insisted that if new protected areas were created as part of their settlement with the federal government, they should be established on terms set by the Inuvialuit themselves. Given the range of competing interests at play in the western Arctic during these years, it remained unclear in 1978 whether Inuvialuit demands would eventually be fulfilled through the negotiating process. But in the face of growing resistance to their land claim proposal, COPE officials remained committed to protecting local harvesting lifestyles and asserting Inuvialuit rights as their particular region of the North changed quickly around them.

Opposition and Compromise

As political ecologists and other scholars of conservation have often demonstrated, protected areas have frequently been sites of social and political conflict, pitting state managers against local peoples and other organized interests.[39] Indeed, many of the essays in this volume highlight how national parks have become terrains of struggle in battles over identity, ideology, and authority. In the wake of the signing of the AIP, the deliberations of the National Wilderness Park Steering Committee epitomized such feuding. From the outset, the group was deeply divided over key aspects of the management regime proposed for the Yukon North Slope. For one thing, the Yukon territorial government refused to participate, arguing that any park proposal designed to block industrial activity along the Arctic coast was non-negotiable. In addition, Aboriginal and federal committee members had conflicting ideas about the best way to manage the area and disagreed on where its boundaries should lie. Parks Canada felt the area should be managed under the *National Parks Act* and should cover approximately eighty-two hundred square miles in the western half of the northern Yukon (Fig. 3). In contrast, Inuvialuit officials, by this point resigned to the idea that some form of protected area would be established in the region, argued that existing park legislation was inadequate for safeguarding wildlife and insisted that a more appropriate legal instrument was required. For its part, the Canadian Wildlife Service felt that even the fifteen thousand square miles of the northern Yukon withdrawn from development by DIAND in 1978 was inadequate. Motivated by an overriding concern for the protection of the Porcupine caribou herd, CWS officials argued that the boundaries of the conservation regime should be extended into the Northwest Territories and that the entire region should be managed as a National Wildlife Area.[40]

In addition to disagreements over appropriate boundaries and legislative mechanisms, heated disputes broke out among committee members over the finer details of management. In particular, the Inuvialuit demand for exclusive harvesting rights within the boundaries of any protected area established on the North Slope generated determined resistance from the Departments of Environment and Fisheries and Oceans. In response to pressure from southern First Nations for amendments to the *Indian Act* and federal wildlife laws in the mid-1970s, both of these agencies developed departmental policies opposing 'special privileges' for Aboriginal people. At the end of the decade, they remained firmly committed to these policies, fearing that wildlife regulations based on ethnic or racial considerations inevitably generated social tensions and undermined conservation efforts.[41] Likewise, the Inuvialuit demand that a primary objective of the wilderness park should involve the "recognition, elaboration, and protection" of Aboriginal rights did not sit well with federal authorities. In the late 1970s, debates over the constitutional status of indigenous peoples were prominent on the national stage, and the Inuvialuit drew on them in negotiations. Their demand for broad group entitlements suggests that they regarded the committee as more than merely a forum for addressing technical and managerial issues, but rather as a platform for airing historic grievances and a vehicle for political empowerment. However, for Parks Canada and CWS officials, such a suggestion raised fundamental questions of governance that lay outside the mandate of the committee and threatened to bog it down in ideological debate.[42] In the end, such disputes effectively derailed the NWPSC, forestalling early efforts at joint management in the western Arctic not long after they began. The final committee report, submitted in May 1980 reflected the lack of consensus among Aboriginal and government members and, as a result, was quickly shelved by senior federal bureaucrats.[43]

The resistance the Inuvialuit faced during NWPSC deliberations was mirrored by reaction to the Agreement-in-Principle as a whole. Shortly after the agreement was announced to the public by COPE and the federal negotiating team, vigorous denunciations of it began to surface, seriously jeopardizing further negotiations on the wilderness park. The strongest response to the agreement came from the Yukon government, which regarded the document as fundamentally unconstitutional because territorial officials did not participate in the negotiating process.[44] In addition, industry executives criticized the agreement for obstructing the search for Arctic oil; Dene and Inuit groups argued it infringed upon their own land claim negotiations; non-Aboriginal northerners complained it discriminated against them; and NWT officials insisted it violated their jurisdiction over wildlife matters.[45] In response to these criticisms, federal authorities began to backpedal on their agreement with the Inuvialuit. Following its victory in the May 1979 election, the new Conservative government came to power with a mandate to overhaul federal Aboriginal policy. In subsequent months, the chief federal negotiator on the western Arctic claim made efforts to renegotiate key aspects of the AIP as he received directions from his superiors in DIAND to curb Inuvialuit demands. Senior government bureaucrats seemed particularly determined to meet the needs of the oil and gas industry for greater access to promising reserves in the Mackenzie Delta.[46] Whatever the reasons for the shift in federal strategy, these actions outraged COPE officials, resulting in a complete breakdown in negotiations.

When discussions between COPE officials and their federal counterparts resumed in January 1983, the Inuvialuit were in a much weaker bargaining position than when negotiations broke off. While the Liberals were in power again in Ottawa, formal talks had been stalled for more than two years and community leaders were feeling increasing pressure to reach a settlement as federal funding dried up and industrial activities in the western Arctic intensified. Faced with this situation, Inuvialuit negotiators suggested several trade-offs to federal officials in an attempt to reach a final agreement. Most important, they proposed a new form of conservation area, a National Wilderness Reservation, for the Yukon North Slope. The proposal made significant concessions to oil and gas companies by permitting industrial development within the reservation and by abandoning COPE demands for reversionary ownership of withdrawn lands. On the other hand, it retained a strong emphasis on Inuvialuit harvesting requirements by insisting upon the protection of Aboriginal lifestyles, permitting the establishment of small settlements, and demanding that Inuvialuit beneficiaries receive the same hunting rights in the northern Yukon as they would on the rest of their settlement lands. In exchange for their package of concessions, COPE negotiators wanted federal authorities to reconsider their positions on Inuvialuit land selections and financial compensation.[47]

The fact that COPE officials put forward a proposal for a new kind of protected area in 1983 is a telling indication of how dramatically their attitudes toward bureaucratic conservation had changed in the six short years since their land claim negotiations began. Dead set against any alternative to fee simple land ownership on the North Slope in 1977, they were willing to accept a vast state-managed reserve in the region by the middle of the following decade. However, while the Inuvialuit proposal for the wilderness reservation was received favourably by the chief federal negotiator, senior bureaucrats in DIAND ultimately succeeded in wresting further concessions from COPE. In the end, rather than a single reserve stretching from Alaska to the Northwest Territories along the Yukon coastline, a conservation regime involving several government agencies and emphasizing multiple use was established. Northern Yukon National Park was created in the western portion of the reserved region. A "special conservation area" permitting limited industrial development was established in the eastern portion.[48] Since the southern half of the region remained subject to the land claims of the Vuntut Gwich'in First Nation, decisions on the future of that area were postponed. In part, the decision to divide the region into distinct conservation units was a result of bureaucratic wrangling between federal agencies. In September 1983, Parks Canada demonstrated its renewed interest in the area by announcing a new park boundary proposal for the northwest corner of the territory.[49] The following month, CWS officials made public their desire to see a flexible management approach adopted in the east. In addition, applications by oil and construction companies for permits to build ports and production facilities at locations on the Yukon coast in the summer of 1983 probably reinforced federal efforts to keep the region open to industrial activity. Certainly, Yukon politicians continued to voice their desire for the construction of a development corridor through the area.[50] Whatever the exact configuration of influences leading to the establishment of a mixed conservation regime in the northern Yukon, the creation of the western national park and the eastern development zone effectively ended Inuvialuit hopes for a larger protected area and stronger conservation legislation in the region.

The national park that was ultimately established by the signing of the Inuvialuit Final Agreement (IFA) in June 1984 was dramatically different from most other national parks previously created in Canada. Most importantly, it was distinguished by its accommodation of Inuvialuit interests and cultural values. For instance, park management guidelines provided for the exclusive right of Inuvialuit hunters to harvest game in the park. This right was limited by quotas set by government wildlife biologists, but it effectively reserved the total allowable harvest for Inuvialuit beneficiaries. Moreover, park policies provided a number of additional protections for Inuvialuit hunting and trapping, including the right to use modern technologies and the right to sell animal products. These protections, in combination with economic and employment guarantees, ensured that park regulations did not prevent the Inuvialuit from conducting important cultural activities or contributing to household incomes, as they had in other parks. Finally, the settlement legislation made provision for the establishment of a co-management body comprised of equal numbers of native and government representatives. This arrangement gave the Inuvialuit some control in formulating park policy and a voice in management decisions. To be sure, Inuvialuit influence was restricted in a number of ways, most notably because federal ministers retained final authority over many park matters. Moreover, some park policies were inconsistent with Inuvialuit priorities, especially those that made allowances for industrial activities along the Beaufort Sea coast.[51] Still, when Northern Yukon National Park was established after seven years of negotiating, it reflected the success of COPE officials in gaining recognition for Inuvialuit interests and demonstrated how some of them had come to appreciate its value in accomplishing larger social and cultural objectives.

Indeed, viewed collectively, key sections in the IFA reflect both the desire of the Inuvialuit to preserve wildlife habitats on their traditional territories and their pragmatic understanding that protected areas could serve the long-term needs of their communities. By the end of the first year of negotiations, COPE officials had concluded that the creation of a national park in the northern Yukon could play an important role in fulfilling the broad mandate they had been given by residents of the western Arctic. They appreciated that if Inuvialuit people could jointly manage the land, wildlife, and natural resources in a protected area, they need not own that land. Through a process of conflict and compromise at the negotiating table, they had learned that an appropriately sited national park would allow them to concentrate their limited land selections elsewhere without suffering any significant costs.[52] Moreover, the IFA as a whole demonstrates the determination of the Inuvialuit to ensure that both conservation and industrial development were practised according to a new set of rules on their traditional homelands. Rather than accepting federal efforts to retain full control over land management in the western Arctic, COPE leaders insisted that protected areas created as part of their negotiated settlement should be established on terms set by local hunters and trappers. In the end, such demands suggest that, rather than valuing Northern Yukon National Park for its own sake or regarding it as an inherent good, COPE negotiators came to view it as a vehicle for community survival, using it to 'talk back' to the state during a period of rapid social change.

Rethinking Colonial Conservation in the North

In recent years, environmental historians and other scholars have argued compellingly that state conservation in northern Canada has been closely tied to broader efforts to control the social and economic lives of Aboriginal peoples. Sometimes drawing on research from colonial settings in Africa and South Asia, these scholars have highlighted how a wide range of environmental protection measures, including national parks, game laws, and wildlife education programs, have displaced resident communities and have been used by government authorities to assimilate or acculturate indigenous populations. Most of this research has focused on the late nineteenth and early twentieth centuries, but lately some scholars have extended its central arguments to the present. The most provocative of the new literature argues that recent innovations in conservation planning such as the co-management of natural resources represent only partial, even disingenuous, efforts to de-colonize state environmental protection.[53]

There can be little doubt that government conservation agencies operating in the Canadian North continue to manage land and wildlife in ways that alienate local people and present challenges for Aboriginal communities. Yet the case of Northern Yukon National Park suggests another way to understand the history of conservation in the region, one that highlights how Aboriginal peoples have forced shifts in government policies and how their views of protected areas have changed over time. Through the vehicle of land claim negotiations, the Inuvialuit of the western Arctic challenged the exclusionary conservation practices that state environmental managers have often employed in North America. Their opposition was rooted in deep cultural attachments to their homelands and the conviction that harvesting lifestyles must be protected if their communities were to remain healthy. During the 1970s and 1980s, these efforts contributed in important ways to the emergence of new approaches to protected areas management by forcing Parks Canada officials to question their assumptions about why parks exist and how they should be run. However, much more than mere pleas for inclusion in enduring colonial institutions, Inuvialuit protests were motivated by an alterative vision of conservation itself, one that challenged Canadians to scrutinize their understanding of wilderness and re-imagine the human place in nature.

1   John Sandlos, "Federal Spaces, Local Conflicts: National Parks and the Exclusionary Politics of the Conservation Movement in Ontario, 1900–1935," *Journal of the Canadian Historical Association* 16 (2005): 293–318; ibid., "Not Wanted in the Boundary: The Expulsion of the Keeseekowenin Ojibway Band from Riding Mountain National Park," *Canadian Historical Review* 89, no. 2 (2008): 189–221.

2   See, for example, Roderick P. Neumann, *Imposing Wilderness: Struggles Over Livelihood and Nature Preservation in Africa* (Berkeley: University of California Press, 1998); Nancy Lee Peluso, *Rich Forests, Poor People: Resource Control and Resistance in Java* (Berkeley: University of California Press, 1992); David Anderson and Richard H. Gove, *Conservation in Africa: Peoples, Policies, and Practice* (Cambridge: Cambridge University Press, 1990); Raymond L. Bryant, *The Political Ecology of Forestry in Burma, 1824–1994* (Honolulu: University of Hawaii Press, 1997); Dawn Chatty and Marcus Colchester, eds., *Conservation and Mobile Indigenous Peoples: Displacement, Forced Settlement, and Sustainable Development* (Oxford: Berghahn Books, 2002); Ramachandra Guha, *The Unquiet Woods: Ecological Change and Peasant Resistance in the Himalaya* (New York: Oxford University Press, 1989); James Fairhead and Melissa Leach, *Misreading the African Landscape: Society and Ecology in a Forest Savanna Mosaic* (Cambridge: Cambridge University Press, 1996); Mahesh Rangarajan, *Fencing the Forest: Conservation and Ecological Change in India's Central Provinces, 1860–1914* (Delhi: Oxford University Press,

1996); Mark David Spence, *Dispossessing the Wilderness: Indian Removal and the Making of the National Parks* (New York: Oxford University Press, 1999); John Sandlos, *Hunters at the Margin: Native People and Wildlife Conservation in the Northwest Territories* (Vancouver: UBC Press, 2007); ibid., "From the Outside Looking In: Aesthetics, Politics, and Wildlife Conservation in the Canadian North," *Environmental History* 6, no. 1 (2001): 6–31; Tina Loo, *States of Nature: Conserving Canada's Wildlife in the Twentieth Century* (Vancouver: UBC Press, 2006); Karl Jacoby, *Crimes against Nature: Squatters, Poachers, Thieves, and the Hidden History of American Conservation* (Berkeley: University of California Press, 2001).

3   Binnema and Niemi have argued that exclusionary wilderness values did not play a central role in the establishment of Banff National Park. See Theodore Binnema and Melanie Niemi, "'Let the Line be Drawn Now': Wilderness, Conservation, and the Exclusion of Aboriginal People from Banff National Park in Canada," *Environmental History* 11, no. 4 (2006): 724–50.

4   Paul Kopas, *Taking the Air: Ideas and Change in Canada's National Parks* (Vancouver: UBC Press, 2007): 37–66. On high modernism, see James C. Scott, *Seeing Like a State: How Certain Schemes to Improve the Human Condition Have Failed* (New Haven, CT: Yale University Press, 1998).

5   For a scholarly development of this criticism, see Richard West Sellars, *Preserving Nature in the National Parks: A History* (New Haven, CT: Yale University Press, 1997).

6   On agency plans to expand the park system into the North in the 1960s, see Lloyd Brooks and Harold Eidsvik, *National Park Potentials: Northwest Territories and Yukon: Report of Field Operations and Recommendations* (Ottawa: Department of Northern Affairs and National Resources, National Parks Branch, 1963). See also W.M. Baker, *Prospects for National Park Development in Parts of the Yukon and Northwest Territories.* Report prepared for the National Parks Branch, Department of Northern Affairs and National Resources, May 1963. On public concerns about the fragility of the Canadian Arctic during this period, see P. Whitney Lackenbauer and Matthew Farish, "The Cold War on Canadian Soil: Militarizing a Northern Environment," *Environmental History* 12 (2007): 932–36, and John Livingston, *Arctic Oil: The Destruction of the North?* (Toronto: CBC Merchandising, 1981). On the impact of the creation of Rocky Mountains Park, later Banff National Park, on the Stoney Indians, see Binnema and Niemi, "'Let the Line be Drawn Now'," and Janet Foster, *Working for Wildlife: The Beginnings of Preservation in Canada*, 2nd ed. (Toronto: University of Toronto Press, 1998), 30, 84. On the exclusion of Aboriginal peoples and other local residents from Point Pelee, Georgian Bay Islands, and Riding Mountain National Parks, see Sandlos, "Federal Spaces, Local Conflicts" and "Not Wanted in the Boundary." On the impact of the creation of Wood Buffalo National Park on Aboriginal peoples, see Sandlos, *Hunters at the Margin*, 23–108.

7   Peter Kulchyski and Frank James Tester, *Kiumajut (Talking Back): Game*

Management and Inuit Rights, 1900–1970 (Vancouver: UBC Press, 2007). For criticisms of co-management arrangements with northern Aboriginal peoples, see Paul Nadasdy, *Hunters and Bureaucrats: Power, Knowledge, and Aboriginal-State Relations in the Southwest Yukon* (Vancouver: UBC Press, 2003); ibid., "Re-evaluating the Co-Management Success Story," *Arctic* 56, no. 4 (2003): 367–80; Sandlos, "Wildlife Conservation in the North: Historic Approaches and their Consequences; Seeking Insights for Contemporary Resource Management" (paper presented at the Canadian Parks for Tomorrow Conference, Calgary, Alberta, 8–12 May 2008).

8   For seminal works in subaltern studies, see the scholarship of Ranajit Guha and Gayatri Chakravorty Spivak. In recent years, historians of conservation in North America have drawn from the work of subaltern scholars. See, especially, Jacoby, *Crimes against Nature*; Spence, *Dispossessing the Wilderness*; Loo, *States of Nature*; Sandlos, *Hunters at the Margin*; Louis S. Warren, *The Hunter's Game: Poachers and Conservationists in Twentieth-Century America* (New Haven, CT: Yale University Press, 1997); Sherrill E. Grace, *Canada and the Idea of North* (Montreal: McGill-Queen's University Press, 2001), 229–60; Julie Cruikshank, *The Social Life of Stories: Narrative and Knowledge in the Yukon Territory* (Vancouver: UBC Press, 1998); ibid., *Do Glaciers Listen? Local Knowledge, Colonial Encounters, and Social Imagination* (Vancouver: UBC Press, 2005).

9   Theodore Catton, *Inhabited Wilderness: Indians, Eskimos, and National Parks in Alaska* (Albuquerque: University

of New Mexico Press, 1997); Spence, *Dispossessing the Wilderness*.

10   On the trend toward managing protected areas as cultural landscapes in Canada, see Guy S. Swinnerton and Susan Buggey, "Protected Landscapes in Canada: Current Practice and Future Significance," *George Wright Forum* 21, no. 2 (2004): 78–92. On the international dimensions of this trend, see Richard W. Longstreth, ed., *Cultural Landscapes: Balancing Nature and Heritage in Preservation* (Minneapolis: University of Minnesota Press, 2008); Stan Stevens, ed., *Conservation through Cultural Survival: Indigenous Peoples and Protected Areas* (Washington, DC: Island Press, 1997); Vasant Saberwal, Mahesh Rangarajan, and Ashish Kothari, *People, Parks, and Wildlife: Towards Coexistence* (New Delhi: Orient Longman, 2001); Patrick C. West and Steven R. Brechin, eds., *Resident Peoples and National Parks: Social Dilemmas and Strategies in International Conservation* (Tucson: University of Arizona Press, 1991).

11   Kevin A. McNamee, "The Northern Yukon," *Probe Post* 13 (1984): 13–16; *A National Wildlife Area in the Northern Yukon and Northwest Territories* (Ottawa: Canadian Wildlife Service, 1979); *Northern Yukon – A Natural Area of Canadian Significance* (Ottawa: Parks Canada, 1978); "What Future for Northern Yukon?" *Beaufort Outlook* 1 (1982): 1–8; Constance Hunt, Rusty Miller, and Donna Tingley, *Wilderness Area: Legislative Alternatives for the Establishment of a Wilderness Area in the Northern Yukon* (Ottawa: Canadian Arctic Resources Committee, 1979); George W. Calef, "The Urgent Need for a Canadian Arctic Wildlife Range," *Nature Canada* 3, no.

3 (1974): 3–10; Parks Canada and the Canadian Wildlife Service, "Why the Yukon North of the Porcupine River Should be Protected as a Wilderness Area," 29 June 1978; Beaufort Sea Alliance, *The Northern Yukon: A National Priority*, 2 December 1983.

For broader discussions of resource development in the Canadian North during the 1960s and 1970s, see Robert Page, *Northern Development: The Canadian Dilemma* (Toronto: McClelland & Stewart, 1986); Edgar J. Dosman, *The National Interest: The Politics of Northern Development, 1968–1975* (Toronto: McClelland & Stewart, 1975); Richard Rohmer, *The Arctic Imperative: An Overview of the Energy Crisis* (Toronto: McClelland & Stewart, 1973); Gurston Dacks, *A Choice of Futures: Politics in the Canadian North* (Toronto: Methuen, 1981).

12   Peter A. Coates, *The Trans-Alaska Pipeline Controversy: Technology, Conservation, and the Frontier* (Anchorage: University of Alaska Press, 1993), 95–110; John M. Kauffmann, *Alaska's Brooks Range: The Ultimate Mountains* (Seattle: The Mountaineers, 1992), 97–111; Margaret Murie and Terry Tempest, *Two in the Far North* (Alaska Northwest Books, 2003).

13   "Proceedings of the Arctic International Wildlife Range Conference, October 20–22, Whitehorse, Yukon Territory," *University of British Columbia Law Review* 6, no. 1 (1971), 1–107.

14   Letter from Chief Alfred Charlie to Jean Chrétien, 29 October 1969, Library and Archives Canada (hereafter LAC), RG 108, acc. 1989-90/079, box 47, file 9192-82/12, pt. 1.

15   Thomas R. Berger, *Northern Frontier, Northern Homeland: The Report of the*

Mackenzie Valley Pipeline Inquiry, rev. ed. (Toronto: Douglas & McIntyre, 1988), 58–79.

16 Parks Canada, *The Firth River, Yukon Territory: A Wild Rivers Survey Descriptive Report* (Ottawa: National Parks Service Planning Division, 1972); Ian McNeil, *Firth River Area: New Park Resource Analysis Report* (Ottawa: Indian and Northern Affairs, 1977).

17 Berger, *Northern Frontier, Northern Homeland*, 127–62, 213–56; Martin O'Malley, *The Past and Future Land: An Account of the Berger Inquiry into the Mackenzie Valley Pipeline* (Toronto: P. Martin Associates, 1976).

18 Many scholars have examined the links between the northern environment and Canadian national identity. For fresh and sophisticated perspectives, see Eric Kaufmann, "'Naturalizing the Nation': The Rise of Naturalistic Nationalism in the United States and Canada," *Comparative Studies in Society and History* 40 (1998): 666–95; Renisa Mawani, "Legalities of Nature: Law, Empire, and Wilderness Landscapes in Canada," *Social Identities* 13, no. 6 (2007): 715–34; and Grace, *Canada and the Idea of North*, 45–75. See also Renée Hulan, *Northern Experience and the Myths of Canadian Culture* (Montreal: McGill-Queen's University Press, 2002); and John Moss, *Enduring Dreams: An Exploration of Arctic Landscape* (Concord, ON: House of Anansi Press, 1996).

19 Parks Canada, *The Firth River*; Ian McNeil, *Firth River Area*; Terry Fenge, "National Parks in the Canadian Arctic: The Case of the Nunavut Land Claim Agreement," *Environments* 22 (1993): 22; Department of Indian Affairs and Northern Development,

National Parks System Planning Manual (Ottawa: Parks Canada, 1971). For an analysis of the System Plan, see Kopas, *Taking the Air*, 53–63.

20 "Faulkner Announces Public Consultation for Six Arctic Wilderness Areas in National Parks System," *Communiqué* 1–7792 (Ottawa: Department of Indian and Northern Affairs, 23 January 1978).

21 Department of Indian Affairs and Northern Development, *Living Treaties, Lasting Agreements: Report of the Task Force to Review Comprehensive Claims Policy* (Ottawa: DIAND, 1985); J.R. Miller, *Skyscrapers Hide the Heavens: A History of Indian-White Relations in Canada*, 3rd ed. (Toronto: University of Toronto Press, 2000), 343; Christa Scholtz, *Negotiating Claims: The Emergence of Indigenous Land Claim Negotiation Policies in Australia, Canada, New Zealand, and the United States* (New York: Routledge, 2006), 68–72.

22 Peter Kulchyski, *Like the Sound of a Drum: Aboriginal Cultural Politics in Denendeh and Nunavut* (Winnipeg: University of Manitoba Press, 2005); Ailsa Henderson, *Nunavut: Rethinking Political Culture* (Vancouver: UBC Press, 2008); Ken S. Coates, *Best Left As Indians: Native-White Relations in the Yukon Territory, 1840–1973* (Montreal: McGill-Queen's University Press, 1991), 231–43; Robert McPherson, *New Owners in their Own Land: Minerals and Inuit Land Claims* (Calgary: University of Calgary Press, 2003), 57–87, 121–58, 203–68; Peter Cumming, "Canada's North and Native Rights," in *Aboriginal People and the Law: Indian, Metis and Inuit Rights in Canada*, ed. Bradford W. Morse, 695–764 (Ottawa: Carleton University

Press, 1985); John David Hamilton, *Arctic Revolution: Social Change in the Northwest Territories, 1935–1994* (Toronto: Dundurn Press, 1994).

23   On the origins of COPE, see Peter Usher, *History of COPE* (Ottawa: COPE, 1973), 20–23; COPE, *Our Land, Our Life: COPE Information Kit*, n.d. (ca. December 1972), copy in Committee for Original Peoples Entitlement Archives (hereafter COPE Archives), Inuvik, Northwest Territories, 8–9; Barry A. Hochstein, "New Rights or No Rights?: COPE and the Federal Government of Canada" (MA thesis, University of Calgary, 1987), 49–106; Barry Scott Zellen, *Breaking the Ice: From Land Claims to Tribal Sovereignty in the Arctic* (Lanham, MD: Lexington, 2008), 140–43, 156–60.

24   Peter J. Usher, *The Bankslanders: Economy and Ecology of a Frontier Trapping Community* (Ottawa: Information Canada, 1971); Gary William Wagner, "Implementing the Environmental Assessment Provisions of a Comprehensive Aboriginal Land Rights Settlement," (MA thesis, University of Waterloo, 1996), 22; Douglas Pimlott, Dougald Brown, and Kenneth Sam, *Oil under the Ice* (Ottawa: Canadian Arctic Resources Committee, 1976); Zellen, *Breaking the Ice*, 193–94; COPE press release, 9 September 1971, COPE Archives.

25   Peter J. Usher, *Eskimo Land Use and Occupancy in the Western Arctic*. A report submitted to the Inuit Land Use and Occupancy Project, 24 September 1974.

26   Sandlos, *Hunters at the Margin*.

27   Tungavik Federation of Nunavut, "Land Claims, National Parks, Protected Areas, and Renewable Resource Economy," in *Proceedings of the Arctic Heritage Symposium, 24–28 August 1985, Banff, Alberta, Canada*, ed. Gordon Nelson, Roger D. Needham, and Linda Norton, 285–97 (Waterloo, ON: Heritage Resource Centre, University of Waterloo, 1985); Inuit Tapirisat of Canada, *Inuit Tapirisat of Canada Report on Proposals to Establish National Wilderness Parks in Inuit Nunangat* (Ottawa: Inuit Tapirisat of Canada, 1979); Nicholas Lawson, "Where Whitemen Come to Play," *Cultural Survival* 9 (1985): 54–56; Rosemarie Kuptana, *An Inuit Perspective on the Establishment of National Parks Within Canada's Arctic*. A Presentation to Parks Superintendents, 3 October 1994, copy in the administrative files of the Western Arctic Field Unit, Parks Canada, Inuvik, Northwest Territories (hereafter WAFU files); Sandlos, *Hunters at the Margin*, 23–78.

28   Fenge, "National Parks in the Canadian Arctic," 23; Kopas, *Taking the Air*, 83–84, 86–88; J.G. Nelson, "The Future of Conservation Reserves in the Arctic," *Contact* 8, no. 4 (1976): 76–116; *Bill S-4, An Act to Amend the National Parks Act*, 1st Session, 29th Parliament, 1973; Canada, House of Commons, Standing Committee on Indian Affairs and Northern Development, Minutes, no. 29 (Whitehorse, Yukon, 12 December 1973), 31.

29   Northern Parks Working Group, *Northern Parks: Issues and Options*, June 1979, copy in WAFU files; "Northern Parks Working Group," n.d. (ca. March 1979), copy in WAFU files.

30   Kopas, *Taking the Air*, 79–83; Gerald V. La Forest and Muriel Kent Roy,

Report of the Special Inquiry on Kouchibouguac National Park (Ottawa:
Government of Canada and Government of New Brunswick, 1981); Alan
MacEachern, Natural Selections: National Parks in Atlantic Canada, 1935–
1970 (Montreal: McGill-Queen's
University Press, 2001), 237–38.

31 Parks Canada, Parks Canada Policy
    (Ottawa: Department of the Environ-
    ment, 1979), 37, cited in Fenge, "Na-
    tional Parks in the Canadian Arctic,"
    24. On the development provisions for
    local consultation in the 1979 policy
    statement, see Kopas, Taking the Air,
    88–91.

32 Inuvialuit Nunangat: The Proposal for
    an Agreement-in-Principle to Achieve
    the Settlement of Inuvialuit Land
    Rights in the Western Arctic Region of
    the Northwest and Yukon Territories
    between the Government of Canada
    and the Committee for Original Peoples'
    Entitlement, 13 May 1977, iv.

33 Ibid., 46, 55–65, schedule D.

34 Paul Sabin, "Voices from the Hydro-
    carbon Frontier: Canada's Mackenzie
    Valley Pipeline Inquiry (1974–1977),"
    Environmental History Review 19, no. 1
    (1995): 17–48.

35 Inuvialuit Nunangat, iv.

36 Letter from Warren Allmand to Sam
    Raddi, 5 August 1977, copy in COPE
    Archives.

37 Ibid.

38 Inuvialuit Land Rights Settlement
    Agreement in Principle, 31 October
    1978, 61–66.

39 The literature on the political ecology
    of conservation is vast. Four works
    that have proven indispensable in
    framing this chapter are: Roderick P.

Neumann, "Nature-State-Territory:
Toward a Critical Theorization of
Conservation Enclosures," in Liberation Ecologies: Environment, Development, Social Movements, 2nd ed., ed.
Richard Peet and Michael Watts,
195–217 (London: Routledge, 2004);
ibid., Imposing Wilderness; Jim Igoe,
Conservation and Globalization: A
Study of National Parks and Indigenous Communities From East Africa to
South Dakota (Belmont, CA: Thomson
Wadsworth, 2004); and Dan Brockington, Fortress Conservation: The Preservation of the Mkomazi Game Reserve,
Tanzania (Oxford: James Currey,
2002).

40 "Minutes of the National Wilder-
    ness Park Steering Committee, First
    Meeting, Whitehorse, Yukon, 12–13
    September 1979," Parks Canada West-
    ern Service Centre files, Whitehorse,
    Yukon; Letter from C.W. Pearson to
    the Honourable John Fraser, 11 Febru-
    ary 1980. LAC, RG 108, vol. 47, box
    148, file 5600-36/N112, pt. 1.

41 "Minutes of the National Wilder-
    ness Park Steering Committee, First
    Meeting," 20; Memorandum from
    the Assistant Deputy Minister, En-
    vironmental Management Service to
    Deputy Minister re: "Interdepart-
    mental meeting on federal position on
    Indian hunting, trapping, and fishing
    rights," 21 March 1978, and "The
    Treaty Rights of Hunting, Fishing,
    Trapping, and Gathering: Concerns of
    the Department of Fisheries and the
    Environment," 30 March 1978, LAC,
    RG 108, vol. 111, file 1165-36/C242.

42 "Minutes of the National Wilderness
    Park Steering Committee, First Meet-
    ing," 20-1; Letter from Lloyd Brooks
    to Steve Kun, 24 October 1979, LAC,

RG 84, acc. 89-90/006, vol. 6, box 197, file 1165-219, pt. 3.

43 Lloyd Brooks, *The Northern Yukon National Wilderness Park Proposal: Report of the Chairman of the National Wilderness Park Steering Committee*, 1 May 1980.

44 Letter from Dan Lang to the Honourable John Roberts, 19 November 1980, LAC, RG 108, acc. 1989-90/079, box 60, file 9440-34-1, vol. 2; letter from C.W. Pearson to the Honourable John Fraser, 11 February 1980; "YTG Slams Feds for Park Approach," *Whitehorse Star*, 27 April 1978; "COPE Claim Thwarts Yukon 2 MLAs Say," *Whitehorse Star*, 25 July 1978.

45 "NWT Wants Own Parks," *Whitehorse Star*, 17 February 1978; "No Hope in COPE," *Whitehorse Star*, 9 August 1978; "Mutual Claim Blame," *Whitehorse Star*, 21 November 1978; "COPE No Model for Yukon Say Native Leaders," *Whitehorse Star*, 17 July 1978.

46 Letter from Maurice LeClair, Treasury Board, to Arthur Kroeger, DIAND, 10 March 1978, LAC, RG 108, vol. 111, file 1165-36/C242; DIAND, "Native Claims Policy – Comprehensive Claims," 20 July 1979, copy in COPE Archives; DIAND, "Discussion Paper: Native Claims Policy – Comprehensive Claims," 5 November 1980, copy in COPE Archives.

47 Letter from Bob DeLury, Chief COPE Negotiator, to Simon Reisman, Chief Federal Negotiator, 17 February 1983, COPE Archives; letter from DeLury to Reisman, 21 February 1983, COPE Archives; letter from DeLury to Reisman, 28 February 1983, COPE Archives.

48 Indian and Northern Affairs Canada, *The Western Arctic Claim: The Inuvialuit Final Agreement* (Ottawa: DIAND, 1984), 18–19.

49 Frances Rennie, *Northern Yukon National Park Boundary Proposal* (Ottawa: National Parks System Division, 16 September 1983); Parks Branch and Canadian Wildlife Service, *Environment Canada's Conservation Interests in the Northern Yukon: The National Park Proposal and Other Conservation Requirements*. Submission prepared for the Beaufort Sea Environmental Assessment Panel, October 1983, 6–24, 26–27; Socio-Economic Division, Parks Canada, *Socio-Economic Base Study for the Proposed Northern Yukon National Park Reserve*, August 1983.

50 Indian and Northern Affairs Canada, *Report of the Yukon North Slope Project Review Group*, vol. 1: *Summary Report* (Ottawa: DIAND, 31 December 1983), 11–17, 57–63.

51 Indian and Northern Affairs Canada, *The Western Arctic Claim*, 18–22.

52 Terry Fenge, "Political Development and Environmental Management in Northern Canada: The Case of the Nunavut Agreement," *Etudes/Inuit/Studies* 16 (1992): 115–41; ibid., "National Parks in the Canadian Arctic," 26; B. Sadler, "National Parks, Wilderness Preservation, and Native Peoples in Northern Canada," *Natural Resources Journal* 29 (1989): 185–204.

53 Sandlos, "Wildlife Conservation in the North"; Nadasdy, *Hunters and Bureaucrats*; ibid., "Re-evaluating the Co-Management Success Story."

Archaeology in the Rocky Mountain National Parks: Uncovering an 11,000-Year-Long Story

꙳

E. Gwyn Langemann[1]
Parks Canada

Today there is a strong program of archaeological research in the Rocky Mountain national parks, as indeed there is throughout Parks Canada. But only forty years ago, it was still possible to find serious publications that claimed the mountains were too difficult a place for people to have lived and so there would be no archaeology to be done. Even though the first formally protected archaeological site in Canada was set aside in Banff on the eve of the First World War, no serious archaeological research happened in the mountain parks for the next fifty years, until Brian Reeves of the University of Calgary showed effectively that archaeological sites were present throughout the backcountry as well as in the major montane valleys, and that mountain passes had long been major travel corridors.

This paper is not going to present the results of archaeological research or the details of the eleven thousand years of culture history that has been reconstructed for the Rocky Mountains.[2] Rather, it will consider the history of archaeological research in the mountain parks and its place within Parks Canada. Initially an academic but amateur pursuit, the field of cultural resource management (CRM) archaeology grew rapidly in Canada in the 1970s in response to the passage of new heritage legislation in all the provinces. Archaeology in the national parks grew in a similar manner. In the 1970s, Parks Canada archaeologists from Ottawa were carrying out excavations at major historic sites in the west, such as Rocky Mountain House National Historic Site. By the early 1980s, the regional offices in Calgary and Winnipeg also had permanent archaeology staff, and a program of inventory and research in the national parks had begun in earnest. In Banff, this was linked to such major development projects as the twinning of the Trans-Canada Highway, which affected a series of deeply stratified, highly significant precontact campsites. Their excavation produced the first culture history sequence for Banff. In all the parks, archaeologists worked to provide a basic inventory and analysis of archaeological and historic resources for the park resource descriptions, as a complement to the park-wide natural resource inventories that were being completed.

Today, there are some two thousand sites known in the mountain park block, and Parks Canada archaeologists carry out a wide variety of research, mitigation, and interpretation projects. This work has established a basic inventory and culture history sequence for the mountain parks, and the spatial patterning of sites is integrated with the GIS natural resource databases for each park. CRM is a strong part of the work being done to protect and present the natural and cultural resources of the parks, and archaeological data is being used to address paleoecological questions: How have people used plant and animal resources in the past, and how has this changed over time? How have people had an impact on the distribution of plants and animals over time? How can this information help parks managers? If one research stream in archaeology as a discipline has been anthropological, another equally strong research focus has always sought to place people in a landscape, and look at the patterns people have made on the land through going about their daily lives. We are beginning to understand that human actions and resource use over the millennia have played a large role in shaping the park ecosystems that we are trying to restore and preserve today. Through archaeological and ecological research, it is becoming clear that people have always been present as an integral part of the landscape.

The First Prehistoric Remains to Be Preserved in Canada

Banff townsite has been a focus of occupation for a very long time, and a place of contact where people from the British Columbia Interior Plateau have met people from the plains. But we didn't know this at first. When Rocky Mountains Park was established in 1885 around the Cave and Basin hot springs, and as Banff townsite developed to provide services for the miners, loggers, and tourists, there was little knowledge of what had been there before. Some residents with an interest in Aboriginal history and knowledge collected their handicrafts and artefacts; these collections eventually became a part of the Whyte Museum of the Canadian Rockies and the Banff Park Museum. Norman Bethune Sanson, curator of the Banff Park Museum (built in 1903), collected a magpie variety of objects pertaining to natural history, including archaeological and anthropological items. In 1913, Harlan I. Smith was asked to write a handbook for the Rocky Mountain Parks Museum.[3] Smith was the first full-time archaeologist in the federal civil service, hired in 1911 by the Geological Survey of Canada to work at the new Victoria Memorial Museum in Ottawa.[4] The wide variety of objects that he describes in the handbook can still be seen very much as they were then, displayed in all their profusion in splendid Edwardian cases, because the Banff Park Museum National Historic Site has been preserved as a museum of museums.[5]

In his handbook, under "Antiquities," Smith also described an archaeological housepit village site that he had recorded earlier near the Banff Springs golf course: the first formal archaeological work in Alberta. Based on his earlier anthropological research in the British Columbia Interior as a member of the Jesup North Pacific Expedition, Smith immediately recognized these circular depressions as the archaeological traces of Shuswap semi-subterranean winter pithouses. Even before going to Banff, Smith wrote to James B. Harkin, the Commissioner of the new Dominion Parks Branch, to request the preservation of the site. Harkin took a strong interest, and wrote to Superintendent Clarke of Rocky Mountains Park on 27 May 1913, instructing him to set aside the housepit site and erect a protective sign reading "Indian Circular House Pits. They mark the easterly limit of such pits. Penalty for damaging them – $100.00" – a serious penalty in 1913 dollars.

FIG. 1. LOOKING TOWARDS MOUNT RUNDLE, ACROSS GROUNDS AND ROAD WAY, TO THE SEMI-SUBTERRANEAN HOUSE SITES NEAR BANFF. [© CANADIAN MUSEUM OF CIVILIZATION, HARLAN I. SMITH, 1913, NO. 25654.]

FIG. 2. SEMI-SUBTERRANEAN HOUSE SITES BETWEEN MOUNT RUNDLE AND BOW RIVER NEAR THE GOLF GROUNDS, BANFF. [© CANADIAN MUSEUM OF CIVILIZATION, HARLAN I. SMITH, 1913, NO. 24014.]

Smith, Harkin, and park staff worked over the next year and a half[6] to restore the pits to their original condition and to withdraw the lots from townsite development. As Smith reminded Harkin on 28 May 1914, "I believe these are the first prehistoric remains to be preserved in Canada, and I am anxious that they should be both protected and kept as near as possible in their original condition." Unfortunately, this protection only lasted until 1928, when an expansion of the Banff Springs golf course destroyed the remaining pits.

Smith's work at the housepits demonstrates the value that the new national parks system was willing to ascribe to archaeological remains. Although it was the first professional archaeological work in the mountain parks, recording the group of housepits was a minor incident as far as archaeological fieldwork goes; Smith did not even have the chance to excavate before the First World War intervened. However, an interest in the housepits is a thread that we can follow through the more recent research in Banff National Park. Today, we know of seven similar sites in the park, dating from the last three thousand years: the only such sites recorded in the Canadian Rockies, distinct from the usual range of precontact campsites, killsites, and quarry sites.[7] They speak to the Rocky Mountains as a crossroads of cultures from the British Columbia Plateau and the Plains, and to people arriving from the west and making a substantial investment of time and labour in excavating and building these structures with the intent of returning. In the late precontact period, Banff was already a village.

1955–64: Creating a Discipline

After the initial interest in the Banff housepits, there was virtually no formal archaeological work done in Alberta, through years of war and depression.[8] In 1955, however, the Glenbow Foundation of Calgary, started by oilman Eric L. Harvie, funded an archaeological survey for the province. Richard Forbis was hired in the first full-time professional position on the Canadian prairies and began a systematic program of excavations at key late prehistoric sites in southern Alberta.[9] Many of these sites are now commemorated as National Historic Sites, including Old Women's Buffalo Jump, Writing on Stone, the British Block cairn, Cluny Earthlodge, and Rocky Mountain

Fig. 3. University of Calgary archaeological field school at site DgPl-10 in Waterton, 1971. From B.O.K. Reeves, *DgPl-10, A Winter Base Campsite in Waterton Lakes National Park, 114* (Ottawa: Environment Canada, Canadian Parks Service, Microfiche Report Series 345, 1980). Parks Canada.

House. In 1965, Forbis and Marie Wormington wrote *An Introduction to the Archaeology of Alberta, Canada*, offering "a very tentative introduction ... the presentation of a casual acquaintance whom one scarcely knows."[10] There is absolutely no mention of any mountain sites in this volume.

Although the Archaeological Society of Alberta was founded in 1960, reflecting a strong public and amateur interest, professional archaeology in Alberta was limited to the work of the Glenbow Foundation until 1963. That year, two archaeologists joined the Department of Sociology and Anthropology at the University of Alberta, and Forbis moved across town to found the Department of Archaeology at the University of Calgary.[11] This was the first Canadian university department devoted to archaeology, and it soon made the southern Rocky Mountains a focus for research. Brian Reeves, one of its first graduate students, stayed on to teach in the department, and became an influential figure in southern Alberta and mountain archaeology.

1964–78: Archaeological Research in the Mountains Begins

Reeves had grown up in Waterton Lakes National Park. He visited local archaeological sites with Waterton residents who had been collecting artefacts, and, in a series of contracts with the National Parks Branch from 1964 through 1970, systematically surveyed the entire park.[12] Because of his training in both geography and archaeology, Reeves was able to combine human history with environmental history and discuss the patterns of human use of Waterton as they changed through the post-Pleistocene era. This linking of human history and environment was of a piece with the ecological thinking of the time. In this work Reeves had the enthusiastic support of national park interpreters, themselves a new addition to the national parks (as Jim Taylor notes in his essay), such as Kurt Seel. The Parks Canada archaeological map collection at Calgary has a topographic map from the late 1960s on which Seel has drawn in all of the major archaeological sites in Waterton, annotating the relationships between the various campsites, bison kill sites, and drive lanes; it suggests an ecological thinking, interpreting human use as a web of life. Seel also maintained a collection of archaeological artefacts, catalogued in the same way as natural history specimens. In his mind at least, human sites and artefacts were very much a part of the same system and landscape as any other natural phenomenon and were to be understood and inventoried in the same way.

In the late 1960s, it was still possible to find statements about how little prehistoric peoples had used the impenetrable mountains.[13] In fact, the language of doubt and difficulty, of seeing the mountain passes as too arduous, and the resources as too scarce, was more the language of the European settlement experience. It was extremely difficult for the early fur traders and explorers to work their way through the Rockies, and for the Canadian Pacific Railway to build a practical route through the Kicking Horse Pass and Rogers Pass. It took some time before early ranchers and farmers in the foothills were able to work out a practical knowledge of the local conditions. The Aboriginal peoples, of course, had worked this out some time ago: Reeves' work in Waterton proved that humans had a long and continuous presence in the region. But outside of Waterton, Reeves told the 1968 Canadian

National Parks: Today and Tomorrow conference, the Rocky Mountain region was "largely unexplored," and "most people conceive of the parks as an uninhabited landscape, a 'living museum of nature' in which aboriginal man played little or no role."[14] He called for better interpretation of the long human involvement with the mountain landscape in the national parks. By reconstructing the palaeoenvironments, park visitors would regain a sense of the environment as a dynamic system and make an emotional connection to the people of the past. (This reads today as a very modern argument, as Parks Canada is being asked to foster meaningful visitor experiences and connections after a period of decreased emphasis on communications.)

The 1968 conference was a landmark event that galvanized efforts to manage natural resources in a more formalized, research-based program.[15] It is significant that an archaeological voice was included here, as it reinforced the role of archaeology as a discipline that places people in a landscape. While Reeves went on to survey the Crowsnest Pass,[16] his pioneering work sparked survey efforts in other mountain areas. By the early 1970s, surveys carried out under contract with the National Historic Sites Service provided a basic archaeological resource inventory of Banff, Yoho, and Jasper national parks and the Ya Ha Tinda Ranch. The work was done largely by Reeves' graduate students from the Department of Archaeology at the University of Calgary but also by students from the University of British Columbia. At this time there was no local archaeological staff with Parks Canada and no body of independent archaeological contractors to call on.

In Banff, a cursory survey in 1966 of the Bow River Valley between Castle Mountain and Cochrane had noted a small number of sites.[17] However, the first archaeological investigations of any duration were those carried out by Ole Christensen of the University of Calgary under Reeves' direction.[18] Four months were spent with a small crew locating visible sites in high potential areas of the park, although, in accordance with the standards of the day, little subsurface testing was done, and the survey was not intensive or systematic. Unfortunately, the data from the 123 precontact sites found were summarized in Christensen's 1973 MA thesis on a park-wide basis, making it difficult to determine what was found at any one site in particular. These data were reworked into recommendations for conservation and interpretation of the sites in specific management areas,[19] but no more substantial work was done until the mid-1970s. Similar surveys were carried out in Jasper and the Ya Ha Tinda.[20] As in Banff, the method was to search areas that could be easily reached in a wide and little-known area, using local informants, without any attempt to be systematic or intensive in coverage. A Yoho survey discovered only five precontact sites and a number of historic sites.[21]

The 1970s was a period of enormous growth in archaeological research in Alberta, resulting in part from the creation of the Archaeological Survey of Alberta and passage of the landmark *Alberta Heritage Act* in 1973 (later named the *Alberta Historical Resources Act*). The Act was passed after a public consultation process (led by Forbis) on the conservation of historical and archaeological resources was able to demonstrate strong public concern about the rapid loss of historic resources in the face of burgeoning economic development. At the time, such public recognition of the need to protect heritage resources was without precedent in Canada; similar heritage legislation was subsequently passed in all provinces and territories.[22] The legislation does not cover the federal lands of the national parks, but we have used the relevant provincial standards as a guideline for best practices, particularly for work at precontact sites, and we do share our data with the provincial and territorial archaeological bodies. The *Alberta Historical Resources Act* generated enough business in Alberta and British Columbia to support full-time archaeological consulting companies because it required development projects to do a heritage resources impact assessment prior to destructive work. Assessments began to be done for work within the national parks as well, on behalf of clients who were now accustomed to the need for similar assessments of their projects outside park boundaries. For example, proposed modifications of the CPR line in Lake Louise were assessed for their impact on any historic or precontact sites.[23]

Meanwhile, researchers from the University of Calgary undertook a systematic surface collection and test excavation at the Minnewanka site, an extensive and highly significant multicomponent precontact site where Clovis spear points had been found.[24] This was an attempt to see if there were any parts of the site that were undisturbed and not damaged by the wartime construction and subsequent operation of the reservoir. In 1978, before the construction of the Muleshoe parking and day-use area in Banff National Park, mitigative excavations at two deeply stratified sites along the Bow Valley Parkway identified a series of occupations going back about eight thousand years (although the strata were not as clearly separated as one might like).[25] Along with the Minnewanka project, these represent the first excavations of consequence in Banff.

During this period, the few archaeologists with the National Parks Branch were in the east. In 1961, John Rick had joined the National Historic Sites Service in the newly created position of staff archaeologist.[26] He built up an archaeological staff in Ottawa to fill the need for expertise in historic archaeology and the study of material culture remains. They were needed to do the applied research behind the major reconstructions at such historic sites as the Fortress of Louisbourg and the Fortifications of Quebec. Historic archaeology was not very visible in Canadian universities then, but the research and expertise developed by the Branch was at the forefront of the discipline.[27] Indeed, the Society for Historical Archaeology later honoured Parks Canada with an Award of Merit for developing the field of historical archaeology for an entire nation; in 1994 award plaques were presented to each of its archaeology offices across the country. Archaeologists with the Branch came west in the late 1960s and early 1970s as part of similar reconstruction projects planned at three fur trade sites: Lower Fort Garry, Fort St. James, and Rocky Mountain House. This was the optimistic centennial era of "the big project," and one archaeologist has argued that such public projects were chosen more to reinforce national pride, and social and economic goals, than strictly for their importance as fur trade sites.[28]

Archaeological research was meant to inform substantial projects of reconstruction and interpretation at these sites, then called National Historic Parks. The name is telling; the goal was to provide living history, a full measure of activities and interpretation for the visitors, at an historic site with a large land base, in a manner analogous to the national parks. Archaeological excavations were a vital part of this effort; they located the exact spot of the fur trade buildings, discovered construction details, and found artefacts that could be used to lend authenticity for animated interpretation. But the work was tightly focussed on the fur trade structures. Today, such a project would also consider it necessary to test as deeply as possible to find any precontact remains below the fur trade era, and to test more widely across the landform, to look at questions about First Nations camps around the fort itself. The fur trade era would be seen as one component in the larger evolution of the site, and in the larger cultural landscape. Archaeologists today would be seeing their role as researchers of culture and ecological adaptation in their own right, and not just as the handmaiden of history or historical reconstruction.

While the National Parks Branch developed a strong specialty in historic archaeology, staff with expertise in precontact archaeology were not hired. The idea was still that any precontact field or analytical work could be best done through contracts with the universities or one of the growing number of firms specializing in archaeological and heritage work to satisfy the demands of the new provincial legislation. The absence of precontact specialists was of particular concern in Western Canada. Parks Canada holdings in the east are dominated by the large national historic sites, and archaeological research needs are more skewed to the historic period. Within the mountain park block, the historic sites are largely related to railways, transportation corridors, and tourism; rather than significant built structures, we have a lot of space, a lot of backcountry, and an 11,000-year-long record of human use that has not left standing structures. Unable to rely on the national collections that had been developed for quite a different purpose, we have had to develop our own research specialities and reference collections.

1979–88: A Full-Time Parks Canada Archaeological Presence

In 1980, the Alberta Archaeological Society organized a forum to review the state of archaeology at the time of Alberta's 75th anniversary. Brian Reeves reviewed the eastern slopes area, including the foothills and mountains, and noted an explosive increase in the number of projects that had been done, mostly as Historic Resources Impact Assessments (HRIA) mandated under the terms of the 1973 Act.[29] This had greatly expanded the numbers of recorded sites, but Reeves was concerned that the pace of development and the reporting requirements of the Act meant that this knowledge was neither well reported in the professional literature nor available in a form accessible to the public. This applied to the surveys within the national parks, published in very limited editions in the National Historic Sites Service Manuscript Report Series. (Later this was continued as the microfiche report series, making it even less accessible. The series and indeed all archaeological publications were cancelled in the mid-1990s, a period of public service restraint.) Reeves also called for a regional management strategy; while key sites within Waterton Lakes National Park were zoned for maximum protection in the park management plan, and areas within the national parks were generally protected, he was deeply concerned that there was no wider regional strategy for site research and management, integrated across municipal, provincial, and federal jurisdictions. This is still lacking today. Finally, he noted that, outside Waterton and the main valleys of Banff and Jasper, few excavations had been done in the mountain region, so there was still no culture history for Banff or Jasper, or indeed for any of the eastern slopes north of the Crowsnest and Waterton Lakes. This was urgent, given the huge industrial and recreational development pressures that the entire area was facing in this economic boom.

Reeves' 1980 review coincides with the beginnings of full-time professional archaeological staff in the Calgary Regional Office of Parks Canada, hired to work in the national parks and national historic sites in B.C. and Alberta. In 1963, the National Parks Branch decentralized into regional offices in Calgary, Cornwall, and Halifax, joined by additional offices in Quebec City and Winnipeg ten years later.[30] By the late 1970s, they each had their own archaeologists, historians, curators, and collections staff. In part, this decentralization from Ottawa was the result of the volume of work related to the large excavation projects that supported fur trade site restoration in the 1970s, such as at Rocky Mountain House. In the Calgary regional office, a full-time archaeologist was hired in 1978 when it became apparent that a number of major inventory and mitigation projects were coming on stream. Most work in the mountain parks since then has been done by archaeological staff with Parks Canada. At first, most were term staff or summer students; over time, more permanent staff have been hired, as the workload was demonstrated to be constant and steady. There have been two basic streams of research. One has been aimed at salvage work or conducting impact assessments of proposed projects within the national parks; this involves a high number of sites or projects with perhaps little work at each. The second has been more intensive, with excavation of key sites threatened by a development or by erosion or for research purposes. A separate focus has been compilations of the results for use in management plans.

Twinning the Trans-Canada Highway through the eastern part of Banff National Park presented an opportunity for a major program of site survey and excavation in the early 1980s.[31] In many cases the design of the highway was altered to avoid the most important sites; where impact was unavoidable, excavations were done. The Vermilion wetlands in particular were ringed by a number of significant, deeply stratified sites, and between 1982 and 1986 there was an intensive program of excavation led by Daryl Fedje.[32] The emphasis was both on developing a culture history and using the palaeo-ecological information present in the site to reconstruct past environmental conditions in the lower Bow Valley. In an echo of Smith's early project at the housepits, palaeoecologist James White from the Geological Survey of Canada was hired for the duration of the project. In the mountain landforms, with active and often violent episodes of erosion and deposition, cultural deposits can be found many metres below the surface; older methods of shovel testing or surface surveys are not adequate, and some sort of backhoe or deep testing must be used. At the Vermilion Lakes site, archaeologists dug through three metres of deposits, finding a 10,700-year-old occupation at the base, with butchered bison and mountain sheep bones along with lithic waste flakes in their hundreds. The sheep were a post-glacial species larger than modern sheep.[33]

As visitors drive through Banff, heading west on the Trans-Canada highway along the Vermilion Lakes and onto the Bow Valley Parkway, they pass through a concentration of alluvial fan and dune landforms that were some of the earliest to appear as the glaciers retreated. This is one of the most significant concentrations of deeply stratified archaeological sites in the mountain parks. This is partly due to it being one of the earliest areas open for occupation, and to a favourable combination of dry sunny landforms and montane grasses where game and plant resources could be found, and partly to the way in which the landforms were built up, rapidly covering and sealing off the traces people left behind so they were preserved from erosion and decay. We have found no sites elsewhere in Banff or Jasper with such a long and detailed record of human occupation, although there are many smaller sites to be found with records from various time periods.

The culture history developed during the excavations at these key sites was used in the Banff Archaeological Resource Description and Analysis (ARDA), the first substantial regional analysis of Banff prehistory.[34] Parks naturalists and wildlife experts had been writing inventories of natural resources as part of the push to a more scientifically based management process. In 1985, a brief chapter on archaeological resources and park history

FIG. 4. PROFILE OF THE 1984 EXCAVATIONS AT THE DEEPLY STRATIFIED
VERMILION LAKES SITE, IN ADVANCE OF TRANS-CANADA HIGHWAY TWINNING.
SUCCESSIVE EPISODES OF ALLUVIAL FLOODING, AEOLIAN DEPOSITION, AND
VIOLENT ROCKFALL EPISODES HAVE BUILT UP A DEEPLY STRATIFIED SITE; A
WHITE VOLCANIC TEPHRA IS VISIBLE JUST ABOVE THE CENTRAL ROCKY LAYER,
AND METAL TAGS REPRESENT DIFFERENT CULTURAL LAYERS. SCALE BAR IS I
METRE. [CALGARY CRS 153R203E. PARKS CANADA.]

was included in the Banff National Park Resource Description and Analysis (RDA), a detailed inventory of all the natural and cultural features contained in the park.[35] In response to this brevity, cultural resources staff in Calgary developed ARDAs as a way of making the growing body of archaeological data available to park managers. For each park as a whole, ARDAs were an opportunity to consider thoughtfully the results of archaeological research on a regional scale and make recommendations for cultural resource management. The work in the early 1980s had been focussed on answering pressing development needs, such as the twinning of the Trans-Canada Highway, so most work had been in the more developed parts of the parks. But as they began to write ARDAs, Parks Canada archaeologists realized there were some sizeable gaps in the research and began more intensive survey programs in the more remote areas of the park. In 1987, a contract was let to inventory the Red Deer River watershed within Banff National Park.[36] This was the first serious look at this area since Christensen's 1969 survey, and the first intensive survey undertaken outside the Bow River valley. Significant finds included a third pithouse village site at McConnell Creek and a site with evidence of microlithic technology, suggesting influences from the Interior Plateau; the result was a general picture of the archaeological record that showed use of the area to have been long-term and almost as intensive as the Bow Valley. We think of it today as backcountry, but that concept relates to our own transportation patterns. Certainly people in the past have used the Red Deer valley consistently and repeatedly.

In that same year, Fedje surveyed other parts of the Banff backcountry, which either had never been assessed previously or which had not been visited since Christensen's work two decades earlier. These included the Clearwater River valley, the junction of Divide Creek and the Red Deer River, and Bryant Creek. In Jasper, Rod Pickard directed an intensive survey of the Athabasca River valley over three seasons and directed excavations at Jasper House National Historic Site.[37] These are examples of several wide-ranging survey projects that were undertaken in advance of writing ARDA documents for the mountain parks. They gave a useful overview of the sites in each park, but, in retrospect, they attempted far too much work in too short a time, resulting in a number of analysis and database problems that we are still clearing up. It would have been better to undertake less field work to allow more time for the necessary report writing and data entry.

Fig. 5. Using GIS to make an interactive clickable base map of the Bar U Ranch National Historic Site. The aerial base map contains hot buttons that are linked to a nested series of databases, which include historic photos, built heritage history, and excerpts from archaeological and historical reports. These underlying databases can be indefinitely expanded, as more relevant information is discovered. The user clicks on the buttons to bring up pages from these other databases, as seen in Figure 6. [Calgary CRS. Parks Canada.]

The Banff and Jasper ARDAs were approved in 1989; ARDAs have since been written for all the mountain block parks, as well as for other parks and historic sites that are served by the Calgary Service Centre.[38] In 2002 an extensive revision of the original Banff ARDA was approved, incorporating recent work, a substantial program of GIS site modelling and mapping, and a long-term work plan. So far, this is the only ARDA that has been updated, and, in the course of these revisions, my conception of a useful ARDA has changed. The trick is to combine a regional overview and discussion, for professional archaeologists and researchers, with a "one-stop shop" useful to

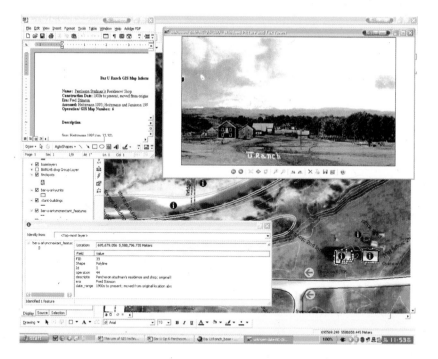

Fig. 6. An expanded version of the Bar U Ranch NHS desktop archaeological GIS database. [Calgary CRS. Parks Canada.]

park managers and interpreters: two rather different aims and audiences. We have dealt with this by treating the ARDA as a base document, with annual updates provided to the park in the form of digital, searchable GIS databases. The desktop user can click on each point on the map and bring up linked databases that display the site forms, visit history, reports, photographic archives, historic aerial views, and plans. This has made the archaeological and historic information much more accessible to the park manager and the public user. Calgary staff are pioneering work in the digital and spatial display and analysis of data for CRM purposes.

1989–2010: Integrating Cultural and Ecological Research in Park Management

Since the first ARDAs were written, the archaeological program in Banff National Park has involved less impact assessment and more basic inventory, site monitoring, and threatened-site excavation. This is partly because there are fewer development and recapitalization projects in these days of leaner budgets, and more are being deferred. Specialist staff are called in when appropriate. In the early 1990s, staff from the Ottawa Marine Archaeology Unit came to Lake Minnewanka to inventory submerged features associated with the former Minnewanka townsite and the various dams that have enlarged the lake.[39] They also recorded the submerged *Gertrude* in Emerald Bay in Waterton, and the World War II-era *Habbakuk* in Jasper. Archaeological staff have been much more involved with CRM training and management and with public archaeology programs. University archaeology field schools have been held at threatened sites where a large block excavation needs to be done.[40] In 1992, Brian Vivian from the University of Calgary began a two-year program of high-elevation survey under contract.[41] High-elevation areas had been surveyed incidentally, but this was the first systematic effort to examine the upper subalpine and alpine areas.

Archaeologists spend considerable time working with other Parks Canada staff in environmental assessment, ecological restoration, and cultural resource management. In 1993, Banff and Jasper National Parks each created the position of a warden responsible for CRM issues. While riding through the backcountry with these wardens, hearing the stories, and participating in the daily routines of riding and camp life, I gained a much stronger understanding of how and why the historic sites were distributed across the landscape in the way they were. In the smaller parks, the warden's responsibilities for CRM have often been combined with Environmental Assessment. This makes a certain amount of sense, as archaeological survey or salvage excavations are often part of the mitigations asked for during an environmental assessment. Passage of the *Canadian Environmental Assessment Act* (CEAA) in 1995 required cultural resources to be considered as part of environmental impact assessments; archaeological sites are often identified as one of the valued environmental components that must be considered. Parks Canada is able to use the CEAA requirements as a minimum and may require stronger reaction to cultural impacts than other projects in less-well-protected areas.

It became particularly important to have strong support for the cultural resources after 1994, when Parks Canada was extensively re-organized. The Regional Office at Calgary now became a Service Centre, responsible for answering requests for professional services from the individual parks. Archaeological staff no longer had an envelope budget to spend as they saw fit but rather received money from each park's budget to do work that the park requested. This continues to present a challenge for our work in the smaller parks, as they have many other needs that can seem more pressing than CRM. The mid-1990s were also a time of extensive cuts in staff and services in Western Canada, as the federal government worked through a period of deficit reduction. But that same year, the new *Parks Canada Guiding Principles and Operating Policies* included for the first time a specific CRM policy, which required parks and historic sites to look after their cultural resources through inventory, evaluation, and monitoring and to consider the impact of all management decisions on these resources.[42] Though much of the policy was tailored for built heritage, and questions of restoration and reconstruction, the mountain parks responded by incorporating CRM concerns into their management plans and in some cases by creating specific CRM plans that cover built heritage, archaeology, and interpretation.[43]

Parks Canada still has to consider these archaeological sites along with its other mandates for national parks: resource management, public interpretation, and, above all, ecological integrity. This has some implications for archaeological research, not the least of which is funding: we can feel like the poor cousins, desperately grateful for any help we can get from our much richer ecological relations. How can we define acceptable and appropriate levels of human use that will at the same time ensure that ecological integrity is maintained? In Banff, for example, the planning process involves modelling a complex mixture of ecological information and information on modern uses and social needs. This is placed in the context of an ever-increasing level of human use of the park and a rapidly expanding regional population that is putting heavy pressure on the ecological integrity of the park.

Where does archaeological information fit in this process? First, archaeological and cultural resources are damaged by human use of the park. In an environment such as the high mountains, the locations for people's activities

Fig. 7. Quartz crystal and chert artefacts from site 1329R, Banff National Park. A modern high-elevation backcountry campsite is built directly on top of a precontact period site, and quartz crystal artefacts have been mistaken for broken glass, and cleaned up by well-meaning visitors. [Calgary CRS RAW 4240E. Parks Canada.]

are constrained. Many modern roads, trails, and campsites are located in the same place as an ancient site, and for the same reasons. If modern users are diverted from one area to another, it is possible that the increased traffic will damage a site to the point where mitigative measures are needed.

Second, past human activity has had an impact on the current ecological conditions: deliberate burning and plant-gathering over the years has formed vegetation communities and therefore affected animal distributions. The zooarchaeological and botanical evidence preserved within datable archaeological deposits can be of use to other disciplines.[44] The great strength of archaeology lies in its ability to look at changes over time. Ecologists and park managers seek to preserve ecological integrity, but what exactly does that mean? What is the range of variation in plant and animal communities that has existed over time? One very good way to examine that question is through the palaeoenvironmental data contained in the soils, animal bones, and artefacts of archaeological sites. In the deep sites near Banff townsite, layers on top of layers have built up over time, containing plant and animal remains that reflect the environmental conditions of that time. Zooarchaeological and archaeobotanical analysis can give an idea of species that were there in the past, in what proportions or communities, and how these proportions have changed over time.

Bison provide one example of the possibilities for ecological study. Bison are a species that came perilously close to extinction and yet were once present in great numbers. For a park such as Waterton Lakes, with a large grassland area and montane valleys reaching deep into the mountains, bison must have been a significant component of the ecosystem. How is it possible to maintain ecological integrity now without having bison present? Park staff have recently considered whether or not it is desirable (and practical) to reinstate free-ranging bison or whether it is possible to mimic the ecological effects of bison through management of fire and other ungulates. Archaeological finds of bison, like a 3,700-year-old skull site at high elevation in Blakiston valley, can speak to the presence of bison in particular places at particular times. In addition, isotopic studies of their bone and teeth have shown patterns of seasonal migration between the fescue grasslands of the montane and the drier grasslands of the high prairies.[45] It would make a difference to a bison recovery strategy if you knew the proportion of a herd that spent all their days in the park as compared to that which spent their time in seasonal migrations, or whether bison had been completely absent from an area for long periods. Waterton has recently decided not to proceed with bison reintroduction, but it remains a stated long-term goal in the Banff Management Plan.

Another example is my excavation of a 720-year-old elk kill site on the Banff Springs golf course, very near Smith's housepits site. At least four individual elk were butchered at this site. Elk are extremely uncommon in precontact sites in the mountain parks, despite being highly visible animals today. As park scientists have been considering how and where to reintroduce or control modern elk populations, as part of a larger suite of measures to restore ecological integrity in the montane, they have been interested in evidence about where elk were in the past.[46] At this site, the bones were sufficiently well-preserved that mitochondrial DNA could be used to show that one of the long bone fragments was in fact moose, and not elk.[47] Often in mountain sites the bones are not well enough preserved for traditional zooarchaeological techniques to visually identify fragments beyond the most general level. The use of DNA evidence could be extremely important for identifying uncommon remains.

Smith's house pits were not forgotten. We discovered more in the Red Deer River valley, at the Drummond Glacier, Divide Creek, and McConnell Creek sites. This housepit research reflects the changing priorities in CRM work: from Smith's concern to preserve and interpret an instructive ruin to the public, to Christensen's park-wide inventory, to Fedje's and my own targeted excavations designed to uncover the cultural history preserved within the pit features, to using the remains of butchered bison preserved in the site as part of an ecological argument for bison restoration in the Red Deer backcountry. A series of five radiocarbon dates obtained from charcoal layers in the central hearth of one single housepit at Drummond ranges between 920 and 2,560 years BP, suggesting a long period for reuse of this same feature.[48] Stratified sites of any kind in the subalpine are rare, and this is a significant sequence. People have been coming back to this very same hearth, time after time, cleaning it out and rebuilding their shelter, for nearly two thousand years. Why? Perhaps to hunt the bison attracted to the small meadows kept open by deliberate burning. Archaeological work at these sites has been done as part of a multidisciplinary program with the fire and vegetation ecologists and their interest in restoring bison to the ecosystem.

Where Have We Been? Where Are We Going?

Much of the archaeological work in the mountain park block has been done in order to establish a basic culture history framework in an unknown area, and as a CRM response to development pressures, with little in the way of explicit theoretical thought.[49] This has been the position of many CRM archaeology workers in Alberta and British Columbia: seeing the immediate need as one of salvaging all that we can learn from a site before it is destroyed by road construction or erosion. There has also been much less of an emphasis on recreating human behaviour in the past, on the anthropological side of things, and more on studying the adaptations people have made to changing environments and resources or the palaeoecological side of things. This is partly because the mountain parks were established very early on, and there were few Aboriginal populations still physically living in these places for the early archaeologists and anthropologists to study. This is very different from other national parks, particularly on the British Columbia coast and in the north, where (as David Neufeld and Brad Martin discuss in this volume) national park reserves have been recently created in the context of modern treaty negotiations, and where culture and cultural resource management issues are a very strong part of the treaty and park establishment framework. In these cases, archaeologists and historians have been working much more closely with First Nations populations. This is beginning to come, though, for the mountain parks as well.

While archaeology has a long history as a discipline, it is hard to over-emphasize how very recent it is as a recognized and supported research activity in the mountain parks. We currently have a staff member in Calgary who has been on staff for the *entire* time that there has been a regional Parks Canada archaeology program. In forty years, we have gone from having no knowledge at all of the archaeology of our mountain parks to having a very comprehensive and well-documented inventory. Excavations have let us define a culture history and describe the changes over time in lifeways and tool manufacture. Advances in mapping and GIS technology have let us model the changing patterns of human use of the landscape and integrate cultural data with other kinds of management planning and resource management issues. Cultural resources are now considered in environmental assessment programs, and, although this can be a bit of a struggle, there is a growing realization that these resources cannot be considered in isolation but rather as one part of an integrated landscape. This emphasis on understanding the cultural landscapes will surely continue in the next decades, along with a much stronger voice for Aboriginal people and other communities who wish to tell their own stories about their history.

NOTES

1   I would like to thank James Taylor, for providing me with references concerning the correspondence between Harkin and Sibbald about the housepits at the Banff Springs Golf Course. I thank wardens Don Mickle, Rob Watt, Cal Sime, Rod Wallace, Mike Dillon, and many others for guiding me to the sites and for their enthusiastic support of the archaeological program in the National Parks. I thank warden Mike Dillon for finally teaching me the diamond hitch. I have been fortunate in being a student of both Richard Forbis and Barney Reeves at the University of Calgary. I thank Martin Magne and Claire Campbell for their comments.

2   An annotated chronology of archaeological projects carried out in Banff National Park is presented in E. Gwyn Langemann and William Perry, *Banff National Park of Canada Archaeological Resource Description and Analysis* (Calgary: Parks Canada, Cultural Resource Services, Western and Northern Service Centre, 2002), and for Waterton Lakes in William Perry, E. Gwyn Langemann, and Brian Reeves, *Archaeological Resource Description and Analysis, Waterton Lakes National Park* (Calgary: Parks Canada, Cultural Resource Services, Western and Northern Service Centre, 1997). A good portion of the archaeological literature about the mountain parks is unpublished, in the form of reports produced by consultants or by in-house staff. Parks Canada in Ottawa also published archaeological and historic research in a Manuscript Report series, which later became a Microfiche Report series, but this has been discontinued. The grey literature reports and the published series can be accessed by contacting the librarian at the Parks Canada Western and Northern Service Centre, in Calgary.

3   Harlan I. Smith, *Handbook of the Rocky Mountains Park Museum* (Ottawa: Government Printing Bureau, 1914), 108–9.

4   Ian Dyck, "Toward a History of Archaeology in the National Museum of Canada: The Contributions of Harlan I. Smith and Douglas Leechman, 1911–1950," in *Bringing Back the Past: Historical Perspectives on Canadian Archaeology*, ed. Pamela Jane Smith and Donald Mitchell (Hull, QC: Canadian Museum of Civilization, Archaeological Survey of Canada Mercury Series Paper 158, 1998), 115–33. Barnett Richling, "Archaeology, Ethnology and Canada's Public Purse 1910–1921," in *Bringing Back the Past*, 103–14.

5   The Commemorative Integrity Statement for the Banff Park Museum National Historic Site of Canada, Banff National Park, approved in 1999, presents the reasons why it is of national historic significance, and the key heritage elements that must be preserved and communicated.

6   The 1913 to 1915 correspondence concerning the Banff housepit site, between Rocky Mountains Park and Harlan I. Smith, Department of Mines, Geological Survey, is found in RG 84, vol. 2073, file A 4128-1, vol. 1, National Archives of Canada. A description of the various developments that have affected the golf course lands over the years can be found in Daryl W. Fedje and Alison J. Landals, *Archaeological Resource Impact Assessment, Banff Springs Hotel Golf Course*

and *Staff Housing Expansion* (Ottawa: Environment Canada, Canadian Parks Service Microfiche Report Series No. 411, 1987).

7   Recent archaeological research at the Banff housepit sites is presented in E. Gwyn Langemann, "Zooarchaeological Research in Support of a Reintroduction of Bison to Banff National Park, Canada," in *The Future from the Past: Archaeozoology in Wildlife Conservation and Heritage Management,* ed. Roel C.G.M. Lauwerier and Ina Plug, 79–89 (Oxford: Oxbow Books, 2004). Proceedings of the 9th Conference of the International Council of Archaeozoology, Durham, August 2002, Umberto Albarella, Keith Dobney and Peter Rowley-Conwy, Series Editors. E. Gwyn Langemann, "A Description and Evaluation of Eight Housepit Sites in Banff National Park, Alberta" (paper presented at the 31st annual meeting of the Canadian Archaeological Society, Victoria, May 1998). E. Gwyn Langemann and Sheila Greaves, "House Hunting in the High Country: Recent Archaeological Research at Housepit Sites in Banff National Park" (paper presented at the 30th annual meeting of the Canadian Archaeological Association, Saskatoon, May 1997). For a discussion of the Plateau Pithouse Tradition of the dry British Columbia Interior, see Thomas H. Richards and Michael K. Rousseau, *Late Prehistoric Cultural Horizons on the Canadian Plateau* (Burnaby: Department of Archaeology, Simon Fraser University Publication No. 16, 1987).

8   H. Marie Wormington and Richard G. Forbis, *An Introduction to the Archaeology of Alberta, Canada* (Denver: Proceedings of the Denver Museum

of Natural History Number 11, 1965). They can cite only four publications concerning Alberta archaeology before 1955.

9   Dyck, "A History of Archaeology in the National Museum," (1998). Ian Dyck, "Canadian Prairies Archaeology, 1857–1886: Exploration and Self Development," *Canadian Journal of Archaeology* 33 (2009): 1–39.

10 Wormington and Forbis, *Archaeology of Alberta,* v.

11 William J. Byrne, "The Archaeological Survey of Alberta: Prospects for the Future," in *Alberta Archaeology: Prospect and Retrospect,* ed. T.A. Moore,15–20 (Lethbridge: University of Lethbridge, Archaeological Society of Alberta, 1981). Robert Janes, "Smith-Wintemberg Award: Richard G. Forbis," *Canadian Journal of Archaeology* 8 (1984): 1–2.

12 Brian O.K. Reeves, "Culture Change in the Northern Plains, 1,000 B.C. – A.D. 1,000" (PhD dissertation, University of Calgary, 1970). This was later published as *Culture Change in the Northern Plains: 1,000 B.C. – A.D. 1,000* (Edmonton: Alberta Culture, Archaeological Survey of Alberta Occasional Paper No. 20, 1983). See also *The Archaeology of Pass Creek Valley, Waterton Lakes National Park* (Ottawa: Manuscript Report Series No. 61, National Historic Sites Service, 1972). "Early Holocene Prehistoric Land/Resource Utilization Patterns in Waterton Lakes National Park, Alberta," *Arctic and Alpine Research* 7 (1975): 237–48.

13 For example, in A. Roger Byrne, *Man and Landscape Change in the Banff National Park Area Before 1911* (Calgary: University of Calgary, Studies in Land

Use History and Landscape Change, National Park Series No. 1, 1968. J.G. Nelson, Director).

14 Brian O.K. Reeves, "Man and his Environment, the Past 10,000 Years: An Approach to Park Interpretation," in *Canadian Parks in Perspective*, ed. J.G. Nelson, 137–52 (Montreal: Harvest House, 1970).

15 See Taylor, this volume.

16 Brian O.K. Reeves, *Crowsnest Pass Archaeological Project 1973 Salvage Excavations and Survey Paper No. 2, Preliminary Report* (Ottawa: Archaeological Survey of Canada, National Museum of Man Mercury Series No. 24, 1974).

17 Roscoe Wilmeth, "Current Research: The Plains," *American Antiquity* 32 (1967): 276–77.

18 Ole Christensen, "Banff National Park Prehistory: Settlement and Subsistence." MA thesis, University of Calgary, 1973. Ole Christensen, *Banff Prehistory: Prehistoric Settlement and Subsistence Technology in Banff National Park, Alberta* (Ottawa: Parks Canada Manuscript Report Series No. 67, 1971).

19 Brian O.K. Reeves, *An Inventory of Archaeological Sites in Banff National Park and the Ya Ha Tinda Ranch* (Ottawa: National Historic Sites Service, National and Historic Parks Branch Manuscript Report Series No. 68, 1972).

20 Jack Elliot, *Jasper National Park and Ya-Ha-Tinda Ranch Archaeological Survey* (Ottawa: National Historic Sites Service, National and Historic Parks Branch Manuscript Report Series No. 44, 1971). Ross Anderson and Brian O.K. Reeves, *An Archaeological*

Survey of Jasper National Park (Ottawa: National Historic Sites Service Manuscript Report Series No. 158, 1975).

21 Thomas H. Loy, *Archaeological Survey of Yoho National Park: 1971* (Ottawa: National Historic Parks and Sites Branch, Parks Canada Manuscript Report No. 111, 1972).

22 W.J. Byrne, Archaeological Survey of Alberta; Janes, "Smith-Wintemberg Award; Marc Denhez, *Unearthing the Law: Archaeological Legislation on Lands in Canada* (Ottawa: Prepared by SynParSys Consulting Inc. for the Archaeological Services Branch, Parks Canada Agency, 2000). Denhez summarizes the provincial and territorial legislation, but there is no federal legislation covering archaeology on federal lands.

23 This resulted in recording the remnants of sawmills at Holt City, the early CPR construction boom town. Colin Poole and Ross Anderson, *Archaeological Survey and Inventory of Proposed Modifications to the Canadian Pacific Railway in the Lake Louise Area, Alberta* (Calgary: Consultant's report, 1975. Copies available from Parks Canada, Cultural Resource Services, Western and Northern Service Centre, Calgary).

24 M. McIntyre and B.O.K. Reeves, *Archaeological Investigations: Lake Minnewanka Site (EhPu-1)* (Calgary: Consultant's report, 1975. Copies available from Parks Canada, Cultural Resource Services, Western and Northern Service Centre, Calgary). Brian O.K. Reeves, *1975 Archaeological Investigations, Lake Minnewanka Site (EhPu-1)* (Calgary: Consultant's report prepared for Western Region Parks Canada, 1976. Copies available

from Parks Canada, Cultural Resource Services, Western and Northern Service Centre, Calgary).

25   Jonathan E. Damp, Catherine E. Connolly, and Thayer V. Smith, *Conservation Archaeological Studies at EhPw-2 and EhPw-4 Banff National Park* (Ottawa: Environment Canada, Parks Service Microfiche Report Series No. 335, 1980).

26   John H. Rick, "Archaeological Investigations of the National Historic Sites Service, 1962 – 1966," *Canadian Historic Sites: Occasional Papers in Archaeology and History*, No. 1 (1970): 9–44.

27   Archaeology departments – as separate from Anthropology – were established at the University of Calgary and Simon Fraser University in the 1960s. For decades, these were the only two in Canada offering degrees specifically in archaeology; as a result, students from these two departments have dominated the professional contracting world in Alberta and B.C.

28   Olga Klimko, "Nationalism and the Growth of Fur Trade Archaeology in Western Canada," in *Bringing Back the Past*, ed. Pamela Jane Smith and Donald Mitchell, 203–13.

29   Brian O.K. Reeves, "The Rocky Mountain Eastern Slopes: Problems and Considerations," in *Alberta Archaeology: Prospect and Retrospect*, ed. T.A. Moore, 31–38 (Lethbridge: University of Lethbridge, Archaeological Society of Alberta, 1981).

30   W.F. Lothian, *A History of Canada's National Parks*, vol. 2 (Ottawa: Parks Canada, 1977), 28.

31   For example, see Donald N. Steer and John E.P. Porter, *Heritage Resources*

Impact Assessment Trans-Canada Highway Kilometres 13 to 26 Banff National Park (Ottawa: Parks Canada Microfiche Report Series 174, 1982).

32   Daryl W. Fedje, "Early Human Presence in Banff National Park," in *Early Human Occupation in British Columbia*, ed. Roy L. Carlson and Luke Dalla Bona, 35–44 (Vancouver: UBC Press, 1996). Daryl W. Fedje, "Banff Archaeology 1983–1985," in *Eastern Slopes Prehistory: Selected Papers*, ed. Brian Ronaghan, 25–62 (Edmonton: Alberta Culture, Archaeological Survey of Alberta Occasional Paper No. 30, 1986). Daryl W. Fedje and James M. White, *Vermilion Lakes Archaeology and Palaeoecology: Trans-Canada Highway Mitigation in Banff National Park* (Ottawa: Environment Canada, Parks Service Microfiche Report Series No. 463, 1988).

33   Daryl W Fedje, James M. White, Michael C. Wilson, D. Erle Nelson, John S. Vogel, and John R. Southon, "Vermilion Lakes Site: Adaptations and Environments in the Canadian Rockies During the Latest Pleistocene and Early Holocene," *American Antiquity* 60 (1995): 81–108.

34   Daryl W. Fedje, *Archaeological Resource Description and Analysis, Banff National Park* (Calgary: Archaeological Research Services Unit, Western Region, Environment Canada, Canadian Parks Service, 1989).

35   K.E. Seel and J.E. Strachan, *Banff National Park Resource Description and Analysis* (Calgary: Parks Canada, Western Region, 1985).

36   Stanley Van Dyke, *Final Report: Archaeological Survey and Assessment, Upper Red Deer River Valley, Banff National Park, 1987* (Ottawa:

Environment Canada, Parks Service Microfiche Report Series No. 386, 1987).

37 R.J. Pickard, *Historical Resources Inventory, Jasper National Park* (Ottawa: Environment Canada, Parks Service Microfiche Report Series No. 202, 1984); Rod J. Pickard and Heather D'Amour, *Archaeological Investigations at the National Historic Site of Jasper House* (Calgary: Archaeological Services, Parks Canada, 1987).

38 For Banff, see Langemann and Perry *Banff ARDA* (2002), which is an extensive revision of the 1989 Fedje *Banff ARDA*, incorporating more recent work, as well as a substantial program of GIS site modelling and mapping. William Perry, "The Use of GIS for Predictive Modelling at Banff National Park, Canadian Rocky Mountain Parks World Heritage Site, Canada," in *GIS and Cultural Resource Management: A Manual for Heritage Managers*, ed. Paul Box, 113–17 (Bangkok: UNESCO, 1999). Rod J. Pickard, *Jasper National Park Archaeological Resource Description and Analysis* (Calgary: Archaeological Research Services Unit, Western Region, Environment Canada, Canadian Parks Service, Calgary, 1989); Wayne Choquette and Daryl W. Fedje, *Yoho National Park Archaeological Resource Description and Analysis* (Calgary: Archaeological Services, Canadian Parks Service, Environment Canada, 1993); Wayne Choquette and Rod Pickard, *Archaeological Resource Description and Analysis, Kootenay National Park* (Calgary: Archaeological Research Services Unit, Western Region, Environment Canada, Canadian Parks Service, 1989); Peter D. Francis and William Perry, *Archaeological Resource Description and Analysis: Mount Revelstoke and*

Glacier National Parks (Calgary: Cultural Resource Services, Western and Northern Service Centre, Parks Canada Agency, 2000). For Waterton Lakes, see Perry and Langemann *Waterton Lakes ARDA* (1997).

39 Marc-André Bernier, *Underwater Archaeology Survey of the Minnewanka Submerged Townsite Banff NP, 1992* (Ottawa: National Historic Parks and Sites Branch, Canadian Heritage, Parks Canada, 1994).

40 Peter D. Francis and E. Gwyn Langemann, *Cultural Resource Management and Archaeological Research Initiatives at the Christensen Site, Banff National Park* (Ottawa: Environment Canada, Parks, Research Bulletin No. 303, 1994). Alison Landals, *Lake Minnewanka Site 2000 Mitigation Program, Interim Report* (Calgary: Consultant's report, 1994. Copies available from Parks Canada, Cultural Resource Services, Western Canada Service Centre, Calgary). Caroline Hudecek-Cuffe, *Final Report, Department of Anthropology University of Alberta Archaeological Field School, Jasper National Park, July 15 – August 20, 1997. Permit No. WRA 97-03* (Edmonton: Consultant's report, 1994. Copies available from Cultural Resource Services, Western and Northern Service Centre, Parks Canada, Calgary).

41 Brian Vivian, "Draught Report, A High Altitude Survey of Prehistoric Cultural Resources in Banff National Park," (Calgary: Consultant's report, 1997. Copies available from Parks Canada, Cultural Resource Services, Western and Northern Service Centre, Calgary).

42 Parks Canada, *Parks Canada Guiding Principles and Operating Policies*

(Ottawa: Minister of Supply and Services, 1994).

43 For example, Parks Canada, *Banff National Park Cultural Resource Management Plan* (Banff: Canadian Heritage – Parks Canada, 1998).

44 Martin Magne, "Archaeology and Rocky Mountain Ecosystem Management: Theory and Practice,"*George Wright Forum* 16, no. 4 (1999): 67–76. Martin Magne, Kurtis Lesick, Peter Francis, Gwyn Langemann, and Rod Heitzmann, "Archaeology – A Crucial Role in Ecosystem Management.," in *Parks Canada – Archaeology and Aboriginal Partners*, ed. Martin Magne, *CRM* 20, no. 4 (1997): 9–11 (Washington, DC: National Parks Service, U.S. Department of the Interior, 1997). Langemann, "Reintroduction of Bison to Banff" (2004).

45 E. Gwyn Langemann, "Recent Zooarchaeological Research in Banff and Waterton Lakes National Parks, Alberta," in *Learning from the Past: A Historical Look at Mountain Ecosystems* (Revelstoke: Parks Canada and the Columbia Mountains Institute of Applied Ecology, Proceedings from the 1999 conference, 2000), 99–108. E. Gwyn Langemann, "Stable Carbon Isotopic Analysis of Archaeological Bison Bone; Using zooarchaeology to address questions of the past ecology of bison," *Research Links* 8, no. 1 (2000): 4, 12. E. Gwyn Langemann, "Archaeological Evidence of Bison in the Central Canadian Rockies," in *Proceedings of the Rocky Mountain Bison Research Forum, October 28th, 1999, Rocky Mountain House, Alberta*, ed. Todd Shury, 6–12 (Banff: Banff National Park Ecosystem Secretariat, 2000). Tamara L. Varney, M. Annie Katzenberg, and Brian Kooyman,

Where Do the Bison Roam? A Stable Isotopic Study of Bison Grazing Behaviour in Waterton Lakes and Banff National Park (Calgary: Consultant's report prepared for Waterton Lakes National Park, 2001. Copies available from Parks Canada, Cultural Resource Services, Western and Northern Service Centre, Calgary).

46 Charles E. Kay, Cliff A. White, Ian R. Pengelly, and Brian Patton, *Long-Term Ecosystem States and Processes in Banff National Park and the Central Canadian Rockies* (Ottawa: Parks Canada National Parks Branch, Occasional Paper No. 9, 1999).

47 M.V. Monsalve, D.Y. Yang, and E.G. Langemann, "Molecular analysis of ancient cervid remains from two archaeological sites: Banff National Park and Rocky Mountain House National Historic Site, Alberta," in *Tools of the Trade: Methods, Techniques and Innovative Approaches in Archaeology*, ed. Jayne Wilkins and Kirsten Anderson, 167–81. Proceedings of the 2005 Chacmool Archaeological Conference, Department of Archaeology, University of Calgary (Calgary: University of Calgary Press, 2009).

48 E. Gwyn Langemann, *Final Report, 1995–1996 Archaeological Resource Management Programme, Banff National Park* (Calgary: Parks Canada, Cultural Resource Services, Western and Northern Service Centre, 1996).

49 This puts Parks Canada archaeology in the position of much of Canadian archaeology, still dominated by theoretical interests in culture-history and processual studies. Bruce G. Trigger, *A History of Archaeological Thought*, 2nd ed. (New York: Cambridge University Press, 2006), 132.

Rejuvenating Wilderness: The Challenge of Reintegrating Aboriginal Peoples into the "Playground" of Jasper National Park

৯৳

I.S. MacLaren
Department of History and Classics
and
Department of English and Film Studies
University of Alberta

All 11,228 km² of Jasper National Park (JNP) have always had what the International Union for Conservation of Nature (IUCN) classifies as Category II designation. This category privileges its national park status and the preservation of ecological integrity. But constant use by humans and animals of the park's congested Upper Athabasca River Valley (UARV) renders it much more characteristic of what the IUCN calls a Category V protected area, managed chiefly for conservation and recreation, "where the interaction of people and nature over time has produced an area of distinct character with significant aesthetic, ecological and/or cultural value, and often with high biological diversity. Safeguarding the integrity of this traditional interaction is vital to the protection, maintenance and evolution of such an area."[1] Balancing human and non-human life in the UARV is an ongoing challenge in managing Canada's fifth national park, by far the largest of the seven located in the mountains along the boundary of Alberta and British Columbia. Even more than the bedeviling binaries inherent in what earlier chapters have called the utilitarianism and preservation, use and conserve, and development and preservation duality of Parks Canada's mandate, the ones inherent in this challenge pit not only humans against non-human life, but also non-Natives against Natives, and well-to-do urban tourists against labouring locals. The interstices of these binaries only stiffen the challenge, foregrounding perhaps even more than what James Morton Turner meant in coining the phrase (quoted in George Colpitts's chapter) "paradoxes of popular wilderness."

All seven mountain national parks – Banff (1885), Yoho (1886), Glacier (1886), Waterton Lakes (1895), Jasper (1907–09), Mount Revelstoke (1914), and Kootenay (1920) – are, as the editor's introduction notes, children of Yellowstone, western North America's and the world's first national park. The Romantic notion of wilderness gave rise to its establishment by the U.S. Congress on 1 March 1872 "as a public park or pleasureing-ground [sic] for the benefit and enjoyment of the people,"[2] the beneficiaries of the park's geysers and hot springs, should a profitable tourism industry develop. Regulations precluded permanent human presence – by local Bannocks, Crow, Blackfeet, Shoshone, or anyone else – in its 9,000 km², so that visitors to comparatively remote realms could behold Nature in its sublime purity and experience supernatural spiritual enrichment unmediated – unperverted – by a human dimension. Axiomatic in the Yellowstone model,[3] then, is the protection of wilderness by the outlawing of permanent human residence. Following on the heels of Romanticism and, although prompted by additional motivations, early twentieth-century conservation continued to practise a policy of exclusion long enough that only about fifteen years, the 1950s and early 1960s, separated the effects of its policies from environmentalists' call – identified as the second conservation movement – to position ecological integrity as the priority in the management of protected areas in western North America.[4] But although most of us "windshield visitors" to mountain national parks cherish the Yellowstone model, it is no longer tenable. Nowhere is this clearer than in the UARV. Moreover, in all such regions of Canada where non-Native populations outnumber Natives, the *wilderness playground* paradox favours majoritarian white culture and precludes Aboriginal presence.[5] We have reached a juncture where untenability and injustice coincide. Jasper Forest Park (1907) became Jasper Park in 1909. Its first acting superintendent, John W. McLaggan, lost no time in ordering all hunters' guns sealed and deputing Lewis Swift, the lone white homesteader, to ensure they were.[6] McLaggan offered and paid compensation for buildings and other improvements to six families of mixed blood (Métis [Cree and white, or Iroquois and white]) inhabiting homesteads in the UARV and told them all to leave. Only their departure, not their destination, concerned him. These homesteaders – four families named Moberly, one Joachim, and another Findlay/Finlay – were only the latest inhabitants of the UARV, for, as it does today, the valley had served many centuries of travellers and seasonal residents as an east/west thoroughfare through the Rocky Mountains. With the Athabasca and Miette rivers forming the relatively low Yellowhead Pass, the UARV played this role in superior fashion, as did the north-south route that the Snake Indian and Rocky rivers provide by meeting the Athabasca within a few kilometres of one another, and only a day's ride by horse downstream from the tri-valley confluence of the Athabasca, Maligne, and Miette. While it is doubtful that over the past eleven centuries hunter-gatherers often practised the sedentary lifeway of erecting permanent habitations in the UARV, archaeological evidence makes plain that the valley had long witnessed an active human presence at different points of the annual cycle.[7] That two dozen groups have signed on as members of the Aboriginal Forum that JNP began establishing a decade ago clarifies how so many peoples, including Cree, Stoney, Shuswap, Ojibwe, several groups of Métis, Sekani, Carrier, Iroquois, and white consider the valley a part of their abiding heritage.

The IUCN's Category V designation aims to *retain* cultural practices that are ongoing in a landscape, not, as would be the case with Aboriginal or Métis groups, *rejuvenate* a cultural practice curtailed by the park's establishment. Any proposal to rejuvenate a cultural practice – whether annually practising ceremonial rites at locations identified by different groups as spiritually significant, or seasonally or permanently homesteading – challenges both the IUCN's categorization and current practice by Parks Canada Agency (PCA), which (as Brad Martin's chapter shows) has for some time worked closely with First Nations in the establishment and management of new parks and park reserves (especially the northern twelve, which cover 173,000 km^2, nearly 65 per cent of the national total), but which has yet to invite evicted people or their descendants to return and take up residence in existing parks. In the case of the UARV, to act on any proposal for permanent re-settlement of any Aboriginal people would embroil Parks Canada in the thorny questions of prioritizing the rights of different Native groups and of prioritizing eras of past occupation. Dendroarchaeological evidence shows that the first of the evicted homesteaders' cabins in the UARV was built no earlier than 1897, so accommodating homesteaders' descendants would mean highlighting little more than two decades – 1897–1909 – of human history.[8] Why should such a brief and recent period receive precedence? Why should particular people receive special attention when, according to one source, more than a hundred people were in the valley in 1907, only two years before the eviction of the six families that had built permanent structures left a unique paper trail because they were paid compensation?[9] But is such thorniness grounds for denying occupation by *any* Native group? These questions face the staff of JNP at a time when Alan Latourelle, the agency's chief executive officer, is on record as stating that

> a Skins golf tournament on a heritage golf course that golfers have been competing on for more than a century, or a dragon boat race on a hydroelectric reservoir already being used for power boating and scuba [*sic*] are not likely to impair a national park nor the idea of national parks. The environmental assessments and public review of those and other events ensure they are responsibly planned and carefully delivered. And these events enable participants and spectators not just to enjoy exciting moments in spectacular settings, but to discover and connect to Canada's protected *heritage*. There are many ways to discover a national park and these events are among them. We very much want Canadians to discover and connect to these places.[10]

Managing people – "all Canadians," as Latourelle is fond of repeating – remains as much a part of the mandate of national parks as the protection of ecological integrity.

Co-management initiatives between a national park in southern Canada and its neighbours would have to deploy a policy that Parks Canada has championed and trumpeted only in seldom-visited, remote national parks and park reserves established in the past four decades.[11] There is common ground between the past and the future, but, at least in terms of the international parks movement's understandings about the management of protected areas, Parks would need to re-designate land in order to mend the discontinuity that a century of Category II designation has imposed. Even a re-designation of what is called the frontcountry of JNP from Category II to Category V necessitates reconsideration of the Yellowstone model and the values that lie behind the concept of wilderness protection established by Canada's first national parks act in 1887, which required that, insofar as "[n]o person shall ... locate, settle upon, use or occupy any portion of the said public park," management of Rocky Mountains (later, Banff National) Park would require "[t]he removal and exclusion of trespassers."[12] This requirement was reiterated in the *National Parks Act* of 1930, which – in wording paraphrased from the United States' *Organic Act* of 1926 and reiterated as recently as Canada's *National Parks Act* of 2000 – maintains that "[t]he Parks are hereby dedicated to the people of Canada for their benefit, education and enjoyment, ... and ... shall be maintained and made use of so as to leave them unimpaired for the enjoyment of future generations."[13]

The interpretation of this ideal follows both its spirit and its letter: according to the principles that guided Parks Canada from 1994 to 2006, "[w]ilderness, is an enduring natural area of sufficient size to protect pristine ecosystems which may serve physical and spiritual well being. It is an area where little or no persistent evidence of human intrusion is permitted so that ecosystems may continue to evolve."[14] Slightly paraphrased, this definition followed one articulated by the IUCN after its Fourth World Wilderness Congress, held in Colorado in 1987.[15] Intentionally or not, it emphasized enjoyment of the non-human by humans. As was noted a decade ago, and repeatedly in chapters of this volume,[16] a paradox inheres in this definition that effectively precludes its enforcement as a management policy in a park with Category II designation. The implicit understanding that some forms of recreation are permissible within a mandate to protect ecosystems acknowledges the ongoing presence of humans; that is, *someone's* "physical and spiritual well being" prospers, but it does so because *some* human activity and activity by *some* humans are privileged, and others are outlawed. The privileging runs along economic lines: those who can afford to prosper do so: snowboarding trumps ranching, for example; hiking trumps hunting (in most parks, at least[17]). But the economic privileging has a habit of going unacknowledged. John Marsh's paper from the 1968 conference, Canadian National Parks: Today and Tomorrow, called for parks to be maintained in order "to provide most wilderness users with a satisfying high-quality experience."[18] So, the matter becomes a question of which individuals, which consumers of wilderness, can afford the "high-quality experience."[19] That the economic lines often resemble ethnic lines that separate Natives from non-Natives is a commonplace of Canadian history, Latourelle's emphasis on "all Canadians" notwithstanding.

Rendering all Canadians as identical when it came to enjoying a national park was merely the rhetorical manœuvre that the first piece of protectionist legislation made in 1887 and that subsequent acts of legislation have repeated. It persists because not to discriminate for and against users seems appropriate for the federal management of a protected area for national benefit. However, we know that we are patently not all equal in our use and enjoyment of JNP or any other national park. Marvin Henberg provoked his audience at the Fifth World Wilderness Congress in 1995 by arguing that to support the above-quoted 1987 IUCN definition of wilderness "tacitly supports the genocide and dispossession of Native Americans."[20] Not just a federal agency, then, but all of us who tacitly support its mandate are complicit. Practically, the definition involves ethnicity and class, not just nationalism. If the Aldo Leopolds of the environmental movement that emerged in the middle of the last century managed, by "see[ing] the environment as a set of interactive relationships between humans and the rest of nature," to "transcend dramatically the more limited national consciousness of the [early twentieth-century] conservationists," then it behooves those in the early twenty-first century to attempt to transcend not just nation but also ethnicity and class in appreciating, evaluating, and managing the formal relationships that occur in protected areas between human and non-human life.[21] As was the case for Leopold and his colleagues, so for Canadians today, the challenge – or might we regard it as inspiration? – comes, as will be shown, from abroad.[22]

Human rights certainly have been upheld in negotiations for the establishment of national parks since 1969, when 1,500 people, 85 per cent of

REJUVENATING WILDERNESS

them Acadians, were summarily evicted at the time that Kouchibouguac National Park was established in eastern New Brunswick.[23] Human rights certainly would figure prominently in negotiations for a new park today. So, one must ask: how is Parks Canada's policy of wilderness protection in the mountain parks still tenable except from the point of view of pure science? Apart from managing a park as though it were a laboratory field station, protected from *all* human intrusion, what could be meant by *wilderness*? Perhaps some sort of reserve could succeed in isolation from humans, but, if looked at dispassionately, a national park that accommodates highways, fibre-optics cables, train tracks, and a recently twinned pipeline could never hope to do so. Increasingly, it appears as if the concepts of wilderness and wilderness protection that were born and bred in western North America are doing JNP a disservice.[24] While Parks Canada has adopted a classification of five zones that recognize degrees of human presence and use,[25] Canadian parks are responding slowly to progressive thinking about the management of protected areas. Fifteen years ago, William Cronon's anthology *Uncommon Ground* articulated criticism of this traditional practice in American parks.[26] Its subtitle, *Rethinking the Human Place in Nature*, sounded a reasonable – if to wilderness devotees a diabolical and heretical – note of insistence on the human role in non-human nature and prompted a new wave of conceptions of protected landscapes that had "aim[ed] to conserve tangible and intangible landscape values that are the outcome of the interaction of people and nature."[27] North Americans loyal to early twentieth-century conservationism (the Yellowstone model) thought such an aim belonged properly only in western Europe, where proponents of protected areas simply had no choice but to manage long-inhabited and long-worked landscapes.[28] That it was a "Eurocentric concept" meant, then, that the IUCN's Category V had no place in western North America[29]; it was precisely the openness, the vacancy of large areas of the West that early preservationists and conservationists had been determined to see protected. As Joseph Sax argued three decades ago, one of the problems for North Americans in our attitude to the West is our inability to cope with landscapes that fail to dissociate people from natural areas; to combine them, we think, is to taint if not pervert non-human nature.[30] According to this thinking, if "protected landscapes often have goals of preserving the traditional local culture and encouraging a lively sustainable economy," the Yellowstone model wants nothing to do with them.[31] Just ask visitors to mountain parks.

One hundred and more years ago, officials with the Department of the Interior could not see Aboriginal people, any more than the general populace could; their view of a vacant wilderness depended upon this myopia and a subscription to the doctrine of the vanishing Indian, undergirded by a deterministic and what was regarded as a "progressive" view of history. Moreover, the emerging authority of science could not offer an antidote to the myopia since *wilderness* is not a scientific concept but a human construct, a non-Native human construct.[32] Generally speaking, the century-old North American understanding of wilderness erected an apartheid between the human and non-human realms, such that people essentially constitute a *problem* for managers of protected areas. Cronon's edition of essays relentlessly showed its readers facets of that apartheid and reasons why proponents of wilderness insisted on it. As well, it showed how such apartheid perpetuated a ban on all permanent settlement. But that ban had established other instances of apartheid, ones between tourists and permanent occupants (whites and Natives, thereafter visitors to and inhabitants of towns like Banff and Jasper) and between well-heeled tourists and labourers – merciless binaries. Protected landscapes are heralded for the species they protect but are seldom examined for the ideologies or cultural values that they protect and project.

Propounding *wilderness* is escapist; malaise with the world inhabited by humans (well, urbanites) prompts us to suppose and desire a better place, one untrammelled by what disturbs and disgusts us about our created world. This anti-modernist spirit held sway when Jasper Forest Park was established in the midst of the great early twentieth-century shift of Canada's population from overwhelmingly rural to – and for the first time – urban and rural evenly split.[33] Wilderness parks in the Rocky Mountains, *playgrounds* as they were then called, became the realm for Canadians who could afford to perceive protected areas as an escape from urban blight. "Safe and inviolate" from "the power of man," these refuges/sanctuaries appear, in the words of the guidebook to Jasper written by Mabel Williams (see Alan MacEachern's chapter, above), "new" because newly "made accessible to beauty lovers of the world."[34] Beauty did not inhere in human life; exclusive to the non-human, it precluded signs of 'sordid' toil by humans of other class or ethnicity than the beholder's.

REJUVENATING WILDERNESS

The implicit European criticism of this perspective ultimately prompted the IUCN's categorization of protected areas.[35] With its seven categories of designation, the graduated European view is influencing North American thinking about biosphere protection (though still more in the east than in the west) just as it is gradually gaining favour around the world, in part because as a species we are coming to the recognition that "strict protection measures alone are … inadequate to secure the biodiversity values of protected areas."[36] If we take people out of the landscape, we also take out people's interest in and commitment to protecting it, cherishing it, and maintaining it (as well, admittedly, as some people's interest in putting it to uses that appear ecologically hostile or imperiling). We evict its most obvious stewards. Assigning it to humans employed to manage it might have made sense at one time in the West, but those managers do not enjoy robust support from the country's citizenry. The national identity of JNP and its fellow parks is muted: as Lyle Dick notes in his epilogue, Canadians do not exhibit a widespread, vital engagement with the challenge of managing national parks; most of us assume their perpetual existence rather as we do an infinite supply of potable water.[37] And yet, the idea of reinstating an ongoing Aboriginal or Métis presence – that is, residence – in the UARV still sounds untenable. It does so, not because the perception remains unchanged that First Nations and Métis associations lack a cultural history worthy of showcasing in the nation's southern parks,[38] but because a reintegration of a hunting-gathering lifeway poses a potential safety risk to other park users. As well, although it encourages Parks Canada staff to consult with Native people, the federal Department of Justice admonishes against establishing a precedent of accommodating them in any way that involves their ongoing occupation of national parks. Co-management occurs as an idea bandied around in meetings, not a practice out on the land.[39]

What remains wrong with the scene depicted in figure 1, such that its viewer would be shocked to learn that it was photographed in JNP? Cattle lowing in an alpine meadow along the edge of which runs a road that permits access to Lac de Gaube by tourists and school children might not strike most people as appropriate for JNP.[40] What would the cost be to the prevailing sense of Jasper, were a portion of it occupied by someone other than tourists/ outdoor sports enthusiasts and something other than "wild" animals? What would be the cost to the prevailing sense of Jasper if the school children were

Fig. 1. Parc national des Pyrénées, Lac de Gaube. June 2007. [Photo: I.S. MacLaren.]

Fig. 2. Parc national des Pyrénées, Lac de Gaube (detail). June 2007. [Photo: I.S. MacLaren.]

on a week-long course at a culture camp operated by a First Nation (a different one each year) teaching the history of its human occupation of the UARV and traditional ecological knowledge (TEK)? If the concept of wilderness acknowledged the longstanding cultural presence of First Nations and Métis cultures, JNP would, at least in the montane and perhaps in selected locations in the backcountry, have to be re-zoned if not re-designated as a park protecting both ecological and cultural values, but it might also pique the interest of a new generation of visitors at a time when park visitation and use of the backcountry are decreasing lower than ever.

The scene in figures 1 and 2 was photographed in June 2007 in the Parc National des Pyrénées, a park of 457 km² established in 1967, which proclaims itself as "protected nature in balance with man." Official wording mentions that "[t]he imposing landscapes were colonized little by little by vegetation and animals. Man also, over the course of centuries, has shaped these spaces by grazing his flocks there, by harvesting the forests, and by practicing prescribed burning ... [ellipsis in original]. Today, with the creation of the National Park of the Pyrénées, new rules of balance have been established between man and wild life."[41] This is a typical description for Category V protected areas and one that accords well with a photograph showing a steep-sloped boulder-bedecked alpine meadow, tourists, a narrow cinder road, school children, and cows. Backing into the Spanish border, Lac de Gaube provides its visitor with hikes as "wild" as, if rather busier than, those available in JNP, but also, at the lakeshore, a human presence such as one finds in many parts of the UARV as part of Jasper's mix of the human and non-human. In Canadian practice, if not in policy, only an inconsiderable stretch separates the current situation from one that included an Aboriginal/Métis presence. Both park staff and visitors are already comfortable with many permanent human constructs lying well outside the townsite of Jasper: the Palisades Centre, Columbia Icefields interpretive centre, Marmot Basin ski resort, Tekarra Lodge, Beckers Bungalows, Pocahontas Cabins, accommodation at Pyramid and Patricia lakes, cottages on Lake Edith, and, most prodigious of all, Jasper Park Lodge, the largest leasehold ever granted in a Canadian national park, which, at 365 hectares (900 acres), is half as big again as the townsite of Jasper (243 hectares [600 acres]).[42]

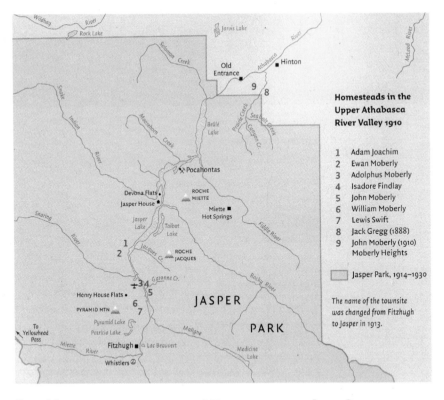

Figure labels within map:

Homesteads in the
Upper Athabasca
River Valley 1910

1 Adam Joachim
2 Ewan Moberly
3 Adolphus Moberly
4 Isadore Findlay
5 John Moberly
6 William Moberly
7 Lewis Swift
8 Jack Gregg (1888)
9 John Moberly (1910)
   Moberly Heights

☐ Jasper Park, 1914–1930

*The name of the townsite
was changed from Fitzhugh
to Jasper in 1913.*

FIG. 3. MAP SHOWING THE LOCATION OF MÉTIS HOMESTEADS IN JASPER PARK, 1910.
Culturing Wilderness in Jasper National Park, 124. FITZHUGH WAS THE NAME OF THE
VILLAGE UNTIL 1914, WHEN THE NAME CHANGED TO JASPER. [COURTESY OF FOOTHILLS
RESEARCH INSTITUTE AND PETER MURPHY.]

Situated on the land (see no. 2 in Fig. 3) once worked by Evan Moberly
(Fig. 4) and his family, for example, a living homestead would not have to
be regarded as obtruding on the experience of Jasper to the same extent that
many other sites selling and exhibiting human values already are.[43] Similarly,
a seasonal cultural camp erected, say, at the confluence of the Miette and
Athabasca rivers would only complement the human/non-human balance
that is pervasive in the frontcountry montane areas.

In terms of preserving the cultural values of Euro-Canadian Jasperites,
the park has done well enough, but what about the now relict cultural values
of Métis and fur-trade era First Nations people, let alone cultural practices
from millennia prior to the arrival of a fur-trade presence in the 1790s? Apart

Fig. 4. Ewan (a.k.a. Evan) Moberly (ca.1860–1919). Anon., no date. [Courtesy of Glenbow Archives, na-3187-16.]

from some plaques and signage, the fur-trade history of the park is not well commemorated on the land. Few visitors realize that this historical dimension is one that distinguishes Jasper from the other Rocky Mountain national parks, any more than they realize that the Athabasca has Heritage River designation because its still-undammed upper 300 kilometres served as part of the transcontinental route during the acme of the continental fur trade (1810–55).

It was as part of the effort to turn the valley into a "playground" for recreationists that its most recent occupants were removed. Identifying this shift is intended less to cast aspersions on majoritarian white society[44] – it operated on the prevailing values of its times – than to insist that, from its inception, JNP has been predicated on human cultural values. In other words – words that echo from a French park with Category V designation – humanity has, over the course of a century, shaped Jasper, by outlawing the grazing of flocks, the harvesting of forests, and the practising of prescribed burning; then by grooming trails, operating tour boats, horse camps, and a golf course, and developing downhill skiing facilities, not to mention managing a town of 4,700. Is it any wonder that the Panel on Ecological Integrity noted in 1999 that some acknowledgment of cultural values had to be made even in plans that aim at safeguarding biodiversity?

As Parks Canada recognizes that many aspects of national parks' ecosystems – wildlife migration routes, for example – extend beyond park boundaries, it now acknowledges that "the ecological integrity of national parks can be maintained only by working within a greater ecosystem context." Such work requires partnerships with people formed into associations and organizations who are willing to act on behalf of the environment.[45] The same should hold for people striving to conserve cultural heritage. Olivier Craig-Dupont's and Ronald Rudin's chapters in this volume offer examples of the much more recent eradication, in the name of ecology, of vestiges of cultural heritage in other national parks, La Mauricie and Kouchibouguac, both in Eastern Canada. Has the time not come to reverse such history in at least one of the mountain parks?

One of the agency's proposed linkages with humans is accelerated and sustained collaboration with First Nations:

This, too, is part of Parks Canada's long-term strategy. With new funds, the first priority would be to build effective ecological integrity partnerships through a process of healing, education and cultural awareness. Workshops and gatherings would be held to develop a shared vision for managing national parks and embracing nearby Aboriginal communities as a part of greater ecosystems. Cooperation on educational projects would involve public education about the role of Aboriginal peoples in ecosystems, Parks Canada staff awareness about Aboriginal culture and its role in ecological integrity and Aboriginal communities' awareness about ecosystem issues. With these building blocks in place, opportunities for Aboriginal communities to be engaged in ecosystem issues would be pursued.[46]

It appears that, on paper, it aims to restore an Aboriginal presence, if not permanent residence, in national parks. The "Healing Broken Connections" program in Kluane National Park is a good example. Although people of the Aishihik Champagne First Nations are not entitled to inhabit the park, they have re-established annual camps on the land and teach TEK to younger generations.[47] All such initiatives help decrease antagonisms between First Nations and Parks Canada (even if non-Native residents of Haines Junction expelled from Kluane when it was established in 1972 continue to resent it). The will is not lacking, but the statement confirms that the necessary funding *is*, and that, unless and until it is forthcoming, work with First Nations communities will not reach beyond consultation to accommodation. And yet, one of the recommendations issuing from the Panel on Ecological Integrity suggests a responsibility by Parks Canada to "ensure protection of the current cultural sites, sacred areas and artifacts" under its jurisdiction.[48] The operative word in the recommendation is probably "current," because Parks Canada has interpreted it to mean the repatriation of "moveable" sacred objects and the like, not the restitution of portions of parks to the descendants of those who inhabited them and were expelled from them. Three other of the Panel's recommendations pertain to fostering relationships and developing educational projects, but not to putting First Nations people on land from which they or their ancestors were removed. The staff of JNP are exploring this possibility through the Aboriginal Forum, but the effort involved requires participants to collaborate, not to contend with, one another.[49] As is not the case with Kluane and most of the parks in the North, with JNP the paramount challenge is contending with multiple groups' varied interests, including groups with no interest at all.

Not part of Jasper's Aboriginal Forum because it has enjoyed preferential status with two successive superintendents of JNP is a group called the Elders of the Descendants of Jasper National Park (EDJNP). Its interests exemplify those of many of the twenty-seven groups that have participated to date at meetings of the Forum. (As EDJNP has no – certainly, it deserves to have no – greater claim to accommodation than do the other members of the Forum, placing it on view on this occasion does not imply precedence or priority.) One of the contributions that a selection of historical essays titled *Culturing Wilderness in Jasper National Park* (2007) aimed to make to the collective human history of JNP and the UARV is the publication of the interview that Ed Moberly (1901–1992) gave in 1980 to Peter Murphy, then professor of forest history at the University of Alberta.[50] Ed spent the first decade of his life on his Métis parents' homestead (no. 5 in Fig. 3) prior to eviction and resettlement outside the park (no. 9 in Fig. 3). Some members of the EDJNP are Ed's kith and kin. From the interview, one gains a strong familial perspective on the workings of a homestead in the UARV during the first years of the twentieth century and what could serve as somewhat of a blueprint for the restored operation of one or more homesteads.[51] According to the experience of the National Park Service in the United States, "[t]ell[ing] the stories of people and place, providing accurate, well-focussed information," numbers among eleven "principles for forging long-term, sustainable partnerships" between parks and engaged citizens.[52] So, an initiative to rejuvenate a *working* homestead in JNP would meet such a principle, as does the park's completed restoration of the exterior of the farmhouse of Ewan Moberly, Ed's uncle (Fig. 5), and the series of meetings that past-superintendent Ron Hooper and current superintendent Greg Fenton have held with the EDJNP. Similarly helpful are the photographs of the homesteads in 1915, five years after their abandonment (e.g., Fig. 6, *left*). The photos were inadvertently captured in the systematic phototopographical survey photos shot by crews under the direction of Dominion Land Surveyor Morrison Parsons Bridgland (1878–1948).[53] Thanks to the work of the Rocky Mountains Repeat

Fig. 5. Restored, unoccupied house of Ewan Moberly, Jasper National Park. May 2002. [Photo: I.S. MacLaren.]

Fig. 6. *Left:* Morrison Parsons Bridgland (1878–1948), DLS. Station 62 (Mt. Esplanade), no. 504, southeast, 1915. Clearly visible are the tracks of each of the Canadian Northern Railway (nearer) and Grand Trunk Pacific Railway (farther; visible is its bridge across the Athabasca River, which is where the Yellowhead Highway presently crosses it, beneath Mt. Morro, at the northern end of the Colin Range). In this photograph, the Ewan Moberly homestead's fields stand between the braided river and ponds above and to the left of them, and the rock of the peak of Mt. Esplanade below them, in the immediate foreground. [Courtesy of Mountain Legacy Project. Digital image copyright 2000, University of Alberta.]

Right and inset: Jeanine Rhemtulla and Eric Higgs. Station no. 62 (Mt. Esplanade), no. 504, southeast, 1999. [Courtesy of Mountain Legacy Project. Copyright, J.M. Rhemtulla and E.S. Higgs, University of Alberta.]

Photography Project, which has also re-taken the entire Jasper survey (e.g. Fig. 6, *right and inset*), these photos are now available in digitized form, so that they may be enlarged sufficiently to provide a valuable visual record of the presence on the land of several homesteads.[54]

As far as the written historical record is concerned, little is known beyond the well-rehearsed version of events concerning Chief Forest Ranger and Acting Superintendent John W. McLaggan's role in evicting the homesteaders. The UARV had not been fully surveyed and title to land had not been made available before the fall of 1907, so homesteaders could not have had title to their land before it was turned into a playground, "a perpetual possession of the people ..., a region, too, of green loveliness, of grassy valleys and thick pine forests, of emerald alplands bright with flowers, of lakes, pure and brilliant in colour as precious gems[, and] an animal paradise, too, with guarded frontiers, from which the vandal and the destroyer are shut out, where many thousands of wild creatures roam, unmolested and unmolesting, learning a new relationship with man."[55] By 1913, a planned townsite had been furnished (Fig. 7),[56] and within fifteen years a championship golf course and other amenities deemed more appropriate to wilderness were imposed on the valley.[57] The point is that, from the start, people trained to deal with trees found themselves dealing with people, who often posed for them far knottier challenges. For people with science degrees, degrees in disciplines which in the twentieth century exalted the positivity of existence and the accountability for all variance, having to deal with people has been as foundational a challenge for the maintenance of protected areas as has been the thorny problem of providing "all Canadians" with access to wilderness while controlling the impact of human nature on non-human nature.

Nothing further is known about McLaggan; he arrived on the scene, played a brief role in confirming the homesteaders' identity as "trespassers" (according to the terminology of the *Rocky Mountains Park Act* of 1887, or "half-breed squatters," according to the account published in the Toronto *Globe* in January 1910[58]), and then seems to have vanished from the historical record.[59] But the identity stuck to the "Moberly breeds," as the Métis families were called by one official, and, when some of the homesteaders were found to have moved to the area of Victor Lake, southeast today of the site of the town of Grande Cache, they were dogged by McLaggan's colleagues working out of the Alberta office of the Dominion Forestry Branch.[60]

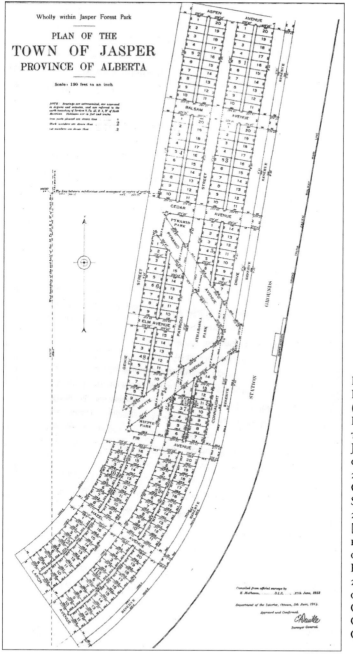

Fig. 7.
H[ugh]. Matheson
(1879–1959),
DLS. Plan of
the town of
Jasper, Province
of Alberta,
27 June 1913.
Canada Lands
Survey Records,
21221 CLSR AB.
[Reproduced
by permission
of Natural
Resources Canada
2010; courtesy
of Surveyor
General Branch,
Government of
Canada.]

Evicted homesteader Evan Moberly decided to move his heavy farming equipment 200 kilometres up the eastern slopes to Victor Lake. It is not certain that the eastern boundary of the Athabasca Forest Reserve was altered purposely to take in Victor Lake, but it is known that the lake did not form part of the reserve when McLaggan told Moberly to leave the UARV.[61] Peter Murphy's study of the shifting boundaries of the Rocky Mountain national parks and the five-forest Rocky Mountains Forest Reserve indicates that in 1910 the unsurveyed boundary ran south and west of Victor Lake.[62] By 1913, however, new legislation, based on a by-then-completed survey, took in Victor Lake.[63]

So, although Moberly and his contingent would see no survey stakes in 1910 or the first half of 1911, they would later learn that they were again in violation of federal legislation, since, like parks, forest reserves precluded permanent settlement.[64] It must have hardly mattered to Moberly whether McLaggan and his colleagues represented the Department of the Interior's Dominion Forestry Branch (est. 1906) or the later Dominion Parks Branch (est. 1911). According to one source, James Shand-Harvey, a sometime forest ranger, packer, surveyor, resident of Entrance, Muskeg River, and Moberly Creek, and not altogether reliable (because sympathetic) witness, "J.J. McCluggen [sic], Government Commissioner, sent to Jasper to make arrangements with the squatters, … Mr. McCluggen stated that he had bought out their rights and made a cash settlement with each one…. He [McLaggan] stated in my hearing that he had told them they could move anywhere they wanted to, outside of the Jasper Park Boundaries. Nothing was said about any Forest Reserve."[65]

By choosing to go north into the watershed of the Smoky River instead of that of the Athabasca outside the park, Moberly was certainly not breaking new ground, for the area was already home to a number of mixed-blood families: Gladieux, McDonalds, Gauchiers, Wynyandies, Plantes, among them. Perhaps they were joined in their move by others from the UARV, people who were not named in documents because, having made no "improvements," they received no compensation.[66] The surviving written record leaves unclear when exactly Moberly and the others who took up residence on the south and southwest side of Victor Lake learned of their violation, since few if any agents of government visited the area in the 1911–15 period. Forestry Branch staff might have, but their numbers were low during the war, as was their

REJUVENATING WILDERNESS

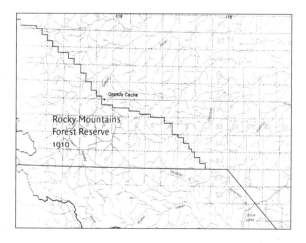

FIG. 8. 1902–1910–ROCKY
MOUNTAINS PARK, JASPER
FOREST PARK, AND THE
ROCKY MOUNTAINS
FOREST RESERVE,
*Culturing Wilderness in
Jasper National Park*, 79
(DETAIL). VICTOR LAKE
IS THE SMALL BODY OF
WATER LOCATED ON THE
MAP TO THE RIGHT OF THE
BLACK DOT INDICATING
THE LOCATION OF THE
TOWN OF GRANDE
CACHE, ESTABLISHED
IN 1966. [COURTESY
OF SUSTAINABLE
RESOURCE DEVELOPMENT
(GOVERNMENT OF
ALBERTA) AND PETER
MURPHY.]

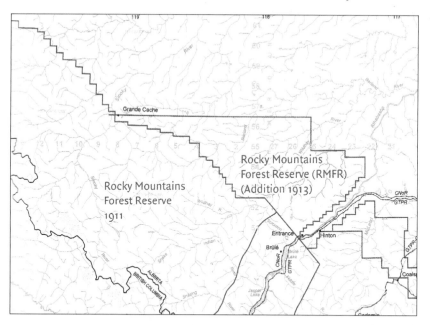

FIG. 9. 1911–1913–DIMINISHED PARKS, EXPANDED FOREST RESERVE, *Culturing
Wilderness in Jasper National Park*, 81 (DETAIL). (A SMALL PORTION OF JASPER PARK, AS
IT THEN WAS DRAWN, IS REPRESENTED ON THIS MAP BY THE TRIANGLE THAT INCLUDES
THE COMMUNITY OF BRÛLE.) [COURTESY OF SUSTAINABLE RESOURCE DEVELOPMENT,
(GOVERNMENT OF ALBERTA) AND PETER MURPHY.]

priority for the Athabasca Forest Reserve. G.H. Edgecombe had nominal charge when it was first formed, but assigning a crew to survey the boundary in 1911 was the extent of his work. Both Ernest Finlayson, on the eastern boundary in the summer of 1911, and Charles H. Morse, in the mountains and along the headwaters of the reserve's various rivers in the summer of 1913, submitted reports, but these reports did not bring a problem of homesteaders to the attention of their superiors.[67] Indeed, before 1915, nothing much seems to have come to the attention of officials in decision-making roles. In that year, a campaign of harassment began, one that issued in no decision and no further removal, but also in the acceptance of no claims of title.[68] To this day, the descendants of Ewan Moberly, whom one wealthy white eastern seaboard alpinist and hunter had called "very pleasant and ... one of the nicest and most willing Indians I ever saw" when he met him at Grande Cache in late July 1914, and who died in December 1917 when the Spanish Flu epidemic ravaged the area, enjoy no title to land.[69]

So, in reverting to the matter of managing wilderness as a matter of human rights: what role could Parks Canada play in the lives of subsequent generations left bereft by previous federal policies towards their forebears? Although the prospect of rejuvenating UARV homesteads possesses an undeniable romantic, nostalgic dimension, would it be improper to invite descendants of the six expelled Métis homesteading families to consider re-situating to the UARV, if the restoration and rejuvenation of their homesteads were offered as part of a redesignation to Category V of a portion of the valley within JNP? Even if it were appropriate, logic demands that this interest-based initiative be balanced by the accommodation of the interests of groups whose presence in the UARV long preceded the short-lived eras of Métis homesteaders, of the fur trade before them, and of Métis people altogether. The challenge of balancing various people's interests, however, is not grounds for inaction. Guy Swinnerton, together with Parks historian Susan Buggey, has analyzed and consulted on Category V initiatives in Canada. A useful western example on which advances have been made is the 97 km² Cooking Lake–Blackfoot Grazing, Wildlife and Provincial Recreation Area, east of Edmonton. It marks a good demonstration that advocates of Category V are not poaching on Category II parks. The area is "managed in an integrated fashion to accommodate cattle grazing, wildlife management, trapping, natural gas extraction, and a wide range of year-round recreation pursuits."[70]

If it has become *de rigueur* for Parks Canada to negotiate with local First Nations peoples when establishing a *new* national park or even reserve,[71] restoring and helping to reinvigorate an Aboriginal presence in a park from which it had been excluded does not lie beyond the realm of possibility in administrative, conceptual, ethical, or political terms that espouse the protection of cultural heritage. That said, although an impressive series of recently erected, detailed, and historically accurate panels recounts the history at the former homestead of Ewan Moberly, such an undertaking has yet to take shape, and one can imagine a host of objections to any attempt. However, the objections focus, like the devil, on the details. Were one to keep an eye on the larger picture, then rejuvenating the valley with various forms of Aboriginal and Métis presence remains worthy of consideration and adoption: biodiversity includes a human presence – and not just the presence of privileged recreationists and other tourists – as well as the commemoration of cultural values and practices that the historical oral and written records justify. Does Parks Canada have the mindset to manage Category II parks and Category V historic sites/landscapes/zones within them as a demonstration that the maintenance and enhancement of biodiversity and the healthy maintenance of cultural values can co-exist? It has usually kept these two mandates separate (although the Abbott Pass Refuge Cabin, Cave and Basin, Skoki Ski Lodge, Sulphur Mountain Cosmic Ray Station, and Banff Park Museum – all in Banff National Park – mark examples of historic sites maintained within a Category II park, commemorating some cultural values, if not the ones that, say, internment camps and abandoned mines would commemorate).[72] In the midst of an always-evolving concept of conservation, a shift in bureaucracy would enable Parks Canada Agency to see this as an opportunity. Bringing to an end the illusionary apartheid that has been steadfastly maintained between human and non-human nature, as between protected areas and their neighbours, is the key. Willmore Wilderness Park, contiguous to JNP and established by the Alberta government in 1959, successfully permits trapping and hunting and yet has not lost its integrity as a protected area.[73] The traditional activity of grazing cattle within the boundaries of Dinosaur Provincial Park has not marred or compromised its UNESCO World Heritage Site designation.[74] If Canadian policy could leave behind the long-held dichotomous idea that parks and cultural activity are antithetical, portions of some national parks could, on an interest-based, not a rights-based, understanding, be re-designated with less difficulty than the current process of consultation invariably experiences. We have graduated beyond early twentieth-century concepts of conservation, so why might we not evolve beyond the concept of parks that the *National Parks Act* of 1930 bestowed with the best of intentions on us, only to end up leaving Canada in the wake of today's progressive thinking about the management of protected areas?

Buggey wrote a decade ago that "the concept of cultural landscapes is a relatively new one in the heritage conservation movement."[75] In the interim, has the concept advanced far enough that Parks Canada could countenance such an initiative? The UARV, unlike most stretches of the transcontinental fur trade route, remains intact on a river that remains undammed and enjoys Heritage River designation. Because of fire suppression and prevention policies, the vegetation is much changed, but ecological restoration could be effected to alter that surmountable hurdle. As the fate of cormorants in Point Pelee National Park shows well, ecological restoration can achieve almost anything.[76] Since 2002, the Beaver Hills Ecosystem east of Edmonton, which includes Elk Island National Park, has partially accommodated integrated management between Parks, local communities, and other stakeholders.[77] Even if, as the Beaver Hills Partnership shows, negotiations for such management are anything but straightforward, does not it suggest that the rejuvenation of the heritage of Aboriginal activities lies within reach? Or would Parks Canada be chary about the prospect of eventually losing, through judicial proceedings, entire control of the land to the Aseniwuche Winewak Nation of Grande Cache, the EDJNP, or another of the more than two dozen groups that have represented themselves at the park's Aboriginal Forum?

Meanwhile, what concept of wilderness must be entertained to make sense of a river valley in a national park that excludes an Aboriginal presence but is managed by policies that include prescribed burning of vegetation, and which includes a townsite, outlying motels, inns and cabins, recreational development, a horse paddock, highway and other paved roads, railway, airstrip, training centre, power station, sewage treatment plant, fibre-optics cable, and twinned pipeline with attendant pumping stations? Given that government agencies cannot garner widespread support as silos, should PCA play the role of an *agent-provocateur*? If it played that role, would it not challenge Canadians to undertake "a fundamental shift in thought and practice" about conservation and stewardship?[78] Expecting PCA to take a leading role in influencing humans seems a tall order, but, if the matter is seen from a global perspective, there appears to be little choice. For the view of 'all Canadians' to avoid looking increasingly unenlightened a century after the view of the nascent Dominion Parks Branch at least *appeared* progressive, the agency will have to marshal resources to put more than words into initiatives that Jasper espouses in its just-approved management plan for the next decade and beyond. Three of that plan's seven commitments, as summarized in its "Highlights" document, are to connect more Canadians "to inspiring experiences that are grounded in Jasper National Park's distinctive natural and cultural characteristics," to "raise the profile of Jasper's rich human history, national historic sites, Canadian Heritage River and World Heritage Site status," and to "strengthen relationships with Aboriginal communities with historic associations with the park and facilitate their increased participation in Parks Canada's activities."[79]

NOTES

1   As early as 1978, the IUCN's system of protected area management categories included a protected area category called "Protected Landscapes" (Elisabeth M. Hamin, "Western European Approaches to Landscape Protection: A Review of the Literature," *Journal of Planning Literature* 16 [2002]: 341 [339–58]). One IUCN website – http://www.unep-wcmc.org/protected_areas/categories/index.html (accessed Oct. 2010) – provides the definition for Category V quoted in the text, and the following definition of Category II–National Park: protected area managed mainly for ecosystem protection and recreation: "[n]atural area of land and/or sea, designated to (a) protect the ecological integrity of one or more ecosystems for present and future generations, (b) exclude exploitation or occupation inimical to the purposes of designation of the area and (c) provide a foundation for spiritual, scientific, educational, recreational and visitor opportunities, all of which must be environmentally and culturally compatible." Areas protected by a Category V designation, which Harvey Locke and Philip Dearden, who take a dim view of it, argue "was created to deal with an anomaly, the English national park system, which did not fit well into categories I–IV," must be committed to the preservation of biodiversity; that said, they have a role reciprocally to provide recreational tourism within a protected working landscape. They usually have multijurisdictional governance, arising from a mix of public and private ownership (Harvey Locke and Philip J. Dearden,

"Rethinking protected area categories and the new paradigm," *Environmental Conservation* 32, no. 1 [2005], 2 [1–10]). Use of the land and management of it are ongoing and active, not historical. As Guy S. Swinnerton and Susan Buggey have characterized them, "category V areas are lived-in landscapes that demonstrate the on-going interaction between people and their means of livelihood that is primarily dependent on the basic resources (natural and cultural) of the area." ("Protected Landscapes in Canada: Current Practice and Future Significance," *The George Wright Forum* 21, no. 2 [2004]: 79 [78–92]). In Great Britain and Japan, most national parks have Category V designation.

With a revision in 2008 to the definitions of IUCN categories, changes in wording for Category V have both narrowed the focus somewhat to emphasize matters ecological and expanded the possible interpretation of the meaning of protection by dropping the term "biological diversity": "an area where the interaction of people and nature over time has produced an area of distinct character with significant ecological, biological, cultural, and scenic value; and where safeguarding the integrity of this interaction is vital to protecting and sustaining the area and its associated nature conservation and other values." This new wording, which has replaced the earlier (1994) version on the IUCN's website (http://www.iucn.org/about/work/programmes/pa/pa_products/wcpa_categories/pa_categoryv/ ; accessed 1 Oct. 2010) but not on the site shared by the IUCN and the World Commission on Protected Areas (http://www.unep-wcmc.org/protected_areas/

categories/index.html ; accessed 1 Oct. 2010), replaces "aesthetic" with "scenic" value, which might foreground the tourist over other humans, and introduces the amorphous term "nature conservation," which, as Nigel Dudley has remarked in providing and assessing the new definitions "is more generally open to different cultural interpretations of what constitutes 'nature.'" ("Why is Biodiversity Conservation Important in Protected Landscapes?" *The George Wright Forum* 26, no. 2 [2009]: 34, 33 [31–8].) In Great Britain and Japan, most national parks have Category V designation.

2   United States, Congress, *Yellowstone National Park Act*, 16 USC, Stat. 32.

3   Paul Kopas, *Taking the Air: Ideas and Change in Canada's National Parks* (Vancouver: UBC Press, 2007), 8. Karl Jacoby, *Crimes against Nature: Squatters, Poachers, Thieves, and the Hidden History of American Conservation* (Berkeley: University of California Press, 2001), 80–146.

4   On Romanticism and Yellowstone, see Michael Bess, *The Light-Green Society: Ecology and Technological Modernity in France, 1960–2000* (Chicago: University of Chicago Press, 2003), 67; and Chris J. Magoc, *Yellowstone: The Creation and Selling of an American Landscape, 1870–1903* (Albuquerque: University of New Mexico Press, 1999). I thank my colleague Liza Piper for directing me to Bess's book. On post-war environmentalism as the "second conservation movement," see Leslie Bella, *Parks for Profit* (Montreal: Harvest House, 1987) and C.J. Taylor's piece in this volume.

5   See Waiser's chapter, which analyses a good example of a club in Prince

Albert National Park, and Craig-Dupont's and Rudin's chapters, which discuss how interest groups were disenfranchised in La Mauricie and Kouchibouguac national parks. See Martin's chapter for an analysis of how a club of sorts, the Committee for Original Peoples' Entitlement, exerted its influence through land claims processes to bring a national park – Ivvavik – into being.

6 Probably because McLaggan required it of him, Swift kept a brief diary, which has survived: Jasper-Yellowhead Museum and Archives, Jasper, AB, JYMA 84.72.09.

7 Roderick Pickard, *Historical Resources Inventory: Jasper National Park*, typescript, Microfiche Report Series, no. 202 (Ottawa: Parks Canada, 1984).

8 Karen Jacqueline Brelsford, "Dendroarchaeological and contextual investigations of remote log structures in Jasper, Banff, and Kootenay national parks, Canada," MSc thesis, University of Victoria, 2004, 55–68. The date of 1877 for one of the structures on Ewan Moberly's homestead is given at 55 and 67; the statement–"the main structure dates from 1899 to 1904" – and supporting documentation for it occur at 63 and 64.

9 A.P. Coleman, *The Canadian Rockies: New and Old Trails* (Toronto: Henry Frowde, 1911), 278. In 1890, the "Jasper House Indians" were described as "rang[ing] within a radius of about 150 miles from that point [the UARV at Jasper House], north to the Smoky and south to the Brazeau, coming east to trade at Lake St. Ann, or going to the west side of the mountains at Tete Jaune Cache. They number about 40 tents or perhaps 400 souls. They are not Indians properly speaking, being descended from Iroquois brought from Eastern Canada many years ago by the Hudson's Bay Compnay to set as hunters and voyageurs" ("Local," *Edmonton Bulletin*, 14 Dec. 1890, 1, cols. 2–3).

10 "What are parks for?" Interview with Alan Latourelle, CEO, Parks Canada, *Canadian Wilderness* 6, no. 1 (2010): 4 [3–5]; emphasis added.

11 One experience in southern Canada that prompted Parks Canada to act less unilaterally and more collaboratively occurred with the establishment in October 1969 of Kouchibouguac National Park, New Brunswick. As Ronald Rudin's chapter in this volume discusses, between 1968 and 1976, about 1,500 people, representing more than two hundred families were evicted from the eight villages overtaken by the park. (As they were not permanent residents on the park lands, Native people did not form part of this eviction, which comprised mainly people of Acadian descent.) The protest over their removal began in June 1971; authorities were unable to open Kouchibouguac National Park until 1979. In the same year, Parks changed its policy to removal from new parks only if residents approved. On earlier cases of eviction from parks in Ontario, see John Sandlos, "Federal Spaces, Local Conflicts: National Parks and the Exclusionary Politics of the Conservation Movement in Ontario, 1900–1935," *Journal of the Canadian Historical Association* 16 (2005): 293–318.

12 *Rocky Mountains Park Act*, Statutes of Canada, 50–51 Victoria, assented to 23 June 1887, c. 32, ss. 3, 4.

13 *The National Parks Act*, Statutes of Canada, 20–21 George V 1930,

assented to 30 May 1930, c. 33, s. 4. *The National Parks Act*, assented to 20 Oct. 2000, c. 34, s. 4(1). The Parks Canada Agency currently words its objective as aiming "[t]o protect for all time representative natural areas of Canadian significance in a system of national parks, and to encourage public understanding, appreciation, and enjoyment of this natural heritage so as to leave it unimpaired for future generations" (*Guiding Principles and Operational Policies*, "Part II–Activity Policies: National Parks Policy," 24 Oct. 2006, http://www.pc.gc.ca/docs/pc/poli/princip/sec2/part2a2_E.asp; accessed June 2010).

14 Parks Canada, *Guiding Principles and Operational Policies* (Ottawa: Canadian Heritage; Parks Canada; Minister of Supply and Services Canada, 1994), 123. It is noteworthy that this wording does not appear in the 2006 edition of *Guiding Principles*, cited above.

15 The original wording is as follows: "Wilderness is an enduring natural area, legislatively protected and of sufficient size to protect the pristine natural elements which may serve physical and spiritual well-being. It is an area where little or no persistent evidence of human intrusion is permitted, so that natural process may begin to evolve" (qtd. in Marvin Henberg, "Pancultural Wilderness," in *Wild Ideas*, ed. David Rothenberg, 61 [59–70] [Minneapolis: University of Minnesota Press, 1995]; and in *Encyclopedia of Environmental Science*, ed. David E. Alexander and Rhodes W. Fairbridge, 698 [Dordrecht: Kluwer Academic, 1999]).

16 I.S. MacLaren, "Cultured Wilderness in Jasper National Park," *Journal of*

Canadian Studies 34, no. 3 (1999): 20 [7–58].

17 One First Nations band is permitted hunting privileges in Wood Buffalo National Park. See *The National Parks Act*, c. 34, assented to 20 Oct. 2000, s. 37: "permits for hunting, trapping and fishing by members of the Cree Band of Fort Chipewyan in the traditional hunting grounds of Wood Buffalo National Park of Canada shall be issued in accordance with regulations of the Wildlife Advisory Board."

18 John S. Marsh, "Maintaining the Wilderness Experience in Canada's National Parks," in *Canadian Parks in Perspective*, ed. J.G. Nelson and R.C. Scace, 124 [123–36] (Montreal: Harvest House, 1970).

19 Locke and Dearden, "Rethinking Protected Area Categories and the New Paradigm," argue that the Category V definition involves "linguistic gymnastics" (4); while this criticism is uncontestable, its implication – that some definitions avoid being similarly fraught – is implausible: applying language to non-human nature ineluctably imposes on it an articulation of human-derived values. The terms *wild biodiversity* and *ecosystems* are hardly pure, value-free. Neglecting to acknowledge as much, Locke and Dearden mount an argument over whose terminology has greater cultural and political purchase. Surely, no one would hold that the successes of any conservation movement have occurred outside cultural and political arenas of engagement, that conservation biology is conducted by humans who have no investment in the outcomes of their research, or that the imposition of conservation measures does not render

nature what humans think it ought to be.

20 Henberg, "Pancultural Wilderness," 61. In his study of the forced removal of Keeseekoowenin Ojibwe from Riding Mountain National Park, Manitoba, in 1936, John Sandlos has identified an "authoritarianism and racism that was often associated with conservation initiatives in Canada during the early twentieth century." ("Not Wanted in the Boundary: The Expulsion of the Keeseekoowenin Ojibway Band from Riding Mountain National Park," *Canadian Historical Review* 89 [2008], 219 [189–221]).

21 For a useful survey of the relation between parks and nationalism in Canada at different historical points, see Catriona Mortimer-Sandilands, "The Cultural Politics of Ecological Integrity: Nature and Nation in Canada's National Parks, 1885–2000," *International Review of Canadian Studies* nos. 39–40 (2009): 161–89.

22 Donald Worster, *Nature's Economy: A History of Ecological Ideas*, 2d ed. (Cambridge: Cambridge University Press, 1994), 352.

23 See note 11, above.

24 For an analysis that explores why "[t]he plight of Jasper is very real" (55), see the penetrating and wide-ranging study by Eric Higgs, *Nature by Design: People, Natural Process, and Ecological Restoration* (Cambridge, MA: MIT Press, 2003).

25 As C.J. Taylor notes, zoning became a standard element of parks management in the mid-1960s. The five zones defined by Parks Canada are: Special Preservation (I), Wilderness (II), Natural Environment (III), Outdoor

Recreation (IV), and Park Services (V). See Appendix 2 for a fuller definition of each. Parks Canada Agency, *Guiding Principles and Operational Policies*, "Part II – Activity Policies: National Parks Policy," 24 Oct. 2006, http://www.pc.gc.ca/eng/docs/pc/poli/princip/sec2/part2a/part2a4.aspx; accessed June 2010.

While this classification lends the IUCN's Category II greater refinement, it does not accommodate landscapes permanently inhabited by humans, despite the recurrence of the term "cultural" in the current definitions of the first three zones.

26 *Uncommon Ground: Rethinking the Human Place in Nature*, ed. William Cronon (New York: W.W. Norton, 1995).

27 Elizabeth Hughes, "Building Leadership and Professionalism: Approaches to Training for Protected Landscape Management," in *The Protected Landscape Approach: Linking Nature, Culture and Community*, ed. Jessica Brown, Nora Mitchell, and Michael Beresford, 219 (219–30) (Gland, Switz., and Cambridge: International Union for Conservation of Nature, 2005). An example of new human/non-human initiatives in protected areas in North America is the five-corridors National Heritage Corridor program partnered by the National Park Service and other groups in the United States (see, for example, http://www.nps.gov/history/rt66/news/Charls_Pres.htm; accessed June 2010), and similar "partnership parks" designations.

28 Some qualification of this description is required: "There is a general tendency for countries [comprising

western Europe] with relatively more areas of 'wild' land – Norway, Ireland, Finland – to use the more strict categories of designation [that is, IUCN's categories I, II, and III], while countries that have more intensively used all of their lands – Austria, France, England, and Wales – rely on the protected-landscape designation" (Hamin, "Western European Approaches to Landscape Protection," 343).

29   Guy S. Swinnerton and Susan Buggey, "Protected Landscapes in Canada," 90.

30   Joseph L. Sax, *Mountains without Handrails: Reflections on the National Parks* (Ann Arbor: University of Michigan Press, 1980). See also Richard White, "From Wilderness to Hybrid Landscapes: The Cultural Turn in Environmental History." *The Historian* 66, no. 3 (2004): 557–64.

31   Hamin, "Western European Approaches to Landscape Protection," 340. Adrian Phillips notes in the guidelines that he wrote for the IUCN's category that "[t]he focus of management of category V areas is not conservation *per se*, but about [*sic*] guiding human processes so that the area and its resources are protected, managed and capable of evolving in a sustainable way" (Adrian Phillips, *IUCN Category V Protected Areas Guidelines – Protected Landscapes/Seascapes* [Gland, Switz. and Cambridge: IUCN, 2002], 10).

32   Henberg claims that "wilderness is more like human rights than like a concept from natural science" ("Pancultural Wilderness," 60); his distinction influences the one that is drawn here.

33   "Remarkable as was the settlement of the Prairies, Canada's rural population rose by only 17 per cent between 1901 and 1911 whereas the urban figure climbed by 62 per cent, resulting in the near-balance of the city and country populations by 1914" (Michael Simpson, *Thomas Adams and the Modern Planning Movement: Britain, Canada and the United States, 1900–1940* [London and New York: Mansell, 1985], 71). I am grateful to Meghan Power, archivist of the Jasper-Yellowhead Archives, for directing me to this item.

34   M. B. Williams, *Jasper National Park* (Ottawa: Department of the Interior, 1928), 1.

35   One must note that Canada has 765 Category V sites listed on the IUCN database, and they represent over 1 million hectares (10,000 km^2) and 14% of the world's total of Category V sites (the figures are slightly greater for the United States: 1.319 sites, 17% of the world total, twelve million hectares). In providing these figures, Nora Mitchell et al. note that "[b]oth of these percentages are double the 6.4% of the world's 6,555 protected areas that are listed as Category V.... Category V areas in Canada, that are included on the IUCN List, embrace a considerable diversity of designations, including provincial parks, conservation authority areas, wildlife management areas, regional parks, recreation sites, and the National Capital Green Belt around Ottawa" (Nora Mitchell et al., "Collaborative Management of Protected Landscapes: Experience in Canada and the United States of America," in *The Protected Landscape Approach: Linking Nature, Culture and Community*, ed. Jessica Brown et al., 190 [189–202] [Gland, Switz.: IUCN, 2005], citing S. Chape et al.,

compilers, *2003 United Nations List of Protected Areas* [Gland, Switz., and Cambridge: IUCN and UNEP-WC-MC, 2003]). However, the Canadian Council on Ecological Areas, although it recognizes the existence in Canada of Category V areas, offers no case studies of a Category V area in its first guidebook, *Canadian Guidebook for the Application of IUCN Protected Area Categories*, CCEA Occasional Paper no. 18 (Ottawa: CCEA Secretariat, 2008; http://www.ccea.org/en_order. html; accessed June 2010), 45. By contrast, Environment Canada's publication, *Canadian Protected Areas Status Report 2000–2005*, lists, province by province, 171 Category V areas, covering a total area of 218,154 hectares (electronic monograph [Ottawa]: Environment Canada, 2006, 41, 43, 45, 47, 49, 51, 53, 55, 57, 59, 61, 63, 65–9 http://www.ec.gc.ca/Publications/default.asp?lang=En&xml=218B3CD1-CB5A-4061-84F2-752B7F03EBB0&p rintfullpage=true&nodash=1; accessed 10 June 2010). Of these, none are administered by Parks Canada (69) (e-mail correspondence, Guy Swinnerton, 30 Apr., 1, 12 May 2008).

36 Hughes, "Building Leadership and Professionalism," 219. For a prime example of the promulgation of a policy of enforcing strict protection measures, see Canada, Banff–Bow Valley Task Force, *Banff–Bow Valley: At the Crossroads*, 2 vols. (Ottawa: Minister of Supply and Services, 1996). This landmark but incendiary report called for no educational programs and identified humans chiefly as a threat to ecological welfare.

37 In the United States, by contrast, since 1978, engaging the citizenry by fostering partnerships between people

and government agencies has spawned "many new units of the National Park System with a variety of nontraditional formulas" (*Collaboration and Conservation: Lessons Learned in Areas Managed through National Park Service Partnerships*, Conservation and Stewardship Publication, no. 3 [Woodstock, VT: Conservation Study Institute, 2001], 4). In short, Category V landscapes are complementing if not making inroads into Category II protected areas in that country. The same can be said only to a very limited degree for Parks Canada. As Alan MacEachern has explained, in the Maritimes and Newfoundland, pragmatic thinking began earlier than elsewhere in the country to reflect "a better ecological understanding that park lands had their own cultural history which had shaped their nature, and staff could not erase this history just by wiping away reference to past inhabitation. Staff in the Atlantic parks began in fact to grow interested in showcasing this cultural history" (MacEachern, *Natural Selections*, 234).

38 Recently, Alan Latourelle, CEO, Parks Canada Agency, listed the "mak[ing of] effective relations with aboriginal communities" as one of eight matters on which "action is required" across the agency's system of parks ("The National Parks System: A View from Parks Canada," Canadian Parks for Tomorrow: 40th Anniversary Conference, Assessing Change, Accomplishment and Challenge in Canadian Parks and Protected Areas, University of Calgary, 8–12 May 2008). See also Canadian Parks Council, *Aboriginal Peoples and Canada's Parks and Protected Areas: Case Studies* ([Ottawa]: Canadian Parks Council, [2008]).

39 In "Not Wanted in the Boundary," Sandlos clarifies that the Kees-eekoowenin Ojibway, evicted by force from Riding Mountain National Park, Manitoba, in 1936, had their reserve returned to them between 1994 and 2004, "though hunting and trapping rights and formal co-management agreements have not been extended" (220).

40 The presence of school children in the French park *does* in fact resonate with Jasper in 2010. In its 2007 Development Plan, Parks Canada adopted education for the first time as part of its mandate. Based at the Palisades Centre in the park, PCA Education Steward-ship leader James Bartram has initiated a pilot project that involves on-site teaching of secondary-school level students. As well, internet hook-ups to classrooms permit virtual learning that complements the teaching of courses accredited by Alberta Education. This educational mandate has a distinctly natural science-oriented bias, but an extension of it to the teaching of cultural heritage, including Aboriginal cultures, has not been discounted as a possibility.

The impetus behind this paradigm shift in the thinking of PCA is the concern that the next generation of urban Canadians will not support the parks system if not educated about it. (As matters stand, visitation to nation-al parks drastically under-represents urban youth.) The education idea has what Parks is calling a 100-year hor-izon. To the question – what must the educational mandate comprise in order for parks to be in vital, viable shape at the beginning of the twenty-second century? – Parks thinks for the first time that the answer lies in education.

"Building Active Ambassadorship for the Future" coincides with the rise in popularity of Richard Louv's book, *Last Child in the Woods: Saving our Children from Nature-Deficit Disorder* (2005; 2d ed., Chapel Hill, NC: Al-gonquin Books, 2008), copies of which Bartram distributes as he disseminates the new vision. (Author's discussion with James Bartram, Palisades Centre, 16 June 2009.)

41 The original wording may be found on panels at the park's interpretive centre in Cauterets. Almost needless to say, the romantic caste of this description ignores other signs of human presence (beyond the roofs of shepherd huts), such as a chair lift, a lakeshore restau-rant and rental store, parking lots, and trails that include chiselled steps.

42 The hotel facility is concentrated on 120 hectares (296.5 acres); the golf course and other facilities occupy the remaining two-thirds of the leasehold.

43 In collaboration with Métis advisors, JNP staff have restored the two build-ings on the Ewan Moberly site. As well, they have mounted six panels interpreting the homestead's history. Their 1,500 words, two maps, and twenty illustrations issued from a Parks Canada–Métis collaboration.

44 Even so, it is noteworthy that, in intro-ducing visitors to Jasper Park in 1928, Williams's guidebook took recourse to the tropes of innocence and of originary status: it made no mention of removal but instead remarked both that "the bands of Indian hunters and half-breeds sought other hunt-ing grounds" implicitly of their own volition, and that "James [*sic*: Lewis] Swift," the only white homesteader and the only one *not* subjected to removal

from the UARV, was the valley's "first settler" (2, 34). For a discussion of Williams's references to Natives, see Alan MacEachern's chapter in this volume.

45 *Parks Canada: First Priority: Progress Report on Implementation of the Recommendations of the Panel on the Ecological Integrity of Canada's National Parks* (Ottawa: Minister of Public Works and Government Services Canada, 2001), 24; available at http://www.pc.gc.ca/docs/pc/rpts/prior/sec3/progres-progress5f_e.asp; updated 15 Nov. 2006; accessed June 2010.

46 *Parks Canada: First Priority*, 24; http://www.pc.gc.ca/docs/pc/rpts/prior/sec3/progres-progress5f_e.asp; updated 15 Nov. 2006; accessed June 2010.

47 See *Time for Nature: Healing Broken Connections: Restoring Historic Links between People and the Land in Kluane National Park and Reserve of Canada*, 10 Dec. 2007; http://www.pc.gc.ca/canada/pn-tfn/itm2-/2007/2007-12-10_e.asp; accessed June 2010.

48 *Parks Canada: First Priority*, 49; available in updated forms at http://www.pc.gc.ca/docs/pc/rpts/prior/sec4/mesures-actions7a_e.asp; updated 15 Nov. 2006; accessed June 2010.

49 *Parks Canada: First Priority*, 48. Another initiative that has involved First Nations people to a limited degree arose out of the crisis that Banff National Park is experiencing with too many elk in its montane areas, where they invariably interact with humans. According to Cliff White, Environmental Sciences Coordinator for Banff National Park, from twenty to forty of the most human-habituated animals are culled each year. The policy by which this practice occurs requires consultation with neighbouring First Nations people (Parks Canada Agency, "Management of Hyperabundant Wildlife Populations in Canada's National Parks," Management Directive 4.4.11, Dec. 2007; contacts Stephen Woodley and John Waithaka). In the case of Banff, this has resulted in the involvement of Stoney and Siksika both at workshops about determining ecosystem management and at cullings, where they butchered and took home the meat (e-mail correspondence, Cliff White, 11 June 2008).

50 See Peter J. Murphy, "Homesteading in the Athabasca Valley to 1910: An Interview with Edward Wilson Moberly, Prairie Creek, Alberta, 29 August 1980," in *Culturing Wilderness in Jasper National Park: Studies in Two Centuries of Human History in the Upper Athabasca River Watershed*, ed. I.S. MacLaren, 127 (123–53) (Edmonton: University of Alberta Press, 2007).

51 Peter J. Murphy, "Homesteading in the Athabasca Valley to 1910."

52 *Collaboration and Conservation*, 11.

53 I.S. MacLaren, with Eric Higgs and Gabrielle Zezulka-Mailloux, *Mapper of Mountains: M.P. Bridgland in the Canadian Rockies 1902–1930* (Edmonton: University of Alberta Press, 2005).

54 The website at which the photographs may be consulted is http://bridgland.sunsite.ualberta.ca/main/index.html. Of related interest is the original project's subsequent (and current) developments: http://mountainlegacy.ca/.

55 Williams, *Jasper National Park*, 2, 3.

56 Hugh Matheson, DLS, "Plan of the Town of Jasper Province of Alberta," Canada Lands Survey Records, 21221, Canada Lands Survey Records Alberta, Edmonton; reproduced in

Judy Larmour, *Laying down the Lines: A History of Land Surveying in Alberta* (Edmonton: Brindle and Glass, 2005), 136. Text in the lower right-hand corner of the plan dates it: "Compiled from official survey by H. Matheson DLS 27th June, 1913. Department of the Interior, Ottawa, 5th June, 1914. Approved and Confirmed E Deville [signed] Surveyor General."

57 Further details are provided in I.S. MacLaren, "Introduction," *Culturing Wilderness in Jasper National Park*, xxv–xxix. As to the emphasis on the townsite as the site of community in the park, the *Jasper National Park of Canada Management Plan* mentions only the townsite of Jasper in section 7.0, which bears the title "place for community" (seehttp://www.pc.gc.ca/docs/v-g/jasper/plan/plan5-7_e.asp; updated 3 April 2005; accessed June 2010).

58 In contrast, during the fur trade these families were known as the "Jasper House Indians." D.J. Benham, "Jasper Park in the Canadian Rockies: Canada's New National Playground," *The Globe*, Saturday Magazine section, 15 Jan. 1910: 9 (4, 9); and *Edmonton Bulletin* (14 Dec. 1890), 1.

59 The last printed evidence of McLaggan's employment appears in the 1911–12 list of "Forest Rangers" in the federal auditor-general's report. It lists him as a "chief forest ranger" stationed at "Strathcona: salary 10 m. to Jan. 31 at $150" (Canada, Sessional Paper no. 1, George V, *Auditor General's Report 1911–1912*, "Part J, Interior Department, Details of Expenditure and Revenue"). I thank Peter Murphy for generously sharing this identification. Investigation of two obvious possibilities – that McLaggan was hired by the

British Columbia Forest Service when it was established in 1912–13, or that he became a soldier – have uncovered no further information.

60 A photo of Ewan Moberly's homestead at Victor Lake, 1914, is reproduced in *Mountain Trails: Memoirs of an Alberta Forest Ranger in the Mountains and Foothills of the Athabasca Forest 1920–1945. By Jack Glen Sr.*, ed. Robert Mueller, Peter J. Murphy, and Bob Stevenson (Hinton, AB: Foothills Research Institute, and Alberta Department of Sustainable Resource Development, 2008), 68. See also Peter J. Murphy, with Robert W. Udell, Robert E. Stevenson, and Thomas W. Peterson, *A Hard Road to Travel: Land, Forests and People in the Upper Athabasca Region* (Hinton, AB: Foothills Model Forest; Durham, NC: Forest History Society, 2007), 224–27; and *People and Peaks of Willmore Wilderness Park, 1800s to mid-1900s*, ed. Susan Feddema-Leonard, Estella Cheverie, and Roger Blunt (Edmonton: Willmore Wilderness Foundation and Whitefox Circle, 2007), 7–9.

61 On the relationship between forest reserves and park and the Forestry and Parks branches of the Department of the Interior in the 1910s, see MacEachern's chapter in this volume. The boundary of Athabaska Forest Reserve as it was first proclaimed by Order in Council 939 on 13 May 1910 indicates that the land in question (Tp 56 R8 W6, sections 25–29 and 32–36) did not form part of the forest reserve during its first years of existence, when the Athabasca homesteaders moved into the area. Thus, when the *Dominion Forest Reserves and Parks Act* was assented to on 19 May 1911, its description of the Rocky Mountains

Forest Reserve's boundary was the same as the description in the 13 May 1910 Order in Council (Canada, *Orders in Council* [1911], 1–2 George V, vols. I–II, lxxx–lxxxi; *Canada Gazette*, vol. 43 [1910], 28 May 1910, 3684–86; specifically, 3686, right col.; and Canada, *Dominion Forest Reserves and Parks Act, Acts of the Parliament of the Dominion of Canada*, 1–2 George V [1911], chap. 10, 133–78; the forest reserves in Alberta are listed beginning at 163, with the five forming the Rocky Mountains Forest Reserve on 165; the land around Grande Cache Lake and the 15th baseline [Tp 56 Ranges 6, 7, and 8 W6] are found beginning at mid-175, where the boundary, from east to west, is described as follows: "to the northeast corner of section 12, township 56, range 7, west of the sixth meridian; thence due north 81 chains, more or less, to the northeast corner of section 13, township 56, range 7, west of the sixth meridian; thence due west 486 chains, more or less to the northeast corner of section 13, township 56, range 8, west of the sixth meridian; thence due north 80 chains, more or less, to the northeast corner of section 24, township 56, range 8, west of the sixth meridian; thence due west 324 chains, more or less, to the northeast corner of section 20, township 56, range 8, west of the sixth meridian; thence due north 242 chains, more or less, to the northeast corner of section 5, township 57, range 8, west of the sixth meridian; thence due west" [175]).

The boundary did not change until well after the summer and early fall of 1911. At that time, a boundary survey was conducted by Dominion Forestry Branch staff S.H. (Stan) Clark and E.H. (Ernest Herbert) Finlayson under the direction of forester G.H. Edgecombe. The surveyors began at Entrance, AB, in the UARV, and worked on the eastern boundary until they reached the 15th baseline. At that easternmost extent of the reserve, however, the surveyors were *east*, not west, of the sixth meridian. It is unclear how far west along the 15th baseline they proceeded before ending their work on 1 October. This survey formed the basis of the 6 June 1913 amendment to the 1911 *Dominion Forest Reserves and Parks Act*. With this amendment, Victor Lake and the Ewan Moberly and Adam Joachim homesteads to the south of it came within the reserve for the first time, for the amendment extended the boundary along the 15th baseline through the relevant portion of Tp 56 R8 W6. The *Act to Amend the Dominion Forest Reserves and Parks Act*, assented to on 6 June 1913, added the Brazeau and the Athabaska forest reserves to the Rocky Mountains Forest Reserve. Following Clark and Finlayson's 1911 survey, it amended paragraph 24 of the *Dominion Forest Reserves and Parks Act*, Canada, *Acts of the Parliament of the Dominion of Canada*, 3–4 George V (1913), chap. 18. The sections bearing on the new homesteads of some of the homesteaders evicted from the UARV reads as follows: "Paragraph 24 is amended by adding at the end thereof the following: ... all the sections in township 56, range 7, except sections 1, 2, 3, 4, 5, 6, 7, 8, 9, 10, 11, 12, 13, 14, 15, 16, 17 and 18; the following sections of township 56, range 8:–sections 25, 26, 27, 28, 33, 34, 35 and 36" (271).

Although other motives prompted this change of boundary, the surveyors, had they covered all the ground that their boundary report touched on, would have understood the implications for the homesteaders around Victor Lake of the changes to the existing boundary that their report would recommend. Correspondence in subsequent years shows, however, that Finlayson, who had become inspector of forest reserves for Alberta, seems not to have been aware of this implication. It is noteworthy that the surveyors also took notice of the timber in the regions where their survey took them, but – and this might offer some evidence that they did not come too far west along the 15th baseline – Finlayson wrote in 1917 to the superintendent of the Forestry Branch in Ottawa that "in 1911 when we were working on the boundary survey of the Athabasca [Forest Reserve] several maps were prepared roughly showing the conditions between the Athabasca and the 15th Base Line; more particularly in the *eastern* part of the Reserve."

62 Peter J. Murphy, "'Following the Base of the Foothills': Tracing the Boundaries of Jasper Park and its Adjacent Rocky Mountains Forest Reserve," in *Culturing Wilderness in Jasper National Park*, 79 (71–121).

63 Murphy, "'Following the Base,'" 81. All six of Murphy's maps are available in digital form at http://www.uap.ualberta.ca/CulturingWilderness/.

64 LAC, RG 39, vol. 416 – "Forest Reserves–Regulations and Legislation 1901–1916" – (no file number) contains a copy of the published pamphlet containing the relevant regulation: Superintendent of Forestry R.H. Campbell and Inspector of Forest Reserves, A. Knechtel, *Regulations for Dominion Forest Reserves* (Ottawa: Government Printing Bureau, 1908).

65 Qtd. in Hazel Hart, *History of Hinton* (Hinton, AB: by the author, 1980), 32 (original source not given). See Gertude Nicks, *Demographic Anthropology of Native Populations in Western Canada, 1800–1975*. PhD dissertation, University of Alberta, 1980.

On 8 March 1967, Mark Truxler and his wife interviewed then eighty-seven-year-old James Shand-Harvey fourteen months before his death on 6 May 1968. His long response to several related questions provides details from his somewhat erratic recollection of the arrangements that McLaggan struck with the homesteaders. One response was as follows: "Yes, McLaggan made the deal, and McLaggan paid for their buildings, but he did not tell them where to go, outside of the fact that they could settle anywhere they liked outside the Park. You see there was no surveyed land this side of the Pembina, and that is what all my affidavits state. I made 4 or 5 affidavits for Ottawa and the Roman Catholics, stating what they were told. (N.B.–McLaggan states in his report 'that settlement was reached with these squatters by mutual agreement between myself and them, Feb. 19, 1910')" ("Transcript of Tape Recording of Interview with James Shand-Harvey, March 8th, 1967," typescript, Jasper-Yellowhead Museum and Archives, Jasper, AB, JYMA 78.01.41, 6. See also James G. MacGregor, *Pack Saddles to Tête Jaune Cache* [Edmonton: Hurtig, 1962], 151–53).

66 As far as can be determined, only those residents of the UARV who had built permanent structures were offered compensation.

67 [Charles H. Morse,] "Forest Types Mountain Section of Athabasca Forest" (bearing a stamped date, 17 Nov. 1913); LAC, RG 39, vol. 285, file 40594. Finlayson refers to his 1911 boundary survey in E.H. Finlayson to R.H. Campbell, 20 Apr. 1917; LAC, RG 39, vol. 285, file 40594. For an analysis of that survey, see Murphy, "'Following the Base,'" 116–17n70.

68 The details from the written record of the interactions between the Grande Cache people and Forestry Branch and other government officials appear in I.S. MacLaren, "Removal of 'Squatters' from the Athabasca River Valley (1909–10) and Attempts to Remove 'Trespassers' from Athabasca Forest Reserve and Environs (1912–22)," typescript report for Ackroyd, Piasta, Roth, and Day, LLP, Edmonton, 2006.

69 The Forgotten Explorer: Samuel Prescott Fay's 1914 Expedition to the Northern Rockies, ed. Charles Helm and Mike Murtha (Victoria, BC: Rocky Mountain Books, 2009), 31, 32.

70 Swinnerton and Buggey, "Protected Landscapes in Canada," 82. The Cooking Lake–Blackfoot Area is one of several protected areas within the more recently evolved Beaver Hills glacial moraine partnership, which includes such other designated protected areas as Miquelon Lake Provincial Park, the Strathcona Wilderness Centre, the Ministik Bird Sanctuary, and a number of "natural areas" with provincial governmental designation. On the map in Environment Canada, *Canadian Protected Areas Status Report 2000–2005*, a map to which the Canadian Council on Ecological Areas (CCEA) contributed and the "first attempt to present nationally the

categorization of Canada's protected areas according to the internationally-recognized World Conservation Union (IUCN) protected areas classification system," Cooking Lake–Blackfoot Area is shown as Category V (3; http://www.ec.gc.ca/Publications/default. asp?lang=En&xml=218B3CD1-CB5A-4061-84F2-752B7F03EBB0&print fullpage=true&nodash=1 [accessed June 2010]; brought to my attention in e-mail correspondence with Guy Swinnerton, 12 May 2008).

71 More than a thirty-year tradition of involvement has existed between First Nations and various governmental agencies charged with protecting northern areas (Canadian Parks Council, *Aboriginal Peoples and Canada's Parks and Protected Areas: Case Studies* (Ottawa: Canadian Parks Council, 2008); http://www.parks-parcs.ca/english/cpc/aboriginal.php; accessed June 2010.

72 Apart from the superintendent's house in Jasper, now the park's information centre, Jasper National Park has no active historic sites: Athabasca and Yellowhead passes have plaques posted to commemorate their role in the transcontinental fur trade, and a plaque across the river from the site of Jasper House II commemorates its archaeological and historical value. A plaque for Henry House, the whereabouts of which is unknown, is vaguely posted. For a list of the 158 national historic sites, see http://www.pc.gc.ca/apps/lhn-nhs/lst_e.asp; accessed June 2010.

73 At present, thanks to an overture from the United Nations Educational, Scientific, and Cultural Organization (UNESCO) to the federal government in 2006, Willmore Wilderness Park,

along with other contiguous areas in Alberta and British Columbia, is being considered for inclusion under World Heritage Site designation that UNESCO conferred on four of the Rockies' national parks (Jasper, Banff, Yoho, and Kootenay) in 1984 because of their exceptional natural beauty and their representation of stages of the planet's geological history. (The designation underwent an expansion in 1990, when Mt. Robson, Mt. Assiniboine, and Hamber – provincial parks in British Columbia contiguous to the national parks – were added to the Rocky Mountain World Heritage Site.) Chris Wearmouth, "Willmore Wilderness Considered for World Heritage Designation," *Wild Lands Advocate: The Alberta Wilderness Association Journal* 15, no. 6 [Dec. 2007]: 14–15). The initiative for expansion remains part of the management plans for Jasper and Banff national parks, but no application has yet been submitted by the provincial governments of British Columbia and Alberta or the federal government (e-mail correspondence, Sheila Luey, Banff National Park, to author, 1 Oct. 2010).

74 See Wearmouth, "Willmore Wilderness," 15.

75 Susan Buggey, *An Approach to Aboriginal Cultural Landscapes* (Ottawa: Parks Canada, 1999); http://www.pc.gc.ca/docs/r/pca-acl/susan_e.asp and http://www.pc.gc.ca/eng/docs/r/pca-acl/index.aspx; accessed June 2010.

76 See Sharon Oosthoek, "Condemned to Death: What happens when a rescue

plan works too well?" *Globe and Mail,* 22 August 2009, F5.

77 Mitchell et al., "Collaborative Management of Protected Landscapes," 194; Swinnerton and Buggey, "Protected Landscapes in Canada," 82–83; Guy S. Swinnerton and Stephen G. Otway, "Collaboration across Boundaries – Research and Practice: Elk Island National Park and the Beaver Hills, Alberta," in *Making Ecosystem Based Management Work: Connecting Researchers and Managers,* ed. Neil Munro (Wolfville, NS: Science and Management of Protected Areas Association, 2004), published only as CD; n.p. (chap. 2); also at http://www.sampaa.org/publications/conference-proceedings-1991-2000/2003-proceedings; accessed June 2010.

78 Mitchell et al., "Collaborative Management of Protected Landscapes," 202.

79 http://www.pc.gc.ca/eng/pn-np/ab/jasper/plan.aspx; accessed June 2010. In attaching two documents complementing the new plan, "Highlights" of the management plan (here quoted) and "Jasper's Best Kept Secrets," Superintendent Greg Fenton announced that "the management plan for Jasper National Park of Canada was approved by the Minister of the Environment, the Honourable Jim Prentice, and with its tabling in both houses of Parliament on Tuesday June 15th, 2010, is now a public document. The updated plan replaces the 2000 management plan and completes the plan review process that began in March 2009" (e-mail circular, 23 June 2010).

Epilogue

LYLE DICK
PARKS CANADA

National parks are maintained for all the people – for the ill that they may be restored; for the well that they may be forti-fied and inspired by the sunshine, the fresh air, the beauty, and all the other healing, ennobling agencies of Nature. They exist in order that every citizen of Canada may satisfy his craving for Nature and nature's beauty; that he may absorb the poise and restfulness of their forests; that he may fill his soul with the brilliance of the wild flowers and the sublimity of the mountain peaks; that he may develop the buoyancy, the joy, and the activity that he sees in the wild animals; that he may stock his brain and mind with great thoughts, noble ideals; that he may be made better, be healthier, and happier.

James B. Harkin, quoted in Mabel Williams,
The Banff-Jasper Highway: Descriptive Guide
(Hamilton, ON: Larson, 1928), 15–16.

I don't think there is an institution in Canada that pays as big a dividend as the Canadian national parks.... National Parks provide the chief means of bringing to Canada a stream of tourists and streams of tourist gold.

James B. Harkin, 1922, quoted in Kevin McNamee,
National Parks in Canada (Toronto: Key Porter, 1994), 23.

Canada still has vast untouched areas out of which more wilderness parks could be carved. Future generations may wonder at our blindness if we neglect to set them aside before civilization invades them. What is needed today is an informed public opinion which will voice an indignant protest against any vulgarization of the beauty of our national parks or any invasion of their sanctity. Negative or passive good-will that does nothing is of little use. We need "fierce loyalties" to back action. The National Parks of Canada are a source of untold pleasure and pride to our people. Every principle of enlightened patriotism should inspire us to keep them inviolate.

James B. Harkin, "Reflections of a Parks Administrator:
From the Papers of James B. Harkin, first Commissioner of
the National Parks of Canada from 1911 to 1936,"
Park News (Journal of the National and Provincial
Parks Association of Canada), January 1966, 16.

Surveys suggest that national parks rank among Canadians' most-valued symbols of identity.[1] But what is it about our national parks that we value or identity with? Is it their natural landscapes, opportunities to view wildlife or the chance to commune with nature? Is it their role in protecting ecosystems? Do our highest values for national parks lie in recreational opportunities, such as backcountry hiking, or alpine skiing? Or do we embrace the tamer fare of scenic drive-throughs, golfing, and quasi-urban vacations at tourist resorts? Do we place a premium on the economic or monetary contributions of national parks as revenue generators for tourism and related sectors of the economy? Or are there other values that resonate? Are these assorted values for national parks in some way compatible or, as some have suggested, incommensurable, the outgrowth of completely different and irreconcilable ideological sets?

The diversity of viewpoints underscores major challenges as we are about to enter the second century of the national parks system. We do not yet know the answers to these questions, but what can be said is that the soundness of national parks programs in future will depend on the success of park administrators in engaging a broad range of constituencies in supporting and sharing the stewardship for these special places. National parks must be seen to work for all groups of Canadians if they are to continue to play an important role in our shared culture and identity.

Public support for the protection of national parks and other protected areas has always been important, but in Canada it lagged historically behind initiatives by administrators to protect and present these protected areas. As Alan MacEachern notes in his essay on M.B. Williams, Canada's national parks system was born in 1911 in relative obscurity, and, as John Sandlos elaborates, most Canadians were not engaged with issues of park establishment and administration in the formative period. Rather, Canada's early policies regarding national parks were largely shaped by James B. Harkin, whose influence is still apparent in the parks system he guided through its first quarter-century. Harkin was fortunate to have the support of a small but dedicated staff, including the remarkable Mabel Williams, who emerges in MacEachern's account as the principal publicist and popularizer of the national parks system in its formative era. However, Harkin knew that the realization of his vision of a country-wide system of national parks depended on more than talented staff – he needed a core of advocates for protected areas from outside the government. He found his essential constituency in a group of committed wilderness enthusiasts centred around the Alpine Club of Canada.[2] Arthur Wheeler, its founder, was an early advocate of banning commercial development within the parks, and he also pushed for the inclusion of the Columbia Icefield within the expanded boundaries of Jasper National Park. Perhaps more importantly, the Alpine Club provided a core preservationist philosophy that helped Harkin make the case for setting aside areas for national parks.[3] In the absence of a broadly based constituency for protected areas, Harkin knew that he needed to muster other arguments in favour of dedicating these lands – some of these are summarized in the passages quoted at the beginning of this epilogue. Prominent among these arguments were his assertions that national parks had the potential to be major drivers of commercial activity, economic development, and generators of wealth for the country. The simultaneous promotion of conservation and recreational tourism was certainly paradoxical and, in Sandlos's interpretation, it embodied "contradictory philosophies," giving rise to recurrent debates between its different constituencies as to whether to extend or restrict development, promote visitation or set limits on park use.

It was Harkin's genius that he was able to incorporate both idealistic and pragmatic strains in his vision and approach, a reflection in microcosm of the larger forces bearing on the country's national parks. Further, he was able to articulate a range of compelling arguments in favour of national parks drawn from notions of both intrinsic and instrumental value. Harkin's hybrid vision expressed the pressures under which the parks system was then operating, but also his sensitive understanding of his audiences, especially the parliamentary representatives and governments to whom he directed his appeals for funding the new system. Harkin was keenly aware that in order to develop a broadly based constituency for national parks, it would be necessary to expand the system across the country so that people in all regions of Canada could experience wilderness areas and their values first-hand. During his tenure, the National Parks Branch also made it a priority to develop roads, tourist attractions, and commercial facilities within the national parks, especially in Banff and Jasper, but also in younger national parks such as Riding Mountain, Prince Albert, and others featuring townsites offering a wide range of quasi-urban amenities for visitors. By 1930 his success was evident in the addition of twelve new national parks in eight of Canada's provinces, effectively transforming the country's national parks into a national system. Further success came with his establishment of Canada's national commemorative program through the inauguration of the Historic Sites and Monuments Board of Canada in 1919. Since that date, more than two thousand persons, places, and events of national historic significance have been commemorated across the country.[4] Harkin thereby was the architect of two national systems for the protection and presentation of Canada's heritage – both natural and cultural.

Harkin also presided over drafting the first comprehensive legislation governing the establishment and management of Canada's national parks, including the well-known words from Section 4 of the 1930 *National Parks*

Act, asserting that national parks "are hereby dedicated to the people of Canada, for their benefit, education and enjoyment."[5] Notwithstanding numerous amendments over time, this phrase still encapsulates the guiding philosophy of national parks and its dual mandate of protection and presentation, predicated on the belief that each is unattainable without the other. Harkin knew that, unless the natural values of national parks were protected, they could lose the special qualities most valued by many Canadians. What he strongly also believed was that without the values of "benefit, education and enjoyment," national parks could not build a constituency of support among the Canadian public for continued protection. In his view, then, the dual mandate was not only integral but indispensable to the continued success and survival of the national parks system.

The dialectic between the different strains of intrinsic and instrumental value is well represented in successive stages of development at Canada's first and most famous national park. Thirty years ago, in a thoughtful essay surveying the history of Banff's first century, the landscape architect Roger Todhunter discerned that the cultural landscape of its townsite displays evidence of three different eras of national park philosophy and practice. In the initial era, 1885–1910, the town developed around the hot springs as a spa, accessed primarily via rail transportation by an elite clientele and isolated from the larger park. The amenities of Banff National Park were largely the product of joint marketing and development by the Government of Canada and the Canadian Pacific Railway. In that era, the park's natural areas were little more than spectacular scenery to be viewed from within the safe, tame confines of the town. In the second phase of development, 1910–1945, Banff developed into a full-fledged resort. Largely corresponding to Harkin's tenure as commissioner, in this phase Banff was positioned to take advantage of automobile access, an expanding regional population, and the emergence of middle-class tourism as the town and park developed into a major international resort. In the third phase, between the Second World War and ca. 1980, Banff expanded exponentially following the building of the Trans-Canada Highway, major ski resorts, and a full range of urban facilities in the town, including hotels and restaurants.[6]

Since Todhunter's essay appeared in 1981, we have witnessed two further phases in the evolution of national parks. The first of these was a period of ecosystem-oriented programming following the placement of Parks Canada within the Department of the Environment in 1979, a public outcry following years of unconstrained development at Banff, efforts by park administrators to address a range of concerns relating to threatened or endangered species, and the continued degradation of ecosystems across the country. By the late twentieth century, national parks were primarily focussed on ensuring ecological integrity within national parks as recommended by the Panel on Ecological Integrity. More generally, Parks Canada confronted challenges of working with other government agencies, non-governmental organizations, and other constituencies to protect the biological diversity of the larger ecosystems of which our national parks form a part. The areas of concern, as enumerated in a recent compilation of Canadian environmental policy, extended beyond federal stewardship and included a collective responsibility of Canada's provincial and federal governments to protect 12 per cent of the country's natural environment, which as of 2003, still lagged at 10 per cent. In 2000, the Panel on Ecological Integrity reported that thirty-eight of Canada's thirty-nine parks established to that point were under serious ecological stress. Indeed, several national parks among Canada's World Heritage Sites were reportedly in danger of losing their World Heritage commemorative status if unconstrained development of these parks were to continue.[7] Such concerns were reflected in the stress placed on ecological values in the *Parks Canada Agency Act* of 2000.[8]

The ecosystem-based model, strongly influenced by the American environmental movement, combined the ethics and ideologies of intrinsic value with an aversion and opposition to most forms of instrumental use. It moved beyond conservationist notions of wise use of natural resources to a preservationist model emphasizing that nature should be "left alone and untouched."[9] In the assessment of one observer, a problem was that it tended to separate humans from nature: "people and their impacts are perceived as foreign influences on the environment."[10] In this paradigm people were often viewed as the problem, virtually an alien invader intruding upon and negatively affecting the ecosystems of protected areas.[11] While successful in influencing Parks Canada to promulgate ecological integrity as its primary mandate and focus for national parks in the late twentieth century, it was less apparent that wilderness conservationists had succeeded in connecting with the Canadian public, whose support they needed to build a broadly based constituency for ecological preservation.[12] In a comparative study of wilderness and nature conservation in Canada, the United States, and Britain, the historian Norman Henderson argued that in Canada, "there has never been a powerful national conservation design."[13]

A shortcoming of earlier concepts was that protection of the natural environment was sometimes accorded greater value than either the cultural resources documenting the human imprint on the land or the people whose histories are written in this heritage. Fortunately, the policy framework for national parks has evolved beyond notions of privileging nature at the expense of culture. Today, Parks Canada's *Guiding Principles and Operational Policies* and its current integrated mandate requires park managers to address the values of both heritage realms in the delivery of their programs.[14] Ronald Rudin has provided a particularly instructive example of this evolution in Kouchibouguac National Park, where the histories of the Acadian people who lived and worked in the park before expropriation of their properties were previously ignored. Concepts of the park's values changed following issuance of the 1981 report of a Special Inquiry into the expropriations, and more recent films documenting this history have influenced Parks Canada to seek to more fully engage the Acadian community. Despite past injustices, Rudin discerns both good will on the part of park administrators and an emerging willingness of members of the Acadian community to explore ways of reclaiming their history through integration of their stories into Kouchibouguac's programs. In his essay on Kluane National Park Reserve, David Neufeld identifies a similar change of attitudes and values arising from political action by Yukon First Nations, contributing to a greater awareness by park administrators of the value and importance of cultural pluralism as an organizing principle of national parks establishment and administration. Also in Yukon, Brad Martin gives a valuable account of how through land claims negotiations concerning Ivvavik National Park of Canada, the Inuvialuit succeeded in shaping the park's establishment into a tool for their own cultural survival, with positive results for both the Inuvialuit and the national parks system.

The history of Aboriginal peoples reminds us that the human presence in our national parks is very deep, often extending back to remote antiquity. Gwyn Langemann's essay on archaeology in the Rocky Mountains reveals that our national parks contain numerous archaeological sites documenting a remarkable time depth, some extending as far back as 10,700 Before the

Present, or earlier. These sites, coupled with many post-contact archaeological sites, buildings, landscapes, and other cultural resources, are among the important heritage values of our national parks and must continue to receive the highest level of protection alongside safeguarding their natural environments. In his essay, I.S. MacLaren suggests that the time depth can pose its own problems, as approved uses of national parks may privilege some users over others, or some groups or cultures over other groups. He poses some very interesting reflections and ideas as to how the participation and presence of Aboriginal peoples might be reintegrated into programs at Jasper and other national parks.

In 2006, as Parks Canada approached the centenary of the national parks system, it embarked on a further phase – a major new initiative focussed on marketing and visitor experience. In part, this development was prompted by declining visitor numbers, a trend discernible over the last decade in museums, historic sites, and natural parks programs across the continent. This initiative apparently also reflected a recognition by Parks Canada's senior managers that its programs would soon not be sustainable without a concerted effort to connect more tangibly with the country's diverse constituencies. The larger context bearing on visitor experience included major demographic changes in Canada over the previous two decades, including the burgeoning populations of communities of new Canadians, many with little prior experience or awareness of national parks, national historic sites, and national marine conservation areas of Canada. As well, the concentration of Canada's population in urban communities has continued to accelerate, while national parks are almost invariably situated in rural and sometimes very remote areas. These demographic changes posed further challenges for Parks Canada to find ways to reach and deliver programs to the great mass of Canadians, which visitor experience and marketing initiatives are now being designed to do. It is to be hoped that the visitor experience initiative will encourage Canada's diverse citizenry to encounter more directly our natural and cultural heritage, learn about its many values, support its continued protection and presentation, and actively join in its stewardship.

The point to draw from this historical progression is that, viewed in the long term over a 125-year span, no single approach to national parks policy seeking to supersede other core aspects of mandate was able to do so indefinitely. After a period within which certain policies were emphasized, the national parks agency recurrently sought to rebalance park programs by addressing other, less well represented aspects of the mandate. Claire Campbell's perceptive comment in the introduction to this volume that "state initiative" and "public participation" cannot be neatly divided seems particularly apt. However paradoxical or unsatisfying from some perspectives, the national parks system more or less reflects the different interests that have weighed in regarding park development and conservation over the course of its first century.

It is also true, as the contributors to this volume have shown, that over the last century Canada's national parks did not enjoy an unproblematic evolution but rather manifested a recurrent and ongoing struggle between diverging interests and viewpoints, centred on competing notions of instrumental and intrinsic use.[15] Ben Bradley shows how politics played out in the unsuccessful quest to integrate Hamber Provincial Park in British Columbia's Big Bend Country into the federal system. Hamber was one of several would-be national parks; others, such as the former Buffalo National Park in Alberta, set up to aid in the renewal of buffalo and antelope populations on the prairies, were short-lived, withdrawn from the system after only a few years: victims of the political climate of the 1920s. In his cogent examination of the portable cabin issue in Prince Albert National Park, Bill Waiser suggests that powerful local interests sometimes exerted an inordinate influence on park administration beyond the expressed will or interests of the larger Canadian population. At the same time, we must recognize that the dialectic between different interests has also generated positive results for the national parks system and the country. Jim Taylor's essay on Banff in the 1960s shows that different visions of the national park ideal came to a head in that decade, in the process energizing a new generation of environmental advocates devoted to ecological preservation by 1970.

Perhaps it might appropriately be acknowledged that political dynamics are integral to the establishment of national parks, an element with the potential for either negative or positive consequences, but an unavoidable part of the process nevertheless. As in other liberal democracies, public policy in Canada has generally been shaped through the interplay between the executive branch, parliamentary representatives, non-governmental interests, and the public service – and the policies and practices adopted for national parks are no exception. It was these diverse players, animated by diverging ideologies and interests, who influenced the evolution and development of this country's national parks system. The system we have today is the result of park authorities' efforts to steer between these competing interests, and the degree to which they have succeeded continues to be debated.

From Harkin to the present, the central question for parks administrators has not been a matter of choosing which components of the mandate to address, but rather: how to strike the right balance. A complicating factor, as pointed out in several essays in this book, was the periodic politicization of the national parks establishment in the twentieth century. It underscores the complexity of setting aside protected areas, a process that may take years and which must often be supported by different levels of government, non-governmental agencies, First Nations, and assorted other constituencies. In our political system, politicians must face the voters every four to five years, or even more often in a minority parliament. Governments understandably desire new initiatives to report to voters, so it is to be expected that political factors will continue to enter into the creation of new parks. However, the issues are now so urgent that citizens must assume a greater role in helping ensure that national parks respect the natural environment while serving the needs of Canadians to experience these magnificent places and icons of Canadian identity. Given the diverse mandates and expectations of the twenty-first century, the continued health and survival of the national parks system will depend on a much more broadly based dialogue in the public sphere than we have witnessed to date. Canada's success in meeting these challenges will depend in large measure on the effectiveness of national parks administration in encouraging a broadly based engagement with diverse constituencies in the public sphere, while building a general ethos of stewardship for the national parks system.

Fulfilling Parks Canada's mandates for national parks will also depend on successful integration of the wide range of professional inputs available to the agency since the professionalization of its research and planning units in the 1960s and 1970s. A major milestone was the production of the first National Parks System Plan in 1970, which established a systematic process for classification of Canada's natural regions and for identifying candidate areas for protection within each of the thirty-nine identified regions.[16] This plan established a basis for much of the research on the natural and cultural heritage of national parks carried out since its inauguration. The System Plan has found support among major non-governmental heritage agencies, such as the Canadian Parks and Wilderness Society and the Sierra Club. Its publication and widespread dissemination perhaps has done more to mitigate the politicization of park establishment than any other factor because governments are aware than any major departure from the established process could well be subject to public censure from influential advocates of national parks conservation. This is not to suggest that the National Parks System Plan cannot be critiqued or that other methodologies of classification are not relevant to the establishment or administration of national parks. In his essay in this volume, Olivier Craig-Dupont makes several cogent observations regarding the System Plan and argues that these ecological regions are cultural rather than natural constructs.

In the past, issues arising from controversies were often addressed in a reactive way, such as the Banff–Bow Valley study, which launched the Panel on Ecological Integrity and prompted extensive public discussion of important issues confronting Banff National Park and the wildlife for which its serves as steward. In the past the national parks agency was sometimes less successful in taking proactive measures, that is, anticipating the future needs of protection and presentation, putting in place plans to implement these goals, and maintaining a clear focus through changing administrations and shifting governmental priorities. A notable exception appears to be the current "visitor experience" initiative, a multi-year program that promises to reshape the development of Parks Canada's brand and vision for many years to come. The new emphasis on outreach and engagement – offering Canadians the opportunity to participate in biological research in national parks or archaeological projects at national historic sites, for example – is designed to win champions or supporters for the continued dedication of protected areas. For public agencies such as Parks Canada, dependent on governmental appropriations, enlisting the support of parliamentary representatives has always been important, but equally critical in the current context will be the support of the citizens who elect the parliamentarians. Achieving their support will require sustained leadership in the years ahead.

In an increasingly complex political environment, addressing its mandate will require Parks Canada to build broadly based constituencies for the protection and presentation of national parks and other protected areas and to navigate between these different constituencies in ongoing dialogue and problem-solving. In an emerging paradigm people might more usefully be viewed not as the problem but as the solution to the myriad challenges confronting Canada's national parks and national marine conservation areas programs today. In this regard, James B. Harkin's goal of fostering an "informed public opinion" seems all the more pressing and critical to ensuring the sustainability and continued health of Canada's national parks system over its second century.

NOTES

1   See, for example, the Environics poll, "Patriotism and Canadian Identity," which showed that in 2003, 62 per cent of Canadians polled ranked national parks as important symbols of national identity, exceeded only by the Canadian flag, at 68 per cent. A similar poll in 2000 showed national parks and the flag tied at the top of the poll, both garnering the support of 73 per cent of respondents. See: http://www.acs-aec.ca/oldsite/Polls/Poll40.pdf.

2   See the discussion in PearlAnn Reichwein, "Beyond the Visionary Mountains: The Alpine Club of Canada and the Canadian National Park Idea, 1906 to 1969," PhD dissertation, Carleton University, 1995.

3   As in Canada, the early conservation movement in the United States was initially driven by dedicated amateur naturalists, especially its central figure and leading philosopher, John Muir. See Stephen Fox, *The American Conservation Movement: John Muir and His Legacy* (Madison: University of Wisconsin Press, 1981), 333–57.

4   See C.J. Taylor, *Negotiating the Past: The Making of Canada's National Historic Parks and. Sites* (Montreal: McGill-Queen's University Press, 1990).

5   For a useful discussion of the evolution of the 1930 Act, see C.J. Taylor, "Legislating Nature: The National Parks Act of 1930," in *To See Ourselves / To Save Ourselves: Ecology and Culture in Canada*, ed. Rowland Lorimer et al., 125–37 (Montreal: Association for Canadian Studies, 1991).

6   Roger Todhunter, "Banff and the National Park Idea," *Landscape 25*, no. 2 (1981): 33–39. On the evolution of the townsite, see also Robert C. Scace, "Banff Town Site: A Historical-Geographical View of Urban Development in a Canadian National Park," in *Canadian Parks in Perspective*, ed. J.G. Nelson, 197–208 (Montreal: Harvest House).

7   David R. Boyd, *Unnatural Law: Rethinking Canadian Environmental Law and Policy* (Vancouver: UBC Press, 2003), 168–69.

8   C. Lloyd Brown-John, "Canada's National Parks Policy: From Bureaucrats to Collaborative Managers," Unpublished paper, Canadian Political Science Association Conference, York University, Toronto, 2006; http://www.cpsa-acsp.ca/papers-2006/Brown-John.pdf; accessed 18 October 2009.

9   Joseph Petulla, *American Environ-mental History: The Exploitation and Conservation of Natural Resources* (San Francisco: Boyd and Fraser, 1977), 219. Quoted in PearlAnn Reichwein, "Beyond the Visionary Mountains: The Alpine Club of Canada and the Canadian National Park Idea, 1906 to 1969," 26. On the problematic character of traditional notions of wilderness, see William Cronon, "The Trouble with Wilderness; or, Getting back to the Wrong Nature," in *Uncommon Ground: Toward Reinventing Nature*, ed. William Cronon, 69–90 (New York: W.W. Norton, 1995).

10   Norman Henderson, "Wilderness and the Nature Conservation Ideal: A Comparative Analysis, Britain, Canada and the United States" CSERGE Working paper GEC 92-22, University College, London, United Kingdom, n.d.

11   For example, Parks Canada's Chief Scientist has argued: "In an ideal world, protected areas would be very large and managed with no human interference." Stephen Woodley, "Planning and Managing for Ecological Integrity in Canada's National Parks," in *Parks and Protected Areas in Canada: Planning and Management*, 3d ed., ed. Philip Dearden and Rick Rollins (Toronto: Oxford University Press, 2009), 129.

12   Parks Canada's policy of ecological integrity has recently been critiqued by scientists arguing that it conforms to a "wilderness-normative" concept that does not include humans. See Douglas A. Clark, Shaun Fluker, and Lee Risby, "Deconstructing Ecological Integrity in Canadian National Parks," in *Transforming Parks and Protected Areas: Policy and Governance in a Changing World*, ed. Kevin S. Hanna, Douglas A. Clark, and D. Scott Slocombe, 54–68 (New York: Routledge, 2008).

13   Norman Henderson, "Wilderness and the Nature Conservation Ideal: A Comparative Analysis. Britain, Canada, and the United States," CSERGE Working Paper GEC 92-22, University College, London, United Kingdom, n.d.

14   Parks Canada, *Guiding Principles and Operational Policies* (Ottawa, 1994); http://www.pc.gc.ca/eng/docs/pc/poli/princip/index.aspx; accessed 4 July 2010.

15   See Rosalind Warner, "A Comparison of Ideas in the Development and Governance of National Parks and Protected Areas in the US and Canada," *International Journal of Canadian Studies* 37 (2008): 13–40.

16   For the current iteration, i.e., the third edition of the National Parks System Plan, see: http://www.pc.gc.ca/eng/docs/v-g/nation/nation1.aspx; accessed 4 July 2010.

Appendix A:
Canada's National Parks and National Park Reserves

PARK NAME	DATE ESTABLISHED
BANFF	1885
GLACIER	1886
YOHO	1886
WATERTON LAKES	1895
ST. LAWRENCE ISLANDS	1904
JASPER	1907
BUFFALO	1911
ELK ISLAND	1913
MOUNT REVELSTOKE	1914
POINT PELEE	1915
KOOTENAY	1918
NEMISKAM	1920
MENISSAWOK	1922
WAWASKESEY	1922
WOOD BUFFALO	1922
PRINCE ALBERT	1927
GEORGIAN BAY ISLANDS	1929
RIDING MOUNTAIN	1929
CAPE BRETON HIGHLANDS	1936
PRINCE EDWARD ISLAND	1937
FUNDY	1948
TERRA NOVA	1957
KEJIMKUJIK	1968
KOUCHIBOUGUAC	1969
FORILLON	1970
LA MAURICIE	1970
PACIFIC RIM (RESERVE)	1970
KLUANE (PARK AND RESERVE)	1972
GROS MORNE	1973
NAHANNI (RESERVE)	1976
PUKASKWA	1978
GRASSLANDS	1981
IVVAVIK	1984
MINGAN ARCHIPELAGO (RESERVE)	1984
BRUCE PENINSULA	1987
GWAII HAANAS (RESERVE)	1988
AULAVIK	1992
VUNTUT	1995
TUKTUT NOGAIT	1996
WAPUSK	1996
AUYUITTUQ	2001
QUTTINIRPAAQ	2001
SIRMILIK	2001
GULF ISLANDS (RESERVE)	2003
UKKUSIKSALIK	2003
TORNGAT MOUNTAINS	2005

Appendix B:
National Parks Zoning System, Parks Canada Agency

From Parks Canada Agency, *Guiding Principles and Operational Policies*, 2006.

The national parks zoning system is an integrated approach by which land and water areas are classified according to ecosystem and cultural resource protection requirements, and their capability and suitability to provide opportunities for visitor experiences. It is one part of an array of management strategies used by Parks Canada to assist in maintaining ecological integrity through providing a framework for the area-specific application of policy directions, such as for resource management, appropriate activities, and research. As such, zoning provides direction for the activities of park managers and park visitors alike. The application of zoning requires a sound information base related to both ecosystem structure, function and sensitivity, as well as the opportunities and impacts of existing and potential visitor experiences.

The zoning system provides a means to reflect principles of ecological integrity by protecting park lands and resources and ensuring a minimum of human-induced change. In certain national parks not all zones will be represented. Where zones which permit a concentration of visitor activities and supporting services and facilities are required (i.e., Zones IV and V), they will occupy no more than a small proportion of a national park.

In some cases, environmentally or culturally sensitive areas or sites may warrant special management but do not fit the zoning designations below. Park management plans will include the guidelines necessary for the protection and use of such areas or sites. Their designation complements the zoning system and is important to the protection of the full range of valued resources in certain national parks. Likewise, a temporal zoning designation may be considered for certain areas as part of the management planning program. Ecosystem management requirements will be paramount in consideration of any temporal zones.

The national parks zoning system will apply to all land and water areas of national parks, and to other natural areas within the Parks Canada system as appropriate. It does not preclude resource harvesting activities which are permitted by virtue of national park reserve status, land claim settlements and/or by new park establishment agreements.

Zone I – Special Preservation

Specific areas or features which deserve special preservation because they contain or support unique, threatened or endangered natural or cultural features, or are among the best examples of the features that represent a natural region. Preservation is the key consideration. Motorized access and circulation will not be permitted. In cases where the fragility of the area precludes any public access, every effort will be made to provide park visitors with appropriate off-site programs and exhibits interpreting the special characteristics of the zone.

Zone II – Wilderness

Extensive areas which are good representations of a natural region and which will be conserved in a wilderness state. The perpetuation of ecosystems with minimal human interference is the key consideration. Zones I and II will together constitute the majority of the area of all but the smallest national parks, and will make the greatest contribution toward the conservation of ecosystem integrity.

Zone II areas offer opportunities for visitors to experience, first hand, a park's natural and cultural heritage values through outdoor recreation activities which are dependent upon and within the capacity of the park's ecosystems, and which require few, if any, rudimentary services and facilities. Where the area is large enough, visitors will also have the opportunity to experience remoteness and solitude. Opportunities for outdoor recreation activities will be encouraged only when they do not conflict with maintaining the wilderness itself. For this reason, motorized access and circulation will not be permitted, with the possible exception of strictly controlled air access in remote northern parks....

Parks Canada will use a variety of other direct and indirect strategies for managing public use, and will evaluate the effectiveness of these strategies on a regular basis.

A CENTURY OF PARKS CANADA

Zone III – Natural Environment

Areas which are managed as natural environments, and which provide opportunities for visitors to experience a park's natural and cultural heritage values through outdoor recreation activities requiring minimal services and facilities of a rustic nature. While motorized access may be allowed, it will be controlled. Public transit that facilitates heritage appreciation will be preferred. Park management plans may define provisions for terminating or limiting private motorized access.

Zone IV – Outdoor Recreation

Limited areas which are capable of accommodating a broad range of opportunities for understanding, appreciation and enjoyment of the park's heritage values and related essential services and facilities, in ways that impact the ecological integrity of the park to the smallest extent possible, and whose defining feature is direct access by motorized vehicles. Park management plans may define provisions for limiting private motorized access and circulation.

Zone V – Park Services

Communities in existing national parks which contain a concentration of visitor services and support facilities. Specific activities, services and facilities in this zone will be defined and directed by the community planning process. Major park operation and administrative functions may also be accommodated in this zone. Wherever possible, Parks Canada will locate these functions to maintain regional ecological integrity.

⅔⅔

Notes on Contributors

Ben Bradley is a doctoral candidate in the Department of History at Queen's University. He studies the social, cultural, and environmental history of western Canada, focusing primarily on twentieth-century British Columbia. His dissertation examines how British Columbians' experiences of nature and history in the province's Interior were shaped by the automobile, the highway network, and the practice of driving in the period 1925–75.

Claire Elizabeth Campbell is an associate professor of History and Canadian Studies at Dalhousie University, where she also teaches in the College of Sustainability. She is the author of *Shaped by the West Wind: Nature and History in Georgian Bay* (UBC Press, 2004). Her work centres on the relationship between the natural environment, regional identity, and Canadian history at designated historic places.

George Colpitts teaches environmental history at the University of Calgary and researches animals in human history from the era of the western fur trade to the twentieth century. Among his publications is *Game in the Garden: A Human History of Wildlife in Western Canada to 1940* (UBC Press, 2002).

Olivier Craig-Dupont is a PhD candidate in Aménagement at the Université de Montréal. After an undergraduate degree in Science and Technology Studies (STS) from Université du Québec à Montréal, he completed a MA in Études Québécoises at the Université du Québec à Trois-Rivières. During the course of this program, he analyzed the environmental history of La Mauricie National Park. He has made numerous presentations about his research and received a Royal Society of Canada Award for one of them. He is currently working on a SSHRC-funded PhD research project on the political ecology challenges of private protected areas in rural landscapes.

Lyle Dick is the West Coast Historian with the Parks Canada Agency in Vancouver and the recipient of three Parks Canada awards of excellence. Author of *Muskox Land: Ellesmere Island in the Age of Contact* (University of Calgary Press, 2001; winner of the Harold Adams Innis Prize in 2003) and *Farmers "Making Good": The Development of Abernethy District, Saskatchewan, 1880–1920* (co-winner of the Canadian Historical Association's Clio Prize in 1990; rev. ed., University of Calgary Press, 2008), he has also published thirty refereed articles or book chapters on aspects of Canadian, Arctic, and American history and historiography. He is the president elect of the Canadian Historical Association.

Gwyn Langemann is a senior archaeologist with Parks Canada's Western and Northern Service Centre. Educated at the University of Calgary and Simon Fraser University, she has worked on a wide variety of archaeological projects in southern Alberta, British Columbia, and Saskatchewan. In the backcountry of Banff, Waterton Lakes, and Jasper, she works with parks staff who share their wide knowledge and love of the mountains.

Alan MacEachern teaches History at the University of Western Ontario and is the Director of NiCHE: Network in Canadian History and Environment. He has written extensively on Canadian environmental history, including *Natural Selections: National Parks in Atlantic Canada, 1935–1970* (McGill-Queen's University Press, 2001).

I.S. MacLaren teaches at the University of Alberta in the departments of History and Classics, and English and Film Studies. Circumpolar Arctic history, the genres of exploration and travel literature from Richard Hakluyt to the Lonely Planet, the history of the Rocky Mountain national parks, and early North American literature comprise the foci of his teaching and research. The study of the art and writing of and the ethnohistory engendered by artist-traveller Paul Kane during his travels across British North America (1845–48) remain ongoing subjects of research.

Brad Martin is a doctoral candidate in the department of history at Northwestern University. He is currently completing his dissertation, "Landscapes of Power: Native Peoples, National Parks, and the Making of a Modern Wilderness in the Yukon Territory and Alaska, 1940–2000."

Since 1986 **David Neufeld** has worked on Yukon protected heritage areas for Parks Canada. Using a combination of archival study and community-based collaborative research, his work focuses on how the history of protected areas illustrates the changing relationships between the state and indigenous peoples in north western Canada. His findings contribute to positive working relationships between Parks Canada and Yukon First Nations. His co-authored *Chilkoot Trail* (Lost Moose, 1996) was awarded the Canadian Historical Association's Clio Prize for Northern history. In 2004–5 he was a Visiting Scholar at the Scott Polar Research Institute, Cambridge University.

Ronald Rudin is a professor of History at Concordia University. He is the author of six books and producer of two documentary films that touch upon the economic, social, intellectual, and cultural history of French Canada. He has long had an interest in questions of public memory, most recently in *Remembering and Forgetting in Acadie: A Historian's Journey through Public Memory* (University of Toronto Press, 2009) and the associated website (rememberingacadie.concordia.ca), winner of the 2010 book award of the National Council of Public History. He is also a Fellow of the Royal Society of Canada.

John Sandlos is an associate professor of history at Memorial University of Newfoundland. His interest in protected areas stems from work as an interpreter in Georgian Bay Islands and Pukaskwa National Parks. He is the author of *Hunters at the Margin* (UBC Press, 2007), a history of conflict between Native hunters and the state over wildlife resources, which includes large sections devoted to Wood Buffalo National Park and the Thelon Game Sanctuary. He has also published case studies on the expulsion of natives and non-natives from Point Pelee, Georgian Bay Islands, and Riding Mountain National Parks.

C.J. Taylor is a graduate of Simon Fraser and Carleton universities. He worked as an historian for Parks Canada in Ottawa and Calgary, where he developed his interest in both the history of national historic sites and national parks. He is the author of *Negotiating the Past: The Making of Canada's National Historic Parks and Sites* (McGill-Queen's University Press, 1990) and *Jasper: A History of the Place and Its People* (Fitzhenry & Whiteside, 2009). He is now retired in Calgary.

W.A. (Bill) Waiser is professor of History and A.S. Morton Research Chair at the University of Saskatchewan. He is the author of several books, including the award-winning *Saskatchewan: A New History* (Fifth House, 2005). Waiser was awarded the Saskatchewan Order of Merit, the province's highest honour, in 2006, and elected a fellow of the Royal Society of Canada the following year. Prior to his Saskatchewan appointment in 1984, he was Yukon historian for the Canadian Parks Service.

Select Bibliography

Archival Sources

NATIONAL ARCHIVES OF CANADA:

Harkin, J.B., papers. MG 30 E169, vol. 2

Records of the Canadian Park Service. RG 84

Records of the Department of Indian Affairs, RG 10; of the Department of Indian and Northern Affairs, RG 22; Northern Affairs Program, RG 85.

Records of the Canadian Wildlife Service. RG 109.

Records of the Department of the Interior. RG 39.

Williams, M.B., Government of Canada personnel papers. RG 32, vol. 480.

Williams, M.B., papers. R12219-0-3-E

Whyte Museum of the Canadian Rockies, H.U. Green Papers, M2 43.

Jasper-Yellowhead Museum and Archives, Lewis Swift Fonds (84.72) and Constance Peterson Fonds (78.01).

Yukon Archives, Records of the Yukon Government, YRG1, Series 2.

Girling, Frances. Oral interview with Alan MacEachern, 28 January 2006.

Williams, M.B. Oral interview with Wertheimer, Ruth and Len. October 1969 and June 1970. In possession of Alan MacEachern.

Secondary Sources

Abbey, Edward. *Desert Solitaire: A Season in the Wilderness*. New York: Touchstone, 1968.

Abrams, G.W.P. *Prince Albert: The First Century, 1866–1966*. Saskatoon: Modern Press, 1966.

Alderson, Lucy, and John Marsh. "J.B. Harkin, National Parks and Roads." *Park News* 15 (Summer 1979): 9–16.

Anderson, David, and Richard H. Gove, eds. *Conservation in Africa: Peoples, Policies, and Practice*. Cambridge: Cambridge University Press, 1990.

Anderson, Ross, and Brian O.K. Reeves. *An Archaeological survey of Jasper National Park*. Ottawa: National Historic Sites Service Manuscript Report Series No. 158, 1975.

Apostle, Alisa. "Canada, Vacations Unlimited: The Canadian Government Tourism Industry, 1934–1959." PhD dissertation, Queen's University, 2003.

Armstrong, Christopher, and H.V. Nelles. *The Painted Valley: Artists Along the Bow River, 1845–2000*. Calgary: University of Calgary Press, 2007.

Banff–Bow Valley Task Force. *Banff–Bow Valley: At the Crossroads*, 2 vols. Ottawa: Minister of Supply and Service, 1996.

Battin, J.G., and J.G. Nelson. *Man's Impact on Point Pelee National Park*. National and Provincial Parks Association of Canada, 1978.

Bella, Leslie. *Parks for Profit*. Montreal: Harvest House, 1987.

Bellefleur, Michel. *L'évolution du loisir au Québec: essai sociohistorique*. Québec: Presses de l'Université du Québec, 1997.

Belliveau, Joel. "Acadian New Brunswick's Ambivalent Leap into the Canadian Liberal Order." In *Creating Postwar Canada: Community, Diversity, and Dissent 1945–75*, edited by Magda Fahrni and Robert Rutherdale, 61–88. Vancouver: UBC Press, 2008.

Berger, Thomas R. *Northern Frontier, Northern Homeland: The Report of the Mackenzie Valley Pipeline Inquiry*, rev. ed. Toronto: Douglas & McIntyre, 1988.

Bernard, David, et al. *State of the Banff–Bow Valley*, rev. ed. Banff: Banff–Bow Valley Study, 1996 [1995].

Bernier, Marc-André. *Underwater Archaeology Survey of the Minnewanka Submerged Townsite Banff National Park, 1992*. Ottawa: National Historic Parks and Sites Branch, Parks Canada, 1994.

Berton, Pierre. *Hollywood's Canada: The Americanization of our National Image*. Toronto: McClelland & Stewart, 1975.

Bess, Michael. *The Light-Green Society: Ecology and Technological Modernity in France, 1960–2000*. Chicago: University of Chicago Press, 2003.

Biel, Alice Wondrak. *Do (Not) Feed the Bears: The Fitful History of Wildlife and Tourists in Yellowstone*. Lawrence: University of Kansas Press, 2006.

Binnema, Theodore, and Melanie Niemi. "'Let the Line be Drawn Now': Wilderness, Conservation, and the Exclusion of Aboriginal People from Banff National Park in Canada." *Environmental History* 11 (2006): 724–50.

Bostock, H.S. *Pack Horse Tracks: Recollections of a geologist's life in British Columbia and the Yukon, 1914–1954*. Whitehorse: Geoscience Forum, 1990.

Bouin, Thierry. *Aménagement et exploitation faunique antérieurs à la création du parc national de la Mauricie (1970)*. Ottawa: Parks Canada, 1979.

Boyd, David R. *Unnatural Law: Rethinking Canadian Environmental Law and Policy*. Vancouver: UBC Press, 2003.

Brelsford, Karen Jacqueline. "Dendroarchaeological and contextual investigations of remote log structures in Jasper, Banff, and Kootenay national parks, Canada." MSc thesis, University of Victoria, 2004.

Brockington, Dan. *Fortress Conservation: The Preservation of the Mkomazi Game Reserve, Tanzania*. Oxford: James Currey, 2002.

Brower, Jennifer. *Lost Tracks: Buffalo National Park, 1909–1939*. Edmonton: AU Press, 2008.

Brown, Jessica, Nora Mitchell, and Michael Beresford, eds. *The Protected Landscape Approach: Linking Nature, Culture and Community*. Gland, Switz., and Cambridge: International Union for Conservation of Nature, 2005.

Brown, Lorne Alvin. "The Bennett Government, Political Stability, and the Politics of the Unemployment Relief Camps, 1930–1935." PhD dissertation, Queen's University, 1983.

Brown-John, C. Lloyd. "Canada's National Parks Policy: From Bureaucrats to Collaborative Managers." Paper presented at the Canadian Political Science Association Conference, York University, Toronto, 2006.

Bryant, Raymond L. *The Political Ecology of Forestry in Burma, 1824–1994*. Honolulu: University of Hawaii Press, 1997.

Buggey, Susan. *An Approach to Aboriginal Cultural Landscapes*. Ottawa: Parks Canada, 1999.

Burns, Robert J., with Mike Schintz. *Guardians of the Wild: A History of the Warden Service of Canada's National Parks*. Calgary: University of Calgary Press, 2000.

Byrne, A. Roger. *Man and Landscape Change in the Banff National Park Area before 1911*. Studies in Land Use History and Landscape Change. Calgary: University of Calgary, 1968.

Byrne, William J. "The Archaeological Survey of Alberta: Prospects for the Future." In *Alberta Archaeology: Prospect and Retrospect*, edited by T.A. Moore, 15–20. Lethbridge: University of Lethbridge, Archaeological Society of Alberta, 1981.

Calef, George W. "The Urgent Need for a Canadian Arctic Wildlife Range." *Nature Canada* 3 (1974): 3–10.

Canada. *Regulations for Dominion Forest Reserves*. Ottawa: Government Printing Bureau, 1908.

————. Auditor-General. Annual Reports. 1911–30.

————. Commissioner of National Parks. Annual Report. 1912–30.

————. House of Commons. Debates. 1885–.

————. *Politique des parcs nationaux/National Parks Policy*. 1969.

————. Environment Canada. *Canadian Protected Areas Status Report 2000–2005*. 2006.

Canadian Council on Ecological Areas. *Canadian Guidebook for the Application of IUCN Protected Area Categories*. Occasional Paper no. 18. Ottawa: 2008.

Canadian Parks Council, *Aboriginal Peoples and Canada's Parks and Protected Areas: Case Studies*. Ottawa: 2008.

Carr, Ethan. *Mission 66: Modernism and the National Park dilemma*. Amherst: University of Massachusetts Press, in association with Library of American Landscape History, 2007.

Catton, Theodore. *Inhabited Wilderness: Indians, Eskimos, and National Parks in Alaska*. Albuquerque: University of New Mexico Press, 1997.

Cavell, Edward. *Legacy in Ice: the Vaux Family and the Canadian Alps*. Banff: Whyte Foundation, 1983.

Chatty, Dawn, and Marcus Colchester, eds. *Conservation and Mobile Indigenous Peoples: Displacement, Forced Settlement, and Sustainable Development*. Oxford: Berghahn Books, 2002.

Chrétien, Jean. *Straight from the Heart*. Toronto: Key Porter, 1985.

Chris, Cynthia. *Watching Wildlife*. Minneapolis: University of Minnesota Press, 2006.

Christen, Catherine A., and Lisa Mighetto. "Environmental History as Public History." *The Public Historian* 26 (2004): 9–19.

Christensen, Ole. *Banff Prehistory: Prehistoric Settlement and Subsistence Technology in Banff National Park, Alberta*. Ottawa: Parks Canada Manuscript Report Series No. 67, 1971.

————. "Banff National Park Prehistory: Settlement and Subsistence." MA thesis, University of Calgary, 1973.

Choquette, Wayne, and Daryl W. Fedje. *Yoho National Park Archaeological Resource Description and Analysis*. Calgary: Archaeological Services, Canadian Parks Service, Environment Canada, 1993.

————, and Rod Pickard. *Archaeological Resource Description and Analysis, Kootenay National Park*. Calgary: Archaeological Research Services Unit, Western Region, Environment Canada, Canadian Parks Service, 1989.

Coates, Ken S. *Best Left As Indians: Native-White Relations in the Yukon Territory, 1840–1973*. Montreal: McGill-Queen's University Press, 1991.

Coates, Peter A. *The Trans-Alaska Pipeline Controversy: Technology, Conservation, and the Frontier*. Anchorage: University of Alaska Press, 1993.

Coleman, A.P. *The Canadian Rockies: New and Old Trails*. Toronto: Henry Frowde, 1911.

Colpitts, George. *Game in the Garden: A Human History of Wildlife in Western Canada to 1940*. Vancouver: UBC Press, 2002.

Crawford, K.G., et al. *Banff, Jasper and Waterton Lakes National Parks: A Report prepared for the Department of Northern Affairs and National Resources respecting certain aspects of the operation of these National Parks and the Townsites therein*. Kingston: Institute of Local Government, Queen's University, 1960.

Cronin, Keri. J. "Manufacturing National Park Nature: Photography, Ecology and the Wilderness Industry of Jasper National Park." PhD dissertation, Queen's University, 2004.

———. "'The Bears are Plentiful and Frequently Good Camera Subjects': Postcards and the Framing of Interspecies Encounters in the Canadian Rockies." *Mosaic* 39 (2006): 77–92.

Cronon, William, ed. *Uncommon Ground: Toward Reinventing Nature*. New York: W.W. Norton, 1995.

———. "The Trouble with Wilderness: Or, Getting Back to the Wrong Nature." *Environmental History* 1 (1996): 7–28.

Cruikshank, Julie. *The Social Life of Stories: Narrative and Knowledge in the Yukon Territory*. Vancouver: UBC Press, 1998.

———. *Do Glaciers Listen? Local Knowledge, Colonial Encounters, and Social Imagination*. Vancouver: UBC Press, 2005.

Cumming, Peter. "Canada's North and Native Rights." In *Aboriginal People and the Law: Indian, Metis and Inuit Rights in Canada*, edited by Bradford W. Morse, 695–764. Ottawa: Carleton University Press, 1985.

Cypher, Jennifer, and Eric Higgs. "Colonizing the Imagination: Disney's Wilderness Lodge." *Capitalism, Nature, Socialism* 8 (1997): 107–30.

Dacks, Gurston. *A Choice of Futures: Politics in the Canadian North*. Toronto: Methuen, 1981.

Damp, Jonathan E., Catherine E. Connolly, and Thayer V. Smith. *Conservation Archaeological Studies at EhPw-2 and EhPw-4 Banff National Park*. Ottawa: Environment Canada, Parks Service Microfiche Report Series No. 335, 1980.

Dawson, Michael. *Selling British Columbia: Tourism and Consumer Culture, 1890–1970*. Vancouver: UBC Press, 2004.

Day, John Chadwick, et al., eds. *Protected Areas and the Regional Planning Imperative in North America: Integrating Nature Conservation and Sustainable Development.* Calgary: University of Calgary Press, 2003.

Dearden, Philip, and Rick Rollins, eds. *Parks and Protected Areas in Canada: Planning and Management,* 3rd ed. Toronto: Oxford University Press, 2009.

Denhez, Marc. *Unearthing the Law: Archaeological Legislation on Lands in Canada.* Ottawa: Prepared by SynParSys Consulting Inc. for the Archaeological Services Branch, Parks Canada Agency, 2000.

Dick, Lyle. "Forgotten Roots: The Gardens of Wasagaming." *NeWest Review* 12 (1986): 10–11

———. *Muskox Land: Ellesmere Island in the Age of Contact.* Calgary: University of Calgary Press, 2001.

Dosman, Edgar J. *The National Interest: The Politics of Northern Development, 1968–1975.* Toronto: McClelland & Stewart, 1975.

Dudley, Nigel. "Why is Biodiversity Conservation Important in Protected Landscapes?" *George Wright Forum* 26 (2009): 31–38.

Dunlap, Thomas R. "Wildlife, Science, and the National Parks, 1920–1940." *Pacific Historical Review* 59 (1990): 187–202.

Dyck, Ian. "Canadian Prairies Archaeology, 1857–1886: Exploration and Self Development." *Canadian Journal of Archaeology* 33 (2009): 1–39.

Elliot, Jack. *Jasper National Park and Ya-Ha-Tinda Ranch Archaeological Survey.* Ottawa: Department of Indian Affairs and Northern Development, National Historic Sites Service, National and Historic Parks Branch Manuscript Report Series No. 44, 1971.

Fairhead, James, and Melissa Leach. *Misreading the African Landscape: Society and Ecology in a Forest Savanna Mosaic.* Cambridge: Cambridge University Press, 1996.

Feddema-Leonard, Susan, Estella Cheverie, and Roger Blunt, eds. *People and Peaks of Willmore Wilderness Park, 1800s to mid-1900s.* Edmonton: Willmore Wilderness Foundation and Whitefox Circle Inc., 2007.

Fedje, Daryl W. *Archaeological Resource Description and Analysis, Banff National Park.* Calgary: Archaeological Research Services Unit, Western Region, Environment Canada, Canadian Parks Service, 1989.

———. "Early Human Presence in Banff National Park." In *Early Human Occupation in British Columbia,* edited by Roy L. Carlson and Luke Dalla Bona, 35–44. Vancouver: UBC Press, 1996.

———, and James M. White. *Vermilion Lakes Archaeology and Palaeoecology: Trans-Canada Highway Mitigation in Banff National Park.* Ottawa: Environment Canada, Parks Service Microfiche Report Series No. 463, 1988.

————, et al. "Vermilion Lakes Site: Adaptations and Environments in the Canadian Rockies During the Latest Pleistocene and Early Holocene." *American Antiquity* 60 (1995): 81–108.

Feit, Harvey A. "Re-cognizing Co-management as Co-governance: Visions and Histories of Conservation at James Bay." *Anthropologica* 47 (2005): 267–88.

Fenge, Terry. "National Parks in the Canadian Arctic: The Case of the Nunavut Land Claim Agreement." *Environments* 22 (1993): 21–36.

————. "Political Development and Environmental Management in Northern Canada: The Case of the Nunavut Agreement." *Etudes/Inuit/Studies* 16 (1992): 115–41.

Fiege, Mark. *Irrigated Eden: The Making of an Agricultural Landscape in the American West.* Seattle: University of Washington Press, 1999.

Fluker, Shaun. "Ecological integrity and the law: The view from Canada's National Parks." Paper presented at the Parks for Tomorrow 40th Anniversary Conference, Calgary, 2008.

Foster, Janet. *Working for Wildlife: The Beginnings of Preservation in Canada*, rev. ed. Toronto: University of Toronto Press, 1998.

Fox, Stephen. *The American Conservation Movement: John Muir and His Legacy.* Madison: University of Wisconsin Press, 1981.

Francis, Daniel. *A Road For Canada: An Illustrated History of the Trans-Canada Highway.* Vancouver: Stanton, Atkins, and Dosil, 2006.

Francis, Peter D., William Perry, and E. Gwyn Langemann. *Cultural Resource Management and Archaeological Research Initiatives at the Christensen Site, Banff National Park.* Ottawa: Environment Canada, Parks, Research Bulletin No. 303, 1994.

————, and William Perry. *Archaeological Resource Description and Analysis: Mount Revelstoke and Glacier National Parks.* Calgary: Cultural Resource Services, Western and Northern Service Centre, Parks Canada Agency, 2000.

Gagnon, Serge. *L'échiquier touristique québécois.* Sainte-Foy: Presses de l'Université du Québec, 2003.

Gillis, R. Peter, and Thomas R. Roach. *Lost Initiatives: Canada's Forest Industries, Forest Policy, and Forest Conservation.* Westport, CT: Greenwood, 1986.

————. "The American Influence on Conservation in Canada 1899–1911." *Journal of Forest and Conservation History* 30 (1986): 160–74.

Gittings, Christopher E. *Canadian National Cinema: Ideology, Difference and Representation.* London: Routledge, 2002.

Grace, Sherrill E. *Canada and the Idea of North.* Montreal: McGill-Queen's University Press, 2001.

Guha, Ramachandra. *The Unquiet Woods: Ecological Change and Peasant Resistance in the Himalaya.* New York: Oxford University Press, 1989.

Hamilton, John David. *Arctic Revolution: Social Change in the Northwest Territories, 1935–1994.* Toronto: Dundurn Press, 1994.

Hamin, Elisabeth M. "Western European Approaches to Landscape Protection: A Review of the Literature." *Journal of Planning Literature* 16 (2002): 339–58.

Hanna, Kevin S., Douglas A. Clark, and D. Scott Slocombe. *Transforming Parks and Protected Areas: Policy and Governance in a Changing World.* New York: Routledge, 2008.

Hardy, René, and Normand Séguin, eds. *Histoire de la Mauricie.* Québec: Institut québécois de recherche sur la culture, 2004.

Harkin, J.B. *The Origin and Meaning of the National Parks of Canada, Extracts from the Papers of the Late Jas. B. Harkin, First Commissioner of the National Parks of Canada.* Compiled by Mabel B. Williams. Saskatoon: H.R. Larson, 1957.

Harp, Elmer. *North to the Yukon Territory via the Alaska Highway in 1948: Field notes of the Andover-Harvard Expedition.* Whitehorse: Yukon Tourism and Culture, 2005.

Harris, Richard. *Creeping Conformity: How Canada became Suburban, 1900–1960.* Toronto: University of Toronto Press, 2004.

Hart, E.J. *The Selling of Canada: The CPR and the Beginnings of Canadian Tourism.* Banff: Altitude, 1983.

——. "See This World before the Next: Tourism and the CPR." In *The CPR West: The Iron Road and the Making of a Nation,* edited by Hugh A. Dempsey, 151–70. Vancouver: Douglas & McIntyre, 1984.

——. *J.B. Harkin: Father of Canada's National Parks.* Edmonton: University of Alberta Press, 2010.

Hart, Hazel. *History of Hinton.* Hinton: by the author, 1980.

Harvey, Mark W.T. *A Symbol of Wilderness: Echo Park and the American Conservation Movement.* Seattle: University of Washington Press, 2000.

Harvey, R.G. *Carving the Western Path: By River, Rail, and Road through BC's Southern Mountains.* Surrey, BC: Heritage House, 1998.

Fay, Samuel Prescott. *The Forgotten Explorer: Samuel Prescott Fay's 1914 Expedition to the Northern Rockies.* Edited by Charles Helm and Mike Murtha. Victoria, BC: Rocky Mountain Books, 2009.

Henberg, Marvin. "Pancultural Wilderness." In *Wild Ideas,* edited by David Rothenberg, 59–70. Minneapolis: University of Minnesota Press, 1995.

Henderson, Ailsa. *Nunavut: Rethinking Political Culture.* Vancouver: UBC Press, 2008.

Henderson, Gavin. "James Bernard Harkin: The Father of Canadian National Parks." *Borealis* 5 (1994): 28–33.

Henderson, Norman. "Wilderness and the Nature Conservation Ideal: A Comparative Analysis, Britain, Canada and the United States." The Centre for Social and

Economic Research on the Global Environment (CSERGE) working paper GEC 92-22. University College, London, n.d.

Herrero, Stephen. "Introduction to the Biology and Management of Bears." In *Bears: Their Biology and Management*. Papers of the International Conference on Bear Research and Management, Calgary, Canada, November 1970. Morges, Switzerland: International Union, 1972.

——. *Bear Attacks: Their Causes and Avoidance*. Piscataway, NJ: Winchester Press, 1985.

Higgs, Eric. *Nature by Design: People, Natural Process and Ecological Restoration*. Cambridge, MA: MIT Press, 2003.

Hildebrandt, Walter. "Historical Analysis of Parks Canada and Banff National Park 1968–1995." Unpublished report prepared for the Banff–Bow Valley Study, December 1995.

Hilliker, John. *Canada's Department of External Affairs*, vol.1: *The Early Years, 1909–1946*. Montreal: Institute of Public Administration of Canada and McGill-Queen's University Press, 1990.

Hochstein, Barry A. "New Rights or No Rights?: COPE and the Federal Government of Canada." MA thesis, University of Calgary, 1987.

Hudecek-Cuffe, Caroline. *Final Report, Department of Anthropology University of Alberta Archaeological Field School Jasper National Park July 15 – August 20, 1997. Permit No. WRA 97-03*. Edmonton: Consultant's report for Parks Canada, 1994.

——, and Alison J. Landals. *Archaeological Resource Impact Assessment, Banff Springs Hotel Golf Course and Staff Housing Expansion*. Ottawa: Environment Canada, Canadian Parks Service Microfiche Report Series No. 411, 1987.

Hulan, Renée. *Northern Experience and the Myths of Canadian Culture*. Montreal: McGill-Queen's University Press, 2002.

Hunt, Constance, Rusty Miller, and Donna Tingley. *Wilderness Area: Legislative Alternatives for the Establishment of a Wilderness Area in the Northern Yukon*. Ottawa: Canadian Arctic Resources Committee, 1979.

Igoe, Jim. *Conservation and Globalization: A Study of National Parks and Indigenous Communities from East Africa to South Dakota*. Belmont, CA: Thomson Wadsworth, 2004.Ingold, Tim. *The Perception of the Environment: Essays in livelihood, dwelling and skill*. London: Routledge, 2000.

International Union for Conservation of Nature. Protected Areas Management Categories. Last updated 10 September 2010. http://www.iucn.org/about/work/programmes/pa/pa_products/wcpa_categories/pa_categoryv/.

Inuit Tapirisat of Canada. *Inuit Tapirisat of Canada Report on Proposals to Establish National Wilderness Parks in Inuit Nunangat*. Ottawa: Inuit Tapirisat of Canada, 1979.

Isenberg, Andrew. *The Destruction of the Bison: An Environmental History, 1750–1920*. Cambridge: Cambridge University Press, 2000.

Jackson, Kenneth. *Crabgrass Frontier: The Suburbanization of the United States.* New York: 1987.

Jacoby, Karl. *Crimes Against Nature: Squatters, Poachers, Thieves, and the Hidden History of American Conservation.* Berkeley: University of California Press, 2001.

Janes, Robert. "Smith-Wintemberg Award: Richard G. Forbis." *Canadian Journal of Archaeology* 8 (1984): 1–2.

Jasen, Patricia. *Wild Things: Nature, Culture, and Tourism in Ontario, 1790–1914.* Toronto: University of Toronto Press, 1995.

Jean, Bruno. "La 'ruralité' bas-laurentienne: développement agricole et sous-développement rural." *Recherches sociographiques* 29 (1998) 239–63.

———. "Les études rurales québécoises entre les approches monographiques et typologiques." *Recherches sociographiques* 47 (2006): 503–29.

Jones, D.B. *Movies and Memoranda: An InterpretiveHistory of the National Film Board.* Toronto: Canadian Film Institute, 1981.

Kaufmann, Eric. "'Naturalizing the Nation': The Rise of Naturalistic Nationalism in the United States and Canada." *Comparative Studies in Society and History* 40 (1998): 666–95.

Kauffmann, John M. *Alaska's Brooks Range: The Ultimate Mountains.* Seattle: The Mountaineers, 1992.

Kay, Charles E., et al. *Long-Term Ecosystem States and Processes in Banff National Park and the Central Canadian Rockies.* Ottawa: Parks Canada National Parks Branch, Occasional Paper No. 9, 1999.

Killan, Gerald, and George Warecki. "J.R. Dymond and Frank A. Macdougall: Science and Government Policy in Algonquin Provincial Park, 1931–1954." *Scientia Canadensis* 22 (1998): 131–56.

Kopas, Paul. *Taking the Air: Ideas and Change in Canada's National Parks.* Vancouver: UBC Press, 2007.

Kraulis, J.A., and Kevin McNamee. *National Parks of Canada*, rev. ed. Toronto: Key Porter, 2004.

Krause, M., and V. Golla. "Northern Athapaskan Languages." *Handbook of the Northern American Indians.* Vol. 6: Subarctic. Ed. June Helm. Washington: Smithsonian Institution, 1981.

Kretch III, Shepard. *The Ecological Indian: Myth and History.* New York: W.W. Norton, 1999.

Kulchyski, Peter. *Like the Sound of a Drum: Aboriginal Cultural Politics in Denendeh and Nunavut.* Winnipeg: University of Manitoba Press, 2005.

———, and Frank James Tester. *Kiumajut (Talking Back): Game Management and Inuit Rights, 1900–1970.* Vancouver: UBC Press, 2007.

La Forest, Gerald V., and Muriel Kent Roy. *Report of the Special Inquiry on Kouchibouguac National Park.* Ottawa: Government of Canada and Government of New Brunswick, 1981.

Lackenbauer, P. Whitney, and Matthew Farish. "The Cold War on Canadian Soil: Militarizing a Northern Environment." *Environmental History* 12 (2007): 920–50.

Landals, Alison. *Lake Minnewanka Site 2000 Mitigation Program, Interim Report.* Calgary: Consultant's report for Parks Canada, 1994.

Langemann, E. Gwyn., *Final Report, 1995–1996 Archaeological Resource Management Programme, Banff National Park.* Calgary: Parks Canada, Cultural Resource Services, Western and Northern Service Centre, 1996.

———. "A Description and Evaluation of Eight Housepit Sites in Banff National Park, Alberta." Paper presented at the 31st annual meeting of the Canadian Archaeological Society, Victoria, May 1998.

———. "Archaeological Evidence of Bison in the Central Canadian Rockies." In *Proceedings of the Rocky Mountain Bison Research Forum, October 28th, 1999, Rocky Mountain House, Alberta,* edited by Todd Shury, 6–12. Banff: Banff National Park Ecosystem Secretariat, 2000.

———. "Stable Carbon Isotopic Analysis of Archaeological Bison Bone: Using zooarchaeology to address questions of the past ecology of bison." *Research Links* 8, no. 1 (2000): 4, 12.

———. "Recent Zooarchaeological Research in Banff and Waterton Lakes National Parks, Alberta." In *Learning from the Past: A Historical Look at Mountain Ecosystems,* 99–108. Revelstoke: Parks Canada and the Columbia Mountains Institute of Applied Ecology, Proceedings from the 1999 conference, 2000.

———. "Zooarchaeological Research in Support of a Reintroduction of Bison to Banff National Park, Canada." In *The Future From the Past: Archaeozoology in wildlife conservation and heritage management,* edited by Roel C.G.M. Lauwerier and Ina Plug, 79–89. Oxford: Oxbow, 2004.

———, and Sheila Greaves. "House Hunting in the High Country: Recent Archaeological research at Housepit Sites in Banff National Park." Paper presented at the 30th annual meeting of the Canadian Archaeological Association, Saskatoon, May 1997.

———, and William Perry. *Banff National Park of Canada Archaeological Resource Description and Analysis.* Calgary: Parks Canada, Cultural Resource Services, Western and Northern Service Centre, 2002.

Larmour, Judy, *Laying down the Lines: A History of Land Surveying in Alberta.* Edmonton: Brindle and Glass, 2005.

Lascelles, Tony, and Grey Owl [Archibald Belaney]. "A Philosophy of the Wild." *Forest and Stream* (December 1931): 15–16.

Lawson, Nicholas. "Where Whitemen Come to Play." *Cultural Survival* 9 (1985): 54–56.

Lears, T.J. Jackson. *No Place of Grace: Antimodernism and the Transformation of American Culture, 1880–1920*. New York: Pantheon, 1981.

Livingston, John. *Arctic Oil: The Destruction of the North?* Toronto: CBC Merchandising, 1981.

"Local." *Edmonton Bulletin*, 14 Dec. 1890, 1, cols. 2–3.

Locke, Harvey. "Civil Society and Protected Areas." Paper presented at the Parks for Tomorrow 40th Anniversary Conference, Calgary, 2008.

————, and Philip J. Dearden. "Rethinking protected area categories and the new paradigm." *Environmental Conservation* 32 (2005): 1–10.

Longstreth, Richard W., ed. *Cultural Landscapes: Balancing Nature and Heritage in Preservation*. Minneapolis: University of Minnesota Press, 2008.

Loo, Tina. "Making a Modern Wilderness: Conserving Wildlife in Twentieth-Century Canada." *Canadian Historical Review* 82 (2001): 91–121.

————. *States of Nature: Conserving Canada's Wildlife in the Twentieth Century*. Vancouver: UBC Press, 2006.

Lorimer, Rowland, et al., eds. *To See Ourselves / To Save Ourselves: Ecology and Culture in Canada*. Montreal: Association for Canadian Studies, 1991.

Lotenberg, Gail. "Recognizing Diversity: An Historical Context for Co-managing Wildlife in the Kluane Region, 1890 – Present." Parks Canada research manuscript, March 1998.

Lothian, W.F. *A Brief History of Canada's National Parks*. Ottawa: Environment Canada, 1987.

Louter, David. *Windshield Wilderness: Cars, Roads, and Nature in Washington's National Parks*. Seattle: University of Washington Press, 2006.

Louv, Richard. *Last Child in the Woods: Saving our Children from Nature-Deficit Disorder*, 2nd ed. Chapel Hill, NC: Algonquin Books, 2008 [2005].

Loy, Thomas H. *Archaeological Survey of Yoho National Park: 1971*. Ottawa: National Historic Parks and Sites Branch, Parks Canada Manuscript Report No. 111, 1972.

Lutts, Ralph H. "The Trouble with Bambi: Disney's 'Bambi' and the American Vision of Nature." *Forest and Conservation History* 36 (1992): 160–71.

Luxton, Eleanor G. *Banff: Canada's First National Park, a History and a Memory of Rocky Mountains Park*. Banff: Summerthought, 1974.

MacEachern, Alan. "Rationality and Rationalization in Canadian National Parks Policy." In *Consuming Canada: Readings in Environmental History*, edited by Chad Gaffield and Pam Gaffield, 197–212. Toronto: Copp Clark, 1995.

————. *Natural Selections: National Parks in Atlantic Canada, 1935–1970*. Montreal: McGill-Queen's University Press, 2001.

————. "Voices Crying in the Wilderness: Recent Works in Canadian Environmental History." *Acadiensis* 31 (2002): 215–26.

————. "Writing the History of Canadian Parks: Past, Present, and Future." Paper presented at the Parks for Tomorrow 40th Anniversary Conference, Calgary, 2008.

MacGregor, James G. *Pack Saddles to Tête Jaune Cache.* Edmonton: Hurtig, 1962.

Machabée, Louis. "La double nature de la nature: une analyse sociologique de la naturalisation des espaces verts en milieu urbain." Thèse du doctorat, Université du Québec à Montréal, 2002.

MacLaren, I.S. "Cultured Wilderness in Jasper National Park," *Journal of Canadian Studies* 34 (1999): 7–58.

————. "Removal of 'Squatters' from the Athabasca River valley (1909–1910) and Attempts to Remove 'Trespassers' from Athabasca Forest Reserve and Environs (1912–1922)," typescript report for Ackroyd, Piasta, Roth, and Day, LLP, Edmonton, 2006.

————, with Eric Higgs and Gabrielle Zezulka-Mailloux. *Mapper of Mountains: M.P. Bridgland in the Canadian Rockies, 1902–1930.* Edmonton: University of Alberta Press, 2005.

————, ed. *Culturing Wilderness in Jasper National Park: Studies in Two Centuries of Human History in the Upper Athabasca River Watershed.* Edmonton: University of Alberta Press, 2007.

Magder, Ted. *Canada's Hollywood: The Canadian State and Feature Films.* Toronto: University of Toronto Press, 1993.

Magne, Martin. "Archaeology and Rocky Mountain Ecosystem Management: Theory and Practice." *George Wright Forum* 16 (1999): 67–76.

————, et al. "Archaeology – A Crucial Role in Ecosystem Management." *Cultural Resource Management* 20 (1997): 9–11.

Magoc, Chris J. *Yellowstone: The Creation and Selling of an American Landscape: 1870–1903.* Albuquerque: University of New Mexico Press, 1999.

Mair, W.W. "Natural History Interpretation: Key to the Future of the National Parks." In "Fifth Annual Naturalists Workshop: Palisades National Parks Training Centre, Jasper National Park [1964]." Unpublished manuscript, Canadian Parks Service, 1969.

Marsh, John S., and Bruce W. Hodgins, eds. *Changing Parks: The History, Future and Cultural Context of Parks and Heritage Landscapes.* Toronto: Natural Heritage/Natural History, 1998.

Martin, Paul-Louis. *La chasse au Québec.* Montréal: Éditions du Boréal, 1990.

Marty, Sid. *A Grand and Fabulous Notion: The First Century of Canada's Parks.* Toronto: NC Press, in co-operation with Cave and Basin Project, Parks Canada, and Supply and Services Canada, 1984.

————. *The Black Grizzly of Whiskey Creek.* Toronto: McClelland & Stewart, 2008.

Mawani, Renisa. "Legalities of Nature: Law, Empire, and Wilderness Landscapes in Canada." *Social Identities* 13 (2007): 715–34.

McCandless, Robert. *Yukon Wildlife: A Social History*. Edmonton: University of Alberta Press, 1985.

McClellan, Catharine. *Part of the Land, Part of the Water: A History of the Yukon Indians*. Vancouver: Douglas & McIntyre, 1987.

McIntyre, M., and B.O.K. Reeves. *Archaeological Investigations: Lake Minnewanka Site (EhPu-1)*. Calgary: Consultant's report for Parks Canada, 1975.

McKay, Ian. *Quest of the Folk: Antimodernism and Cultural Selection in Twentieth Century Nova Scotia*. Montreal: McGill-Queen's University Press, 1994.

McNamee, Kevin A. "The Northern Yukon." *Probe Post* 13 (1984): 13–16.

McPherson, Robert. *New Owners in their Own Land: Minerals and Inuit Land Claims*. Calgary: University of Calgary Press, 2003.

Miller, J.R. *Skyscrapers Hide the Heavens: A History of Indian-White Relations in Canada*, 3rd ed. Toronto: University of Toronto Press, 2000.

Mitman, Gregg. *Reel Nature: America's Romance with Wildlife in Film*. Cambridge, MA: Harvard University Press, 1999.

Monaghan, David W. *Canada's 'New Main Street': The Trans-Canada Highway as Idea and Reality, 1912–1956*. Ottawa: Canadian Science and Technology Museum, 2002.

Monsalve, M.V., D.Y. Yang, and E.G. Langemann. "Molecular Analysis of Ancient Cervid Remains from Two Archaeological Sites: Banff National Park and Rocky Mountain House National Historic Site, Alberta." In *Tools of the Trade: Methods, Techniques and Innovative Approaches in Archaeology*, edited by Jayne Wilkins and Kirsten Anderson, 167–81. Proceedings of the 2005 Chacmool Archaeological Conference, Department of Archaeology, University of Calgary. Calgary: University of Calgary Press, 2009.

Moquay, Patrick. "La référence régionale au Québec. Les visions étatiques de la région et leurs incarnations." In *L'institutionnalisation du territoire au Canada*, edited by J.P. Augustin, 85–127. Québec: Presses de l'Université Laval, 1996.

Mortimer-Sandilands, Catriona. "The Cultural Politics of Ecological Integrity: Nature and Nation in Canada's National Parks, 1885–2000." *International Journal of Canadian Studies* 39/40 (2009): 161–89.

———. "Calypso Trails: Botanizing on the Bruce Peninsula." *Dalhousie Review* 90 (2010): 7–22.

Moss, John. *Enduring Dreams: An Exploration of Arctic Landscape*. Concord, ON: House of Anansi Press, 1996.

Mueller, Robert, Peter J. Murphy, and Bob Stevenson. *Mountain Trails: Memoirs of an Alberta Forest Ranger in the Mountains and Foothills of the Athabasca Forest*

1920–1945. By *Jack Glen Sr*. Hinton, AB: Foothills Research Institute, and Alberta
Department of Sustainable Resource Development, 2008.

Murie, Margaret, and Terry Tempest. *Two in the Far North*. Alaska Northwest Books,
2003.

Murphy, Peter J., et al. *A Hard Road to Travel: Land, Forests and People in the Upper
Athabasca Region*. Hinton, AB: Foothills Model Forest; Durham, NC: Forest
History Society, 2007.

Nadasdy, Paul. *Hunters and Bureaucrats: Power, Knowledge, and Aboriginal-State Relations
in the Southwest Yukon*. Vancouver: UBC Press, 2003.

——. "Re-evaluating the Co-Management Success Story," *Arctic* 56 (2003): 367–80.

Nash, Roderick. "The American Invention of National Parks." *American Quarterly* 22
(1970): 726–35.

Naske, Claus M. "The Taiya Project." *BC Studies* 91–92 (1991–92): 5–50.

Nelson, J.G. "The Future of Conservation Reserves in the Arctic," *Contact* 8 (1976):
76–116.

——, and R.C. Scace, eds. *The Canadian National Parks: Today and Tomorrow*. Calgary:
National and Provincial Parks Association of Canada and the University of
Calgary, 1969.

——, with R.C. Scace, eds. *Canadian Parks in Perspective: Based on the Conference the
Canadian National Parks: Today and Tomorrow, Calgary, October 1968*. Montreal:
Harvest House, 1970.

——, et al., eds. *The Canadian National Parks: Today and Tomorrow Conference II: Ten
Years Later*. Waterloo: University of Waterloo, Faculty of Environmental Studies,
1979.

Neufeld, David. "The Development of Community-Based Cultural Research and
Management Programs: The Canadian Parks Service (CPS) Experience in the
Northwest." *Canadian Oral History Association Journal* 12 (1992): 30–33.

——. "Parks Canada and the Commemoration of the North: History and Heritage."
In *Northern Visions: New Perspectives on the North in Canadian History*, edited by
Kerry Abel and Ken S. Coates, 45–76. Peterborough, ON: Broadview, 2001.

——. "Imposed by the Current: The Yukon River as a Cultural Route." *Momentum* 10
(2002): 34–39.

Neumann, Roderick P. *Imposing Wilderness: Struggles Over Livelihood and Nature
Preservation in Africa*. Berkeley: University of California Press, 1998.

——."Nature-State-Territory: Toward a Critical Theorization of Conservation
Enclosures." In *Liberation Ecologies: Environment, Development, Social Movements*,
2nd ed., edited by Richard Peet and Michael Watts, 195–217. London: Routledge,
2004.

Nicks, Gertude. "Demographic Anthropology of Native Populations in Western Canada, 1800–1975." PhD dissertation, University of Alberta, 1980.

Nicolson, Marjorie Hope. *Mountain Gloom and Mountain Glory: The Development of the Aesthetics of the Infinite*. Ithaca, NY: Cornell University Press, 1959.

O'Malley, Martin. *The Past and Future Land: An Account of the Berger Inquiry into the Mackenzie Valley Pipeline*. Toronto: P. Martin Associates, 1976.

Oberlander, Peter H. *Urban Development Plan: Banff, Alberta*. Ottawa: National Parks Branch, Dept. of Northern Affairs and National Resources, 1961.

Owram, Doug. *Born at the Right Time: A History of the Baby Boom Generation*. Toronto: University of Toronto Press, 1999.

Outram, James. *In the Heart of the Canadian Rockies*. London: Macmillan, 1905.

Page, Robert. *Northern Development: The Canadian Dilemma*. Toronto: McClelland & Stewart, 1986.

Parks Canada [National Parks Branch]. "Winter Recreation and the National Parks: A management policy and a Development Program." Unpublished manuscript, 1965.

———. [National Parks Service]. "Yukon National Park Proposal: Background Data Report," Planning Report 72. Ottawa: National Parks Service, Planning Division, 1969.

———. *Banff National Park provisional master plan – Plan directeur provisoire*. Ottawa: National Parks Service, Planning Division, 1968 [1967].

———. "Economic Aspects of the Proposed St. Maurice National Park, March 1970." J. Hendry. Québec: National Parks Service, Planning Division, 1970.

———. *L'aménagement d'un parc en Mauricie*, 24 March 1971. Québec: National Parks Service, 1971.

———. *Manuel de planification du réseau des parcs nationaux/National Parks System Planning Manual*. Ottawa: National and Historic Parks Branch, 1972.

———. *Guiding Principles and Operational Policies*. Ottawa: Canadian Heritage and Parks Canada, 1994.

———. *National Park System Plan*, 3rd ed. Hull, QC: Canadian Heritage and Parks Canada, 1997.

———. *Banff National Park Cultural Resource Management Plan*. Banff: Canadian Heritage – Parks Canada, 1998.

———. *Commemorative Integrity Statement, Banff Park Museum National Historic Site, Banff National Park*. Banff, AB: Parks Canada, 1999 [1998].

———. *State of the Parks Report*; continued as *State of Protected Heritage Areas*. Ottawa: Parks Canada, 1991–98; 1999–2009.

———. *First Priority: Progress Report on Implementation of the Recommendations of the Panel on the Ecological Integrity of Canada's National Parks*. Ottawa: Parks Canada, 2001.

————. "Evolution of Bear Management in the Mountain National Parks." Ottawa: Parks Canada, 2003.

————. "Time for Nature: Healing Broken Connections: Restoring Historic Links between People and the Land in Kluane National Park and Reserve of Canada." Ottawa: Parks Canada, 2007.

————. "Management of Hyperabundant Wildlife Populations in Canada's National Parks." Management Directive 4.4.11. Ottawa: Parks Canada, 2007.

————. Parks Canada Agency Corporate Plans, 2008/09 – 2013/14. Gatineau, QC: Parks Canada, 2008, 2009.

Panel on the Ecological Integrity of Canada's National Parks. *Unimpaired for Future Generations? Conserving Ecological Integrity with Canada's National Parks.* Ottawa: Parks Canada, 2000.

Parr, Joy. *Sensing Changes: Technologies, Environments, and the Everyday, 1954–2003.* Vancouver: UBC Press, 2010.

Penfold, Steve. "'Are we to go literally to the hot dogs?' Parking Lots, Drive-Ins, and the Critique of Progress in Toronto's Suburbs, 1965–1975." *Urban History Review* 33 (2004): 8–23.

Peluso, Nancy Lee. *Rich Forests, Poor People: Resource Control and Resistance in Java.* Berkeley: University of California Press, 1992.

Perry, William. "The Use of GIS for Predictive Modelling at Banff National Park, Canadian Rocky Mountain Parks World Heritage Site, Canada." In *GIS and Cultural Resource Management: A Manual for Heritage Managers,* edited by Paul Box, 113–17. Bangkok: UNESCO, 1999.

Pickard, R.J. *Historical Resources Inventory, Jasper National Park.* Ottawa: Environment Canada, Parks Service Microfiche Report Series Number 202, 1984.

————. *Jasper National Park Archaeological Resource Description and Analysis.* Calgary: Archaeological Research Services Unit, Western Region, Environment Canada, Canadian Parks Service, Calgary, 1989.

————, and Heather D'Amour. *Archaeological Investigations at the National Historic Site of Jasper House.* Calgary: Archaeological Services, Parks Canada, 1987.

Pimlott, Douglas, Dougald Brown, and Kenneth Sam. *Oil Under the Ice.* Ottawa: Canadian Arctic Resources Committee, 1976.

Phillips, Adrian. *IUCN Category V Protected Areas Guidelines–Protected Landscapes/Seascapes.* Gland, Switz. and Cambridge: IUCN, 2002.

Poole, Colin, and Ross Anderson. *Archaeological Survey and Inventory of Proposed Modifications to the Canadian Pacific Railway in the Lake Louise Area, Alberta.* Calgary: Consultant's report, 1975. Copies available from Parks Canada, Cultural Resource Services, Western and Northern Service Centre, Calgary.

————, E. Gwyn Langemann, and Brian Reeves. *Archaeological Resource Description and Analysis, Waterton Lakes National Park*. Calgary: Parks Canada, Cultural Resource Services, Western and Northern Service Centre, 1997.

Pringault, Jérémy. "Le parc national de la Mauricie: mise en valeur d'un espace protégé dans la perspective du développement durable." Mémoire de maîtrise, Université de Caen, 1994.

Rangarajan, Mahesh. *Fencing the Forest: Conservation and Ecological Change in India's Central Provinces, 1860–1914*. Delhi: Oxford University Press, 1996.

Reeves, Brian O.K. "Culture Change in the Northern Plains, 1,000 B.C. – A.D. 1,000." PhD dissertation, University of Calgary, 1970.

————. *An Inventory of Archaeological Sites in Banff National Park and the Ya Ha Tinda Ranch*. Ottawa: National Historic Sites Service, National and Historic Parks Branch Manuscript Report Series No. 68, 1972.

————. *The Archaeology of Pass Creek Valley, Waterton Lakes National Park*. Ottawa: Manuscript Report Series No. 61, National Historic Sites Service, 1972.

————. *Crowsnest Pass Archaeological Project 1973 Salvage Excavations and Survey Paper No. 2, Preliminary Report*. Ottawa: Archaeological Survey of Canada, National Museum of Man Mercury Series No. 24, 1974.

————. "Early Holocene Prehistoric Land/Resource Utilization Patterns in Waterton Lakes National Park, Alberta." *Arctic and Alpine Research* 7 (1975): 237–48.

————. *1975 Archaeological Investigations, Lake Minnewanka Site (EhPu-1)*. Calgary: Consultant's report prepared for Western Region Parks Canada, 1976.

————. "The Rocky Mountain Eastern Slopes: Problems and Considerations." In *Alberta Archaeology: Prospect and Retrospect*, edited by T.A. Moore, 31–38. Lethbridge: University of Lethbridge, Archaeological Society of Alberta, 1981.

————. *Culture Change in the Northern Plains: 1,000 B.C. – A.D. 1,000*. Edmonton: Alberta Culture, Archaeological Survey of Alberta Occasional Paper 20, 1983.

————. "Mistakis: The Archaeology of Waterton-Glacier International Peace Park. Archaeological Inventory and Assessment Program 1993–1996, Final Technical Report." Denver: Consultant's report prepared for the National Park Service, 2003.

Reichwein, PearlAnn. "Beyond the Visionary Mountains: The Alpine Club of Canada and the Canadian National Park Idea, 1906 to 1969." PhD dissertation, Carleton University, 1995.

————. "'Hands off our National Parks': The Alpine Club of Canada and Hydro-development Controversies in the Canadian Rockies, 1922–30." *Journal of the Canadian Historical Association* 6 (1995): 129–55.

————. "Holiday at the Banff School of Fine Arts: The Cinematic Production of Culture, Nature, and Nation in the Canadian Rockies, 1945–1952." *Journal of Canadian Studies* 39 (2005): 49–73.

Richards, Thomas H., and Michael K. Rousseau. *Late Prehistoric Cultural Horizons on the Canadian Plateau*. Burnaby, BC: Department of Archaeology Press, Simon Fraser University, Publication No. 16, 1987.

Rick, John H. "Archaeological Investigations of the National Historic Sites Service, 1962–66." *Canadian Historic Sites: Occasional Papers in Archaeology and History* No. 1 (1970): 9–44.

Robertson, Gordon. "Administration for Development in Northern Canada: The Growth and Evolution of Government." *Journal of the Institute of Public Administration in Canada* 3, no. 4 (1960): 354–62.

Robinson, Bart. "A Biographical Portrait of Byron Harmon." In *Byron Harmon: Mountain Photographer*, edited by Carole Harmon, 5–14. Banff: Altitude, 1992.

Rohmer, Richard. *The Arctic Imperative: An Overview of the Energy Crisis*. Toronto: McClelland & Stewart, 1973.

Rome, Adam. *The Bulldozer in the Countryside: Suburban Sprawl and the Rise of American Environmentalism*. Cambridge: Cambridge University Press, 2001.

Ronaghan, Brian, ed. *Eastern Slopes Prehistory: Selected Papers*. Edmonton: Alberta Culture, Archaeological Survey of Alberta Occasional Paper No. 30, 1986.

Rothman, Hall K. *Devil's Bargains: Tourism in the Twentieth-Century American West*. Lawrence: University of Kansas Press, 1998.

Rudin, Ronald. *Remembering and Forgetting in Acadie: A Historian's Journey through Public Memory*. Toronto: University of Toronto Press, 2009.

Saberwal, Vasant, Mahesh Rangarajan, and Ashish Kothari. *People, Parks, and Wildlife: Towards Coexistence*. New Delhi: Orient Longman, 2001.

Sabin, Paul. "Voices from the Hydrocarbon Frontier: Canada's Mackenzie Valley Pipeline Inquiry (1974–77)." *Environmental History Review* 19 (1995): 17–48.

Sadler, B. "National Parks, Wilderness Preservation, and Native Peoples in Northern Canada." *Natural Resources Journal* 29 (1989): 185–204.

Sandlos, John. "From the Outside Looking In: Aesthetics, Politics, and Wildlife Conservation in the Canadian North." *Environmental History* 6 (2001): 6–31.

———. "Federal Spaces, Local Conflicts: National Parks and the Exclusionary Politics of the Conservation Movement in Ontario, 1900–1935." *Journal of the Canadian Historical Association* 16 (2005): 293–318.

———. *Hunters at the Margin: Native People and Wildlife Conservation in the Northwest Territories*. Vancouver: UBC Press, 2007.

———. "Not Wanted in the Boundary: The Expulsion of the Keeseekowenin Ojibway Band from Riding Mountain National Park." *Canadian Historical Review* 89 (2008): 189–221.

————. "Wildlife Conservation in the North: Historic Approaches and their Consequences; Seeking Insights for Contemporary Resource Management." Paper presented at the Canadian Parks for Tomorrow Conference, Calgary, 2008.

Santos, Boaventura de Sousa. "Beyond Abyssal Thinking: From Global Lines to Ecologies of Knowledges." *Eurozine* (2007): http://www.eurozine.com/articles/2007-06-29-santos-en.html .

Sax, Joseph L. *Mountains without Handrails: Reflections on the National Parks.* Ann Arbor: University of Michigan Press, 1980.

Scace, R.C., "Man and Grizzly Bear in Banff National Park, Alberta," MA thesis, University of Calgary, 1972.

Schaeffer, Mary. *Old Indian Trails: Incidents of Camp and Trail Life, Covering Two Years' Exploration through the Rocky Mountains of Canada.* New York: G. Putnam's Sons, 1911.

Schama, Simon. *Landscape and Memory.* Toronto: Random House, 1996.

Scheffer, Victor B. *The Shaping of Environmentalism in America.* Seattle: University of Washington Press, 1999.

Scholtz, Christa. *Negotiating Claims: The Emergence of Indigenous Land Claim Negotiation Policies in Australia, Canada, New Zealand, and the United States.* New York: Routledge, 2006.

Schullery, Paul. *Searching for Yellowstone: Ecology and Wonder in the last Wilderness.* Boston: Houghton Mifflin, 1997.

Scott, Chic. *Powder Pioneers: ski stories from the Canadian Rockies and Columbia Mountains.* Calgary: Rocky Mountain Books, 2005.

Scott, James C. *Seeing Like a State: How Certain Schemes to Improve the Human Condition Have Failed.* New Haven, CT: Yale University Press, 1998.

Searle, M.S., and R.E. Brayley. *Leisure Service in Canada: An Introduction.* Edmonton: Venture Publishing, 2000.

Searle, Rick. *Phantom Parks: The Struggle to Save Canada's National Parks.* Toronto: Key Porter, 2000.

Seel, K.E., and J.E. Strachan. *Banff National Park Resource Description and Analysis.* Calgary: Parks Canada, Western Region, 1985.

Sellars, Richard West. *Preserving Nature in the National Parks: A History.* New Haven, CT: Yale University Press, 1997.

Simpson, Michael. *Thomas Adams and the Modern Planning Movement: Britain, Canada and the United States, 1900–1940.* London and New York: Mansell, 1985.

Skidmore, Colleen, ed. *This Wild Spirit: Women in the Rocky Mountains of Canada.* Edmonton: University of Alberta Press, 2006.

Smith, Harlan I. *Handbook of the Rocky Mountains Park Museum.* Ottawa: Government Printing Bureau, 1914.

Smith, Pamela Jane, and Donald Mitchell, eds. *Bringing Back the Past: Historical Perspectives on Canadian Archaeology*. Hull, QC: Canadian Museum of Civilization, Archaeological Survey of Canada Mercury Series Paper 158, 1998.

Spence, Mark David. *Dispossessing the Wilderness: Indian Removal and the Making of the National Parks*. New York: Oxford University Press, 1999.

A Sprig of Mountain Heather; Being a Story of the Heather and Some Facts about the Mountain Playgrounds of the Dominion. Ottawa: Department of the Interior, 1914.

Stead, Robert. *Canada's Mountain Playgrounds: Banff, Jasper, Waterton Lakes, Yoho, Kootenay, Glacier, and Mt. Revelstoke National Parks*. Department of Mines and Resources, National Parks Bureau, 1941.

Steer, Donald N., and John E.P. Porter. *Heritage Resources Impact Assessment Trans-Canada Highway Kilometres 13 to 26 Banff National Park*. Ottawa: Parks Canada Microfiche Report Series 174, 1982.

Stevens, Stan, ed. *Conservation through Cultural Survival: Indigenous Peoples and Protected Areas*. Washington, DC: Island Press, 1997.

Struthers, James. *No Fault of Their Own: Unemployment and the Canadian Welfare State, 1914–1941*. Toronto: University of Toronto Press, 1983.

Sutter, Paul, *Driven Wild: How the Fight against Automobiles Launched the Modern Wilderness Movement*. Seattle: University of Washington Press, 2002.

Swainson, Neil. *Conflict over the Columbia: The Canadian Background to an Historic Treaty*. Montreal: Institute of Public Administration of Canada and McGill-Queen's University Press, 1979.

Swinnerton, Guy S., and Susan Buggey. "Protected Landscapes in Canada: Current Practice and Future Significance." *George Wright Forum* 21 (2004): 78–92.

———, and Stephen G. Otway. "Collaboration across Boundaries – Research and Practice: Elk Island National Park and the Beaver Hills, Alberta." In *Making Ecosystem Based Management Work: Connecting Researchers and Managers*, edited by Neil Munro. Wolfville, NS: Science and Management of Protected Areas Association, 2004; http://www.sampaa.org/publications/conference-proceedings-1991-2000/2003-proceedings/collaboration-across-boundaries-1/Swinnerton%20and%20Otway%20 2004.pdf/view .

Tanner, Thomas William. "Microcosms of Misfortune: Canada's Unemployment Relief Camps Administered by the Department of National Defence, 1932–1936." MA thesis, University of Western Ontario, 1965.

Taylor, C.J. "A History of National Parks Administration." Unpublished manuscript 1989.

———. *Negotiating the Past: The Making of Canada's National Historic Parks and Sites*. Montreal: McGill-Queen's University Press, 1990.

———. "A History of Automobile Campgrounds in the Mountain National Parks of Canada." Unpublished report, Parks Canada, 2001.

————. *Jasper: A History of the Place and Its People.* Calgary: Fifth House, 2009.

Theberge, John B. "Kluane National Park." In *Northern Transitions*: vol. 1, *Northern Resource and Land Use Policy Study*, edited by E.B. Peterson and J.B. Wright, 153–89. Ottawa: Canadian Arctic Resources Committee, 1978.

————, ed. *Kluane: Pinnacle of the Yukon.* Toronto: Doubleday Canada, 1980.

Thibeault, J.M. "La création d'un premier parc national au Québec: le parc Forillon, 1969–1970." Mémoire de maîtrise, Université de Sherbrooke, 1991.

Thompson, John Herd, and Allen Seager. *Canada, 1922–1939: Decades of Discord.* Toronto: McClelland & Stewart, 1985.

Thoreau, Henry David. *Walden: or, Life in the Woods; and on the Duty of Civil Disobedience.* New York: Signet Classic, 1999 [1854].

Todhunter, Roger. "Banff and the National Park Idea." *Landscape* 25 (1981): 33–39.

Touche, Rodney, *Brown Cows, Sacred Cows: A True Story of Lake Louise.* Hanna, AB: Gorman and Gorman, 1990.

Trigger, Bruce G. *A History of Archaeological Thought*, 2nd ed. New York: Cambridge University Press, 2006.

Tully, James. *Strange Multiplicity: Constitutionalism in an Age of Diversity.* Cambridge: Cambridge University Press, 1995.

Tungavik Federation of Nunavut. "Land Claims, National Parks, Protected Areas, and Renewable Resource Economy." In *Proceedings of the Arctic Heritage Symposium, 24–28 August 1985, Banff, Alberta, Canada*, edited by Gordon Nelson, Roger D. Needham, and Linda Norton, 285–97. Waterloo: Heritage Resource Centre, University of Waterloo, 1985.

Turner, James Morton. "From Woodcraft to 'Leave no Trace': Wilderness, Consumerism, and Environmentalism in Twentieth-Century America." *Environmental History* 7 (2002): 462–84.

Turner, R.D., and W.E. Rees. "A Comparative Study of Parks Policy in Canada and the United States." *Nature Canada* 2 (1973): 31–36.

Tuxill, J.L., and N.J. Mitchell, eds. *Collaboration and Conservation: Lessons Learned in Areas Managed through National Park Service Partnerships.* Conservation and Stewardship Publication No. 3. Woodstock, VT: Conservation Study Institute, 2001.

Urry, John. *The Tourist Gaze.* London: Sage, 2002.

Usher, Peter J. *The Bankslanders: Economy and Ecology of a Frontier Trapping Community.* Ottawa: Information Canada, 1971.

Van Dyke, Stanley. *Final Report: Archaeological Survey and Assessment, Upper Red Deer River Valley, Banff National Park, 1987.* Ottawa: Environment Canada, Parks Service Microfiche Report Series No. 386, 1987.

Varney, Tamara L., M. Annie Katzenberg, and Brian Kooyman. "Where Do the Bison Roam? A Stable Isotopic Study of Bison Grazing Behaviour in Waterton Lakes and

Banff National Park." Prepared for Waterton Lakes National Park, Parks Canada Western and Northern Service Centre, 2001.

Vaughan, Walter. *The Life and Work of Sir William Van Horne*. New York: Century, 1920.

Vivian, Brian. "A High Altitude Survey of Prehistoric Cultural Resources in Banff National Park." Prepared for Parks Canada Western and Northern Service Centre, 1997.

Wagner, Gary William. "Implementing the Environmental Assessment Provisions of a Comprehensive Aboriginal Land Rights Settlement." MA thesis, University of Waterloo, 1996.

Waiser, W.A. *Saskatchewan's Playground: A History of Prince Albert National Park*. Saskatoon: Fifth House, 1989.

———. *Park Prisoners: The Untold Story of Western Canada's National Parks, 1915–1946*. Calgary: Fifth House, 1995.

Wall, Geoffrey, and John Marsh, eds. *Recreational Land Use: Perspectives on Evolution in Canada*. Ottawa: Carleton University Press, 1982.

Warner, Rosalind. "A Comparison of Ideas in the Development and Governance of National Parks and Protected Areas in the US and Canada." *International Journal of Canadian Studies* 37 (2008): 13–40.

Warren, Louis S. *The Hunter's Game: Poachers and Conservationists in Twentieth-Century America*. New Haven, CT: Yale University Press, 1997.

Wearmouth, Chris, "Willmore Wilderness considered for World Heritage Designation," *Wild Lands Advocate: The Alberta Wilderness Association Journal* 15, no. 6 (2007): 14–15.

West, Paige, et al. "Parks and Peoples: The Social Impact of Protected Areas." *Annual Review of Anthropology* 35 (2006): 251–77.

West, Patrick C., and Steven R. Brechin, eds. *Resident Peoples and National Parks: Social Dilemmas and Strategies in International Conservation*. Tucson: University of Arizona Press, 1991.

"What are parks for?" [Interview with Alan Latourelle]. *Canadian Wilderness* 6 (2010): 3–5.

White, Richard. "From Wilderness to Hybrid Landscapes: The Cultural Turn in Environmental History." *The Historian* 66 (2004): 557–64.

Williams, M.B. *The Banff-Windermere Highway*. Ottawa: Department of the Interior, 1923.

———. *Jasper National Park*. Ottawa: Department of the Interior, 1928.

———. *Through the Heart of the Rockies and Selkirks*, 4th ed. Ottawa: Department of the Interior, 1929.

———. *Guardians of the Wild*. London: Thomas Nelson and Sons, 1936.

———. *Waterton Lakes National Park*. Ottawa: Department of the Interior [1927?]

———. *The Kicking Horse Trail*. Ottawa: Department of the Interior, 1930 [1927].

Wilmeth, Roscoe. "Current Research: The Plains." *American Antiquity* 32 (1967): 276–77.

Wilson, Jeremy. *Talk and Log: Wilderness Politics in British Columbia, 1961–1996.* Vancouver: UBC Press, 1998.

Wormington, H. Marie, and Richard G. Forbis. *An Introduction to the Archaeology of Alberta, Canada.* Denver: Proceedings of the Denver Museum of Natural History, No. 11, 1965.

Worster, Donald. *Nature's Economy: A History of Ecological Ideas,* 2nd ed. Cambridge: Cambridge University Press, 1994.

Wright, R.G., ed. *National Parks and Protected Areas: Their Role in Environmental Protection.* Cambridge, MA: Blackwell Science, 1996.

Yaworsky, Arlene. "Preserving the History of Georgian Bay Islands National Park." Unpublished report, Parks Canada, 1976.

Yukon Native Brotherhood. *Together Today for Our Children Tomorrow: A Statement of Grievances and an Approach to the Settlement by the Yukon Indian People.* Brampton: Charters Publishing, 1973.

Zellen, Barry Scott. *Breaking the Ice: From Land Claims to Tribal Sovereignty in the Arctic.* Lanham, MD: Lexington, 2008.

Zellers, Suzanne. *Inventing Canada: Early Victorian Science and the Idea of a Transcontinental Nation.* Toronto: University of Toronto Press, 1988.

Index

A

Abbey, Edward, 71
Abbot Pass Refuge Cabin, 355
Aboriginal challenges to modernism, 10, 13–14, 254–63, 294
Aboriginal Forum, 335, 348, 356
Aboriginal handicrafts and artefacts, 197, 203n51, 305
Aboriginal knowledge of place, 237, 254
Aboriginal land claims. *See* land claims
Aboriginal people, 74n2, 237, 239, 260, 286, 293. *See also* First Nations people
  assimilating or enculturating, 293–94
  challenged conventional thinking about national parks, 10, 14, 197, 257, 294
  cultural attachment to Yukon North Slope, 277
  doctrine of the vanishing Indian, 340
  erasing native presence in parks and protected areas, 42, 260, 346
  expulsion from national parks, 74n2, 77n40, 169, 244, 274, 296n6, 361n20, 364n39
  forced shifts in government policies (*See* Aboriginal challenges to modernism)
  introducing moral questions into conservation debates, 277
  invisible to officials 100 years ago, 340
  IUCN definition of wilderness (1987) and, 338

  objected to tourist orientation of national parks, 283
  reinstating in parks, 341, 347–48, 355, 378
  'special privileges' for, 289
  stakeholders in national park territories, 181
  vote, 245
Aboriginal status as "citizens plus," 260, 271n63
Aboriginal subsistence lifeway. *See* subsistence lifeway
Aboriginal title, 282, 284
Acadians, 14, 207, 211, 339
  acceptance of lives after Kouchibouguac, 223–24, 228
  artistic representations, 207, 211–12, 227–28
  "authentic" residents idea, 216, 230n26
  changes in Acadian society, 208
  deportation, 217, 219, 223, 227
  expropriation, 205, 208, 211–16
  resilience, 227
  willingness to stand up for Acadian interests, 211–12, 230n15
Acadie in twenty-first century, 229
L 'Acadie l'Acadie?!? (1971), 230n15
Acadie nouvelle, 227
Africville, 208
Agreement-in-Principle. *See* Inuvialuit Land Rights Settlement Agreement-in-Principle (AIP)

Agricultural Rehabilitation and Development Act (ARDA, 1966), 183
Aishihik Champlain First Nations annual camps and teaching TEK, 347
Aishihik First Nation, 263, 264n1
Alaska Highway, 101n25, 243, 245, 256
Alberta, 68
expanded highway system, 134
Alberta Archaeological Society, 313
Alberta Heritage Act (1973), 311
Alberta Historical Resources Act, 311
Allmand, Warren, 286
Alpine Club, 55, 67, 373
Aluminum Company of America, 246
animal–human conflicts, 158, 164. *See also* bears
mauling incidents, 160, 164, 168–69
antelope, 5
archaeological research in the Rocky Mountain parks, 303–25, 377
ability to look at changes over time, 322, 325
basic culture history framework, 324–25
focus on placing people in a landscape, 304, 310
funding for, 321
Archaeological Society of Alberta, 308
archaeological staff in the Calgary Regional Office of Parks Canada, 304, 314
Archaeological Survey of Alberta, 311
archaeology, 10
architecture, 135
Arctic International Wildlife Range Society (AIWRS), 278
Arctic National Wildlife Range, 278
Arctic sovereignty, 10
ARDAs (Archaeological Resource Description and Analysis), 318
Arsenault, Aurèle, 228
asbestos mines, 246

Aseniwuche Winewak Nation, 356
Aspen, Colorado, 148
Astotin Lake, 69
Athabasca Forest Reserve, 352, 354
Athabasca Pass, 369n72
Athabasca River, 346, 356
Athabasca River valley survey, 317
Atikamac, Lake, 192
automobile campgrounds, 136, 274
automobile culture, 31, 39, 41, 153
dependence on industrial processes, 73
influence on animal-human relationships, 154
shaping of park design, 5–6
automobile road films, 158
automobile tourism, 5, 13, 60, 62, 71, 73n1, 134, 144, 375
local groups and, 59
priority for federal government for national parks (interwar years), 83
automobile tourism and bears, 154, 158, 164–65, 172
treatment in *Bears and Man* (1978), 170–71
wilderness ideal, 155
automobiles, 35, 41–43
originally prohibited in parks, 31
Auyuittuq, 8, 235, 282
Away from it all (1961), 162

B

back to nature movement, 4, 27, 72, 154
Baffin Island (Auyuittuq), 8, 235, 282
Ballade de Jackie Vautour (Richard), 227
Banff Advisory Council, 137–40, 145
Banff Archaeological Resource Description and Analysis (ARDA), 315, 317–18
Banff hot springs, 3, 15n6, 375
Banff National Park, 41, 334, 355, 381
archaeological resource inventory, 310

Bridgland, Morrison Parsons, 348
  Description of and Guide to Jasper Park,
    34, 38
British Block cairn, 307
British Columbia, 83, 88
  campaign to get Ottawa to build and
    maintain highways, 80, 84 (*See
    also* Big Bend Road)
  created Hamber as a provincial park, 6
  Dominion Railway Belt, 80
  expanded highway system, 134
  process for creation provincial parks
    (1940s), 89
  resource-based economy, 81
  unemployment rate (early 1931), 82
British Columbia Forest Service, 95
British Columbia Parks Branch, 94–95
Brooks, Lloyd, 116
Brown, Robert Craig, "The Doctrine of
  Usefulness," 54
Bruce, R. Randolph, 61
Bryant Creek, 317
buffalo, 5, 244
Buffalo National Park, 68, 102n38, 379
  removed from parks system, 69
Buggey, Susan, 354, 356
Bureau d'aménagement de l'Est-du-
  Québec (BAEQ), 183
Burwash Indian Band, 247, 249–50, 253

C

Calder case (1973), 282
Calgary, 61
Calgary Olympic Development
  Association (CODA), 140
Calgary Regional Office of Parks Canada,
  314, 321
Calgary-Banff chapter of the National
  and Provincial Parks Association,
  144
Cameron, G.I., 253
Campbell, Claire Elizabeth, 379, 391

Campbell, R.H., 29
Canada Land Inventory (1961), 183
Canada National Parks Act (2000), 11
Canada's national parks. *See* national
  parks
Canada's Unemployment Relief Camps,
  82–83, 87, 99n5
Canada's World Heritage Sites, 10, 376
Canadian Arctic Gas Limited, 281
Canadian Audubon Society, 142
Canadian Environmental Assessment Act
  (CEAA), 320–21
Canadian Forest Service, 185
Canadian Government Travel Bureau, 37
Canadian national identity
  parks as symbol of, 340, 361n21, 372,
    382n1
  sentimental links to 'the North,' 281
"Canadian National Parks: Today and
  Tomorrow" (conference, 1968),
  144–45, 183, 309–10, 338
Canadian National Parks Conference
  (Banff, 1978), 148
Canadian Pacific Railway, 15n6, 31,
  99n3, 311
  allure of national parks en route, 3
  Banff Springs Hotel, 134, 136
  Chateau Lake Louise, 136
  marketing of Banff National Park, 375
  mountain passes, 309
Canadian Parks and Wilderness Society,
  16n19, 23, 142, 150, 270n55
  influential environmental lobby, 8
  support for Systems Plan, 381
  veneration of J.B. Harkin, 55
Canadian Parks Service (1984), 2
Canadian Wildlife Service, 135, 146, 161,
  256–57, 289, 292
  opposed giving Indians formal claim
    to any part of a National Park,
    253
  opposition to development on Beaufort
    Sea coast, 277

opposition to industrial activity or hunting, 67
second conservation movement, 142, 334
Consolidated-Bathurst Limited, 185
Cooking Lake-Blackfoot Grazing, Wildlife and Provincial Recreation Area, 354
COPE, 282, 286–87, 293
ambivalence about state conservation, 286, 290
belief that protected areas could serve long-term needs, 293
breakdown in negotiations, 290
committed to conservation, 285
demanded employment opportunities in the park, 287
desire to preserve wildlife habitats, 293
determined to ensure conservation practised according to a new set of rules, 288
distrustful of federal conservation practices, 285
exclusive rights to hunt and trap within park boundaries, 287, 289
importance attached to wildlife and habitat conservation, 288
Inuvialuit land claim, 283
opposition to ideal of 'uninhabited wilderness,' 275
proposed a National Wilderness Reservation for Yukon North Slope, 291
rejected government proposals for protected areas in the region, 283
copper, 246
Cormier, Linda, 225
cormorants, 356
Cornwall, 314
Coudert, J.L., Bishop, 251
Council for Yukon Indians, 262
coyotes, 146–47

CPR. *See* Canadian Pacific Railway
Crag and Canyon, 29, 44, 136–37, 139, 146, 148
'Carolling Coyotes Kapowed,' 147
Craig-Dupont, Olivier, 8, 145, 274, 346, 381, 391
Craighead, John and Frank, 168
Cree, 335
Crerar, Thomas, 87, 110
CRM. *See* cultural resource management (CRM) archaeology
Cronin, Keri, 155
Cronon, William, 340
"The Trouble with Wilderness," 180
Uncommon Ground, 339
Cross, Austin, 88
Crowsnest Pass, 62, 310
Cruikshank, Julie, 275
cultural colonialism, 199
cultural heritage, 196, 260, 292, 335, 339, 343–44, 346, 356, 377–78
cultural landscapes, 10–11, 14, 325, 356, 363n37
protected areas as, 277, 297n10
cultural pluralism, 377
cultural relationships, negotiation of, 263–64
cultural resource management (CRM) archaeology, 304, 320–24
culture
privileging nature over, 377
Culturing Wilderness in Jasper National Park (2007), 348
Cyprus Anvil lead/zinc open pit mine, 246

D

Dalton Post, 244
David Thompson Highway, 141
Davidson, Al, 148
Davis, T.C., 62
Davis, Tommy, 105

Dawson, 246
Dawson News, 245
Dempster, Harry, 115
Dempster Highway, 245
Department of Archaeology at the
  University of Calgary, 308, 310
Department of Fisheries and Oceans,
  287, 289
Department of Heritage, 11
Department of Indian Affairs and
  Northern Development. *See*
  DIAND
Department of National Defence, 83, 87
Department of Northern Affairs and
  National Resources, 7, 116–18,
  135, 163
Department of Sociology and
  Anthropology at the University of
  Alberta, 308
Department of the Environment, 11, 287,
  289
Department of the Interior, 2, 4, 7, 26,
  58, 61, 68, 70
deportation and Kouchibouguac link,
  217, 219, 223, 227
Désaulniers Club, 189
Description of and Guide to Jasper Park
  (Bridgland), 34, 38
Desmeules, Pierre, 191
DIAND, 7, 11, 103, 124, 183, 289–90
  determined to meet needs of the oil
    and gas industry, 277, 290
Dick, Lyle, 274, 341, 392
Diefenbaker, John, 14, 122, 125, 129n13,
  130n43
  "Northern Vision" of development and
    progress, 246
  represented Prince Albert riding, 117
Dieppe, 226
Dinosaur Provincial Park, 355
Dinsdale, Walter, 117–18, 258
Divide Creek, 324
Divide Creek and Red Deer River
  junction, 317

DNA, 323–24
doctrine of the vanishing Indian, 340
"The Doctrine of Usefulness" (Brown),
  54
Dominion Forest Reserves and Parks Act
  (1911), 4, 28, 58, 367n61
  amendments (1913 and 1914), 30
Dominion Forestry Branch, 4
Dominion Lands Act, 58
"Dominion Parks – Their Values and
  Ideals" (Harkin), 32
Dominion Parks Branch, 2, 4–5, 25–27,
  55, 58–59, 71, 181
  accomplishments, 44
  alliance with the landscape artist, 29
  annual reports, 33
  commercial potential, focus on, 68, 72
  created auto-accessible parks, 41, 60
  environmental or resource
    management, 44
  facilitated private sector development
    of resort towns in national
    parks, 60
  guidebooks (1920s), 22, 35, 39
  lobbying from local groups, 60
  parks roadbuilding (1920s), 41
  preservationist and pro-development
    policies (simultaneously), 5, 59
  preservationist philosophy, 5, 59–60,
    68
  promotional literature, 33 (*See also*
    guidebooks)
  promotional literature (1920s), 34
  Publicity Division, 7n407, 35, 37,
    66–67
  road building, 41, 60
  tourism, promotion of, 31, 34, 60, 68
  wildlife protection, 69
Domtar, 185
doublespeak or whitewashing, 206,
  229n2, 364n44
Douglas, Howard, 28, 58
Douglas, Robert, 34

426   A CENTURY OF PARKS CANADA

H

surveyed Waterton Lakes National Park, 309

Reichwein, Pearlann, 55

reinstating an ongoing Aboriginal or Métis presence, 341, 347–48, 356, 378
not beyond realm of possibility, 355
rejuvenating cultural practice, 335, 356
challenge to Parks Canada Agency (PCA) practices, 335, 378

relief work camps, 82–83, 87, 99n5

resource development in national parks, 181
forbidden under *National Parks Act* (1930), 106

resource development in the north, 246, 282. *See also* mineral prospecting; mining interests (Yukon); oil and gas companies

resource management, 321

Resources for Tomorrow Conference, Montreal (1961), 142

Revelstoke, 61, 81

Revelstoke Progress Club, 60

Richard, Zachary, 207, 219–21, 226
Ballade de Jackie Vautour, 227

Rick, John, 312

Riding Mountain National Park, 66–67
approvals for private sector development, 65
draw for automobile travelers from U.S., 63
exclusion of Native people, 77n40, 361n20, 364n39
program of road and golf course construction, 65
shack tents, 118

Riding Mountain National Park Committee, 62

Riding Mountains area
significance as sanctuary for a threatened elk herd, 62

Rimrock Hotel (now the Juniper), 136

roads. *See also* names of specific roads and highways
automobile link between Vancouver and Calgary, 81
automobile roads (late 1920s) in the mountains of western Canada, 80
back to healthier and fuller contact with nature, 41
construction to provide automobile access to ski hill areas, 140
democratic ideal that national parks not be restricted to the wealthy, 66
environmental effects in Point Pelee, 71
national park status and, 105
proposed in Banff provisional master plan, 144–45
wildlife and, 154, 158

roadside timber reserve (Big Bend), 83
between Kinbasket Lake and Boat Encampment, 87
open to logging in anticipation of Mica Dam flooding, 96

Robertson, Gordon, 116–17

Robichaud, Louis, 210–12

Rocky Mountain House National Historic Site, 304, 307, 312, 314

Rocky Mountain Park (1885), 27, 58
exclusion of Native people, 74n2
first open to automobile, 60
little knowledge of what had been there before, 305
shrunk by *Dominion Forest Reserves and Parks Act*, 28
villa or cottage lots in, 104

Rocky Mountains, 80, 97
crossroads of cultures from the BC Plateau and the Plains, 307
people have always been present, 303–4
promotion of (through guidebooks), 22

Université de Moncton, 211–12, 230n15
universities. *See also* names of individual
universities
environmental studies programs, 142
growing influence in shaping
government policy, 134
public advocacy in, 142
second wave of wilderness preservation
and, 154
University archaeology field schools, 320
"University of Banff," 146
University of British Columbia's School
of Community and Regional
Planning, 142
University of Calgary, 144
University of Calgary's Department of
Geography, 142
Upper Athabasca River Valley (UARV),
356
balancing human and non-human life
in, 334
homesteads in, 335
long history of human presence,
334–35
reinstating Métis or Aboriginal
presence (idea), 340–41
use by humans and animals, 333
U.S., 3, 32, 93
bear problem, 159
restrictive corridor on both sides of the
Alaska Highway, 243
U.S. Bureau of Reclamation, 246
U.S. National Park Service, 7, 190, 195,
348
U.S. National Park Service Mission 66
building program, 142
U.S. national parks system, 140
criticism of industrial tourism, 71
U.S. *Organic Act* (1926), 337
use and protection, twinning, 5
use-*versus*-preservation debate, 154, 163,
171. *See also* dual mandate of
development and preservation

V

vacant wilderness. *See* uninhabited
wilderness
Van Horne, William, 3, 15n6
Vancouver Sun, 95
Vautour, Jackie, 212, 225
accepted as permanent presence, 223
arrested for digging clams, 215
centre stage in many artistic creations,
217
contested legality of expropriation, 214
house bulldozed, 207, 213–14, 217,
222
image as agent of resistance, 219
Métis (aboriginal rights), 216
payment to leave, 215, 228
petition, 214–15
provided leadership and a public face,
213
returned as a squatter, 207, 214, 221
Vautour, John L. *See* Vautour, Jackie
Vermilion Lakes site
10,700-years of occupation, 315
Vermilion wetlands excavation, 315
Victor Lake, 367n61
homesteaders move to, 350, 352
shifting boundaries, 352, 367n61,
368n61
Victoria Memorial Museum in Ottawa,
305
visitor experience initiative, 378, 381
Vivian, Brian, 320
Vuntut Gwich'in First Nation, 290–91

W

Waiser, Bill, 5, 14, 138, 273, 379, 394
Walden (Thoreau), 180
Walt Disney Productions, 161
Wapizagonke, Lake, 185
Wardle, J.M., 83
Wasagaming (resort town), 65
Waskesiu campground

crowded conditions, 106, 111, 115
dominated by shack tents and portable
cabins, 117
plan to replace shack tents with trailer
sites, 120
popularity, 107, 110
Waskesiu Lake, 105
Waskesiu redevelopment plan (1967), 119
second thoughts about, 123–24
shock and dismay at, 120–21
Waskesiu summer cottagers
influential in deciding park policy, 127
Waskesiu Tent Cabin and Portable Cabin
Association, 103
campaign to stop redevelopment plan,
121–22
Chrétien's meeting with, 123
complaints "their park" under attack,
124–25
Waskesiu townsite, 65
private cottages, 104
Waterton Lakes National Park, 27, 30,
58, 309, 334
bison, 323
park within a forest reserve, 28
Waterton Lakes National Park (Williams),
35, 42
Watrous, Richard B., 49n28
Wawaskesey, 16n11, 68–69
Weber, Lake, 192
Weekend Magazine, 139
Wheeler, Arthur, 373
Where Has Sanctuary Gone? (1971), 165
Whistler, B.C., 148
White, James, 315
White Paper on Indian Policy, 103, 260,
271n60, 282
White River First Nation, 263
Whitehorse mines, 246
Whyte Museum of the Canadian
Rockies, 305
Whytes, 136
wilderness, 13, 27, 142, 198, 343, 383n9

debate (corruption by over-
development), 159
fundamental component of North
American culture, 180
human rights issues, 334, 338–39, 354
IUCN definition of, 338
justification for parks, 54, 66
popular histories emphasizing, 74n8
questionable in parks established in
long-inhabited lands, 199
redefined, 10
reworking inhabited landscapes into
"pristine" wilderness, 180
Romantic notion of, 334
a social construct, 181, 340
uninhabited, 275, 340, 357
wilderness recreation, 124, 135
"windshield wilderness," 158
Wilderness Act (U.S., 1964), 7
wilderness activism, 54–55
Wilderness and the American Mind (Nash),
142
wilderness conservation in Canada, U.S.,
and Britain
comparative study, 376–77
wilderness movement, 153, 165
wilderness park as alternative to fee
simple ownership, 286
wilderness playground paradox, 334–35,
340
wilderness protection, 144, 274, 334, 337,
339
wilderness recreation, 135
Wilderness Society, 278
wilderness values, 274
wildlife. *See also* bears; coyotes;
subsistence lifeway
economic value of, 247
as tourist attraction, 8, 62, 245, 247
wild animals seemed "tamed" along
roadways, 158
wildlife cinematography, 155, 161
wildlife in the Yukon report (1958), 257